THE WINGS
OF ATALANTA

Studies in American Literature and Culture

MARK RICHARDSON

THE WINGS OF ATALANTA

ESSAYS WRITTEN ALONG THE COLOR LINE

CAMDEN HOUSE
Rochester, New York

Copyright © 2019 Mark Richardson

All Rights Reserved. Except as permitted under current legislation, no part of this work may be photocopied, stored in a retrieval system, published, performed in public, adapted, broadcast, transmitted, recorded, or reproduced in any form or by any means, without the prior permission of the copyright owner.

First published 2019
by Camden House

Camden House is an imprint of Boydell & Brewer Inc.
668 Mt. Hope Avenue, Rochester, NY 14620, USA
www.camden-house.com
and of Boydell & Brewer Limited
PO Box 9, Woodbridge, Suffolk IP12 3DF, UK
www.boydellandbrewer.com

ISBN-13: 978-1-57113-239-0
ISBN-10: 1-57113-239-2

Library of Congress Cataloging-in-Publication Data

Names: Richardson, Mark, 1963–
Title: The wings of Atalanta : essays written along the color line / Mark
    Richardson.
Description: Rochester, N.Y. : Camden House, 2019. | Includes bibliographical
    references and index.
Identifiers: LCCN 2019008511| ISBN 9781571132390 (hardcover : alk. paper) |
    ISBN 1571132392 (hardcover : alk. paper)
Subjects: LCSH: African Americans in literature. | Racism in literature. |
    American literature—History and criticism.
Classification: LCC PS374.N4 R53 2019 | DDC 810.9/896073—dc23 LC record
    available at https://lccn.loc.gov/2019008511

This publication is printed on acid-free paper.
Printed and bound in Great Britain by TJ International Ltd.

If the Reconstruction of the Southern states, from slavery to free labor, and from aristocracy to industrial democracy, had been conceived as a major national program of America, whose accomplishment at any price was well worth the effort, we should be living today in a different world.

—W. E. B. Du Bois, *Black Reconstruction* (1935)

CONTENTS

Acknowledgments		ix
Introduction		1
1:	Frederick Douglass and the Philosophy of Slavery	21
2:	W. E. B. Du Bois and the Redemption of the Body	73
3:	The Mephistophelean Skepticism of Stephen Crane	110
4:	Charles Chesnutt: Nowhere to Turn	164
5:	Richard Wright: Exile as Native Son	204
6:	Peasant Dreams: Reading *On the Road*	238
Conclusion		259
Notes		263
Bibliography		299
Index		313

ACKNOWLEDGMENTS

First, I must say what a pleasure it has been to work with Jim Walker, Jane Best, Gretchen Hitt, and the rest of the staff at Camden House. They do things the good old ways. Second, I acknowledge with gratitude permission from the James Baldwin Estate to quote *The Fire Next Time*, *Nobody Knows My Name*, and *No Name in the Street*; and permission from the University of Texas Press to reprint (in revised form) my essay "Peasant Dreams: Reading *On the Road*," published first in *Texas Studies in Language and Literature* 43, no. 2 (Summer 2001): 218–42. Copyright © 2011 by the University of Texas Press. Extracts from the works of Richard Wright are reprinted by permission of John Hawkins and Associates, Inc. Copyright © 1940 Richard Wright. Portions of the chapters on Douglass, Du Bois, Chesnutt, Crane, and Wright are reprinted here, in revised and expanded form, by permission of *EBK: AMERICAN WRITERS CLASSICS V1* © 2003 Gale, a part of Cengage, Inc., and also by permission of Oxford University Press, USA, to whose *Oxford Encyclopedia of American Literature* I once contributed (at the invitation of Jay Parini, whom I also thank). Excerpts from ON THE ROAD by Jack Kerouac, copyright © 1955, 1957, by John Sampas, Literary Representative, the Estate of Stella Sampas Kerouac; John Lash, Executor of the Estate of Jan Kerouac; Nancy Bump; and Anthony M. Sampas. Used by permission of Viking Books, an imprint of Penguin Publishing Group, a division of Penguin Random House LLC. All rights reserved.

My endnotes register the debts I owe to a host of scholars. All follies, lapses in reason, faults in style, statements of the obvious, and affronts to sensibility I ascribe to the secular Calvinist whose name appears on the title page. And I acknowledge, last, a regret: that I read two books by neuroscientist and primatologist Robert Sapolsky—*Why Zebras Don't Get Ulcers* (2004; third edition) and *Behave* (2016)—only after this book was in production. Anyone hoping to understand the intractable and insidious effects of such systems of oppression as white supremacy—indeed, at endocrinological and neurobiological levels—should read "The View from the Bottom," chapter seventeen in *Zebras*. As for Du Bois's claim that (most) white folk in America have enjoyed a "public and psychological wage" denied (most of) their African-American compatriots: to understand just how right he is we do well to bear in mind—as Sapolsky puts it, summarizing research done by Nancy Adler and Richard Wilkinson—that it is not poverty so much as *being made to feel poor amid plenty* that so degrades such mortals as us. May the recent rapprochement between humanists and science become a more productive embrace. As the physician (and 1848-er) Rudolf Virchow wrote: "Medicine is a social science, and politics is nothing else but medicine on a large scale." Social democracy is generally the best Rx. Here's to Abou Ben Adhem (may his tribe increase!) and to higher marginal tax rates.

INTRODUCTION

This book proceeds from two premises. The first I phrase with a nod to Marianne Moore: America is an imaginary place with real people living in it. Such splendid ideals, and yet so often such sordid realities. My second premise is that slavery and its legacies explain why America should remain so imaginary a place. Both premises assume that slavery and, after it fell, white supremacy generally, were—and to a marked degree remain—essential to American capitalism, which requires, insofar as it can be secured, cheap, unorganized labor. I concur with David Roediger's suggestion in *Class, Race and Marxism* (2017) that "the production of racial . . . differences is itself part of the logic of capital" (7). I take as granted W. E. B. Du Bois's observation in *Black Reconstruction* (1935): "It must be remembered and never forgotten that the civil war in the South which overthrew Reconstruction [1876–90] was a determined effort to reduce black labor as nearly as possible to a condition of unlimited exploitation and build a new class of capitalists on this foundation. The wage of the Negro worker, despite the war amendments, was to be reduced to the level of bare subsistence by taxation, peonage, caste, and every method of discrimination. This program had to be carried out in open defiance of the clear letter of the law" (670)—and therefore entailed an imposture that kept our national promise illusory. Or to put the matter in the cooler phrasing of social psychologists Michael W. Kraus, Julian M. Rucker, and Jennifer A. Richeson in their 2017 study: "Race-based economic inequality is both a *defining* and *persistent* feature of the United States that is *at odds with national narratives regarding progress toward racial equality.* . . . Americans, on average, systematically overestimate the extent to which society has progressed toward racial economic equality, driven largely by overestimates of current racial equality. . . .[Our] findings suggest a profound misperception of and misplaced optimism regarding contemporary societal racial economic equality—a misperception that is likely to have important consequences for public policy" (my emphases).¹ Most Americans, in a word, do not know the nation they inhabit.²

In speaking of white supremacy in America, I have in mind 250 years of chattel slavery—roughly 1620–1865, across both the colonial and national eras³—and convict labor, sharecropping, and related institutional practices dating to the post-Reconstruction years and the first half of the twentieth century (as Douglas Blackmon describes them in *Slavery by Another Name* [2008]). I have in mind also the elaborate, government-sanctioned systems of "redlining" that did much to concentrate wealth derived from real estate in white hands, even in the years *beyond* passage of the Fair Housing Act of 1968 (and *always* in the teeth of the Civil Rights Act of 1866, which provides that "all persons born in the United States . . . shall have the same right, in every State and Territory in the United States, to make and enforce contracts, to sue, be parties, and give evidence, to inherit, purchase, lease, sell, hold, and convey real and personal property, and to full and equal benefit of all laws and proceedings for the security of person and property, as is enjoyed by white citizens. . .").⁴ I have in mind, too, the system of mass incarceration described by Michelle Alexander in *The New Jim Crow* (2012)—a system which disproportionally imprisons people of color. "Human Rights Watch reported in 2000 that, in seven states, African Americans constitute 80 to 90 percent of all drug offenders sent to prison," writes Alexander. "In at least fifteen states, blacks are admitted to prison on drug charges at a rate from twenty to fifty-seven times greater than that of white men. In fact, nationwide, the rate of incarceration for African American drug offenders dwarfs the rate of whites. When the War on Drugs gained full steam in the mid-1980s, prison admissions for African Americans skyrocketed, nearly quadrupling in three years, and then increasing steadily until it reached in 2000 a level more than twenty-six times the level in 1983" (98). Of course, as Alexander points out, "rates and patterns of drug crime do not explain the glaring racial disparities in our criminal justice system. People of all races use and sell illegal drugs at remarkably similar rates. If there are significant differences in the surveys to be found, they frequently suggest that whites, particularly white youth, are more likely to engage in illegal drug dealing than people of color" (99). In many states, as Alexander shows, felons (again, disproportionately African American) are denied job opportunities (148–54), access to federal aid (157–58), access to public housing (144–48), and—most importantly—access also to the franchise (158–61). Until passage of Amendment 4 on November 6, 2018,⁵ ten percent of all Floridians and 21.3% of the state's 2.9 million African American citizens (some 617,000 persons) were permanently ineligible to vote due to felony convictions (see Lai and Lee, 2016)—a metric whose effect is suggested by the fact that Donald Trump won the state in 2016 with a 113,00-vote margin, making possible (among other things) passage of the Republican Tax Cuts and Jobs Act of 2017.[6] After signing the bill, the president departed for his Florida Winter White House, Mar-a-Lago, where he told his wealthy congregants, "You all just got a lot richer."[7] Alexander further documents, in *The New Jim Crow*, the degree to which incarceration has, in recent decades, become a multi-billion-dollar, for-profit industry (230–31)—the market value of which rose sharply after Trump was elected.[8]

I should mention here also voter-suppression efforts disproportionately affecting people of color both before and in the wake of the Supreme Court's decision in *Shelby County (Alabama) v. Eric Holder* (2013). The Roberts Court effectively nullified the requirement—in the Voting Rights Act of 1965—that states and counties with a history of suppressing African American votes obtain "preclearance" from the Department of Justice before amending rules affecting elections.[9] In *The Embattled Vote in America: From the Founding to the Present* (2018), Alan Lichtman details what followed that decision: new measures swiftly adopted in state after Republican-controlled state—most notably in the Deep South—to (in effect) disenfranchise African American and other minority voters (180–230). "The great value of Lichtman's book, writes Michael Tomasky, "is the way it puts today's right-wing voter suppression efforts in their historical setting. He identifies the current push as the third crackdown on African American voting rights in our history," the first dating to the early national period, the second—which I discuss in chapter 2—dating to the post-Reconstruction years (10). In concluding his book, Lichtman writes: "In some ways modern American democracy resembles the economic stakeholder model of more than two centuries ago," when the franchise was chiefly confined to landowners. "Restrictions on registration and voting, and alienation from politics have combined to produce a 'party of non-voters' that is disproportionately minority, young, and economically disadvantaged" (256). "Economic stakeholders" today include billionaire financiers of Super PACs and the energy industry. As for the "party of non-voters"—well, "Rejoice, and be exceeding glad: for great is your reward in heaven." It is quite as if with the fall of each system of disciplining labor—especially black labor—to the needs of industry and capital there arose a new one to replace it, so essential to the economy of the South and the nation has degraded labor been. That is the mean towards which the nation appears to regress, periodic advances—the

Radical Reconstruction, the New Deal, the Great Society, the civil rights movement—notwithstanding.¹⁰

Of course, there is something extraordinary about American white supremacy, something that cannot be accounted for by economic arrangements alone—something, in fact, psycho-pathological (as I suggest in chapters 1, 2, and 4). But I would add here a few words more regarding white supremacy as a function of American capitalism. Consider how, for example, the de-regulationist program advanced so successfully in the Congress for so many decades, through the early to mid-twentieth century, enjoyed as its natural complement, fierce opposition to every civil rights and anti-lynching bill that came before that body until at least 1964–65 (the 1957 Civil Rights Bill, though a victory, was adulterated by compromise); and consider how the same politicians were responsible for advancing the one and for opposing the other (Southern Democrats, at times working in coalition with the Chamber-of-Commerce and Taft wings of the Republican Party in the North).¹¹ Surely it is telling that, in the United States, opposition to civil rights legislation of all kinds so often "presents as" (to use the medical term) a radical defense of private property rights, whether that property is, in fact, human (slaves); or residential properties, the value of which was artificially inflated by the aforementioned redlining and by racially restrictive covenants (one abiding consequence of which is the twenty-fold margin by which the wealth of white households exceeds the wealth of black households);¹² or at places of business where the "right" of a person to associate only with persons of his own race was so long asserted (whether by Robert Bork in 1963, by Barry Goldwater in 1964, or by Texas congressman and perennial presidential aspirant Ron Paul in 2011, or by Ron Paul's son Rand during *his* Senate campaign in 2010.)¹³ Moreover, in mid-twentieth century America, hostility to integration, or to advances in civil rights, or to the expansion of the franchise, were, in their extremist forms, typically coupled with anti-communism—with dogmatic, evangelical, and militant free-market capitalism.¹⁴ Edward Baptist reminds us further that arguments informing and stemming from the 1857 *Dred Scott* decision have cast a dark shadow across American jurisprudence: "the federal judiciary took the [John] Calhounian argument for the independence of slave property from majority control and made it, in the form of the so-called Lochner Doctrine [deriving from the 1905 Supreme Court case of *Lochner v. New York*], a defense of rampant industrial power in the face of attempts to regulate workers' safety, consumer health, and environmental impact" (415). In his celebrated dissent to the *Lochner* decision, Justice Oliver Wendell Holmes, Jr., noted drily that "the Fourteenth Amendment does not enact Mr. Herbert Spencer's *Social Statics*. . . . [A] constitution is not intended to embody a particular economic theory, whether of paternalism and the organic relation of the citizen to the State or of laissez faire" (quoted in Frankfurter 65). And yet there we were, and here we are.

Finally, I would note Jacqueline Jones's observation in *A Dreadful Deceit* (2013): "The devastating impact of the Great Recession of 2008 on black Americans reflects their unique, historic vulnerabilities. Between June 2009 and June 2012, median annual black household income fell 11 percent, compared to 5.2 percent for white households and 4.1 percent for Hispanic households" (290). Here, to be sure, is a pillaging of black wealth by white capital. Consider the case of Countrywide Financial.[15] Jones continues: "The disproportionate number of black households affected by foreclosures after 2008 suggests a dramatic loss of the hard-won gains of the post-1965 generations: between 2005 and 2009 black households' median net worth—an indication of capital accumulation through the generations—declined from $13,124 to $5,677 (53 percent), while the decline for white households was from $134,992 to $113,149 (15 percent)" (290). I have facts such as these in mind when I speak of white supremacy as "integral" to American capitalism; the two forces have remarkably similar redistributive effects. If no single agency may be said to "design" our economy, nevertheless our economy may be said to have designs not simply on the poor and the working class but on working people of color.

But I must now turn to the main chance—to more strictly literary concerns. Many readers will, I expect, find the two guiding premises laid out above in paragraph one non-controversial.[16] For readers who don't, I hope to bear them out in argument insofar as a literary critic can. I work at those points where literature, history, and politics intersect. I trace white supremacy, and resistance to it, at the level of style and rhetoric—in the *texture* of the prose I discuss. What is the relation between, on the one hand, the cool, ironic (even "hip") style of *The Red Badge of Courage* (1895), and, on the other, the spectacularly cynical turn by the Republican Party—and with it the nation—against the promise and early successes of the Radical Reconstruction? Why do metaphors associated with sexuality pervade *The Souls of Black Folks* (1903)? Why and how do motifs evoking late-nineteenth-century "plantation tales" find their way into *On the Road*, of all books, published in 1957, two years after the lynching of Emmett Till (and the exoneration of his killers)? How is Douglass's conversion to political abolitionism registered in the rhetoric of *My Bondage and My Freedom* (1855)? How do the short stories and novels of Charles Chesnutt record the malice and dishonesty of the new order of things, circa 1890–1903, years during which capital, in its novel administrations in North Carolina, disenfranchised black labor and impoverished much of white labor, too? How best to explain the strange incoherence of Crane's novella *The Monster* (1898) (whose central character is an enfeebled black hostler)? I try to answer those questions and also to accord Du Bois's *The Souls of Black Folk* and Douglass's *My Bondage and My Freedom* a thorough literary-critical treatment.[17] I further intend to show how labor relations are represented, reflected upon, and registered—at whatever remove, and with whatever distortions—through resources of metaphor and style. In what follows I say some things about the nature of white supremacy as a system of economic relations, as I have already above. But I am more concerned with it as a disposition and state of mind; as an *attitude* that implies actions, whether taken or not; as a set of assumptions entertained by white men and women about their own bodies, and about the bodies of those on the other side of the color line; as a set of feelings and sentiments tempering (so to speak) both body and mind, and allowing thereby for the reproduction of the relations of production characteristic of a political economy that for centuries rested upon a foundation of slave labor (and the globally traded commodities that slave labor produced). Finally, in my notes I discuss certain contemporary political developments that suggest continuities between such ordeals as Douglass, Du Bois, Chesnutt, and Wright underwent and our current state of affairs. "What's past is prologue" is not only a remark made in *The Tempest* by a man who wrongly deposed his brother and who conspires to commit a murder; it is also engraved in marble just outside the National Archives Building in Washington, DC.

I know no better confessor of the truth of the second of the premises stated at the outset of this introduction than Jefferson Davis, in his *Rise and Fall of the Confederate Government*. The book appeared in 1881, four years after a compromised President Hayes withdrew the last Federal troops from the five departments of the South, leaving the freedmen, and their sons and daughters, to the tender mercies of the Democratic Party and its terrorist constabulary. In the following passage—in language better suited to the Gilded Age during which he penned it than to 1863—Davis reacts afresh to the Emancipation Proclamation and to Lincoln's decision to field black soldiers, thousands of them former slaves, in the Union Army during the final two and a half years of the Civil War. The passage is best taken whole, for its wicked splendor:

The forefathers of these negro soldiers were gathered from the torrid plains and malarial swamps of inhospitable Africa. Generally they were born the slaves of barbarian masters, untaught in all the useful arts and occupations, reared in heathen darkness, and, sold by heathen masters, they were transferred to shores enlightened by the rays of Christianity. There, put to servitude, they were trained in the gentle arts of peace and order and civilization; they increased from a few unprofitable savages to millions of efficient Christian laborers.[18] Their servile instincts rendered them contented with their lot, and their patient toil blessed the land of their abode with unmeasured riches. Their strong local and personal attachment secured faithful service to those to whom their service or labor was due. A strong mutual affection was the natural result of this life-long relation, a feeling best if not only understood by those who have grown from childhood under its influence. Never was there happier dependence of labor and capital on each other. The tempter [i.e., Lincoln] came, like the serpent in Eden, and decoyed them with the magic word of "freedom." Too many were allured by the uncomprehended and unfulfilled promises, until the highways of these wanderers were marked by corpses of infants and the aged. He put arms in their hands, and trained their humble but emotional natures to deeds of violence and bloodshed, and sent them out to devastate their benefactors. What does he boastingly announce? "It is difficult to say they are not as good soldiers as any." Ask the bereaved mother, the desolate widow, the sonless aged sire, to whom the bitter cup was presented by those once of their own household. With double anguish they speak of its bitterness. What does the President of the United States further say? "According to our political system, as a matter of civil administration [as against martial necessity], the General Government had no lawful power to effect emancipation in any State." And further on, as if with a triumphant gladness, he adds, "Thus giving the double advantage of taking so much labor from the insurgent cause, and supplying the places which otherwise must be filled with so many white men." A rare mixture of malfeasance with traffic in human life! It is submitted to the judgment of a Christian people how well such a boast befits the President of the United States, a federation of sovereigns under a voluntary compact for specific purposes. (2: 192–93)

Even the verbs do the work of white supremacy: slaves are "gathered," as huckleberries might be—not seized, not bought, nor taken (what "selling" Davis acknowledges he assigns to *heathen* masters, not Christian ones). "Gathered" may also have a tendentious, congregational/liturgical cast, given what follows in Davis's remarks. Whatever the case, the Middle Passage is here like some salubrious change of cars: Africans weren't stuffed into the pestilential holds of slave ships; they were "transferred" from "malarial swamps." White mischief works hard in these sentences: on our shores, Africans "increased from a few unprofitable savages to millions of efficient Christian laborers." A few? More than 500,000 Africans were brought into British North America alone prior to 1807, and 11,000,000 into the New World.[19] Notice how, in Davis's phrasing, "Christian" and "unprofitable" stand in inverse relation (as in the "seed" ministries run by televangelist hucksters: Christ *pays*). Lincoln, for his heaven-daring part, plays Satan. He appears in the person of "the Tempter," stepping in from the shade of the Tree of the Knowledge of Good and Evil with his "decoy." Which is to say: Lincoln connived at the Fall of an Edenic *ancien régime*. And who could have been his Eve, his devil's doorway, but the slave (or black America) just as Davis says? However indirectly, Davis hints at that *ne plus ultra* of the forbidden—miscegenation. For what is the Fall on which he allegorically depends if not a fall from sexual purity into sexuality as sin, somewhere east of Eden? "Liberty" for the slave is, for Davis and his like, always *libertinism*, always a scandal—in fact, the scandal of scandals (that black men shall rise and be as gods). Of course, Davis isn't thinking or writing very clearly; old agitations stir him. I suspect in all his mythology some inchoate revival of charges promiscuously made, in 1860–61, that Lincoln and his "Black Republicans" sought a "mongrel" republic—an unbounded disorder, a monstrous confusion of black and white. Scareheads like the following appeared in the columns of newspapers across the nation in 1860: "Increase of the Black Republican Party"—always that quasi-sexual, scriptural term: *increase*: "Seventy-two white females were married to negroes in the State of Massachusetts last year!"[20]

Africa, says Davis, is "inhospitable." But inhospitable to whom? Given how often Davis and other pro-slavery apologists spoke of black folk as *naturally* suited to tropical climates, one has cause to wonder. Inhospitable to white folk, of course; that goes without saying. Among the hoariest defenses of slavery was that white men neither could nor would labor too much in the sun. In January 1850, during the Compromise debates, Davis pointed out that "the European races" "engaged in working the mines of California sink under the burning heat . . . to which the African race [is] altogether better adapted" (1: 530). (Slavery expansionism animates that thought.) Yet something about the African continent's *inhospitality* must affront even its natives. Otherwise, why the imperative—indeed, the ancestral duty, as Davis seems to have understood it—to deliver them from Africa's swamps into the embrace of North American Christianity? It doesn't matter that the motives are confused—the one sanitary, the other evangelical. The ministry of the slave trade was total: it saw to body and to soul. What does Davis imply if not that the trans-Atlantic slave trade had been a half-measure? Follow his line of reasoning right on out and it has but one conclusion: depopulation of the dark continent would have been a great desideratum, had white men enjoyed New World enough and time. Surely they'd have taken up more of that burden if they could. Davis has much better English for it than President Trump, but he joins his confederate in judgment: Africa is "a shithole," a continent of "huts."[21] Far better than its "torrid," disease-ridden plains were such happy resorts as the cotton slave-labor camps of Davis's hospitable Mississippi; or (say) the rice plantations of Calhoun's South Carolina;[22] or the cane fields of Louisiana (opened for American business, by purchase, in 1803—and worked in part by slaves "transferred" from Toussaint's newly inhospitable Haiti).

Of course, slavery bestowed on Africans a most cunning—and Christian—gift: redemption from Adam's curse (Eden again). Their labor, as Davis imagines it, is hardly burdensome. "Patient toil" suggests no overseers and summons no whips. Anyhow, slaves did not really *work*; no, they "blessed the land of their abode." The whole enterprise accorded with Africans' natural "servile *instincts*." An asymmetry—white over black—informs that doggish phrase. In late-nineteenth-century discourse, "instincts" were more readily located in animals than in men. "Man, perhaps, has somewhat fewer instincts than those possessed by the animals which come next to him in the series," writes Darwin in *The Descent of Man* (1871). "The fewness and the comparative simplicity of the instincts in the higher animals are remarkable in contrast with those of the lower animals. Cuvier maintained"—and Davis would concur—"that instinct and intelligence stand in an inverse ratio to each other" (65–66). And hear the ringing defense of secession sounded in the last clause of the long passage quoted above: the United States is "a federation of sovereigns under a voluntary compact for specific purposes." Davis yields not an inch to the Union. Why would he, in 1881? He had ample reason to feel vindicated, and to dance round Lincoln's tomb.

But what of *these* details of Davis' apologia? The slaves' "strong local and personal attachment secured faithful service to those to whom their service or labor was due. A strong mutual affection was the natural result of this life-long relation, a feeling best if not only understood by those who have grown from childhood under its influence." Where even to begin? With the familiar Southern claim—that Faulkneresque forestaller—that no one not native to the region will ever rightly understand it? Or with the cool euphemism to which Davis resorts? Speaking of "those [masters] to whom [the slaves'] service or labor was due," he strikes an abstract, legalistic note, quite out of key in a passage otherwise by turns mawkish and lurid (incoherence in tone follows from incoherence in thought, and from certain contradictions latent in American political economies). Of course, Davis has in mind Article IV, Section 2 of the Constitution: "No person held to service or labor in one state, under the laws thereof, escaping into another, shall, in consequence of any law or regulation therein, be discharged from such service or labor, but shall be delivered up on claim of the party to whom such service or labor may be due." In the Senate, Davis argued for the vigorous enforcement, and national recognition, of state laws requiring the return of fugitive slaves; he decried the "personal liberty laws" enacted in northern states opposed to the provisions of the 1850 Fugitive Slave Bill;[23] he sat on the Joint Select Committee charged with investigating the 1859 insurrection at Harpers Ferry (led by John Brown); and during debates associated with the Crittenden Compromise—a congressional measure meant to prevent secession and war—he called for a constitutional amendment *positively affirming* the right of property in men (precisely what the Founders could not bring themselves to do).[24] Had not Davis seen evidence enough that the peculiar institution was hardly self-regulating and organic? Had he not been as vigilant an inquirer into insurrection as any man in the Senate? Still, nothing could inspire in him any doubts, in 1881, as to the "strong personal attachment" slaves had to their masters, so imaginary had his relation to them been. "*White Americans do not take the privileged status of white people for granted,*" writes Albert Murray. "*They work at it.* They pretend that it is natural to their social inheritance. So would they impress others and so perhaps do they reassure themselves, somewhat. But in reality they leave little to nature, and what they inherit is the full-time obligation to keep up social appearances without ever seeming to do so" (italics in the original; 42–43).

Or we might begin instead with Davis's concession that the South was not some such species of "agrarian" society as Thomas Jefferson dreamt on, but a *capitalist* one, which produced commodities—well-leveraged, securitized, and insured—for sale on a vast world market ("Never was there happier dependence of labor and capital on each other").[25] Or we might start instead with the legerdemain that makes slave and master members of the same "household." Or with that perfect moment of ideological inversion whereby Lincoln and the abolitionists, not enslavers, "traffic in human life."[26] Astonishing, but then again not. Marx, in *The German Ideology*:

> The production of ideas, of conceptions, of consciousness, is at first directly interwoven with the material activity and the material intercourse

of men, the language of real life. Conceiving, thinking, the mental intercourse of men, appear at this stage as the direct efflux of their material behavior. The same applies to mental production as expressed in the language of politics, laws, morality, religion, metaphysics, etc., of a people. Men are the producers of their conceptions, ideas, etc.—real, active men, as they are conditioned by a definite development of their productive forces and of the intercourse corresponding to these, up to its furthest forms. Consciousness can never be anything else than conscious existence, and the existence of men is their actual life-process. If in all ideology men and their circumstances appear upside-down as in a camera obscura, this phenomenon arises just as much from their historical life-process as the inversion of objects on the retina does from their physical life-process. (169)

Davis's way of talking about the South—a highly *literary* way of talking about it, with counterparts in the fiction and poetry of the period—is clearly "the direct efflux of [his] material behavior" as a slaveholder, as a defender of slavery in the Senate, and as head of the Confederate States of America. The government of the latter was forthrightly based—as its vice president, Alexander H. Stephens, apprised the world in February 1861—upon the economy of white supremacy. The "foundations" of "our new government," Stephens announced, "are laid . . . upon the great truth that the negro is not equal to the white man; that subordination to the superior race is his natural and normal condition" (quoted in Cleveland 721). Given their investments, and their "material behavior," how could men such as Davis and Stephens not "see" slavery "upside-down as in a *camera obscura*"? "It is not the consciousness of men that determines their being, but, on the contrary, their social being that determines their consciousness," writes Marx in a celebrated maxim (160)—and we might here add: determines also their *conscience*. Davis and Stephens slept well enough at night—until the war came.[27] Again, not the slaveholders but the abolitionists "trafficked" in men. Not Lincoln and the Union Army, but the slaveholders themselves were the "benefactors" of African Americans. As I suggest in chapter one, few things incline one more toward historical materialism than studying the rise of pro-slavery rhetoric—in conjunction with the rise in value of cotton in the American economy—from 1820 to 1861.[28] King Cotton ruled not so much by divine right as by divination. The similes underlying Marx's claim—the one based on the *camera obscura*, the other on the optics of the human eye—seem hardly similes at all. Davis sees black for white, up for down. The planter bears the burden, his slaves garner the benefits. Capital is the paternal, philanthropic mover, and Lincoln—with his claim that real democracy be fulfilled—is a sociopathic agent of evil.[29] In his demonic offices, Lincoln re-channels (or de-sublimates) the "humble but emotional" "nature" of men and women—the slaves, motivated, as always, by Passion rather than Reason—into pathological, violent abuses the better to achieve such un-Constitutional aims as the preservation of the Union (as against such Constitutional aims as the destruction of the Union). The point is not that this actually happened but that Davis sincerely supposes it had. His rhetoric—"Never was there happier dependence of labor and capital on each other"—was bound to warm the hearts of the industrialists and capital investors in the *New* South circa 1881, because they wanted, they *required*, exactly that: a "happy dependence" of (black) labor on (white) capital; and of course that is what the South supposed itself so uniquely suited to offer. Yet Davis *pre*-dates, by some twenty years, the promissory note he offers to those who would build the New South on the basis of industrialization and cheap black labor; he dates it all the way back to the days when Lincoln and his "Black Republicans" were but a gathering cloud, and the Cotton Kingdom sat so apparently secure. *There* and *then* we saw what a "happy" capitalism was and ought to be.

The work Davis's book accomplishes is clear: it advances a way of knowing the Old South (and through it, America) that best reproduces the *relations* of production characteristic of white supremacy (along with the reproduction of the *means* of production, whether agricultural or industrial: cotton seed, land, securitized slave-mortgages, cotton gins, power-looms, railways, barges, and so on). Men and women must be reproduced, regulated, and arrayed as "white" and "black," and the commerce between them policed. Through such misdirections as the "familial" metaphors Davis employs (as did so many), the relations of production (again, white *over* black) are re-described so as to accord them unwarranted prestige. Authorizing Davis's *Rise and Fall* is what C. Wright Mills calls in a 1997 book "the racial contract," which arises from and shores up "norms for cognition"—protocols that govern what is and is not thinkable (10–11, 137–38). When Davis recoils in horror at the memory of black men "decoyed" by "the magic word of 'freedom'" until "the highways of these wanderers were marked by corpses of infants and the aged," he reaches the outer limits of what the racial contract to which he was signatory permits him to know and to feel. Beyond knowledge (and comfort) lie fear, hysteria, horror. Without slavery—without white supremacy generally—the South is, for Davis, a nightmare of broken homes. The alternatives are two: white control or chaos. (The tacit assumption that this is the case has proven remarkably durable: hence the "border-wall," "travel ban," and immigrant "caravan" panics of 2015–18).³⁰ Children and the elderly are left to die, while the thought of the black men who abandoned them—vagrant, "wandering" men of employable age but incapable of forming purposes on their own—summons only the specter of violence (those "corpses of infants and the aged," for whom they apparently do not care: a familiar and spurious charge one still hears in talk of the "pathology" of the black family³¹). As for black Union soldiers during the war itself: "Ask the bereaved [white] mother, the desolate widow, the sonless aged sire, to whom the bitter cup was presented *by those once of their own household*." What infernal ingratitude! Any close reader of Charles Chesnutt's fiction—as I aim to show in chapter 4—will find in it an explosion of the "plantation myth," which we have seen articulated by the top two government officials of the C.S.A., and which (in fresher guise) fascinates the neo-Confederate wing of the contemporary alt-right. Of course, many hoary fables of the Civil War and the Reconstruction pass current yet, as recent debates about Southern "heritage" and the proper disposition of Confederate monuments and memorials suggest.³²

Davis's and Stephens's style of thought remained fashionably American in the early twentieth century (until FDR came with his New Deal). Consider Andrew Carnegie's remarks in *The Gospel of Wealth and Other Timely Essays* (1901): "The problem of our age is the proper administration of wealth, so that the ties of brotherhood may still bind together the rich and poor in harmonious relationship" (1). True. And so it remains in our own era of rising income inequality. But note the bad faith in the metaphor of "brotherhood." This re-description of class relations (capital/labor) as fraternal ones recalls the metaphors Davis deploys to re-describe antagonistic race relations in *familial* ways, with the result that their proper economic relation (owner/slave, landholder/sharecropper) is obscured. Carnegie then contrasts man in what he regards as a state of nature (the Sioux) with "civilized man" when, in point of fact, "civilized man" is a placeholder for "man under capitalism," as what follows makes clear: "The contrast between the palace of the millionaire and the cottage of the laborer with us to-day measures the change which has come with civilization. This change, however, is not to be deplored," notes Carnegie, "but welcomed as highly beneficial. It is well, nay, essential for the progress of the race, that the houses of some should be homes for all that is highest and best in literature and the arts, and for all the refinements of civilization, rather than that none should be so. Much better this great irregularity than universal squalor" (1–2). The notion—the *gospel*—that "great irregularity" in distribution of wealth and "universal squalor" are our only alternatives is, of course, specious (though the folk at Americans for Prosperity, the Koch Industries-funded Super PAC, might demur); so is the use of the word "change" where "cost" or "price" belong. Identify the rise of a "millionaire" class with the progress "of the [human] race," and the trick is done, as surely as it is now done by the Republican Party when its spokespersons reclassify private equity firms and the people who run them as "job creators," as if they answer to and aim chiefly to benefit the working class; or when the same spokespersons re-describe anti-union legislation as "right to work" laws. Many of these habits of thought trace back through Carnegie to Davis and his ilk and, as we have seen, to the Calhounian argument for the complete independence of private property from legislative or majority control.[33]

And we recognize related habits of thought—however moderated by new proprieties—in twenty-first century debates about "makers" and "takers," criminal justice reform, the federal budget, economic stimulus packages, the federal debt, tax policy, the Affordable Care Act (aka Obamacare), the Supplemental Nutrition Assistance Program (SNAP), immigration, policing, "voter fraud," public education, Medicaid, and "entitlement" programs generally. Public debates concerning these issues have become more, not less, racially polarized since the election of Barack Obama in 2008. Political scientist Michael Tesler calls the phenomenon "the spillover of racialization," a process whereby apparently race-neutral public policy debates excite white animosity simply because those policies are associated with our first African American president or his perceived allies (Tesler 29–43, and *passim*).

A few words about Booker T. Washington are in order here. In his famous 1895 Atlanta Exposition Address, Washington says: "To those of the white race who look to the incoming of those of foreign birth and strange tongue and habits for the prosperity of the South, I would repeat what I have said to my own race: 'Cast down your bucket where you are.' Cast it down among the eight millions of Negroes whose habits you know, whose fidelity and love you have tested in days when to have proved treacherous meant the ruin of your fireside. Cast down your bucket among these people who have *without strikes and labor wars* tilled your fields, cleared your forests, builded your railroads and cities, brought forth treasures from the bowels of the earth, just to make possible this magnificent representation of the [industrial] progress of the South" (my emphasis; 138). Having made this practical appeal (no labor unions!), Washington feeds his white auditors a solid dose of Davisonian sentiment, and then makes his great concession: "As we have proved our loyalty to you in the past, nursing your children, watching by the sick-bed of your mothers and fathers, and often following them with tear-dimmed eyes to their graves, so in the future, in our humble way, we shall stand by you with a devotion that no foreigner can approach, ready to lay down our lives, if need be, in defense of yours, interlacing our industrial, commercial, civil, and religious life with yours in a way that shall make the interests of both races one. In all things that are purely social we can be as separate as the fingers, yet one as the hand in all things essential to mutual progress" (139). Washington well suited the purposes of "the rich and dominating North" (as Du Bois puts it in *Souls* [398]) after that 1895 speech, which was one reason (among many) why Andrew Carnegie funded his Tuskegee Institute, and not Du Bois's Atlanta University. Washington agreed to defer demands for political and civil rights in favor of economic development alone. He, however tactically, acceded to segregation. No wonder Du Bois damns Washington with faint praise: he is "the most distinguished Southerner since Jefferson Davis" (*Souls* 393). No strikes, no labor wars, no "happier dependence of capital upon labor"—*and* "social separation" of the races. The circuit is complete. White and (some) black leaders at the turn of the nineteenth century into the twentieth alike invested in their own—in every American's—unhappiness, to borrow a phrase from Terry Eagleton (*Ideology* xiii).

Jefferson Davis, Alexander H. Stephens, Du Bois, Washington: it would be hard to assemble a more fractious panel, and yet all make clear in what they say that discussions of race in America, or of white supremacy, are always discussions of labor relations. Martin Luther King, Jr., saw the logic. When to the struggle for civil rights he added support for striking sanitation workers in Memphis, a fully integrated Poor People's Campaign, and opposition to a neocolonial, anti-communist/pro-capitalist war in Vietnam, he and the movement he led lost much of the patronage they'd enjoyed in Washington. We've been in a holding pattern since he was murdered in 1968; we may never land. Nixon succeeded Lyndon Johnson, the Great Society faltered, Reagan consummated the movement Barry Goldwater helped begin, the Democratic Leadership Council succeeded Walter Mondale (the last Democratic nominee fully to embrace the legacies of the New Deal and the Great Society[34]), and we are where we are: in power, now, in 2019, is an administration white nationalist in disposition, hostile to brown and Islamic immigrants, ruthlessly anti-labor in policy, regressive in taxation, and jubilantly contemptuous of the Black Lives Matter movement and of criminal justice reform. The Black Atlantic hit of the literary season is still Paul Beatty's *The Sellout* (2015)—the first American novel to win Britain's Man Booker Prize. The novel features an African American character named "Me" who attempts to reintroduce segregation and slavery in the United States, starting in Los Angeles, only to find himself, in *Me v. The United States*, before the Supreme Court, smoking weed. More particularly still, smoking weed before Justice Clarence Thomas, the archconservative who flummoxed his opponents—who'd adduced sensational testimony as to his sexual mores—by charging them with commission of "a high-tech lynching." "Sitting here on the steps of the Supreme Court smoking weed, under the 'Equal Justice Under Law' motto, staring into the stars," says Me, "I've finally figured out what's wrong with Washington, D.C. It's that all the buildings are more or less the same height and there's absolutely no skyline, save for the Washington Monument touching the night sky like a giant middle finger to the world" (278). Little wonder that one of the most interesting television series about African Americans—about *America* itself—to have appeared in recent years is Donald Glover's *Atlanta*, by turns comic, surreal, and nihilistic (as is also his music video "This Is America," in which he performs as Childish Gambino).[35]

✶   ✶   ✶

An overview of what follows is now in order. In chapter 1, devoted to Frederick Douglass, I offer a close reading of his 1855 autobiography, *My Bondage and My Freedom*, that explains what I take my first premise to mean (i.e., that America is an imaginary nation with real people living in it). Out of an old book called *The Columbian Orator*—out of the power afforded him there of literacy—Douglass forged for himself a new identity, and *himself* became the essential "Columbian" (or New World) orator of the nineteenth century. He became what Albert Murray would call an "omni-American"—if not *the* omni-American (Murray 22). In the latter phase of his life, Douglass lived in the Anacostia neighborhood of the District of Columbia. Yet his America, his Columbian ideal, remained a thing forever unrealized in politics, a thing forever imaginary, as anyone who visits his house—called Cedar Hill, and held in trust by the National Park Service—must feel, looking out over our capital city, a site still on the wrack of poverty drawn along the color line.

The second chapter, devoted to W. E. B. Du Bois, suggests how African Americans had been reduced to mere *bodies*, both in and after slavery, by what many have come to call patriarchal white supremacy.[36] Du Bois shows how an intra-psychological antagonism that sets soul over body becomes an inter-racial antagonism that sets white over black. A white person, knowing and feeling himself to be white, experiences black persons as he does his own body: they fascinate him, repel him, attract him, excite him, shock him, disgust him—incite him to appalling disciplines. "The white man's un-admitted—and apparently, to him, unspeakable—private fears and longings are," as James Baldwin puts it in *The Fire Next Time*, "projected onto the Negro."[37] That is what made it necessary for Du Bois to write his book about the *souls* of black folk. No one wishing to understand the "spiritual strivings" of black Americans—or of the better sort of all Americans—can ignore this passage from the chapter titled "Of the Training of Black Folk": "The tendency is here, born of slavery and quickened to renewed life by the crazy imperialism of the day, to regard human beings as among the material resources of a land to be trained with an eye single to future dividends. Race-prejudices, which keep brown and black men in their 'places,' we are coming to regard as useful allies with such a theory" (428). For Du Bois, the black American is a "colonized" subject, a person treated merely as a "body," as a "material resource," just as were colonized people of color everywhere on earth in 1903.

In the third chapter, devoted to Stephen Crane, I show how *The Red Badge of Courage* involves a certain mode of "forgetting" the Civil War even as one writes about it. I argue that this mode of forgetting was a product of the post-Reconstruction years, and most especially of the 1890s. That decade marked the "nadir" of race relations (in many respects), as Rayford Logan pointed out years ago. *The Red Badge of Courage*, as I read it, is one among many symptoms of this fact, as is Crane's novella *The Monster*. In the latter we have a book that *appears* to address itself to what, in those days, Americans called The Negro Question. The figure around whom the action of the novel is organized—Henry Johnson—is injured horribly in a fire, and then consigned to such civic neglect as might well constitute homicide (lynching hangs in the shadows of the book). Yet *The Monster* remains equivocal in relation to questions of race, and its language and moods are implicated in those of white supremacy—implicated to such a degree that it becomes hard to understand the real significance of the fact that its central character is black. His suffering is to that degree made race-neutral, as it becomes clear that the object of Crane's satire isn't racism; its object is closer to small-town, suburban bigotry of the kind Sinclair Lewis would later take as his theme.

In chapter 4, I turn to Charles Chesnutt, who, like his best-known creation, Uncle Julius, had nowhere to turn in the post-Reconstruction South, or in post-Reconstruction America. In his first book, *The Conjure Woman*, Chesnutt introduces us to this Uncle Julius, a laborer who must tell tales and "wear the mask" Paul Laurence Dunbar speaks of in order to earn a living (Dunbar 167). Here, I argue, Chesnutt offers us a kind of alter ego, a figure situated as he was himself—that is, as an author writing not simply in the "plantation tale" genre that white authors such as Joel Chandler Harris and Thomas Nelson Page had created, but in the larger world of white-owned and white-dominated American publishing. This explains why his *au revoir* to America as a writer should be such a tale as "Baxter's Procrustes," a brilliant satire of a literary culture where books are judged by the quality of their covers rather than by the character of their contents. I address also the degree to which his two major novels—*The House Behind the Cedars* and *The Marrow of Tradition*—reveal, with extraordinary nuance, the work of white supremacy (as a state of mind, and as a means to discipline labor). In treating the first of these novels I show how the antagonism that sets white over black assimilated and exacerbated an ancient antagonism setting soul (or spirit) over body (or matter)—an antagonism dating to pre-Socratic philosophy and the Pauline scriptures.

Chapter 5 takes up Richard Wright. In an essay offering an overview of his career, I refine arguments laid down in the first two chapters, and also in the fourth; and then suggest how it was that this "native son" wound up in exile. There is a logic to Wright's end, to be found, again, in my first premise: that America is an imaginary place with real people living in it—some of whom simply cannot bear living in a nation so dislocated from its ideals as to have become a soothing fiction for those who benefit from that dislocation, and a fraud for those who do not.

Finally, in a sixth chapter, I turn to Jack Kerouac and *On the Road*. This novel, written as the civil rights movement began, and published as it achieved its first tentative victories, revives that "imaginary America" in which such things as "plantation tales" and the myth of the "happy Negro" are possible. Early on, the book does hold out a promise to free its readers from bondage to an American past that was hardly imaginary, with all its appalling contingencies. But rather than the radical departure it was taken for by many in 1957, *On the Road* devolves into a perfectly familiar and nostalgic sort of fiction—or, as I like to say, a "peasant dream." Yet *the writing of the novel* seems somehow to know more about America than the writer. It bears a guilty conscience for what it does, and for what it fails to do—for its sins of commission and omission. For that reason, despite its "peasant dreaming," the novel can, as with a kind of glamour, make us "citizens, by anticipation, in the world we crave," as George Santayana put it in his *Interpretations of Poetry and Religion* (vi). Mill City, California, as Kerouac describes it in part 1 of the book, always exists as a possibility in *On the Road*: "It was, so they say, the only community in America where whites and Negroes lived together voluntarily; and that was so, and so wild and joyous a place I've never seen since" (61). Yet Kerouac himself couldn't really see this novel American place as he wrote *On the Road*—even as it was beginning to be brought into existence by Martin Luther King, Jr., and others—precisely because his "America" remains, as I have said, an "imaginary" space: *a place we've never seen since*. Like Crane, he had evolved a certain style of forgetting. The better to tie the book up, I bring to bear, in my reading of *On the Road*, both Wright and Chesnutt, and also James Baldwin, whose remarks on the Beat Generation, and whose book *The Fire Next Time*, are, for me, an essential corrective to *On the Road*.

As for my title: I take that from the centerpiece of Du Bois's *The Souls of Black Folk*, the essay that forms the intersection through which every other essay in that book passes and re-passes: "Of the Wings of Atalanta." It is an essay about the New South, and about the new America that allowed it to rise. "Perhaps Atlanta was not christened for the winged maiden of dull Boeotia," Du Bois writes: "You know the tale,—how swarthy Atalanta, tall and wild, would marry only him who out-raced her; and how the wily Hippomenes laid three apples of gold in the way. She fled like a shadow, paused, startled over the first apple, but even as he stretched his hand, fled again; hovered over the second, then, slipping from his hot grasp, flew over river, vale, and hill; but as she lingered over the third, his arms fell round her, and looking on each other, the blazing passion of their love profaned the sanctuary of Love, and they were cursed. If Atlanta be not named for Atalanta, she ought to have been" (416). Then he adds: "The Wings of Atalanta are the coming universities of the South. They alone can bear the maiden past the temptation of golden fruit. They will not guide her flying feet away from the cotton and gold; for—ah, thoughtful Hippomenes!—do not the apples lie in the very Way of Life? But they will guide her over and beyond them, and leave her kneeling in the Sanctuary of Truth and Freedom and broad Humanity, virgin and undefiled" (421). Here, in a fable that takes greed for lust, and lust for greed, Du Bois finds his new myth for America's unquestionably bleak past, and also for its *possibly* bleak future. Shall we "profane" what ought properly be an American "sanctuary of Love," that beloved community where, as Kerouac has his Sal Paradise say, "whites and Negroes" live together "joyously"—shall we defile *this* with "the gambler's code of the bourse," as he puts it (416); or with (say) a prison-industrial complex? Or, instead of stooping for gold, shall we re-imagine our nation out of possibility and into real time and democracy of the kind Du Bois advocated? "Plant deeply and for all time," he says, "centres of learning and living, colleges that yearly would send into the life of the South a few white men and a few black men of broad culture, catholic tolerance, and trained ability, joining their hands to other hands, and giving to this squabble of the Races a decent and dignified peace" (422).

After the 1995 Oklahoma City bombing, carried out by a white supremacist; after Hurricane Katrina in 2005 and its many thousands gone; after predatory lending, sub-prime mortgages, and credit-default swaps zeroed out billions in wealth amongst the poorest Americans; after three decades during which inequality of income has approached what it was in the post-Reconstruction years; after the distortion of the American electorate by a "prison gerrymandering" that eerily recalls electoral distortions effected by the "three fifths" clause of the Constitution; and after the installation of a white nationalist administration in the White House, led by a president who propagated the racist "birther" lie; a president who more readily condemns African American athletes who take a knee than white supremacists who carry a torch for Robert E. Lee; who prefers immigrants from Scandinavia to those from what he calls "shithole" countries in Africa (or the Caribbean); and who repeatedly states, contrary to the truth, that 3–5 million votes were cast for his opponent by non-white "illegals" (a lie that emboldens conservative state legislators bent on passing voter-suppression laws under color of "protecting" the ballot)—in light of all this, the questions I address remain as vital as they were in 1903, when Du Bois first proposed, in speaking of *The Souls of Black Folk*, to lift the veil that estranges us, one from another.[38]

Du Bois might as well have been writing in 2019 as in 1935, when he said, in the "argument" prefixed to chapter 9 of *Black Reconstruction*: "The price of the disaster of slavery and civil war was the necessity of quickly assimilating into American democracy a mass of ignorant laborers in whose hands alone for the moment lay the power of preserving the ideals of popular government; of overthrowing a slave economy and establishing upon it *an industry primarily for the profit of the workers* [both black and white]. It was this price which in the end America refused to pay and today suffers for that refusal" (my emphasis; 325). Whether America will remain a quasi-illusory democracy, or whether it will become the social-democratic nation Du Bois long hoped for, is as open for debate now as it was when the Reconstruction was destroyed, and white supremacy "Redeemed" in the 1870s. A fresh "backward glance o'er [our] traveled roads," as Walt Whitman put it (5), will better help us understand how we got here.

CHAPTER ONE

FREDERICK DOUGLASS AND THE PHILOSOPHY OF SLAVERY

It was doubtless the fact that, at the era of the revolution, many of the Southern states began to feel the burthen of unproductive slaves, and that a growing disposition to be clear of them manifested itself simultaneously with the mammon-prompted philanthropy of England. A great danger was thus springing up, when the inventions of the cotton-gin, the carding machine, the spinning-jenny, and the steam engine, combined to weave that net-work of cotton which formed an indissoluble cord, binding the black, who was threatened to be cast off, to human progress.

—Josiah C. Nott, *DeBow's Review*, 1851

A normal and rounded development can only come from a use of faculties very different from that practiced by the average American since the discovery of the cotton gin.

—John Jay Chapman, *Causes and Consequences*, 1898

Cotton Thread Is the Union

Emerson had, in 1844, much warrant for his sour observation that "Cotton thread holds the union together. Patriotism is for holidays &

summer evenings with music and rockets," he says, "but cotton thread is the union" (*Journals* 356). This is, of course, an observation about slavery. The black slave was the instrument white men used to make the cotton thread that bound the union to their interests. Love of money, not of country, lay at the bottom of it. Music, rockets, holidays, and summer evenings: there is patriotism, and there is the power to which patriotism gives cover. Frederick Douglass had that power in mind when, in Rochester, New York, he took the stage one bunting-bedecked July evening in 1852, eight years after Emerson set down his remark about cotton: "What to the American slave is your Fourth of July?" he asked an audience of white abolitionists. "A day that reveals to him, more than all other days in the year, the gross injustice and cruelty to which he is the constant victim. To him, your celebration is a sham; your boasted liberty, an unholy license; your national greatness, swelling vanity; your sounds of rejoicing are empty and heartless; your denunciations of tyrants, brass-fronted impudence; your shouts of liberty and equality, hollow mockery; your prayers and hymns, your sermons and thanksgivings, with all your religious parade and solemnity, are to him mere bombast, fraud, deception, impiety, and hypocrisy—a thin veil to cover up crimes which would disgrace a nation of savages."[1] How, then, can a thinking man be "patriotic," even for the span of a single summer evening? How can he make a "nation of savages" his own? In fact, the thing can be done, and it was to do precisely this—to denounce the nation that cotton wealth had made, and thereby re-imagine the republic as something other than a nation of mere commerce—that Frederick Douglass wrote *My Bondage and My Freedom* in 1855. But before inquiring into that hymn to American possibilities, we might consider further the implications of Emerson's remark about cotton and the union; it reveals much about the strange career of slavery, and, consequently, about the shape that the movement to abolish slavery took.

Cotton had been cultivated in South Carolina as early as 1767. But not until the 1780s and 1790s, when more profitable varieties were imported from the Bahamas, did large-scale planting take hold. Cotton exports from South Carolina rose from 9,840 pounds in 1790 to 8,000,000 pounds in 1800. The introduction of the cotton gin in 1793 made the processing of cotton cheap, and, with new markets for the commodity widening, investment in the crop expanded quickly, in the early years of the nineteenth century, across the whole of the lower South—territory that had only recently been brought into the union by way of the Louisiana Purchase in 1803 (and secured by Andrew Jackson's victory in the Creek War of 1813–14 and by his defeat of the British at New Orleans in 1815). And with cotton went slavery.

National production rates over the period leading up the Civil War illustrate the growth of the commodity, which, by 1840, came to be known simply as "King Cotton." In 1811, sixty-seven million pounds of cotton were produced; in 1831, 322 million pounds; in 1851, more than one billion pounds; and in 1860, on the eve of the war, 1,536,000,000 pounds. During the period between 1820 and 1861 cotton was consistently the top US export. Cotton accounted for some 61% of all exports and merchandise in the United States when the Civil War began (Baptist 114). Atop this economic base, characterized, as it was, by intensive "mono-crop" agriculture produced by chattel slavery, there arose a body of opinion—theological, political, ethnological, medical, and literary—to support the idea that the South's peculiar institution was not merely profitable for the small class of men who engaged in it on a large scale, but, as South Carolina senator John C. Calhoun said, a "positive good" for the nation as a whole, and even for the world. The new means of producing wealth had given rise to certain mores. These crystallized into a new morality, which was forthrightly white supremacist.

John Jay Chapman rightly pointed out—he was the grandson of Maria Weston Chapman, an associate of the leading abolitionist William Lloyd Garrison—that this new way of thinking would have shocked Americans of Thomas Jefferson's day (Chapman 23). Millions of women and men— slaves—had become, as Frederick Douglass put it on that day of music and rockets in 1852, "food for the cotton field" (*A* 436), whose great maw, at the time, was the Mississippi delta and its adjacent regions. But what of Chapman's claim? How had men of Jefferson's day regarded slavery? Jefferson's own *Notes on the State of Virginia* affords us a fairly accurate view of the matter. "The whole commerce between master and slave," he writes, "is a perpetual exercise of the most boisterous passions, the most unremitting despotism on the one part, and degrading submissions on the other." That man must be "a prodigy" who could escape such a circumstance "with his manners and morals undepraved," Jefferson concludes, as one who should know. Worse still, the mere existence of slavery presents a standing threat to republican institutions. "Can the liberties of a nation be thought secure," Jefferson asks, "when we have removed [by upholding slavery] their only firm basis, a conviction in the minds of the people that these liberties are a gift of God? That they are not to be violated but with his wrath? Indeed I tremble for my country when I reflect that God is just:

that his justice cannot sleep forever.... The Almighty has no attribute," Jefferson says, "which can take side with us in such a contest" (174–75).

Jefferson, himself a slaveholder, and not without an interest in the matter, took it for granted that slavery was morally indefensible. Of course, in his view, practical considerations prevented its immediate abolition. Instead he looked forward, mystically, to the gradual disappearance of the institution as "the spirit of the master" abated, and as the spirit of the slave "rose from the dust" of his abjection (175). A generation or two, it was hoped, would see the business consummated. Yet such is the nature of progress in these matters that, by 1861, when the Confederate States of America was founded, and when investments in cotton as a proportion of the total economy of the South had reached their peak, it was a truth unquestioned in that section of the nation that slavery, rather than a necessary evil, as Jefferson had believed, was a blessing that would "hush the murmur of the world's distress." The words are those of South Carolina poet Henry Timrod in "The Cotton Boll." He believed, quite sincerely, that the South's peculiar institution would "give labor to the poor the whole planet o'er" and "save from want and crime the humblest door." For the extension of all these blessings God himself had made the Confederacy "great and rich" in what Timrod unforgettably calls—in a stunning show of commodity fetishism, as if the crop descended from heaven, abstracted entirely from the real contexts of its production—"the snow of Southern summers" (125–31): cotton.[2] American slavery, or so it appeared to Confederate expansionists like Timrod, was only in its *infancy*. And, Jefferson notwithstanding, men saw in it the one thing needful, if manners and morals were to remain undepraved.

For his part, Alexander H. Stephens, vice president of the new Confederacy, felt quite prepared to chastise the Founding Fathers for having framed a nation on a proposition now discredited by nothing less than "science" itself—to wit, the Jeffersonian proposition that "all men are created equal." I briefly touched on Stephens's "cornerstone" address in my introduction. Revisiting it here allows for a fuller understanding of its audacity. The new Constitution of the Confederate States of America, Stephens said, "put at rest forever all the agitating questions relating to our peculiar institutions—African slavery as it exists among us, the proper status of the Negro in our form of civilization." I quote his speech at length—it was well known in its day—because it tells us much about the struggle in which Frederick Douglass would labor all his long life as an advocate of political and civil rights. "The prevailing ideas entertained by [Jefferson] and most of the leading statesmen at the time of the formation of the old Constitution were," Stephens points out, "that the enslavement of the African was in violation of the laws of nature; that it was wrong in principle, socially, morally and politically." And he continues:

> It was an evil they knew not well how to deal with; but the general opinion of the men of that day was, that, somehow or other, in the order of Providence, the institution would be evanescent and pass away.... Those ideas, however, were fundamentally wrong. They rested upon the assumption of the equality of races. This was an error. It was a sandy foundation, and the idea of a Government built upon it—when the "storm came and the wind blew, it fell." Our new Government is founded upon exactly the opposite ideas; its foundations are laid, its cornerstone rests, upon the great truth that the Negro is not equal to the white man; that slavery, subordination to the superior race, is his natural and moral condition.... The truth of this principle may be slow in development, as all truths are, and ever have been, in the various branches of science. It was so with the principles announced by Galileo—it was so with Adam Smith and his principles of political economy. It was so with Harvey, and his theory of the circulation of the blood. It is stated that not a single one of the medical profession, living at the time of the announcement of the truths made by him, admitted them. Now, they are universally acknowledged. May we not therefore look with confidence to the ultimate universal acknowledgment of the truths upon which our system rests? (quoted in Cleveland 721–22)

Stephens concludes by echoing the Bible, the better to sanctify the new Confederate States of America: "This stone [i.e., of white supremacy] which was rejected by the first builders 'is become the chief stone of the corner' in our new edifice" (Cleveland 723). The passage in question is Matthew 21:42: "Jesus saith unto them, Did ye never read in the scriptures, The stone which the builders rejected, the same is become the head of the corner: this is the Lord's doing, and it is marvellous in our eyes?"[3]

How had so complete a change in public sentiment occurred since 1783, when Jefferson set down his *Notes*? How had men of learning and affairs come to regard "Negro inferiority," and white supremacy, as truths established "scientifically"—truths to be likened, in their claims on our assent, to Harvey's model of the circulatory system, or to the model of the solar system established by Galileo? The explanation must be economic. Sentiment as to the "good" of slavery precisely tracked the rise of the value of the crop that slaves produced. It is enough to make anyone a historical materialist (as I earlier intimated).[4] Consider the intuitive Marxism of John Greenleaf Whittier's poem "The Haschish" (1854), which provides, without aiming at it, an able interpretive framework for the poetry of Henry Timrod:

> Of all that Orient lands can vaunt
> > Of marvels with our own competing,
> The strangest is the Haschish plant,
> > And what will follow on its eating.
>
> What pictures to the taster rise,
> > Of Dervish or of Almeh dances!
> Of Eblis, or of Paradise,
> > Set all aglow with Houri glances!
>
> The poppy visions of Cathay,
> > The heavy beer-trance of the Suabian;
> The wizard lights and demon play
> > Of nights Walpurgis and Arabian!
>
> The Mollah and the Christian dog
> > Change place in mad metempsychosis;
> The Muezzin climbs the synagogue,
> > The Rabbi shakes his beard at Moses! . . .
>
> Such scenes that Eastern plant awakes;
> > But we have one ordained to beat it,
> The Haschish of the West, which makes
> > Or fools or knaves of all who eat it.
>
> The preacher eats, and straight appears
> > His Bible in a new translation;
> Its angels negro overseers,
> > And Heaven itself a snug plantation! . . .
>
> The Judge partakes, and sits erelong
> > Upon his bench a railing blackguard;
> Decides off-hand that right is wrong,
> > And reads the ten commandments backward.
>
> O potent plant! so rare a taste
> > Has never Turk or Gentoo gotten;
> The hempen Haschish of the East
> > Is powerless to our Western Cotton! (254)

In any case, in 1855, Frederick Douglass found arrayed against him in the institution of slavery a political, economic, and social edifice more firmly entrenched, more articulate in its self-defense, more arrogant in its ambitions to extend its influence and territories than Thomas Jefferson had ever conceived. Josiah C. Nott—celebrated physician, proponent of scientific racism and of the "polygenetic" theory of human origins—was certainly sanguine. "The time is . . . rapidly approaching," he wrote in *DeBow's Review* (New Orleans) in 1851, "when the [American] South and West will manufacture the greatest proportion of their own raw products; and that large shipping interest in Europe and the North which depends upon the transport of the raw products, will find itself confined to the carrying of goods; while the markets of the world will come to depend upon the Mississippi valley for wrought fabrics, as they have hitherto done for the raw material. New Orleans may become the Liverpool of America, communicating by the father of waters with that vast region which is to be the Manchester of the world" (142).

And so, writes Du Bois, "in order to maintain its income without sacrifice or exertion, the South fell back on a doctrine of racial differences which it asserted made higher intelligence and increased efficiency impossible for [free] Negro labor." Here entered those ideological developments that arose with and appeared to naturalize the Cotton Kingdom in all its practices and mores. (Josiah Nott was especially active in this field.) Seeking "an excuse," says Du Bois, "for [his] lazy indulgence, the planter easily found, invented and proved it. His subservient religious leaders reverted to the 'Curse of Canaan'; his pseudo-scientists gathered and supplemented all available doctrines of race inferiority [as in the American school of ethnology]; his scattered schools and pedantic periodicals repeated these legends, until for the average planter born after 1840 it was impossible not to believe that all valid laws in psychology, economics and politics stopped with the Negro race" (*Black Reconstruction* 39). Church, science, education, and journalism conspired. These were the ideological state apparatuses necessary to the maintenance of the slave state apparatus proper (to use Althusser's terms). They advanced with arms locked. "The South could say that the Negro, even when brought into modern civilization, could not be civilized," adds Du Bois, "and that, therefore, he and the other colored peoples of the world were so far inferior to the whites that the white world had a right to rule mankind for their own selfish interests" (39). "The whole weight of America was thrown to color caste," as Du Bois puts it elsewhere in *Black Reconstruction* (30).[5] And the larger white world, which hardly needing the prompt, followed suit in Africa and Asia.

We have seen how slavery came to be defended as "a positive good." How did the opposition to slavery evolve—for this never disappeared—between Jefferson's day and the start of the Civil War? We can distinguish several schools of anti-slavery thought in the period, in two of which—and these mutually incompatible—Douglass was a major figure. (In fact, *My Bondage and My Freedom* marks his passage from the one school to the other.) Jefferson's generation, we know, had looked vaguely forward to the "gradual" abolition of slavery, if by no other means than by the work of Almighty God. Obviously, no coherent program of action is associated with this school of thought. But in conjunction with the doctrine of "gradual" emancipation there arose various "colonization" schemes, which sought to "repatriate" slaves, and free persons of color, to Africa, or, as was sometimes suggested, to Haiti or some other Caribbean nation or territory.

Against both "colonization" schemes and "gradualism" arose the Garrisonian school, named for its founder and great animating force, William Lloyd Garrison. After brief flirtations both with gradualism and colonization, for which he publicly (and self-scathingly) repented, Garrison developed the doctrine of "immediate" and "unconditional" emancipation, which he propounded through *The Liberator*, the weekly anti-slavery paper he published in Boston beginning in 1831. Immediacy was not the only novel element in his abolitionism; he also demanded that full citizenship rights be granted to the slaves on their emancipation. He opposed all "colonization" schemes and had nothing but contempt for proposals that slaveholders be compensated for liberating their slaves—some moderate anti-slavery agitators favored a system of compensation—on the grounds that the "ransom" implicitly acknowledged the right of "property" in men. With Garrison's appearance, the character of the anti-slavery movement forever changed. As his doctrine evolved, he grew more radical in outlook.

Revisions to Garrison's doctrine came quickly. In August 1831 a slave called Nat Turner led an insurrection in Southampton, Virginia. More than fifty whites died in the fighting, and more than a hundred blacks. It did not go unnoticed in Massachusetts that Virginia authorities called on the Federal government, as warranted by the Constitution, to assist it in suppressing the rebellion (Article I, Section 8:15). For this reason, and because the Constitution obliged states where slavery did not exist to return fugitive slaves to their owners, Garrison concluded that the Constitution was, both in theory and in practice, a "pro-slavery" instrument. "There is much declamation," Garrison said in the pages of *The Liberator*, "about the sacredness of the compact which was formed between the free and the slave States on the adoption of the Constitution. A sacred compact, forsooth! We pronounce it the most bloody and heaven-daring arrangement ever made for the continuance and protection of a system of the most atrocious villainy ever exhibited on earth." "So long as we continue one body," he added, "as union—as nation—the compact involves us in the guilt and danger of slavery" (Garrison 1:308–9).

It took some years for the new doctrine to be perfected, but here was the beginning of Garrisonian "disunionism": the call for the dissolution of the union, and for non-participation in electoral politics. (Such participation, it was thought, implied consent to the terms of the US Constitution, the document under whose general aegis elections are conducted.) By 1842 the masthead of each number of *The Liberator* bore this banner: "THE UNITED STATES CONSTITUTION IS A COVENANT WITH DEATH AND AN AGREEMENT WITH HELL! NO UNION WITH SLAVEHOLDERS!" With that, Garrisonian abolitionism had matured, and in this shape it would remain until war came in April 1861: 1) immediate, unconditional emancipation; 2) disunion; 3) refusal to participate in electoral politics; 4) non-violence; and 5) exclusive reliance on a policy of "moral suasion," to be effected through propaganda, public debate, and non-political organizations—through, as Garrison's own children put it in their chronicle of his life and works, "the simple fidelity of a remnant pledged to eternal hostility to slavery wherever found and legalized, and to incessant agitation" (Garrison 3:509).

Abolitionists of the Garrisonian school traveled from Maine to Illinois, holding rallies. They debated their opponents, both within and without the wider abolition movement. They distributed pamphlets, books, newspapers. They raised money. And, on occasion, they ritually burned copies of the Constitution in town squares. Frederick Douglass entered the Garrisonian movement—star-struck in its ideals, miraculous in its purity—with astonishing force in 1841. Within months he was its most popular and effective orator. His first autobiography, *Narrative of the Life of Frederick Douglass, an American Slave, Written By Himself*, appeared in 1845 with a preface by Garrison; advertisements for it ran in the pages of *The Liberator*; it was published out of the same office in Cornhill Street, Boston, that printed Garrison's great weekly; and the closing paragraphs of the book take special pains to extol the newspaper. Douglass's debt to the Garrisonians is evident from beginning to end.

We must now consider "political abolitionism." This was organized, initially, in New York State, around the small but influential Liberty Party (founded in 1840), whose central figure and financial backer was the wealthy landholder Gerritt Smith. Smith and the Liberty Party maintained, against the Garrisonians, that the Constitution was, in fact, anti-slavery in "spirit," notwithstanding clauses providing for the return of fugitives and for the (aforementioned) use of Federal power in suppressing insurrections. This position was controversial as a reading of the Constitution as it then stood. But when put into practice it allowed, as Garrisonian "disunionism" did not, for the vigorous pursuit, through the instrument of electoral politics, of a policy of complete and immediate abolition; and it held out the productive promise of perfecting the Constitution. The policy of working within the Constitution had going for it, to boot, one all but unassailable rejoinder to the Garrisonian alternative. "The Garrisonian view of disunion," Douglass said, "if carried to a successful issue, would only place the people of the North in the same relation to American slavery which they now bear to the slavery of Cuba or the Brazils" (*A* 133).[6] And though Garrison was initially loath to concede the point, "political abolitionism" found its validation in the policies of the Lincoln administration in 1863, and, after the war, in the adoption of the 13th, 14th and 15th amendments.

It was toward "political abolition" of this kind that Douglass drifted in the later 1840s and early 1850s. The move was complete in 1851 when Douglass merged his paper, *The North Star*, with the *Liberty Party Paper* and accepted financial backing from Smith in the new enterprise. When *My Bondage and My Freedom* appeared four years later, published by a firm in western New York State, a stronghold of political abolition, it bore, set in the ornate patchwork of typefaces used for such purposes in those days, a dedication to the "Honorable Gerrit Smith as a slight token of esteem for his character, admiration for his genius and benevolence," and in gratitude for his "ranking slavery with piracy and murder," and for "denying it either a legal or constitutional existence" (*A* 104). The break with Garrison was irrevocable, and Douglass suffered much for it in the Garrisonian press, where he was castigated, often in the tawdry ways, as an apostate bought out by Smith (McFeely 180). The view he now took of the Constitution is epitomized in a speech he gave in 1863: "I hold that the Federal Government was never, in its essence, anything but an anti-slavery government. Abolish slavery tomorrow, and not a sentence or syllable of the Constitution need be altered. It was purposely so framed as to give no claim, no sanction to the claim, of property in man. If in its origin slavery had any relation to the government, it was only as the scaffolding to the magnificent structure, to be removed as soon as the building was completed" (*Life and Writings* 3:365). It was of course in tacit acknowledgement of this fact that Alexander H. Stephens and the other architects of the

Confederacy saw fit to lay the foundation of their government on a new "cornerstone": the "scientific truth," as they believed, of white supremacy.

My Bondage and My Freedom: Its Origins and Character

On February 24, 1845, the Garrisonian abolitionist and orator Wendell Phillips wrote to his friend Elizabeth Pease: "Frederick Douglass who is now writing out his story thinks of relaxing by arranging a voyage" (*A* 1078). There is a sly euphemism in this, which Phillips and Pease conspiratorially enjoy: Douglass arranged for his voyage abroad not so much to relax—he never relaxed in those years—as to escape the attentions of any agents his Maryland master might dispatch to Massachusetts now that his whereabouts and identity would be made public in his *Narrative of the Life of Frederick Douglass*. He wrote the book, despite the fact that it would expose him to danger, for reasons later set out in *My Bondage and My Freedom*: "People doubted if I had ever been a slave. They said I did not talk like a slave, look like a slave, nor act like a slave, and that they believed I had never been south of Mason and Dixon's line." Accordingly, Douglass "wrote out the leading facts" connected with his experience, and thus "put it in the power of any who doubted, to ascertain the truth or falsehood" of his story (*A* 367).

Why, then, did Douglass publish a second autobiography a mere ten years later? The question is the more interesting because only seven percent of the new book, by word count, covers ground not already traversed in the 1845 *Narrative*. As this figure suggests, *My Bondage and My Freedom* is not a supplement to the *Narrative*, and not by any means its continuation. It is instead a radical revision of the earlier book. This fact looms the larger when we consider that in preparing his third autobiography, *The Life and Times of Frederick Douglass*, published in 1881 and expanded in 1893, the portion of book devoted to his life through 1855 remains materially unchanged from *My Bondage and My Freedom*. There can be little doubt that the latter is Douglass's "definitive" account of himself, though, curiously, teachers in high schools and universities seldom assign it, so attached are they to the large teaching anthologies, which prefer the shorter, more Garrisonian, and less politically complex text of 1845.[7]

The reader of *My Bondage and My Freedom* soon enough discovers that Douglass's apprenticeship to the Garrisonians was not entirely to his liking. Compare the following two accounts of his watershed inaugural appearance on the podium in Nantucket in 1841, the first from the *Narrative*, the second from *My Bondage*:

[1845:] I had not long been a reader of the "Liberator," before I got a pretty correct idea of the principles, measures and spirit of the anti-slavery reform. I took right hold of the cause. I could do but little; but what I could, I did with a joyful heart, and never felt happier than when in an anti-slavery meeting. I seldom had much to say at the meetings, because what I wanted to say was said so much better by others. But, while attending an anti-slavery convention at Nantucket, on the 11th of August, 1841, I felt strongly moved to speak, and was at the same time much urged to do so by Mr. William C. Coffin, a gentleman who had heard me speak in the colored people's meeting at New Bedford. It was a severe cross, and I took it up reluctantly. The truth was, I felt myself a slave, and the idea of speaking to white people weighed me down. I spoke but a few moments, when I felt a degree of freedom, and said what I desired with considerable ease. From that time until now, I have been engaged in pleading the cause of my brethren—with what success, and with what devotion, I leave those acquainted with my labors to decide. (*A* 96)

[1855:] My speech on this occasion is about the only one I ever made, of which I do not remember a single connected sentence. It was with the utmost difficulty that I could stand erect, or that I could command and articulate two words without hesitation and stammering. I trembled in every limb. I am not sure that my embarrassment was not the most effective part of my speech, if speech it could be called. At any rate, this is about the only part of my performance that I now distinctly remember. But excited and convulsed as I was, the audience, though remarkably quiet before, became as much excited as myself. Mr. Garrison followed me, taking me as his text; and now, whether I had made an eloquent speech in behalf of freedom or not, his was one never to be forgotten by those who heard it. Those who had heard Mr. Garrison oftenest, and had known him longest, were astonished. It was an effort of unequaled power, sweeping down, like a very tornado, every opposing barrier, whether of sentiment or opinion. For a moment, he possessed that almost fabulous inspiration, often referred to but seldom attained, in which a public meeting is transformed, as it were, into a single individuality—the orator wielding a thousand heads and hearts at once, and by the simple majesty of his all controlling thought, converting his hearers into the express image of his own soul. That night there were at least one thousand Garrisonians in Nantucket! (*A* 364–65)

So far, both accounts are friendly to Garrison. In fact, the second is apparently the friendlier of the two—save for one telling remark: after Douglass spoke, Garrison "took [him] as his text," we are told. The metaphor is homiletic. Douglass is the "text" on which Garrison's "sermon" is based; he is the "matter," Garrison the expositor; he is the body, Garrison the mind; he is the story-teller, Garrison the interpreter; he deals in facts, Garrison in theory. This, anyway, is the idea, and in it we see intimated the more patronizing features of Garrison's patronage. All things considered, it is no surprise that, as Douglass confesses in the 1845 account, he felt ill at ease addressing "white people." It was indeed like "taking up a cross." John Collins, a confederate of Garrison, accompanied Douglass on his first lecture tour, and, in introducing him, inevitably called him "a graduate from the peculiar institution" with "his diploma written on [his] back" (*A* 365). Douglass's body was, for the Garrisonians, the originating site of his writing. His scars, and not his words and thoughts, "authenticated" him. The interest his handlers took in that body was, or so at times it appeared, unseemly. They fairly dwelt on it, to the exclusion of taking a proper interest in his mind. Douglass explains: "Among the first duties assigned me, on entering the ranks, was to travel, in company with Mr. George Foster, to secure subscribers to the 'Anti-slavery Standard' and the 'Liberator.' . . . I was generally introduced as a 'chattel'—a 'thing'—a piece of southern 'property'—the chairman assuring the audience that *it* could speak." The "thing" continues:

> During the first three or four months, my speeches were almost exclusively made up of narrations of my own personal experience as a slave. "Let us have the facts," said the people. So also said Friend George Foster, who always wished to pin me down to my simple narrative. "Give us the facts," said Collins, "we will take care of the philosophy." Just here arose some embarrassment. It was impossible for me to repeat the same old story month after month, and to keep up my interest in it. It was new to the people, it is true, but it was an old story to me; and to go through with it night after night, was a task altogether too mechanical for my nature. "Tell your story, Frederick," would whisper my then revered friend, William Lloyd Garrison, as I stepped upon the platform. I could not always obey, for I was now reading and thinking. New views of the subject were presented to my mind. It did not entirely satisfy me to *narrate* wrongs; I felt like *denouncing* them. I could not always curb my moral indignation for the perpetrators of slaveholding villainy, long enough for a circumstantial statement of the facts which I felt almost everybody must know. Besides, I was growing, and needed room. "People won't believe you ever was a slave, Frederick, if you keep on this way," said Friend Foster. "Be yourself," said Collins, "and tell your story." It was said to me, "Better have a little of the plantation manner of speech than not; 'tis not

best that you seem too learned." These excellent friends were actuated by the best of motives, and were not altogether wrong in their advice; and still I must speak just the word that seemed to me the word to be spoken by me. (*A* 366–67)

It was not necessarily gratifying, or so Douglass hinted in 1855, to be "taken as a text" for the expounding of other men. The lecture platform, as Eric Sundquist points out in connection with this passage, soon came to seem like an auction block (104). Douglass felt he had been "pinned down," and also discouraged, at least implicitly, from "thinking" too much. His office was to show himself, and to "obey." To be sure, Douglass was "on display," when he mounted the stage, in a way that neither Collins nor Garrison nor any of the white abolitionists ever was: his "body" was the thing, not his mind. Collins enjoins Douglass to "be himself," but this really means, we are allowed to conclude: Put on blackface; be a white man's idea of what a black man truly is. Otherwise (so goes the unstated argument), no white man will recognize you; to a white audience you will be, in the most literal sense of the word, incredible. The abolitionist lecture hall becomes a theater for the staging of a singularly highbrow sort of minstrel show, with the familiar—and deeply sympathetic, to white hearts and minds—"plantation darky," the sort of black man with whom these white Northerners could most be "at ease." In a word, these white abolitionists were clipping the wings of Atalanta from their fledgling fugitive slave.

At times Douglass seems to suspect that his white readers may suffer from these same debilities. Twice he apologizes to his reader—with ironic humility—for philosophizing unduly, and without portfolio, as it were. After discussing the "self-executing laws of eternal justice"—the sort of matter one might expect to encounter in Emerson's "Compensation"—he says: "But let others philosophize; it is my province here to relate and describe" (*A* 189). And later, after mounting an ingenious defense of the slave's right to steal, and even to take up arms against his master—this latter policy the pacifist Garrisonians would surely have opposed—Douglass says: "But my kind readers are, probably, less concerned about my opinions, than about that which more nearly touches my personal experience" (*A* 248). And so it goes: Give us the facts, Frederick; let the kind (white) reader take care of the "philosophy," which in any case will exclude the notion that theft and armed insurrection are in order.

On the abolitionist lecture circuit, Douglass picked up a certain habit of guarded self-deprecation. And in *My Bondage and My Freedom*, one is made aware of just how peculiar the felt relation of black author to white reader is or can be—at least in American contexts. Black writers would often revisit the problem, as we shall see when we turn to Charles Chesnutt, W. E. B. Du Bois, and Richard Wright later in this book. In any case, it was necessary for Douglass to be unmistakably and conventionally "black" for the Garrisonians to "be themselves"—for them really to feel like "white" men. "Better have a *little* of the plantation manner of speech than not," they told him; "'tis best that you not seem too learned." I suspect the advice was not chiefly meant to fend off accusations that Douglass had not been raised a slave. In fact, it bespeaks a terrible need—a need perhaps not altogether unrelated to the creed espoused by Douglass's Old Master in Baltimore: "Learning will spoil the best nigger in the world" (*A* 217). Here, among the most enlightened and radical of the abolitionists, Douglass had hoped to "forget that [his] skin was dark and [his] hair crisped" (*A* 366). Here he had hoped to find a world in which, as Du Bois might say, "walked souls alone, uncolored and unclothed" (*Souls* 509). And again, he was made to see himself through the medium of his "body"; again, he was made to assume a mask. Where in America could he become, as Whitman puts it in *Leaves of Grass*, published in this same year (1855), "undisguised" (14)?

The Philosophy of Slavery

Who shall "represent" the slave? The question has both political and literary implications, and it was to address both that Douglass wrote *My Bondage and My Freedom*. In it he would lay claim to the main and most productive tradition in American politics. In it he would appear not chiefly as a black man, and certainly not as a sentimental "plantation darky" in contemplation of whom white abolitionists might weep, but as, in the words of James McCune Smith's introduction to the first edition of the book, the "Representative American man"—as, in fact, the very "type" of his countrymen, white and black alike (*A* 132). This required that any trace of the deference he shows in the *Narrative* with respect to the Garrisonians be expunged, the better that he might emerge from behind the mask of white patronage. Instead of authenticating prefaces and letters from white eminences, there appears in *My Bondage* the introduction from which I have just quoted, written by a black, Edinburgh-trained physician, James McCune Smith—a man who ought to figure more prominently in histories of American literature.[8] He puts the matter unforgettably: "The same strong self-hood" that led Douglass "to measure strength with Mr. Covey," the "Negro-breaker" whom Douglass challenged and humiliated while still in his teens, led him to "wrench himself from the embrace of the Garrisonians" (*A* 137). The implied analogy must have stung Garrison to the quick (was Covey's "embrace" also his?). But he and his protégé were at irreconcilable odds—partly for party-political reasons, but also owing to the scandal-mongering attacks against Douglass that had been appearing in the Garrisonian press since 1851. (These went so far as to foment rumors of an affair between Douglass, who was married, and his white British associate Julia Griffiths [McFeely 186–87].) Douglass's pen can be wickedly sharp, but so had been Garrison's. In *My Bondage and My Freedom*, Douglass replies in kind.

The very style in which the new book is written is an index of his mature "self-mastery": it is by turns sardonic, ironic, playful; it is mercurial, in the best sense of the word—and always self-possessed. This style, this extraordinary "literacy," is in fact what gives him over to possession of himself. Even when he narrates the most distressing incidents, his control as a stylist affords him a certain detachment, which he deploys to brilliant effect. And he is careful to attribute whatever "love of letters" he possesses "*not to* [his] admitted Anglo-Saxon paternity, but to the native genius of [his] sable, unprotected, and uncultivated *mother*—a woman, who belonged to a race whose mental endowments it is, at present, fashionable to hold in disparagement and contempt" (*A* 156). These remarks are not present in the 1845 *Narrative*. And one is allowed to suspect, I believe, and even invited so to do, that the Garrisonians, abolitionists though they were, had yielded to this "fashionable" prejudice when they advised Douglass to let them "take care of the philosophy" (*A* 367). In *My Bondage and My Freedom* Douglass detaches the power of reason, and of the word, from "whiteness," and from "race" of any kind; these are for him merely *human* gifts, from which Southern slavery and Northern "caste-slavery" (*A* 128) alike sought to ban men and women of African descent, the better to make them "food for cotton fields," under color of the new "scientific" racism. In *My Bondage and My Freedom*, Douglass presents himself to the reader as a New World figure—a "Columbian," self-emancipated figure who would transcend "color" altogether. This maneuver is authorized by, and also authorizes, his adoption of political abolitionism—his full-hearted embrace of Enlightenment values, as against what struck him as the backward, feudal, and superstitious culture of the Old Worlds of Europe and Africa alike.

The novelty of Douglass's style in *My Bondage and My Freedom* is easily gauged by comparison of its opening sentences to the corresponding passage in the 1845 *Narrative*. The latter begins simply enough: "I was born in Tuckahoe, near Hillsborough, and about twelve miles from Easton, in Talbot county, Maryland" (*A* 15). In 1855 this becomes:

> In Talbot county, Eastern Shore, Maryland, near Easton, the county town of that county, there is a small district of country, thinly populated, and remarkable for nothing that I know of more than for the worn-out, sandy, desert-like appearance of its soil, the general dilapidation of its farms and fences, the indigent and spiritless character of its inhabitants, and the prevalence of ague and fever.
>
> The name of this singularly unpromising and truly famine stricken district is Tuckahoe, a name well known to all Marylanders, black and white. It was given to this section of country probably, at the first, merely in derision; or it may possibly have been applied to it, as I have heard, because some one of its earlier inhabitants had been guilty of the petty meanness of stealing a hoe—or taking a hoe that did not belong to him. Eastern Shore men usually pronounce the word *took*, as *tuck*; *Took-a-hoe*, therefore, is, in Maryland parlance, *Tuckahoe*. But, whatever may have been its origin—and about this I will not be positive—that name has stuck to the district in question; and it is seldom mentioned but with contempt and derision, on account of the barrenness of its soil, and the ignorance, indolence, and poverty of its people. Decay and ruin are everywhere visible, and the thin population of the place would have quitted it long ago, but for the Choptank river, which runs through it, from which they take abundance of shad and herring, and plenty of ague and fever.
>
> It was in this dull, flat, and unthrifty district, or neighborhood, surrounded by a white population of the lowest order, indolent and drunken to a proverb, and among slaves, who seemed to ask, "Oh! what's the use?" every time they lifted a hoe, that I—without any fault of mine—was born, and spent the first years of my childhood. (*A* 139–40)

The style, the address, of this second passage is arch to the point of satire. We sense an excess of facility, a power held in reserve of the sort found in writers of uncommon self-possession. This is evident even in the structure of the sentences, the first of which turns neatly upon its four-fold parallelism, setting in devastating equation desert soil, dilapidated farm, indigent character, and raging fever. And then there is the syntactic wit of the following sentence, which suggests the droll Augustan manner of Pope: "Decay and ruin are everywhere visible, and the thin population of the place would have quitted it long ago, but for the Choptank river, which runs through it, from which they take abundance of shad and herring, and plenty of ague and fever." The verb "take" has two objects, grammatically parallel but semantically disjunctive: one doesn't fish for "ague and fever," unless one is an indigent denizen of a barren land, too shiftless to get up and leave. And consider the playful etymology of the name "Tuckahoe." Here, surely, is a bit of satire carried over from Douglass's immensely popular lectures. As Douglass no doubt knew, Tuckahoe is a common enough place name in the eastern United States. It is of Native American origin, derived—though this Douglass might not have known—from the Algonquin name of an edible root. (Variant forms of the name as applied to the district in Talbot County include: Tochwogh, Tockwhogh, Tockwoghs, and Tukkoho; other "Tuckahoes" exist in Virginia, New York, and New Jersey.) Still, Douglass's intimation that "Tuckahoe" had a comical meaning is not entirely off the mark, and maybe the name was derisively applied to inhabitants of rural Talbot County, though not because they made a habit of stealing hoes. George Stewart's *American Place Names* reports that "the word passed into English, probably in the seventeenth century, and most of the namings would seem to be English rather than Indian, and to be from an acquired meaning, i.e., a backwoods or folksy person, such as might live on wild tubers, but with a humorous more than a derogatory suggestion" (496). But however things stand as to "Tuckahoe," the leisured expansiveness, the "liberty" with which this overture to the book is allowed to unfold characterizes the prose throughout *My Bondage and My Freedom*. The reader at once understands that this is a narrator who will not limit himself merely to giving us "the facts" ("I was born in Tuckahoe, near Hillsborough, and about twelve miles from Easton, in Talbot county, Maryland").

Of course, Douglass undertakes much more than a bit of humor when he sets before us the barren district of Tuckahoe. He means to advance a thesis: the political economy of slavery exhausts not merely the body of the slave, but the "body" of the land itself. "Natural" and "social" environments mirror one another, he suggests, and the reflection so implied works otherwise than at first we might expect: the people do not mirror the land; the land mirrors the people. In Tuckahoe the desolating pestilence of slavery had infected the very waters of the Choptank River. Douglass's description of the soil and land around Tuckahoe is of course "argumentative" (as the lawyers say). But it is not without foundation, as is clear from Eugene Genovese's essay "Cotton, Slavery, and Soil Erosion" in his *Political Economy of Slavery*: the use of slave labor did not sort well with good husbandry (even where cotton wasn't grown). In any case, readers of the 1855 edition of Douglass's book cannot mistake the general idea, here, because it is highlighted by a pair of intricate engravings (done by Nathaniel Orr), one of which stands at the beginning of part 1 of the book, "Life as a Slave" (fig. 1), and the second of which stands at the head of part 2, "Life as a Freeman" (fig. 2). Each engraving features five archetypical scenes. In the first, the center panel depicts a slave auction: a young woman, her head bowed in modesty, stands at the foot of the auctioneer (his gavel is raised), while a group of white men, some wearing top hats, others wearing rural garb of one sort or another, look on; in the deep background stands what obviously is a capitol building, with the stars and stripes hoisted. The auction of this black woman's body suggests prostitution. As Edward Baptist points out, "Starting in the early 1830s, the term 'fancy girl' or 'maid' began to appear in the interstate slave trade. It meant a young woman, usually light-skinned, sold at a high price explicitly linked to her sexual availability and attractiveness: 'For Sale: A coloured girl, of very superior qualifications . . . what speculators call a fancy girl; a bright mulatto, fine figure, straight, black hair, and very black eyes; very neat and cleanly in her dress and person'" (204).[9] The capitol dome in the background merely completes the idea: the slave state is a kind of brothel (and so it was often depicted in abolitionist writing). Above the center panel is one depicting a fugitive pursued by dogs and a mounted slave-catcher, the latter's pistol drawn and smoking; the image needs no explanation, save for the reminder that it likely has particular reference to the Fugitive Slave Bill of 1850, which—despite fierce, at times armed, resistance in certain quarters of the north—had gone some way toward nationalizing the institution of slavery. Beneath the center panel is an engraving illustrating the disparity in wealth at the South: a "Great House" stands at the left of the frame, the hovel of a slave shack at the right. Flanking the auction scene on its left is a picture illustrating the sloth of the "white" population: an overseer leans lazily—and "nondiegetically," as the film theorists say—against the border of the central panel itself (no doubt to suggest that his leisure literally "rests" upon the institution of the auction block); he keeps watch as a group of slaves work the cotton. To the right of the central panel two slaves dance the "juba"—as we learn to call it later in the book—as a white man looks on amused. I will have more to say in due course about this "juba beating," which, to Douglass, sums up the "vernacular" culture of the slave—something he always treats with suspicion, if not disdain: this folk culture, as he sees it, is inextricably bound up with the "priestcraft" of slavery (*A* 306). The essential point of the engraving is this: under slavery the land itself is made unsound; everything about it assumes a wasting air of infection, sensualism, decadence, and corruption. This is the "spirit" of the district of Tuckahoe, and Tuckahoe is, for Douglass, a *representative* American site.

Figure 1. Engraving by Nathaniel Orr (1822–1908) from Douglass's *My Bondage and My Freedom*, part 1, "Life as a Slave" (New York and Auburn: Miller, Orton & Mulligan), 1855.

Figure 2. Engraving by Nathaniel Orr (1822–1908) from Douglass's *My Bondage and My Freedom*, part 2, "Life as a Freeman" (New York and Auburn: Miller, Orton & Mulligan), 1855.

By contrast, the engraving illustrating his "Life as a Freeman" depicts an auction not of a woman but of cattle and sheep (the center panel); a landscape subordinated not to a wasteful and abusive regime of slave agriculture, but to the instruments of industry and technology (in the top panel a train steams across a bridge that spans a canal; telegraph wires stand in the foreground); children gather outside a school, as a steeple rises in the deep background (bottom panel); a farmer drives a sprightly team of horses with a plow (left panel); and a woman sits poised, wearing white robes, with books at her feet and a shield bearing the stars and stripes at her back (right panel). Clearly, "liberty" is associated with industrial progress and with science. We see in these panels the completion of the American Revolution, as this was imagined by such early Republican writers as Joel Barlow, author of *The Columbiad*, which holds out a vision of an empire not of wealth or of military power, but of Reason itself. This second engraving serves well enough to illustrate the town of New Bedford as Douglass soon describes it in a chapter titled "Liberty Attained." "The reader will be amused at my ignorance when I tell the notions I had of the state of northern wealth, enterprise, and civilization," Douglass writes.

> The impressions I had received were all wide of the truth. New Bedford, especially, took me by surprise, in the solid wealth and grandeur there exhibited. I had formed my notions respecting the social condition of the free states, by what I had seen and known of free, white, non-slaveholding people in the slave states. Regarding slavery as the basis of wealth, I fancied that no people could become very wealthy without slavery.... Judge, then, of my amazement and joy, when I found—as I did find—the very laboring population of New Bedford living in better houses, more elegantly furnished—surrounded by more comfort and refinement—than a majority of the slaveholders on the Eastern Shore of Maryland. There was my friend, Mr. Johnson, himself a colored man (who at the south would have been regarded as a proper marketable commodity), who lived in a better house—dined at a richer board—was the owner of more books—the reader of more newspapers—was more conversant with the political and social condition of this nation and the world—than nine-tenths of all the slaveholders of Talbot county, Maryland. Yet Mr. Johnson was a working man, and his hands were hardened by honest toil. Here, then, was something for observation and study. Whence the difference? The explanation was soon furnished, in the superiority of mind over simple brute force. (my emphasis; *A* 355)

The livestock is healthier and stronger, the fields neater and more fertile, the craftsmanship more exact. Labor everywhere exhibits a "superior mental character" (my emphasis; *A* 356). In *My Bondage and My Freedom*, liberty is inevitably associated with "mastery" of the "brutish" body—with the subordination of its unruly "passions" and "appetites," and of its corrupting sensuality, to the management of "mind" and "reason." Having arrived at this idea and having dispensed with the notion that Douglass means simply to give his reader "the facts," we begin to see the outlines of what might be called a "philosophy" of slavery.

Douglass tells us of the time—he was still a mere boy—when it first occurred to him to ask: "Why are some people slaves, and others masters?" (*A* 178). That this question should have overtaken him at all, when slavery everywhere presented itself as "natural," seems to require some explanation. And Douglass takes the view—authorized, if any authority is needed, by the Declaration of Independence—that the will to be "free" is in fact "an inborn dream" of "human nature," and thus a "constant menace to slavery," a menace which "all the powers of slavery" are "unable to silence or extinguish" (*A* 179). Slavery, then, can never relax; it is an institution most "unnatural," whose price is eternal vigilance. Later Douglass will liken it to a temperamental and delicate machine, which requires "conductors or safety valves"—for example, the "holiday" permitted slaves at the turn of the New Year—"to carry off explosive elements inseparable from the human mind, when reduced to the condition of slavery": "woe to the slaveholder when he undertakes to hinder or to prevent the operation of these electric conductors" (*A* 291).

In any case, men and women must be *taught* to be slaves and masters, and the course of instruction, with its constant adjustments and corrections, never concludes. Slavery requires "learned" habits of mind and demeanor, of which children are born "naturally" free. "The equality of nature," Douglass says, "is strongly asserted in childhood, and childhood requires children for associates. *Color* makes no difference with a child. Are you a child with wants, tastes and pursuits common to children, not put on but natural? Then, were you black as ebony you would be welcome to the child of alabaster whiteness" (*A* 169). Young boys, he says, feel a hatred of slavery that "springs from nature, unseared and unperverted" (*A* 224). Nature, in fact, does "almost nothing to prepare men and women to be either slaves or slaveholders" (*A* 222). At such moments Douglass advances what might be termed a Romantic, or Rousseauian, argument: social institutions—in this case, slavery—deform us, pervert our native inclination to charity and fair play. To the hoary question, *Does "civilization" distort or complement human nature?*, he appears to answer: The former.

That is well and good. But the savagery of slavery as it developed in North America, and the intractability, there, of the "scientific" racism that soon underpinned it, seem to require a more worldly explanation—and a bleaker, less reassuring one. This also emerges in Douglass's narrative, though he remains equivocal and circumspect about it. Inborn to us, as well as a love of freedom, is a will to power and cruelty. Douglass's master, we are told, could commit "outrages, deep, dark and nameless" (*A* 171). These outrages, as we know from facts soon narrated, and to which we will later return, are at once erotic and violent; they are nothing less than sadistic. But, lest we see in him a monster, Douglass assures us that his first owner Captain Anthony "was not by nature worse than other men," any one of whom, we are left to conclude, is therefore quite "naturally" capable of binding a young woman to a ceiling joist with her upraised hands, stripping her to the waist, and, after "shocking preliminaries," and to the accompaniment of "tantalizing epithets," lashing her almost to the point of death (*A* 176–77).[10] Such is inborn human "nature" when it is allowed an uninhibited self-expression, when it is allowed free reign to satisfy its darker appetites.

With this notion we hit upon a view of man more Freudian (or Calvinistic) than Rousseauian. Men are by "nature" savage—even depraved. They need the complement of "discipline," of some sort of curb against their "freedom" to act. This discipline may be, to adopt a secular vocabulary, "civilization," notwithstanding its inevitable "discontents" (these latter are simply the price we pay to become something more than "a nation of savages"). Or it may be, to adopt a religious vocabulary, a "redemption" from "original sin." As Douglass sees it—and the mild paradox with which he expresses the point is nicely Freudian—the great desiderata are "the just *restraints* of *free* society" (my emphasis; *A* 171): Reason and Chastity. These effect a sublimation, into more socially useful channels, of the rapacious will-to-power that is, like the love of liberty, also the birthright of men. To realize his humanity, to transcend his animality—to put on the "wings of Atalanta" and transcend both lust and greed—a man must be *disciplined*, but disciplined with the tempering rod of Reason, not the incendiary lash of Passion. The real problem with slavery is not so much that it entails too much "discipline," but that it involves "discipline" of the wrong kind— "discipline" that is in fact an expression of license, not an instrument of control. The "slave system" everywhere "robs its victims," master and slave alike, of every "earthly incentive" to lead "a holy life" (*A* 175). This fact should chasten us, for, as Douglass says, "Capt. Anthony might have been as humane a man, and every way as respectable, as many who now oppose the slave system; certainly as humane and respectable as are members of society generally" (*A* 171).[11] The idea, if I may sum it up, is simply this: 1) Slavery sets the "passions" free, when really they should be "imprisoned," or at least held under close restraint; and 2) "passions" are everywhere the same. These "passions" lead us to "defile the temple of love," as Du Bois has it in his revision of the fable of Atalanta (*Writings* 416).

Essential to slavery, then, is a general-purpose, sensualizing exercise in debauchery that might well gratify lusty Hippomenes. Consider the following account of a typical holiday on the plantation, a holiday that is, in fact, one of those protective "safety valves" built into the machinery of slavery of which I have already spoken:

> Everything like rational enjoyment among the slaves, is frowned upon; and only those wild and low sports, peculiar to semi-civilized people, are encouraged. All the license allowed, appears to have no other object than to disgust the slaves with their temporary freedom, and to make them as glad to return to their work, as they were to leave it. By plunging them into exhausting depths of drunkenness and dissipation, this effect is almost certain to follow. . . . The scenes, brought about in this way, were often scandalous and loathsome in the extreme. Whole multitudes might be found stretched out in brutal drunkenness, at once helpless and disgusting. Thus, when the slave asks for a few hours of virtuous freedom, his cunning master takes advantage of his ignorance, and cheers him with a dose of vicious and revolting dissipation, artfully labeled with the name of LIBERTY. We were induced to drink, I among the rest, and when the holidays were over, we all staggered up from our filth and wallowing, took a long breath, and went away to our various fields of work; feeling, upon the whole, rather glad to go from that which our masters artfully deceived us into the belief was freedom, back again to the arms of slavery. It was not what we had taken it to be, nor what it might have been, had it not been abused by us. It was about as well to be a slave to master, as to be a slave to rum and whisky. (*A* 290–91)

In short, "when a slave is drunk," Douglass concludes, "the slaveholder has no fear that he will plan an insurrection; no fear that he will escape to the north. It is the sober, thinking slave who is dangerous, and needs the vigilance of his master, to keep him a slave" (*A* 292). This is more than a temperance tract, laid into the narrative to appease the Teetotalers among the abolitionists (of whom there were a great many: Douglass himself had taken the pledge while in England in 1845). The point is this: the slave system intoxicates the slave with a delusive sort of "liberty" the better to make "liberty" in general seem toxic. This delusive "liberty" is of course libertinism, or unholy "license." And it involves the slave in a "brutal" descent into the "depths" of sensuality that Douglass always associates with slavery (black and white are alike made "brutes" by the peculiar institution). Slavery, owing to its very laxity, draws us down into a state of "revolting dissipation," an animalistic "wallowing" in the "filth" of the body—of the senses. Demon rum, it turns out, is an efficient "overseer": as does slavery, it "imprisons reason," and makes us thrall to passion. "Sobriety" is what is called for; and sobriety is but another name for chastity—for a principled resistance to "voluptuary" indulgence; it is but another name for the "self-control" by which means only is true "self-possession" attained. A sober slave is therefore a "thinking" slave—a slave who lives his life in the "mind," not in the "body." Master the body and you master the self; banish "libertinism" and "liberty" follows. Freedom, the attaining of a perfect abolition, is a "resurrection" from the "dark and pestiferous tomb of slavery" (*A* 286), from the "blight and mildew" of a chthonic, stupefying, merely bodily existence (*A* 305). To be a slave is to be entombed in the body, buried alive in it—to be bound up altogether by its fate. To be fully "emancipated" is to transcend the limits of corporeality (the idea seems almost Platonic); it is to achieve a chaste, and therefore perfect, "manhood"—to achieve, through Reason, a final "mastery" of Passion. This is no easy struggle, no mid-Victorian parlor jihad, and Douglass is not a prude. Slavery reveals unspeakable things about us; it doesn't "produce" them. True "abolition" is nothing less than a struggle to overcome—for men, anyway—an "inborn" kind of depravity, a vestigial animality, which slavery is peculiarly (though not uniquely) suited to bringing out. At any rate, that is the argument as I understand it.

There is in all this a real challenge—even if Douglass doesn't quite realize it, or pursue its implications—to the more transcendental, the more *Unitarian* foundations of certain strains of New England abolitionism. Douglass at times has more in common, as a thinker, with "pessimistic" writers like Hawthorne and Melville than he does with that great exponent of the "optative mood," Emerson. Emerson could say such things as these about abolition: "Nature will not have us fret and fume. She does not like our benevolence or our learning much better than she likes our frauds and wars. When we come out of the caucus, or the bank, or the Abolition-convention, or the Temperance-meeting, or the Transcendental club, into the fields and woods, she says to us, 'So hot? my little Sir'" (*Essays* 307). I will have occasion later to qualify my view of Douglass's relation to Emerson. But for now, I let the contrast stand, with the additional observation that Douglass's "philosophy" of slavery, in its bleaker phases, may explain his willingness to adopt the worldlier, and much less absolutist, tactic of "political abolitionism." It may explain as well why he could not, at last, accept the Garrisonian proposal that New England "purify" itself of slavery by dissolving the union. Men being what they naturally are, we could "purify" neither them nor any nation they compose simply by cutting the slave states loose. Abolition of "slavery" to instinct, to passion, to intemperance, to the gross sensualism that sees in a man or woman chiefly a "body"—this we can never take for granted as a thing achieved, or so Douglass implies. Why is this so? Because the "plantation," as Douglass imagines it in *My Bondage and My Freedom*, is not so much a site in Maryland or Georgia—though it certainly found a genial habitat there—as it is an uncharted region of the mind. The dark continent was in Mr. Kurtz, not he in it.

The plantation, Douglass tells us, is "a little nation of its own," where, "wrapped in its own congenial, midnight darkness," slavery develops "all its malign and shocking characteristics." On the plantation men can be "indecent without shame." (Rudyard Kipling's London bank clerk has this "plantation" in mind when he says, in "Mandalay": "Ship me somewheres east of Suez, where the best is like the worst, / Where there ain't no Ten Commandments an' a man can raise a thirst" [9]) The plantation, Douglass says, is a "'tabooed' spot," savage and primitive (*A* 158). Call it the great American unconscious, an unspeakable domain of the mind where "taboo" inclinations to rape and torture and "voluptuarian" indulgence find their perfect exhilaration. Only by being brought ever more within reach of the benignly repressive instrument of "reason" will the "plantation" be redeemed from darkness, and men themselves redeemed from bondage to their more "animal" tendencies; only then can we assume the wings of Atalanta. This is as unanswerable an argument against Garrisonian disunionism as might be offered. It is naive to suppose that slavery would wither away if it were denied the protection of the Federal Government—as naive as to suppose that men are better off in a Hobbesian "state of nature," or that the Belgian colonial bureaucrat left all the horror behind him when, departing the Congo, he set sail again for Europe, for a "civilization" that would, in the twentieth century to come, unleash unimaginable savagery.

Douglass never quite belonged in Massachusetts, not in the literary-historical sense, anyway. The great optimism of *My Bondage and My Freedom* is not the somewhat mystical optimism of Emerson and Whitman, the sort that says there really is no death in the world, or that evil will bless and ice will burn. It is instead rationalist, secular, and progressive; it is the Enlightenment "optimism" of such early republican writers as Thomas

Paine, Philip Freneau, and Joel Barlow.[12] Notwithstanding its darker implications as to the "nature" of humanity—in fact, precisely *because* of them—*My Bondage and My Freedom* believes, and simply *must* believe, in the "possibility" of a New World empire of Reason, even if that possibility had as yet never been made real; and even if—what with the Kansas-Nebraska Act of 1854, the *Dred Scott* decision of 1857, rising cotton prices, and the ever more arrogant exertions of the Slave Power—that great possibility appeared, in the 1850s, more farcical than it ever had. Douglass's worldly optimism is a natural corollary of his break with the Garrisonians, a break that opened up for his use—for his practical and imaginative use—the revolutionary tradition of the American "Founding Fathers."

The Columbian Orator

This brings us to a schoolbook called *The Columbian Orator*. Had not Douglass immortalized it in his autobiographies, this volume, together with its author, Caleb Bingham, might have passed into oblivion and the Library of Congress. The book was published first in 1797, when, as we have seen, opinion in America, even in parts of the South, was more or less anti-slavery, at least in principle. The speeches, poems, and extracts it collects, which were memorized by a generation or two of American schoolboys, celebrate liberty and republican ideals, and include forthrightly anti-slavery texts. The book figures prominently in *My Bondage and My Freedom*—having once obtained a copy, Douglass used it to learn to read and write—and its title and contents are altogether to the point. The book espouses "Columbian" ideals. It imagines the New World, in the fashion of Bingham's contemporaries Freneau and Barlow, as the place where liberty, and redemption from the "feudal superstition" of caste, at last were to be effected. Over the course of his narrative, Douglass himself emerges as the essential "Columbian orator." He is a self-emancipated man for a self-emancipated nation, and *My Bondage and My Freedom* is his *Columbiad*—his New World epic. He is the real expositor of the American revolution, the prophet of the New America. "There are to-day," wrote Du Bois in 1903, "no truer exponents of the pure human spirit of the Declaration of Independence than the American Negroes" (*Souls* 370). So it was in 1855. And as the instrument of *The Columbian Orator*, a primer in composition, would imply, Douglass's means of self-emancipation is literacy: he arrives at "self-possession" through mastery of the word—a fact intimated, as I have said, in the nuanced style of the book itself.

Scores of narratives produced by fugitive slaves turn on, and prominently feature accounts of, the acquisition of literacy. *My Bondage and My Freedom* is no exception. When Douglass was nine years old, his master (at this date Thomas Auld) sent him to live with his brother Hugh Auld (and his wife Sophia) in Baltimore. Of this move, Douglass writes: "The ties that ordinarily bind children to their homes had no existence in my case, and in thinking of a home elsewhere, I was confident of finding none that I should relish less than the one I was leaving. If I should meet with hardship, hunger, and nakedness, I had known them all before, and I could endure them elsewhere, especially in Baltimore, for I had something of the feeling about that city that is expressed in the saying that 'being hanged in England is better than dying a natural death in Ireland'" (A 210). Most propitious, though he is as yet unaware of it, is that his new mistress will begin his education in the Word: "The frequent hearing of my mistress reading the Bible aloud, for she often read aloud when her husband was absent, awakened my curiosity in respect to this mystery of reading, and roused in me the desire to learn," Douglass explains. "Up to this time I had known nothing whatever of this wonderful art, and my ignorance and inexperience of what it could do for me, as well as my confidence in my mistress, emboldened me to ask her to teach me to read. With an unconsciousness and inexperience equal to my own, she readily consented, and in an incredibly short time, by her kind assistance, I had mastered the alphabet and could spell words of three or four letters. My mistress seemed almost as proud of my progress as if I had been her own child, and supposing that her husband would be as well pleased, she made no secret of what she was doing for me." He continues: "And here arose the first dark cloud over my Baltimore prospects, the precursor of chilling blasts and drenching storms. Master Hugh was astounded beyond measure, and probably for the first time proceeded to unfold to his wife the true philosophy of the slave system, and the peculiar rules necessary in the nature of the case to be observed in the management of human chattels. Of course he forbade her to give me any further instruction, telling her in the first place that to do so was unlawful, as it was also unsafe" (A 216–17).

At this point, Douglass errs, at least in *one* particular; or, what is likelier, his *master* either errs or bends the truth. Teaching a slave to read was not in itself a criminal offense in Maryland, as Janet Duitsman Cornelius indicates. However, public assemblies for the purpose of educating slaves had, indeed, been criminalized;[13] and the mores of the slave-owning class forbade instruction of any kind. In any case, the report of at least one Maryland slave-holder's reasoning that Douglass proceeds to give is without question true. Auld chides his wife: "If you give a nigger an inch he will take an ell. Learning will spoil the best nigger in the world. If he learns to read the Bible it will forever unfit him to be a slave. He should know nothing but the will of his master, and learn to obey it. As to himself, learning will do him no good, but a great deal of harm, making him disconsolate and unhappy. If you teach him how to read, he'll want to know how to write, and this accomplished, he'll be running away with himself.'" "Such was the tenor of Master Hugh's oracular exposition," quips Douglass, "and it must be confessed that he very clearly comprehended the nature and the requirements of the relation of master and slave. His discourse was the first decidedly anti-slavery lecture to which it had been my lot to listen." He continues: "The effect of his words on me was neither slight nor transitory. His iron sentences, cold and harsh, sunk like heavy weights deep into my heart, and stirred up within me a rebellion not soon to be allayed" (*A* 217–18). The punning ("iron sentences") and the irony—"His discourse was the first decidedly anti-slavery lecture to which it had been my lot to listen"—that characterize this highly literary performance register the mastery of what the master here forbids, and affirm its essential truth. The Auld family horse was already out of the barn; the ell had already been taken. Hugh's blunder lay in not conceiving that a slave, listening in, might *take* what he says to Sophia as the ten-year-old Douglass did. He, not his wife, provides the better education.

As for Douglass: he continued his education with purloined copies of schoolbooks his master's son (whom he served as companion) had cast aside and relied on the neighborhood children: "Seized with a determination to learn to read, at any cost, I hit upon many expedients to accomplish the desired end," he writes. "The plea which I mainly adopted, and the one by which I was most successful, was that of using my young white playmates, with whom I met in the street, as teachers. I used to carry, almost constantly, a copy of Webster's spelling book in my pocket; and, when sent on errands, or when play time was allowed me, I would step, with my young friends, aside, and take a lesson in spelling. I generally paid my tuition fee to the boys, with bread, which I also carried in my pocket. For a single biscuit, any of my hungry little comrades would give me a lesson, more valuable to me than bread.[14] Not every one, however, demanded this consideration, for there were those who took pleasure in teaching me, whenever I had a chance to be taught by them," Douglass says, and then forebears to name names: "I am strongly tempted to give the names of two or three of those little boys, as a slight testimonial of the gratitude and affection I bear them, but prudence forbids; not that it would injure me, but it might, possibly, embarrass them; for it is almost an unpardonable offense to do any thing, directly or indirectly, to promote a slave's freedom, in a slave state." "It is enough to say, of my warm-hearted little play fellows," Douglass adds, "that they lived on Philpot street, very near Durgin & Bailey's shipyard" (*A* 223–34). By the time he published *The Life and Times of Frederick Douglass* (1881), all embarrassments had been removed. Douglass altered the passage: "I would step aside with my young friends and take a lesson in spelling," he writes. "I am greatly indebted to these boys—Gustavus Dorgan, Joseph Bailey, Charles Farity, and William Cosdry" (*A* 531).[15]

But to return to Douglass's philosophy of slavery, as against Hugh Auld's. Douglass argues, in *My Bondage and My Freedom*, that a "free" society alone offers real and proper "restraints" against iniquity: Liberty everywhere banishes libertinism. Slavery, with all its oppressions, actually "sets free" the worst, the most insubordinate, passions of the men it involves. In a word, reason "is imprisoned" under slavery, as Douglass memorably puts it (*A* 171). And as I have suggested, this is another way of saying that slavery reduces men to the condition of "animals," or "brutes." As John Donne would have it in his Holy Sonnets—and he is simply taking the Christian party line—Reason is God's "viceroy" in us.[16] Slavery forces us all, master and slave alike, one link farther down the Great Chain of being; and for that reason it is radically incompatible with the progress and transcendence ritually associated by Americans—and by Douglass in this book—with the New World.

Douglass speaks, as the title to an early chapter has it, of his "Gradual Initiation into the Mysteries of Slave Society." It is as if slavery were a "secret society" concerning which, in *My Bondage and My Freedom*, Douglass were writing an exposé. Certainly, the content of the book is at times erotic and sensational, as was the case with antebellum anti-Catholic exposés of life inside the convent. And it must be said that an anti-clerical, at times anti-Catholic, vein runs through Douglass's writing, as it does through the writing of many abolitionists. The "plantation," as Douglass imagines it, is a Counter-Reformation sort of place. The reader might well miss the ultra-Protestant strain in Douglass's book, but once pointed out it is easy enough to see. Further on in the book Douglass relates a significant episode, in which three "Christian" white men forcibly disperse an informal Sabbath School he had undertaken to run for his fellow slaves in St. Michaels, with the intention of teaching them to read the Bible. "These Christian class leaders were, to this extent, consistent. They had settled the question, that slavery is *right*, and, by that standard, they determined that Sabbath schools are wrong. To be sure, they were Protestant, and held to the great Protestant right of every man to '*search the scriptures*' for himself; but, then, to all general rules, there are *exceptions*. How convenient!" (*A* 299). Slaveholders, then, are insufficiently "reformed." In fact, they constitute a new priesthood in the New World—a class that would control utterly the meaning and delivery of "the word." Of course, the secular "word" of the *Columbian Orator* concerns Douglass more than does the "sacred" word of God. And as had the Puritan founders of the Bay Colony, Douglass conceives of his "errand" in radically "Protestant" terms: he would purge the New World of Old World "priestcraft" (*A* 306); he would put men in an unmediated relation to the Columbian "book" that sets them free; he would give them their wings of Atalanta.

In any case, after "initiating" us into the feudal priestcraft of slavery, Douglass takes up the subject of the "Great House Farm," the home of the Lloyds, who were among the wealthiest families in Maryland in the antebellum period, and who were at the very center of its governing class.[17] Here he presents us with a vision of decadent corruption—a society absolutely inimical to republican institutions and culture. It is an indictment not simply of slavery, but of the whole culture of feudalism with which slavery is inevitably associated in his book. The idea is that wealth is in some sense sensualizing in its effects; it is the sort of thing we must write sumptuary laws against in order to check. And so Douglass alludes, in opening his paragraphs on the Great House, to the parable of the rich man and the beggar Lazarus in the gospel of Luke. Like the rich sinner, the Lloyds go arrayed "in purple and fine linen." This isn't a description; it is an indictment. Most notable in this chapter is the specifically sensual decadence of the Lloyds, associated with the almost Biblical dominion they exercise over every creeping thing:

> The table groans under the heavy and blood-bought luxuries gathered with pains-taking care, at home and abroad. Fields, forests, rivers and seas, are made tributary here. Immense wealth, and its lavish expenditure, fill the great house with all that can please the eye, or tempt the taste. Here, appetite, not food, is the great desideratum. Fish, flesh and fowl, are here in profusion. Chickens, of all breeds; ducks, of all kinds, wild and tame, the common, and the huge Muscovite; Guinea fowls, turkeys, geese, and pea fowls, are in their several pens, fat and fatting for the destined vortex. The graceful swan, the mongrels, the black-necked wild goose; partridges, quails, pheasants and pigeons; choice water fowl, with all their strange varieties, are caught in this huge family net. Beef, veal, mutton and venison, of the most select kinds and quality, roll bounteously to

this grand consumer. The teeming riches of the Chesapeake bay, its rock, perch, drums, crocus, trout, oysters, crabs, and terrapin, are drawn hither to adorn the glittering table of the great house. The dairy, too, probably the finest on the Eastern Shore of Maryland—supplied by cattle of the best English stock, imported for the purpose, pours its rich donations of fragrant cheese, golden butter, and delicious cream, to heighten the attraction of the gorgeous, unending round of feasting. . . . Wines and brandies from France; teas of various flavor, from China; and rich, aromatic coffee from Java, all conspired to swell the tide of high life, where pride and indolence rolled and lounged in magnificence and satiety. (*A* 190–91)

Douglass always highlights the sheer promiscuity of slavery. The Lloyds live in "profuse luxury," in "luxurious extravagance," in "gilded splendor." They are "feverish voluptuaries," vortices of appetite. They are "self-deluded gourmandizers with aches, pains, fierce temper, uncontrolled passions, dyspepsia, rheumatism, lumbago and gout" (*A* 192–93). They are "troubled, like the restless sea." This last phrase Douglass takes from Isaiah 57:20: "The wicked are like the troubled sea, when it cannot rest, whose waters cast up mire and dirt. There is no peace, saith my God, to the wicked." Douglass certainly intends that we think of the "mire and dirt." His slaveholders fairly wallow.[18]

I have spoken already of Douglass's anti-clericalism, and of his implicit suggestion that slaveholders constitute a kind of priesthood, at once mysterious and unanswerable in its machinations. And it is worth mentioning here that nothing else in Douglass's writings so resembles his portrait of the Great House Farm as his description, in *The Life and Times of Frederick Douglass*, of the Vatican. The Catholic Church, we are told, trains young men "to defend dogmas and superstitions contrary to the progress and enlightenment of the age"; it is an institution "too occult" in its operations for ordinary "vision" to penetrate (*A* 1002). Within the Vatican and St. Peter's Basilica one encounters unspeakable "wealth and grandeur": "The fine silks and costly jewels and vestments of the priests of the present could hardly have been dreamed of by the first preacher of Christianity at Rome," St. Paul (*A* 1003). "As in its day pagan Rome drew tribute from all the known world, so the Church of Rome today receives gifts from all the Christian world, our own republican country included," Douglass adds, sounding a note of scandal. "A look into one of these Romish churches will show that even Solomon in all his glory was not arrayed like one of these" (*A* 1003). The result is everywhere "a degrading idea of man's relation to the Infinite Author of the universe" (*A* 1004). The Vatican is certainly a "great house."

It shares with the "plantation," as Douglass portrays plantations, all the essential retrograde features: incompatibility with republican institutions, unaccountability, secrecy, sensual indulgence in luxury, and a superstitious regard for hierarchy. The Catholic Church and the "plantation" are alike perfect in their opposition to the "Columbian" ideals. (The idea was hardly unique to Douglass; one encounters it frequently in anti-slavery writing, which, in its less attractive precincts, recalls mid-nineteenth century anti-Catholic polemics.)

The Root of the Matter

We should consider now the best-known chapter in *My Bondage and My Freedom*, "Covey the Negro Breaker."[19] It is the first in an astonishing series of chapters chronicling Douglass's successful struggle to recreate himself along properly "Columbian," "New World" lines. Douglass will, in this section of the book, be placed in the hands of a "Negro breaker," whom he must either dominate or be dominated by (in the political economy of slavery, men like Covey function as Pinkerton agents would later function in the North: they exist, and are paid, to discipline labor, to keep it disorganized and docile). On Covey's farm, Douglass will come of age, enter "manhood," and thereby evade the fate of the perpetual "infancy" that a life in slavery is for him. He will conspire to escape, and, though the conspiracy fails, he will find himself at last so situated as to make his decisive break for freedom, wage labor, and self-employment. As I have suggested, his achieved self-mastery is registered even in the style of the book, which in these chapters assumes a particularly elegant sort of "literacy." This fluency figures in *My Bondage and My Freedom* as his "Columbian" ideal—as the wings that shall bear him into realms of possibility—and it everywhere distinguishes the highly artful 1855 text from the more spartan narrative of 1845. Throughout these chapters, Douglass writes with urbanity and humor, with a novelist's eye for detail, and with a satirist's eye for the ridiculous.

Consider a few examples. "The morning of the first of January, 1834," Douglass writes, "with its chilling wind and pinching frost, quite in harmony with the winter in my own mind, found me, with my little bundle of clothing on the end of a stick, swung across my shoulder, on the main road, bending my way toward Covey's, whither I had been imperiously ordered by Master Thomas. The latter had been as good as his word, and had committed me, without reserve, to the mastery of Mr. Edward Covey.

Eight or ten years had now passed since I had been taken from my grandmother's cabin, in Tuckahoe; and these years, for the most part, I had spent in Baltimore, where—as the reader has already seen—I was treated with comparative tenderness. I was now about to sound profounder depths in slave life. The rigors of a field, less tolerable than the field of battle, awaited me" (*A* 258). The little bundle of clothes on a stick with which Douglass equips himself as he sets out for Covey's place is pathetic in its suggestion of poverty. But notice something wily even in this. The bundle on a stick was a stereotypical accoutrement of the fugitive slave, as is clear from (among other sources) Tom Sawyer's use of it in the "coat of arms" he makes for Jim in *Huckleberry Finn*. The same image figured in countless antebellum newspaper advertisements soliciting help in the capture of fugitives. In this chapter, Douglass both is and is not that pathetic figure with the bundle on his stick; he is a titan in disguise, and this allows him, in his narration of the episode, an occasional note of whimsy and sport. And the "winter in his mind," as he puts it, laying the scene before us in both its inner and its outer weather, will in due course give way to the "spring" of a "resurrection": "new shoots from the tree of liberty" will begin to "put forth tender buds," we later read (*A* 297). This possibility is always before us, as for example when Douglass nicely exploits the ambiguity of the preposition "of": Master Thomas "had committed me," he says, "to the mastery of Mr. Edward Covey." Is he to master Covey or to be mastered by him? The former, as it happens. By the time he leaves the farm the infamous Negro breaker is "as gentle as a lamb" (*A* 288).

As it takes shape, the episode at Covey's has certain generic elements. It is, among other things, a rural comedy of manners. The sophisticated Douglass, lately of Baltimore, for the first time takes up a career in the "field" of manual labor. Douglass makes the point in an ironic reversal: "I found myself even more awkward than a green country boy may be supposed to be, upon his first entrance into the bewildering scenes of city life" (*A* 260). Covey's farm is of course nothing cosmopolitan, but it is a strange world in its way, with its "in-hand oxen" and "off-hand oxen," and with its arcane language of "woa," "gee," and "hither"—a language that is, as Douglass puts it (quoting *Julius Caesar*), "Greek to me" (*A* 261). The comedy of the scene, as Douglass sets it up, is affecting. Because the sense of discomfort is so precisely understated—"My life, hitherto, had led me away from horned cattle," he drily says (*A* 261)—the writing lets us feel just how fragile the slave's situation is. Douglass's descriptive language makes Covey himself appear at once ridiculous and terrible. Covey has a "wolfish visage," "green eyes," and a "growl, like a dog." When Douglass takes him down, in the great fight scene, he does it on ground that is not "over clean," as he fastidiously puts it, "for we were now in the cow yard. He had selected the place for the fight and it was but right that he should have all the advantages of his own selection" (*A* 284). Douglass parodies the chivalrous generosity of a gentleman fighting a contest of "honor," as the saying used to go. And his facility, his achieved levity, always already suggests the mastery that Douglass will soon achieve over this "Negro breaker." We smile when we read that Covey, after two hours' futile effort to get the better of this sixteen-year-old slave, "gave up the contest," and, "puffing and blowing at a great rate," admonished Douglass: "Now, you scoundrel, go to your work; I would not have whipped you half so much as I have had you not resisted" (*A* 285). In the weeks to come, Covey would sometimes say that "he did not want to have to get hold of" Douglass again, to which admonition the latter smartly rejoins, in an aside to the reader, that it was "a declaration" which he "had no difficulty in believing" (*A* 286). Covey's motives, here, are plainly economic, or so they seem to Douglass. "The reader will be glad to know why, after I had so grievously offended Mr. Covey, he did not have me taken in hand by the authorities," he writes; "indeed, why the law of Maryland, which assigns hanging to the slave who resists his master, was not put in force against me; at any rate, why I was not taken up, as is usual in such cases, and publicly whipped, for an example to other slaves, and as a means of deterring me from committing the same offense again." The answer is simple: "Covey was, probably, ashamed to have it known and confessed that he had been mastered by a boy of sixteen. Mr. Covey enjoyed the unbounded and very valuable reputation, of being a first-rate overseer and negro breaker. By means of this reputation, he was able to procure his hands for very trifling compensation, and with very great ease," an important fact given his aspirations to join the planter class (he already owned six slaves). "His interest and his pride mutually suggested the wisdom of passing the matter by, in silence. The story that he had undertaken to whip a lad, and had been resisted, was, of itself, sufficient to damage him; for his bearing should, in the estimation of slaveholders, be of that imperial order that should make such an occurrence impossible." Had Douglass known that Covey's middle name was Napoleon, he no doubt would have made something of it here. In any case, he winds up with a fine comic flourish: "I judge from these circumstances, that Covey deemed it best to give me the go-by. It is, perhaps, not altogether creditable to my natural temper, that, after this conflict with Mr. Covey, I did, at times, purposely aim to provoke him to an attack, by refusing to keep with the other hands in the field, but I could never bully him to another battle" (*A* 287). Covey was willing to suffer a little humiliation if thereby he could better regulate the relations of production in his little quarter of Maryland's Eastern Shore.

Even the description of the intractable oxen is comic. Douglass, unused to "horned cattle," has a devil of a time managing them; they slip the yoke and damage the wagon; they run headlong into the trees; they get hung up on the gate. They are, in fact, "rascals" on a "spree," who act up when master is absent, and behave themselves when he looks on—all the better, it appears, to embarrass Douglass. "On arriving" at the gate, Douglass explains, "it was necessary for me to let go the end of the rope on the horns of the 'in hand ox'; and now as soon as the gate was open, and I let go of it to get the rope, again, off went my oxen—making nothing of their load—full tilt; and in doing so they caught the huge gate between the wheel and the cart body, literally crushing it to splinters, and coming only within a few inches of subjecting me to a similar crushing, for I was just in advance of the wheel when it struck the left gate post. With these two hair-breadth escapes, I thought I could successfully explain to Mr. Covey the delay, and avert apprehended punishment," Douglass explains.

> But, in this I was disappointed. On coming to him, his countenance assumed an aspect of rigid displeasure, and, as I gave him a history of the casualties of my trip, his wolfish face, with his greenish eyes, became intensely ferocious. "Go back to the woods again," he said, muttering something else about wasting time. I hastily obeyed; but I had not gone far on my way, when I saw him coming after me. My oxen now behaved themselves with singular propriety, opposing their present conduct to my representation of their former antics. I almost wished, now that Covey was coming, they would do something in keeping with the character I had given them; but no, they had already had their spree, and they could afford now to be extra good, readily obeying my orders, and seeming to understand them quite as well as I did myself." (A 263–64)

It is "break and be broken," Douglass ruefully says; "such is life" (A 263). The culture and agriculture of slavery corrupts even the inborn sincerity of oxen.

I rehearse these oddly comic flourishes, not one of which is present in the 1845 *Narrative*, to illustrate the point I have been making: in this second of his autobiographies, Douglass's achieved "self-possession" manifests itself even—and perhaps chiefly—at the level of style. He takes his liberties as a writer, appealing not merely to the moral sense of the reader, but also to his wit—to his feeling for play. There are the events themselves (terrible and overwhelming), and then there are the events as rendered here (nicely contained and mastered); the distance between the two, affectively speaking, is the distance between dispossession and self-possession, between bondage and freedom, between a house of prose and a house of possibility. Yet, notwithstanding his levity, his wit, and his extraordinary range of tone, Douglass always holds before the reader of these chapters the horror of the experience narrated. After he suffers the ordeal with the oxen, after he is worked to the point of heat exhaustion, after he is kicked and cuffed when he collapses in the sun, "Mr. Covey succeeded," he says, "in breaking" him: "I was broken in body, soul, and spirit. My natural elasticity was crushed, my intellect languished, the disposition to read departed, the cheerful spark that lingered about my eye died; the dark night of slavery closed in upon me; and behold," he adds, "a man transformed into a brute!" (*A* 268). Of course, Douglass will rise, Phoenix-like, from the ashes of the abjection into which Covey threw him; that is the business of the two chapters that succeed "Covey, the Negro Breaker." He will flee Covey and appeal to his master to redeem him; he will be succored and advised by his friend Sandy Jenkins. But at last, his only recourse is—as it should be for reasons both personal and narrative—to fight Covey openly. "Who would be free, themselves must strike the blow," as Byron puts it in the lines Douglass quotes at the conclusion to his account of the last flogging he ever suffered.

Now I must attend to Sandy Jenkins, a man to whom Douglass devotes a great deal of attention (more attention, in fact, than he devotes to any other slave). Sandy finds Douglass in the woods, where he has retreated to hide from Covey (the day before, Covey had beaten him into insensibility when he fell ill and could no longer work). Douglass introduces Sandy to us as "an old adviser": "He was not only a religious man, but he professed to believe in a system for which I have no name. He was a genuine African, and had inherited some of the so-called magical powers, said to be possessed by African and eastern nations."[20] Sandy, a man locally renowned for his "good nature," takes Douglass in, feeds him, and persuades him to carry in his pocket a special "root": "He told me further, that if I would take that root and wear it on my right side, it would be impossible for Covey to strike me a blow; that with this root about my person, no white man could whip me." For proof, Sandy offers his own case: he had, he assures Douglass, "never received a blow since he carried it" (*A* 280). Douglass takes the root, but in a spirit of skepticism. The fellowship with Sandy is real. We've no reason to doubt it. But Douglass feels as well, and makes us feel, that the strategies of resistance that the folk culture had evolved—such superstitious magic as Sandy's "root," for example—are unbecoming a "man."

The portrait of Sandy is complex. He appears before us first as a savior of sorts, as "the good Samaritan" (*A* 281). Doubtless we take as praise the affirmations of Sandy's "good nature," and "kind heart" (*A* 279). The business of the root is, of course, presented to us as "superstition"—"very absurd and ridiculous if not positively sinful" (*A* 281). But that alone is not a disgrace. No, the reader's suspicion of Sandy is first aroused, I suspect, when he reads this: "I had," Douglass says, "a positive aversion to all pretenders to '*divination*.' It was beneath one of my intelligence to countenance such dealings with the devil, as this power implied. But, with all my learning—it was really precious little—Sandy was more than a match for me. 'My book learning,' he said, 'had not kept Covey off me,' (a powerful argument just then,) and he entreated me, with flashing eyes, to try this [root]" (*A* 281). This sets Sandy's "genuine Africanism," his conjuring, over against Douglass's New World "book learning"—the instruction he had imbibed from the *Columbian Orator*. Which shall give him his wings? The point is the more urgent in light of certain facts of which we are apprised only a page or so earlier. Douglass tells us that he, "the only slave now in that region who could read and write," is feared by whites and respected by slaves. Literacy is power; the only other literate slave in those parts had been sold South as a menace (*A* 280). And when Sandy disparages "book learning," he reveals a weakness. His African "superstitions," insofar as they discourage a slave from looking toward "book learning" as a source of power and encourage him to put his faith in his "roots," are instruments quite useful to the slaveholder—which is precisely why slaveholders, as presented in *My Bondage and My Freedom*, indulge such superstitious customs as these, seeing in them no threat. And to the extent that Douglass is seduced by Sandy's conjuring, however momentarily, he puts on, again, the mind-forged manacles of slavery.

Douglass wants us to assume that Sandy's celebrated "good nature" is not what it appears to be. It is in fact, at least in certain of its aspects, perfectly unrespectable, a thing not worthy of a man: his meekness is what protects him from floggings, not his root. Sandy, we later learn, is not free of what Douglass—speaking, again, an anti-Catholic sort of language—calls the "priestcraft of slavery." He remains essentially feudal in outlook. Like too many Americans—to borrow a phrase from Joel Barlow's epic *The Columbiad*—Sandy Jenkins "nurse[s] feudal feelings" on "the tented shore" of the New World (265). And his weakness, his distrust of "book learning," his effort to turn Douglass away from it—all of this leads him, in the end, to betray Douglass and his co-conspirators, once they determine to make their escape. Douglass clearly has this sort of weakness in mind when he sums up his account of his great victory over Covey. The "battle with Covey," says Douglass, "undignified" as "I fear my narration of it is"—the literary self-deprecation is certainly conventional—"was the turning point in my *'life as a slave.'* It rekindled in my breast the smouldering embers of liberty; it brought up my Baltimore dreams, and revived a sense of my own manhood. I was a changed being after that fight. I was *nothing* before; I WAS A MAN NOW. It recalled to life my crushed self-respect and my self-confidence, and inspired me with a renewed determination to be A FREEMAN. A man, without force is without the essential dignity of humanity. Human nature is so constituted, that it cannot *honor* a helpless man, although it can *pity* him; and even this it cannot do long, if the signs of power do not arise" (*A* 286). The "signs of power" do not arise in Sandy Jenkins, sympathetic though he may be. Douglass himself finds it hard to "pity" him: this "genuine African" is an Old-World survival, sadly complicit in his own immiseration. In fact, through his actions Sandy had, Douglass intimates, "branded" himself a slave. "I did not forget to appeal to the pride of my comrades," Douglass tells us in the section recounting the conspiracy to run away: "If having solemnly promised to go, as they had done, they now failed to make the attempt, they would, in effect, brand themselves with cowardice, and might as well sit down, fold their arms, and acknowledge themselves as fit only to be *slaves*. This detestable character, all were unwilling to assume. Every man except Sandy (he, much to our regret, withdrew) stood firm" (*A* 315). Sandy Jenkins prefers to rely on his roots.

In *My Bondage and My Freedom*, Douglass wavers between rendering Sandy's speech in his own literary language—the language of what Sandy calls "book learning"—and in the language of the slave's vernacular. Consider the following passage. It recounts a dream Sandy had, which, it turns out, anticipates his Judas-like betrayal of the conspirators:

> In the progress of our preparations [to escape], Sandy, the root man, became troubled. He began to have dreams, and some of them were very distressing. One of these, which happened on a Friday night, was, to him, of great significance; and I am quite ready to confess, that I felt somewhat damped by it myself. He said, "I dreamed, last night, that I was roused from sleep, by strange noises, like the voices of a swarm of angry birds, that caused a roar as they passed, which fell upon my ear like a coming gale over the tops of the trees. Looking up to see what it could mean," said Sandy, "I saw you, Frederick, in the claws of a huge bird, surrounded by a large number of birds, of all colors and sizes. These were all picking at you, while you, with your arms, seemed to be trying to protect your

eyes. Passing over me, the birds flew in a south-westerly direction, and I watched them until they were clean out of sight. Now, I saw this as plainly as I now see you; and furder, honey, watch de Friday night dream; dare is sumpon in it, shose you born; dare is, indeed, honey." (*A* 312–13)

Douglass is a writer of consummate control; his diction is always well modulated. Yet here, in these last sentences, he awkwardly blends "dialect" and "standard" English in rendering the quoted speech of Sandy "the root man," this "genuine African" whose "superstitious" engagement with the "priestcraft of slavery" will lead him to betray his fellow slaves. In *My Bondage and My Freedom*, Douglass's own learned language—his urbane self-possession as a writer—circumscribes and quarantines "vernacular" culture. His touchiness as to the matter is evident at once in the account he gives of his initial conference with Sandy Jenkins: "He told me that he could help me; that, in those very woods, there was an herb, which in the morning might be found, possessing all the powers required for my protection, (I put his thoughts into my own language;) and that if I would take his advice, he would procure me the root of the herb of which he spoke" (*A* 280). Nowhere else does Douglass take pains to ensure that his reader knows how great a distance separates his English from that of an interlocutor, for that alone could be the purpose of the parenthesis. It is quite gratuitous; the plain business of indirect quotation hardly requires it, and makes it superfluous. It is as if the vernacular embarrasses Douglass— and for good enough reason, at least in 1855: rightly enough did he shrink when the Garrisonians said, "Better have a little of the plantation manner of speech than not" (*A* 367). They would prefer a Sandy Jenkins, a meek, "good natured" man, a man who doesn't show too many of the "signs of power." Douglass makes them uneasy. We can forgive him if his portrait of Sandy is tendentious; and we can look instead to Charles Chesnutt, in *The Conjure Woman*, for the first fully nuanced treatment of the "folk culture" of the slave, and of the slave's vernacular (and syncretic religion). Of course, even Chesnutt was "embarrassed," to an extent: having "a little of the plantation manner" in their prose was something white editors still demanded of black authors in 1899, when *The Conjure Woman* first appeared.[21] It was hard work, the work of several generations of African American writers, to redeem the vernacular from bondage to the "priestcraft of slavery." Langston Hughes was still at it in 1925 when he published "The Negro Artist and the Racial Mountain."

For his part, Douglass is "assimilationist" and "rational." He is an "Enlightenment" republican, and, fittingly, his almost neo-classical prose everywhere shows it. He rejects the "folk" culture of the slave, notwithstanding that it has a special relationship to what he calls his "roots." Even "juba dancing," a festivity popular on the plantation, and much encouraged by slaveholders, has its small but invidious role to play in shoring slavery up, and this despite the fact that some of the songs the slaves sing while "juba dancing" illustrate "the meanness of slaveholders":

> We raise de wheat,
> Dey gib us de corn;
> We bake de bread,
> Dey gib us de cruss;
> We sif de meal,
> Dey gib us de huss;
> We peal de meat,
> Dey gib us de skin,
> And dat's de way
> Dey takes us in.
> We skim de pot,
> Dey gib us the liquor,
> And say dat's good enough for nigger.
> Walk over! walk over!
> Tom butter and de fat;
> Poor nigger you can't get over dat;
> Walk over! (*A* 290)

In *To Wake the Nations*, Eric Sundquist suggests that this song, as Douglass presents it here, is itself one of the "safety valves" slavery employs the better to redirect and carry off insubordinate energies (128–29). That is to say: the "letter" of the song may be rebellious, but its rebellion is allegorical, figurative. It is an example of what Kenneth Burke might call "symbolic action"; it is, or can be, a substitute for insurrection, which is presumably why the slaveholders under whom Douglass worked never objected to "juba dancing." To sing "We raise de wheat" while "beating juba" on holiday is—or so Douglass allows us to infer—like carrying a "root" in the pocket, rather than a menace in the eye, to ward off the blows of Old Master. It is to engage in what Douglass calls the "wild and low sports peculiar to semi-civilized people" (*A* 291).

For all of these reasons, then, Douglass will have none of "the plantation" in his manner, though that is what the Garrisonians wanted him either to fabricate or to "retain." He makes himself master of the culture of the master-class; and he'll have nothing to do with a "vernacular" counter-culture whose contours, or so he believed, were dialectically shaped by the needs of that same master-class. He finds his "roots" not in the folk culture of Sandy so much as in an Enlightenment culture unfriendly alike, as he sees it, to slavery and to "Old-World" superstition—to anything that smacks of mystery and irrationality. Douglass's relation to his African "roots" is dubious. He "chooses the west," which is what makes this book so thoroughly "American" in its bearing, as James McCune Smith points out in introducing it:

> And the secret of [Douglass's] power, what is it? He is a Representative American man—a type of his countrymen. Naturalists tell us that a full grown man is a resultant or representative of all animated nature on this globe; beginning with the early embryo state, then representing the lowest forms of organic life, and passing through every subordinate grade or type, until he reaches the last and highest—manhood. In like manner, and to the fullest extent, has Frederick Douglass passed through every gradation of rank comprised in our national make-up, and bears upon his person and upon his soul every thing that is American. And he has not only full sympathy with every thing American; his proclivity or bent, to active toil and visible progress, are in the strictly national direction, delighting to outstrip "all creation." . . . It is not without a feeling of pride, dear reader, that I present you with this book. The son of a self-emancipated bond-woman, I feel joy in introducing to you my brother, who has rent his own bonds, and who, in his every relation—as a public man, as a husband and as a father—is such as does honor to the land which gave him birth. I shall place this book in the hands of the only child spared me, bidding him to strive and emulate its noble example. You may do likewise. It is an American book, for Americans, in the fullest sense of the idea. (A 137)

When Douglass actually confronts Covey, at the moment of crisis, he "forgets his roots," as he puts it, with a pun surely deliberate, and instead stands up in violent protest (A 283). This severs his tie to the Old World, with its un-republican superstitions—superstitions that nurse feudal feelings in Sandy Jenkins. This marks his deracination, his point of passage into the New World, into "Columbia." This is where he first stands before us as the essential Columbian orator, a man who best answers to the portrait James McCune Smith draws of him. The "embryonic" analogy involves parturition: Douglass was born—and then born again (he "passed through every gradation of rank comprised in our national make-up," and so on). "Book-learning" had already freed his mind; now it would free his body. Douglass throws off "humility" and "pacifism," both of which the Garrisonians had required him to sustain: "My hands were no longer tied by my religion," he says (A 282). He forsakes Uncle Tom for Madison Washington and

Denmark Vesey, but also for Patrick Henry, as he makes clear in the chapter called "The Run-Away Plot": "Patrick Henry, to a listening senate, thrilled by his magic eloquence, and ready to stand by him in his boldest flights, could say, GIVE ME LIBERTY OR GIVE ME DEATH, and this saying was a sublime one, even for a freeman; but, incomparably more sublime, is the same sentiment, when practically asserted by men accustomed to the lash and chain—men whose sensibilities must have become more or less deadened by their bondage" (*A* 312). Clearly, this is a defiant reply not only to Covey and to Sandy—involved as they both are in slaveholding "priestcraft"—but to the romantic Christian racialism of a book like *Uncle Tom's Cabin*, as well as to the Christian "non-resistance" of the Garrisonians.[22] This is Douglass's Declaration of Independence: "I was resolved to fight," he says, aligning his personal emancipation with the national emancipation the Founding Fathers achieved (*A* 283). And he would, in realizing that aspiration to liberty, remake the American dream of possibility, taking it to higher and "incomparably more sublime" regions. Douglass's fight marks his passage into the future, into futurity as such—and also into "manhood"; this is where he earns his wings of Atalanta and transcends the fate of the body. *My Bondage and My Freedom* is a coming-of-age story of both personal and "national" dimensions (as James McCune Smith saw). Like so many other works of the American Renaissance, it heralds the coming of a real "Columbia," with the difference that its New American Adam is, of necessity, forged in the crucible of slavery. *My Bondage and My Freedom* is a book dedicated to "unceasing progress," to the ideal of a "republican" Promised Land; dedicated even, as we have seen, to the perfection of the Reformation itself. Douglass engages all of the foundationally "American" narratives.

Plotting Out an American Life

We don't often speak of the "plot" of an autobiography. Lives (we tell ourselves) unfold or happen; they aren't thrown into shape by design. But there is something about peculiarly "American" lives that should give us pause, that should lead us, it may be, to reconsider the relation between storytelling and living, and between the "imagined" and the "real." For ours is a nation of "confidence men," of "self-made" men, of Walt Whitman, Mark Twain, Howard Hughes, Norman Mailer, and Jay Gatsby—of men who are also "characters," and of characters who are also men. (Douglass's most popular oration, the one he delivered more often than any other, was entitled "Self-Made Men.") Ours is a nation where "autobiography" can come first, and the "life" itself second; or—and perhaps this is the better way of putting it—where a life can be written out even as it is lived.

As I have intimated, the "book learning" Sandy Jenkins so easily dismissed secured Douglass his freedom. He writes in the chapter titled "The Run-Away Plot": "To [my friends], therefore, with a suitable degree of caution, I began to disclose my sentiments and plans; sounding them, the while, on the subject of running away, provided a good chance should offer. . . . That (to me) gem of a book, the *Columbian Orator*, with its eloquent orations and spicy dialogues, denouncing oppression and slavery—telling of what had been dared, done and suffered by men, to obtain the inestimable boon of liberty—was still fresh in my memory, and whirled into the ranks of my speech with the aptitude of well trained soldiers, going through the drill" (*A* 306). That last metaphor equates literacy with militancy, the pen with the sword (or, to be strict about it, words with well-trained soldiers). This equation is what Sandy the root man failed to understand, and that failure issues in treason. It is necessary, really, that Sandy Jenkins should betray the conspiracy, and for two reasons. First, Douglass has to force a choice upon the reader—a choice between New World "rationality" and Old World "folk" belief (the two cannot co-exist: the New World must be purged of the Old). Second, the manifest complicity of that folk culture with slavery must be demonstrated, even in the arc of the plot. If Sandy Jenkins had not existed, Douglass would have had to invent him, at least if he were to make his argument genuinely narrative and "literary."

Sandy's "betrayal" of the conspirators' trust alerts us, as most readers will see at once, to another organizing principle in the narrative—the "Christological" plot. First, the abjection at Covey's, even to suicidal despair, is shortly followed by what Douglass calls a "resurrection" from the "tomb" of slavery, an ascension to a "heaven of comparative freedom" (*A* 286). Second, Douglass takes on the role, with respect to his co-conspirators, of savior: it is to him that they look for salvation, since he alone has the Power of the Word—is "*with* the Word," as the scripture has it (John 1:1). And he takes on also the role of the man who freely assumes all responsibility for their transgressions: "I am the man," he says (*A* 309). Third, Douglass appears as a Mosaic figure, leading his men out of Egypt and into Canaan—out of the Old World and into Columbia (*A* 308–9). In the typological reading of the Old Testament favored by the Puritans, Moses prefigures Christ, of course. He frees Israel from bondage to Pharaoh, as Christ frees believers from bondage to death and sin, and in fact from bondage to the body: Christianity has its "wings of Atalanta," too, though in these neither Douglass nor Du Bois had much interest. Fourth, the escape is initially scheduled for Easter, and thus would mark a second "resurrection" for Douglass: the first resurrection, at Covey's, was of the spirit; this second would carry his very person away to Canaan.

Of course, Sandy Jenkins did exist, and we have no reason to doubt that the escape was planned for Easter Sunday. Douglass isn't making these things up, no matter how well the details lend themselves to his narrative purposes. Historians interested in his life have corroborated the principal details of his narratives (as do such census records and slave schedules as I've consulted). Nonetheless, the story he tells is peculiarly overdetermined, strikingly well ordered, and in such a way as to suggest that he was "writing it up," so to speak, even as he acted it out. It is as if he were suggesting that the "word" can set us free precisely because it organizes our lives *in prospect*—not merely in retrospect, when we pen an autobiography. It is impossible to live outside of the stories we tell. The living is the telling, or so Douglass's example seems to suggest. That is why Sandy Jenkins died in bondage: the Old World story he was always telling, the story about his "roots," could end no other way. The Enlightenment Republican story that Douglass learned how to tell so well, the story that organized his life toward "freedom," the story of *The Columbian Orator*—this is the story he wants the nation never to stop telling itself, which is why we still must read *My Bondage and My Freedom*. Like Whitman, Frederick Douglass forever stands somewhere out ahead, waiting for us.

When Douglass called together his fellow slaves at St. Michaels they met as "revolutionary conspirators" (*A* 309). Here is another organizing principle for the plot—the story of the Revolution of 1775–83, to which, as I have indicated, Douglass's embrace of political abolitionism gave him full "literary" access. The slave says "literally" what Patrick Henry said but half-figuratively: "Give me liberty or give me death." The Egypt out of which that slave makes his exodus is more "real" than any Old World "Egypt" the Puritan fathers (and Cotton Mather) thought they had left behind (*A* 312). Here at last, among such "conspirators" as Douglass himself was, is to occur the *real* American revolution—the real Columbiad. The slave's rebellion is "incomparably more sublime," we are told, than the rebellion of 1775–83 (*A* 312). This is so because his "slavery," when compared to the "bondage" against which the Founding Fathers fought, stands as "original" does to "imitation," or as substance does to shadow; these earlier acts were mere anticipations, or pre-figurations, of the "New World" acts to come. Patrick Henry may have played the role of rebel against tyranny (he never served in the Continental Army); that was all well and good—"even for a freeman," as Douglass puts it, with a note of condescension. But Douglass's revolutionary conspiracy is the thing itself—the "*practical* assertion" of an inalienable right (*A* 312). "*Shoot! Shoot me!*" says Henry, one of Douglass's party, when the constables order him to cross his hands for binding. "*You can't kill me but once.* Shoot!—shoot! and be damned. *I won't be tied*" (*A* 318). The echo of Patrick Henry, whom Douglass quotes only a page or two before, is unmistakable. 1776 was a rehearsal for a play that to this day has not been adequately staged, or so Douglass's narrative encourages us to say. Sometimes we rehearse the play, whether on Broadway or elsewhere, simply to keep from acting it out: in our political campaigns, our oratory, our movies, our pageants and parades, our foreign policy. America is a "possibility" neither fulfilled in history, nor yet altogether foreclosed by the unreconstructed, "irrational" Old World survivals that strut and fret their hour upon its stage.

To be "American"—this is one lesson of *My Bondage and My Freedom*—is to fold stories like the ones Douglass tells into the accidents of your life; it is to live "as if" these stories were real or *might be made real*. That is what Douglass did. That is how he plotted out a life for himself even as he lived it: three autobiographies in thirty-six years (1845, 1855, 1881), three self-inventions and self-re-inventions. To be "American," in *My Bondage and My Freedom*, is to "dwell in possibility, a fairer house than prose," as Emily Dickinson once put it (506).[23] The act of dwelling in possibility can seem quite hollow, once the curtain comes down; it did for Jay Gatsby—another self-made man. But it needn't be so. And as for Douglass: slavery compelled him to forge a life for himself. He was, as he tells us, "without an intelligible beginning in the world" (*A* 157)—a curious position for an autobiographer to occupy. If he was to have a "self," he had to win it, to conjure it up; he had to stand as though a man were author of himself and knew no other kin (to borrow a phrase from *Coriolanus*). The luxury of being born with an identity is denied the slave, which may be why slaves led such exemplary American lives (just as James McCune Smith implies): the self-emancipating slave, and his world elsewhere (to borrow yet another phrase from *Coriolanus*), are our characteristic products. When Douglass bestows a new Scottish surname on himself—he had been born Frederick Bailey—he performs an emblematic act.

Tight in Dungeons

I have had occasion to mention—in connection with Douglass—Dickinson, Emerson, and Whitman. These writers, in their several ways, tell a story about bondage and freedom, a story about movement from the one to the other condition. They hold the past in contempt; all would dwell in "possibility." Any story that can somehow accommodate such astonishingly varied experiences as Dickinson, Whitman, Douglass, and Emerson had is, in a sense, a "representative" story of the culture, one to which everyone somehow has imaginative access. But it is a peculiar story, and one not without its costs, if we seriously try to abide by it. "How shall a man escape from his ancestors," Emerson asks in "Fate," "or draw off from his veins the black drop which he drew from his father's or his mother's life? When each comes forth from his mother's womb, the gate of gifts closes behind him. Let him value his hands and feet, he has but one pair. So he has but one future, and that is already predetermined in his lobes, and described in that little fatty face, pig-eye, and squat form" (*Essays* 772–73). Emerson's disgust is expressed physically because bondage to the "past," as we know from reading Douglass, is like bondage to the body—to physicality, as opposed to "spirit" or "soul." The body is fated, but the soul, as Emerson elsewhere says, "becomes" (271). Douglass, in slavery, had been accounted merely a body; he knew well enough about bondage to the past. What had the past to offer him? He knew how, when he issued from a black Maryland mother's womb, "the gate of gifts closed behind him." Dickinson, as feminist readers of her work have pointed out, knew about this too, at least insofar as patriarchy, as it impinged on her, saw in women mere bodies—mere "biology." That is why she says what she does in poem 661. She prefers "to ride indefinite / As doth the Meadow Bee":

> And visit only where I liked
> And No one visit Me
>
> And flirt all Day with Buttercups
> And marry whom I may
> And dwell a little everywhere
> Or better, run away
>
> With no Police to follow . . .
>
> What Liberty! So captives deem
> Who tight in Dungeons are. (509)

The language of bondage and slavery is simply there for her to use; it is what Americans often think of when they think about the "self." "With no police to follow" is the wish of every fugitive soul in the New World, of every soul yet imprisoned in the feudal "dungeons" of the past—caste, color, sex, gender, and blood. We would all "marry whom we may" (as most Americans now can, thanks to *Loving v. Virginia* [1967] and *Obergefell v. Hodges* [2015]). We would select our own society.

So, self-emancipation is a transgressive ordeal: the police are always about. Certainly, it was transgressive for Douglass, who could, quite literally, create a "self" only *outside* the law. And "canonical" American literature often intimates that the representative condition of the American "soul" is, in fact, a condition of bondage. It is a literature of men and women "who tight in dungeons are." To hear our great writers tell the tale, America is, or can be, all but totalitarian in its textures, or (perhaps) some kind of new nightmare state; the "gate of gifts" is always closed.[24] For that sentiment we needn't turn to "tenured radicals," as conservative journalists would have us believe. It is very evidently in the "canon," which is why right-leaning condemnations of "leftists" in our English Departments are curiously misguided. What these leftists say is more or less in harmony with a major strain in our literature. "Demur—you're straightway dangerous and handled with a chain," says Dickinson (337). The "American" soul knows only that it must commit what Mailer calls "socially impossible acts" if it is ever to become real (*Cannibals and Christians* 169).

It is worth emphasizing here what is already plain. Dickinson describes this condition of "dwelling in possibility" or of rootlessness—this absolute break with the fate of the past as it would determine her—in such a way as to make it altogether appealing. That is necessary "ideological equipment" for Americans, and Douglass early on fitted himself out with it. Should we adapt it to the purposes to which he put it, it equips us to accept with good grace, even with a certain satisfaction, a society that can be profoundly unstable—a society of wanderers, drifters, of people on the make; of self-inventors and confidence men; and of slaveholders and slaves. Equipped as Dickinson and Douglass are, we can see in all that instability and indeterminacy, and in the responsibility of self-creation, a higher sort of freedom, rather than, say, isolation, or emptiness; we can ignore the often-gossamer insubstantiality of the ties that bind communities together in America. And, if you really are born a slave, as Douglass was, you can, with this equipment for living, learn to manage even the ordeal of finding yourself "without an intelligible beginning in the world." As I said, Douglass knew how to stand as though a man were author of himself. But he also knew how cunning, how wicked, at times, that culture is that somehow requires this ordeal of its most "exemplary" citizens.

Dickinson is usually affirmative about the ordeal of self-creation. Mark Twain—to take another example—is less so. Huckleberry Finn is, of course, his great "self-authorizing" hero, his boy "without an intelligible beginning in the world" (who makes his escape by staging what is, in effect, a suicide). And every little concession Huck makes to the demands of his "conscience"—to that instrument that requires that he be a good little agent of the slave-power and reproduce its relations of production—every concession so made strikes the reader as disastrous (*Mississippi Writings* 711–12, 832–35). Huck has to stop being "*theirs*," as Dickinson puts it in another poem (389), if he is to realize himself. But at the same time Twain always lets us see how Huck's break with what would limit the progress of his soul—this socializing force he calls a "conscience"—is terrifically hard for the boy to make. Its costs include the abiding "loneliness" of which Huck speaks in every chapter of the novel.

Dickinson achieved her "exodus," her New World crossing at the heels of "the police," in the Amherst that her Whiggish New England family had, in fact, helped create. Sam Clemens achieved his, if ever he really did, by making a long march out of slave-holding Missouri (and the Civil War) and into a second christening, in Nevada and California, as "Mark Twain," whom he sometimes seemed to confuse with himself;[25] and then into a marriage with Olivia Langdon, the genteel daughter of a family of New York abolitionists. (Langdon was, let us say, the "just restraint" that allowed for his passage into a genuinely "free" society, which is why the complaints one still hears about her censorial air are unfair.) The house Sam Clemens built in Hartford out of the money Mark Twain made—extravagant, fanciful, idiosyncratic, unreal—became his world elsewhere. The price of the ticket was high, or so one gathers from the bitter turn his work took after 1890, when his American century drew bleakly to its close with its bloody Philippine adventures and its epidemic of lynching. One would like to ask of Twain a question Allen Ginsberg later put to Walt Whitman in "A Supermarket in California," across the heart-sore gulf of four generations: "Ah, dear father, graybeard, lonely old courage-teacher, what America did you have when Charon quit poling his ferry and you got out on a smoking bank and stood watching the boat disappear on the black waters of Lethe?" Ginsberg, who loved America both wisely and too well, can hardly bear to ask the question, let alone to have it answered (the implication is that Whitman had no America at all). And the truly American crime, as Mark Twain knew, is that Huck Finn had been forced to mistake his own private "Columbia"—those undisguised hours on the Mississippi River with the fugitive slave who was his truest friend this side of the grave—for Hell itself. How could a poor little white boy *not* have been confused? The police had gotten to him early; they had colonized his mind (as the saying goes). What America did *he* have? None: he lights out for Indian Territory (*Mississippi Writings* 912)—for the society of refugees, outlaws, and the footsore casualties of the Trail of Tears.

Douglass, too, might have asked himself that question, when, in 1895, he lived out his last hours in the stately but modest house he bought in 1878 on a hill in Anacostia, in the southeast quarter of the District of Columbia. He called the house "Cedar Hill," and furnished it with a desk once owned by Charles Sumner, the Republican from Massachusetts (the desk at which, in 1856, Sumner was assaulted by the distinguished gentleman from South Carolina, Preston Brooks); and he decorated it with portraits of Garrison, Gerritt Smith, Susan B. Anthony, Elizabeth Cady Stanton, and Lincoln. Of course, he had no portraits of his Maryland family, or of his co-conspirators at St. Michaels. Who can say what price Douglass paid for his passage into the New World, into the District of Columbia? Who knows if he thought he ever arrived?

From his chair on the veranda at Cedar Hill, Douglass could look out over Washington and see the capitol dome. He was separated from the green lawns of the National Mall only by the Anacostia River. But in 1895—surely, he and his friend Ida B. Wells must have felt it—that capitol dome had become the seat of what Twain (or was it Sam Clemens?) would soon call "The United States of Lyncherdom." And the Republican Party for which Douglass had been, some three decades running, a "wheel-horse," and which was temporarily out of power, was now the party of industrialist king-makers like Mark Hanna, not of abolitionist-labor radicals like Thaddeus Stevens.[26] It was a nation of markets, not of men. Too many golden apples lay in the way of our American Atalanta. Patriotism was again a matter of holidays and summer evenings, music and rockets.

These days, more than a century later, Cedar Hill is maintained for the people of the United States by the National Park Service. There is a Visitors' Center at the foot of the long rise leading up to the house; you can buy books there, and souvenirs, or you can "begin your tour by watching a seventeen-minute film," as the brochures say. There is a parking lot outside, which on weekdays is full of yellow school buses on pilgrimage. Inside the house, Douglass's violin rests atop his old piano (he was a lover of music). His books are on the shelves. Sumner's desk is still there, and all the portraits of the nineteenth century. But when the visitor from elsewhere in America crosses the Pennsylvania Avenue Bridge over the Anacostia River—when he steps out on the smoking bank of Lethe to see these cherishably American things—he crosses also a line: it separates black Washington from white, and Frederick Douglass's long looked-for Columbia from itself.[27]

CHAPTER TWO

W. E. B. DU BOIS AND THE REDEMPTION OF THE BODY

The word race encourages me to remember the influence of eroticism on history. For that is what race memorializes.
—Richard Rodriquez, *Brown* (2003)

Sexual chaos was always the possibility of slavery.
—W. E. B. Du Bois, *Black Reconstruction* (1935)

The Civil War Begins Again

In 1872, Ulysses S. Grant, a Republican, was elected to his second term as President of the United States. That year marked the height of the Radical Reconstruction of the South. The Republican Party controlled state legislatures and statehouses in many of what, for a few years back in the early 1860s, had called itself the Confederate States of America. Black voters were registered in the South in numbers never to be seen again until the 1960s. African Americans there held public office at nearly all levels of government, from City Hall to the Senate of the United States. Here, W. E. B. Du Bois would later maintain in *Black Reconstruction* (1935), were the first steps toward a radical labor-democracy ever taken in the New World, or, for that matter, anyplace in the world where white folk and people of color lived together.[1] In 1870 in South Carolina, for example, blacks were elected to the statewide posts of lieutenant governor and attorney general; and of 155 seats in the legislature, 96 would now be filled by former slaves, or by men who shared their complexion. Reactionaries, together with the academic historians who lent their views a mantle of respectability, later attributed this to corruption in the Republican "carpetbag" regime of governor Daniel H. Chamberlain, as if there simply could be no other explanation. But sixty-percent of the South Carolina population was African American in 1872 (the majority was larger still in the lowland counties); the Democratic Party had never been any friend of the slave; the 15th Amendment to the US Constitution had enfranchised African American men; and they voted—to fund public schools and redistribute land (among other things hated by the planter class). This was a time and a place when the logic of the following exchange—made during the investigation of Ku Klux Klan terrorism ordered by President Grant—made a certain kind of sense: "Question. Is he a white man? Answer. No, sir. His father is a senator."[2]

Resistance to Reconstruction had always been bitter in South Carolina, and often violent. By 1875, white South Carolinians, and the state Democratic Party, were prepared to "redeem" the state from Republican rule—from what Du Bois rightly calls, throughout *Black Reconstruction*, "industrial democracy" (by which he means a democracy controlled by and in the interests of labor, not property). Some white Democrats from the planter class had tried to cooperate with certain elements in the Republican Party, during the elections of 1870, for example, when a fusion ticket went down to defeat. Now, their patience exhausted, Democrats decided to act. Led chiefly by reactionaries in Edgefield County, they adopted the "straight-out" policy of opposing all political compromise, and of resorting to violence whenever occasion offered. Their opportunity came in July 1876, as the nation attained its hundredth year. On the 4th, a detachment of state-armed militia, under the command of Dock Adams—a black veteran of the Union Army and a Republican activist—assembled for a Centennial celebration in the town of Hamburg, South Carolina, a settlement populated chiefly by freedmen, situated directly opposite Augusta (and near Edgefield). Two young white men, Henry Getzen and Thomas Butler, found their progress embarrassed by the assembly, and asked that it disperse. Insults were exchanged (details of the confrontation vary, according to whether the historian giving them is kindly disposed toward the "straight-out" Redeemers); and the two white men took the measure of retaining an attorney to press charges against Adams for "blocking the public way." The case was brought before the magistrate in Hamburg, Prince Rivers, an African American, former slave, and native of the state who'd fought with distinction in the Union Army.[3] The attorney for the plaintiffs was former Confederate general Matthew Calbraith Butler, an Edgefield man and a Democratic Party stalwart. Butler set out for the courthouse in Hamburg on July 8, accompanied by a band of heavily armed whites (one of several "rifle clubs" organized in Edgefield). But the matter wasn't resolved by Magistrate Rivers. Instead, by day's end, seven black men lay murdered (the bodies were left in public sight, to point the moral); some thirty more had been summarily imprisoned; and homes and shops belonging to Hamburg's black citizens lay in ruin.[4] Party to the action was a then little-known Edgefield County farmer named Benjamin Tillman; he would later serve as governor of the state and in the US Senate (where he succeeded his fellow townsman General Butler). The "Redemption" of South Carolina was underway, as it was all across the Deep South.[5]

The tactics and tempo varied from state to state, but the result was astonishing. By 1903, when Du Bois published *The Souls of Black Folk*, better than ninety percent of the voting-eligible black population of the South had been disenfranchised; more than a thousand had been murdered; and hundreds of thousands had been returned to a condition of tenant-farming serfdom, well described in two chapters of *Souls* called "Of the Black Belt" and "Of the Quest of the Golden Fleece" and little better than slavery itself. In 1870, US Senate investigations into the activities of the Ku Klux Klan in South Carolina revealed that in one nine-month period during the Reconstruction, and in just six counties, 35 black men were murdered, 262 men and women whipped or otherwise tortured, and the property of 101 black persons vandalized (*Black Reconstruction* 676). As Du Bois would later put it, with an allusiveness that makes his historical writings so literary, "the Civil War began again—indeed had never ceased": the "black Prometheus" was again "bound to the Rock of Ages by hate, hurt, and humiliation," the better that his "vitals" might be "eaten out as they grew" (*Black Reconstruction* 670).

To continue this ongoing Civil War as a literary combatant on all fronts, the young Harvard-trained sociologist and historian sat down in his office at Atlanta University, in the heart of the New South, to write *The Souls of Black Folk*. Du Bois's great book arrived at the dawn of a century whose central problem, he predicted, would be "the problem of the color-line—the relation of the darker to the lighter races of men in Asia, and

Africa, in America and the islands of the sea" (*Souls* 372). He saw that this most intractable of American dilemmas was—always had been—but a "phase," as he puts it (372), of a truly global enterprise that originated with the slave trade; that saw its refinement in a system of colonialism that, even as he wrote in 1903, had attained extraordinary bureaucratic development in most parts of Africa and Asia; and that would not begin to unravel until the British left the Indian subcontinent; until Emmett Till had been murdered in Mississippi; until the Algerians ousted the French; until Martin Luther King, Jr., wrote his "Letter from Birmingham Jail"; until Ghana, the West African country of which this most American of writers would die a citizen, had achieved its independence. Born in the year U. S. Grant was first elected, buried in the year John F. Kennedy was murdered, Du Bois would see it all. His many books, his hundreds of essays and articles, constitute an indispensable record of the making of the world we inhabit now, in the second decade of the twenty-first century, as the nation-states created by the British and French mandates in the Middle East fall into chaos the resolution of which no one can foresee.

The Souls of Black Folk marks something of a change in Du Bois's writing. Prior to 1903, he had lived in scholarly detachment, studying (at Fisk University, Harvard, and the University of Berlin); teaching (at Wilberforce University and Atlanta University); working as a research fellow (at the University of Pennsylvania); and writing history and sociology. But events in the 1890s made this sort of academic life hard for Du Bois to sustain. Several developments deserve mention in this connection, and Du Bois discusses all of them in his autobiography *Dusk of Dawn* (most particularly, in chapters titled "Education in the Last Decades of the 19th Century" and "Science and Empire").

Booker T. Washington's "Tuskegee" philosophy of "industrial training" for blacks, as against traditional "liberal arts" education, had by this time attained its majority. It was underwritten by such men as John D. Rockefeller, of the Standard Oil Trust, and Andrew Carnegie, steel magnate and author of the Social Darwinist-inflected book *The Gospel of Wealth* (1901; quoted in my introduction). Carnegie alone gave the Tuskegee Institute $600,000 in 1903, the year Du Bois published *Souls*. In *Up From Slavery* (1901), Washington tells the story of how, two years earlier, he secured funds for the library at Tuskegee from Carnegie, after whom the building is named (190–92). Carnegie repaid the favor in his own *Autobiography* (1920): "No truer, more self-sacrificing hero ever lived [than Washington]: a man compounded of all the virtues. It makes one better just to know such pure and noble souls—human nature in its highest types is already divine here on earth. If it be asked which man of our age, or even of the past ages, has risen from the lowest to the highest, the answer must be Booker Washington. He rose from slavery to the leadership of his people—a modern Moses and Joshua combined, leading his people both onward and upward" (277). William Baldwin, President of the Long Island Railroad, sat on Tuskegee's board of trustees, and in that capacity once tried to woo Du Bois onto its faculty, a move that would effectively have silenced him as a critic of Washington (*Dusk* 611). These men, and many others like them, sought to reconcile North and South, the better to make the South safe for Northern capital, and the better, as Du Bois came to believe, to weaken the working class everywhere. The philanthropists were unfriendly to unions, and the South, unlike the industrial areas of the Northeast, was almost entirely without them. "It must not be forgotten that this Tuskegee Machine was not solely the idea and activity of black folk at Tuskegee," writes Du Bois in *Dusk of Dawn*. "It was largely encouraged and given financial aid through certain white groups and individuals in the North. This Northern group had clear objectives. They were capitalists and employers and yet in most cases sons, relatives, or friends of the abolitionists who had sent teachers into the new Negro South after the war. These younger men believed that the Negro problem could not remain a matter of philanthropy. It must be a matter of business." And then Du Bois hits his main point: "These Negroes were not to be encouraged as voters in the new democracy, nor were they to be left at the mercy of the reactionary South. They were good laborers and they might be better. They could become a strong labor force *and properly guided they would restrain the unbridled demands of white labor, born of the Northern labor unions and now spreading to the South*" (my emphasis; 607).

Alongside the great industrialists and Washington stood all the exponents of the "New South," chief among them Henry Grady, editor of the *Atlanta Constitution*, and first publisher of Joel Chandler Harris's beloved "Uncle Remus" tales. These men held that traditional "liberal arts" education for blacks would give rise to social tension between the races, and that, moreover, black men and women were not really (or not yet) suited for liberal arts education in the first place; a host of anthropologists, eugenicists, and biologists stood ready to support that belief with scientific evidence, often arguing from the same social Darwinist premises that gladdened the de-regulationist hearts of the great Robber Barons.[6] The "Tuskegee" idea, Du Bois charged, was plainly to "adjust" the education made available to black men and women to the requirements of southern industrialization, which were in turn the requirements of capital generally—and *only* to those requirements (*Souls* 398–99). Washington spoke frankly of these aims in the Atlanta address: "The wisest among my race understand that the agitation of questions of social equality is the extremest folly, and that progress in the enjoyment of all the privileges that will come to us must be the result of severe and constant struggle rather than of artificial forcing. No race that has anything to contribute to the markets of the world is long in any degree ostracized. It is important and right that all privileges of the law be ours, but it is vastly more important that we be prepared for the exercise of these privileges. The opportunity to earn a dollar in a factory just now is worth infinitely more than the opportunity to spend a dollar in an opera-house" (141). And the money flowed down to Tuskegee.

But of course, *The Souls of Black Folk* is much more than a response to crude "social Darwinists," or to Booker T. Washington and the capitalists with whom he'd chosen to treat. The 1880s and 1890s saw a steady rise in lynchings, a trend only worsened by the Long Depression that began in 1873, and by populism's rapid decay in the South into Negrophobia (consider the career of Thomas E. Watson of Georgia, who began as an integrationist and wound up a stone-cold racist). The record logs 235 public lynchings in the Deep South in 1892, a rate of more than four per week. A number of these lynchings were unspeakably brutal, involving torture and genital mutilation, the twisted motivation of which is hinted at, brilliantly, in *Souls*, as I shall argue. In *Dusk of Dawn* Du Bois places the death toll for the nine years between 1885 and 1894 at 1,700 (575). This tide of reaction, which had swollen in force with every passing year since 1876, compelled Du Bois to leave his academic sanctuary and enter the fray. He says in *Dusk of Dawn*: "One could not be a calm, cool, and detached scientist while Negroes were lynched, murdered, and starved" (603)—or while terrorists like Matthew Calbraith Butler or Ben Tillman sat in the Senate. *The Souls of Black Folk* is one result of this decision. It was written to put to rest—at least to those who could read it and would—the slanders against black men and women issuing from every quarter of the country in 1903, and to bring white Americans, generally, to the hard-won insight of a fourteen-year-old character named Huckleberry Finn: namely, that "though it don't seem natural," Jim "cares just as much for his people as white folks does for their'n" (*Mississippi Writings* 777). "Ignorant it may be, and poverty stricken, black and curious in limb and ways and thought," Du Bois writes of the black peasantry of Georgia, "and yet it loves and hates, it toils and tires, it laughs and weeps its bitter tears, and looks in vague and awful longing at the grim horizon of its life,—all this, even as you and I" (Souls 462). *Souls* is, moreover, a book of international reach. Du Bois sets the situation of black Americans in the broader context of colonized peoples across the globe, and in relation to the Spanish-American War, which decisively marked America's entry into the Great Game of empire; this is as important an impetus behind the book as anything just named. In 1903, as he completed *Souls*, the US Army was fighting Filipino republicans for control of a country they, the Americans, had only five years earlier liberated from imperial Spain; the US Senate was investigating war crimes committed by US soldiers there (through what was called at the time the Lodge Committee); and the New England Anti-Imperialist League, which counted Du Bois's former teacher William James among its members, was decrying the whole affair.

Souls is artfully designed. At the head of each essay appears an epigraph, usually from the English poets, and always shrewdly chosen, together with several bars of music, without words, from the Negro spirituals that Du Bois calls, in the concluding chapter of the book, the "sorrow songs." Bracketing everything are two short notes called "The Forethought" and "The Afterthought." The effect is highly literary, and quite distinct from that produced by Du Bois's first two books: *The Suppression of the African Slave Trade to the United States of America, 1638–1870* (a revision of his Harvard thesis) and *The Philadelphia Negro* (a sociological study of black life in the Quaker City). With *Souls*, Du Bois broke from the academic tradition of writing into which he had been trained, and thenceforth even his contributions to history and historiography—notably, *Black Reconstruction*—would challenge the limits of academic writing. *Souls* was something of a sensation: twelve printings were exhausted by June of its first year in print. By October two hundred copies per week were selling—remarkable figures for a book of such uncommon erudition.[7]

"One ever feels his twoness,—an American, a Negro"

I find no better place to begin a reading of *Souls* than with the "Forethought" Du Bois affixed to the book by way of preface:

> Herein lie buried many things which if read with patience may show the strange meaning of being black here at the dawning of the Twentieth Century. This meaning is not without interest to you, Gentle Reader; for the problem of the Twentieth Century is the problem of the color line.
> I pray you, then, receive my little book in all charity, studying my words with me, forgiving mistake and foible for sake of the faith and passion that is in me, and seeking the grain of truth hidden there. (359–60)

There is a mortuary note to the phrase with which Du Bois opens the book: "Herein lie buried many things." *Souls* will be an exhumation. Du Bois and his fellows "within the veil" (*Souls* 359) know best where the American bodies are buried. He also establishes at once that the "color-line" of which he speaks separates not only whites from blacks in America. It also separates him from his reader: "Need I add that I who speak here am bone of the bone and flesh of the flesh of them that live within the Veil?" he says, echoing Genesis (360). Du Bois wonders whether or not he will be read with "charity" or even with "patience" by his implied white reader, and this lends the word "gentle," in the conventional address to the reader, the ever so slightly acid tone that Du Bois is so skilled at deploying. (Richard Wright, less constrained by the market, could afford to be more direct. He titled one of his last books of essays *White Man, Listen!* [1957].) We are made aware, in reading "The Forethought," of an important fact. We too often take it for granted that the "American" reader is "white." The effect of this revelation is all the more complicated if, taking a step further, we imagine a black reader of the book, who, therein, will read not so much about "black folk" as about black folk described as if for a (perhaps) "uncharitable" and "impatient" white reader. This adds to the book a certain complexity in rhetoric and address—a complexity determined, in the last instance, by the political, economic, and social tensions of the new American apartheid. Only white men really knew where they stood; others who would appeal to them did so with a measure of anxiety (a very measured measure in Du Bois's case). It is evident that, in speaking of *The Souls of Black Folk* to white readers, in raising the "Veil" behind which they live, Du Bois lays himself open. The "discomfort" of writing the book is precisely the "discomfort" he would feel on being forced to take his white companion with him into the Jim Crow car of a train (*Souls* 440). He isn't writing out of self-satisfaction, a luxury he'd not be allowed in any case. His is always the discomfort of an affronted dignity. Why should he so expose himself and his people to the gaze of uncharitable eyes? But his is also the discomfort of a frustrating and private sorrow. Why should he constantly be compelled to see himself as a "black" man, rather than merely as a "man"? Why should a "veil" fall even between him and himself-as-the-object-of-his-own-thoughts? Is there no place where he can let fall what Paul Laurence Dunbar called "the mask"? Has he ever really "known" himself? White supremacy, he says, yields an African American "no true self-consciousness" (*Souls* 364). Why else would the author of a book implore the reader to "[study] his words" with him? He is a student of his own writing, and of himself.

When Du Bois startles us into this recognition in the opening pages of *The Souls of Black Folk* he introduces a provocative and fertile idea, the idea for which the 1903 book is so often remembered even by those who haven't read it: the concept of "double consciousness." "After the Egyptian and Indian, the Greek and Roman, the Teuton and Mongolian," Du Bois writes in the first chapter of *Souls*,

> the Negro is a sort of seventh son, born with a veil, and gifted with second-sight in this American world,—a world which yields him no true self-consciousness, but only lets him see himself through the revelation of the other world. It is a peculiar sensation, this double-consciousness, this sense of always looking at one's self through the eyes of others, of measuring one's soul by the tape of a world that looks on in amused contempt and pity. One ever feels his twoness,—an American, a Negro; two souls, two thoughts, two unreconciled strivings; two warring ideals in one dark body, whose dogged strength alone keeps it from being torn asunder. (364)

Double-consciousness is equivocally a gift and a curse. It is a "gift" insofar as it helps those who have it toward a purchase on the world that those without the Veil might never achieve: namely, the intuition (later, the conviction) that the social world we inhabit is not, in fact, of a "natural" kind, but of an "absurd" kind, as the existentialists say—that it is a contingent and historical world, a made world that can and must be remade in turn. But double-consciousness is also a curse because, as Du Bois says, it requires of a man that he "measure his soul" by "the tape" of a white world that holds him in contempt or regards him with amusement and pity. He cannot know himself as in himself he "really" is. The language through which he "thinks" of the world (and the self) is a white-inflected language, and in it he is Object, not Subject; Other, not Same; criminal, not innocent. In it he is seen to act from Passion more than from Reason, to be more readily assimilated to Nature than to Culture.[8] The biological, literary, historiographical, and anthropological writing of the nineteenth century (especially the period after 1830) is everywhere shaped by precisely these assumptions, such that it becomes difficult to think beyond their boundaries. The language even of the most innovative black writers is at times troubled by imperfectly acknowledged "white" assumptions, as when Jean Toomer, in *Cane* (1923), consistently imagines colored "bodies" as uniquely sensual (as opposed to chaste), and "colored" minds as peculiarly intuitive (as opposed to rational), though he does so in order to celebrate, not to belittle, them. And consider the narrator's remarks in Paul Beatty's *The Sellout* (2015): "I understand now that the only time black people don't feel guilty is when we've actually done something wrong, because that relieves us of the cognitive dissonance of being black and innocent, and in a way the prospect of going to jail becomes a relief. In the way that cooning is a relief, voting Republican is a relief, marrying white is a relief—albeit a temporary one" (18).

I want now to consider an idea corollary to the idea of "double consciousness." To read American literature or American history, both of which take for granted a necessarily unscrutinized "white" way of seeing, a white way of being aware of the world—to read this literature is, for black folk, to be educated in self-distrust (absent due care and self-awareness). In "Of the Training of Black Men," an essay about education, Du Bois has a black interlocutor ask a melancholy question (and he stands for his people as a whole): "suppose, after all, the World is right and we are less than men? Suppose this mad impulse within is all wrong, some mock mirage from the untrue?" (425). In that question lurks what Ngugi wa Thiong'o calls the "cultural bomb": "The oppressed and the exploited of the earth maintain their defiance: liberty from theft. But the biggest weapon wielded and actually daily unleashed by imperialism against that collective defiance is the cultural bomb," he writes in *Decolonising the Mind* (2011): "The effect of a cultural bomb is to annihilate a people's belief in their names, in their languages, in their environment, in their heritage of struggle, in their unity, in their capacities and ultimately in themselves. It makes them see their past as one wasteland of non-achievement and it makes them want to distance themselves from that wasteland." The cultural bomb "even plants serious doubts about the moral rightness of struggle," writes Thiong'o. "Possibilities of triumph or victory are seen as remote, ridiculous dreams. The intended results are despair, despondency and a collective death-wish. Amidst this wasteland which it has created, imperialism presents itself as the cure and demands that the dependant sing hymns of praise with the constant refrain: 'Theft is holy.' Indeed, this refrain sums up the new creed of the neo-colonial bourgeoisie in many 'independent' African states." (3)

The project of "de-colonizing the mind" leads Du Bois to conclude *Black Reconstruction* with a devastating review of American historiography titled, simply, "The Propaganda of History." It also leads him mischievously to divide his bibliography for the book, placing the literature in the field into the following unorthodox categories: "Standard—Anti-Negro (These authors believe the Negro to be sub-human and congenitally unfitted for citizenship and suffrage)"; "Propaganda (These authors select and use facts and opinions in order to prove that the South was right in Reconstruction, the North vengeful and deceived, and the Negro stupid)"; "Historians (Fair to Indifferent on the Negro)"; and "Historians (These historians have studied the history of Negroes and write sympathetically about them)" (731–33). We should not forget that the works ranged under the first two of these four headings were the ones in standard use in classrooms across the United States through the early 1960s, when I was myself born in Georgia, in the year of Du Bois's death in 1963. "An American youth attending college today," Du Bois wrote in 1935, "would learn from the current textbooks of history that the Constitution recognized slavery; that the chance of getting rid of slavery by peaceful methods was ruined by the Abolitionists; that after the period of Andrew Jackson, the two sections of the United States had become fully conscious of their conflicting interests. Two irreconcilable forms of civilization [arose]: in the North, the democratic . . . in the South, a more stationary and aristocratic civilization." He would read that "Harriet Beecher Stowe brought on the Civil War; that the assault on Charles Sumner [on the floor of the US Senate] was due to his 'coarse invective' against a South Carolina Senator; and that Negroes were the only people to achieve emancipation with no effort on their part." He would learn further "that Reconstruction was a disgraceful attempt to subject white people to ignorant Negro rule; and that, according to a Harvard professor of history (the italics are ours)"—and here come the words of Frederick Jackson Turner, writing for the *Encyclopedia Britannica*— "'Legislative expenses were grotesquely extravagant; *the colored members in some states were engaging in a saturnalia of corrupt expenditure*'" (*Black Reconstruction* 712–13).

A review of the "popular" American fiction of the period—though what is history, Du Bois seems to suggest, if not popular fiction of a sort?— would yield a similar result. Consider *Gone with the Wind*, which took the Pulitzer Prize for fiction in 1937 (two years after Du Bois published *Black Reconstruction*). Faced with all of this, a black reader of American literature must take pains if he would see himself "directly," without mediation—without refraction through the formulating gaze of white eyes. *Huckleberry Finn* (Twain's good politics notwithstanding) manages to admire a black man, Jim, chiefly by making an innocent, self-sacrificial child of him—and an illogical thinker at that. Faulkner (one suspects) asks us to sympathize with his Dilsey more *because* she "endures" than because *she has been made to*.⁹ For her part, Gwendolyn Brooks appears to suggest, in *A Street in Bronzeville* (1945), that liberal white folk find black *endurance* peculiarly moving. In any case, that's what draws the ladies of the so-called "Ladies Betterment League" into the South Side Chicago ghetto in a poem she collected in a later book, *The Bean Eaters* (1960): "Lovers of the Poor." Its title is ironic. Its form is loose iambic pentameter, with occasional, though never schematic, rhymes; it moves through heavily alliterative, highly stressed rhythms. The vigor of the lines animates the anger that hangs about the poem. There is nothing sweet or sentimental here; something like a well-merited rebuke, directed at the good ladies, is necessary to Brooks's purposes. These ladies want to "better" the poor. But they prefer, truth be told, a fabulous proletariat, the actual one being too grim, crude, and disturbing for them to "love" (and expend their sympathies on). They prefer not to be taken too far behind Du Bois's "Veil." They require a fit object for their solicitude, and the poem concerns the impure motives prompting their charity.

These ladies are consumers of the poor, really; they're buying self-regard with their donations, and want a good return on the investment—the "psychological wage" Du Bois speaks of in *Black Reconstruction* (700). It is interesting to think of the poem as an allegory of Brooks's relationship to *her* "gentle" white readers, the audience for whom she chiefly wrote prior to 1967. She pointed out in interviews dating to the late 1960s that her first patrons were white—editors, publishers, reviewers, and so on. Her early poems often read as if written in the presence of a white auditor (as does Du Bois's "Forethought"). Some of them, in fact, take this situation as their theme. "The Sundays of Satin Legs Smith," collected first in *A Street in Bronzeville*, is a good example, and is perhaps best read in light of what Du Bois says of "double consciousness." The speaker of the poem assumes a mediating role. She is intimate with the world she describes—the South Side Chicago world of Satin Legs Smith, who earned his sobriquet by dressing downtown sharp (in "wonder-suits in yellow and in wine," with "shoulder padding that is wide / And cocky and determined as his pride" [14]).¹⁰ Yet she can see that world as through the eyes of a "higher" and implicitly "white" class (uptown, *Northside* Chicago). This facility is not reciprocal. The poem makes clear that parties to any uptown constituency cannot rightly see Satin Legs Smith—cannot see him, with sympathy, as through the eyes of the speaker ("you forget, or did you ever know, / His heritage of cabbage and pigtails, / Old intimacy with alleys, garbage pails" [13]).

They're limited, ethnocentric, even a little racist, whereas Brooks transcends the antagonism implied in the poem (between speaker and reader). She moves freely across boundaries of class, race, high culture/low culture, and literary tradition—as the eloquence, wide-ranging diction, and well-modulated iambic pentameter lines of the poem suggest. She not only sees Satin Legs Smith; she sees him also *through the eyes of white folk who look on in amused contempt and pity*. One notices at once the poem's conspicuously Latinate phrasings (as in its opening lines: "Inamoratas, with an approbation, / Bestowed his title. Blessed his inclination" [12]). We quickly find that the rococo manner sorts well, if oddly, with the proletarian element in which Satin Legs Smith operates; it perfectly complements the elegance of Satin Legs Smith himself (he is nothing if not a man of style). The speaker of the poem therefore stands in sympathy with him, aesthetically speaking, but in antagonism to the implied white readers of the poem, who are addressed directly in the second person. The poem assumes that *these* readers favor a certain restrained, understated classicism that would alike proscribe wonder suits and wonder *phrases* ("inamoratas with an approbation"): "might his happiest /Alternative (you muse) be, after all, / A bit of gentle garden in the best / Of taste and straight tradition?" (13). The persons here addressed are (as I've suggested) like the ladies of the Ladies Betterment League in "The Lovers of the Poor": a little shocked and disgusted at the character of ghetto life, whether in its sordid or in its extravagant and joyous aspects. "Lovers of the Poor" invites us to re-read Brooks's earliest poems, as for example those collected in *A Street in Bronzeville*. And when we do that, Brooks' white patrons—the ones she later speaks of in her memoir, *Report from Part One*—strike us as *patronizers* of the sort imagined in "Lovers . . ." (and reminiscent of the white patrons under whom Douglass first worked while amongst the Garrisonians). The sarcasm and aggression latent in that poem make perfectly intelligible Brooks's move, late in the 1960s, into the culturally separatist Black Arts Movement. In any event, Brooks's *Selected Poems* (1963)—which reprints both "Satin Legs Smith" and "Lovers of the Poor"—comes complete with its own critical response to its white readers, and to its white literary contexts. It has in it a critical response, in fact, to the *interest* white editors and readers take and have in the poetry of black life, or in *The Souls of Black Folk*. White liberal readers are compelled to say: *Brooks won't really let us off the hook. She won't let us "love" these poems, and the people in them, without taking stock of the uneasy motives that lie behind our fascinations.* (I am aware that Brooks and Du Bois offer white scholars no exemptions.) Du Bois excites similar questions in any white reader's mind in *The Souls of Black Folk*, although, writing at quite a different juncture in American history than did Brooks in "Lovers of the Poor," his guardedness seems more delicate than provocative. Whatever the case, our literature was, for better and for worse, and for much of its history, *constituted* by books like *Huckleberry Finn*. I say so not to impeach American literature so much as to suggest that, as Du Bois saw it, any black reader who would educate himself by reading that literature must undertake to do so (to some degree) oppositionally.

"Truth forever on the scaffold"

Du Bois often speaks a philosophical sort of language ("true self-consciousness," "double-consciousness," etc.). This is no accident. Neither is the eschatological bearing of the title of the essay in which the passage on "double-consciousness" appears: "Of Our Spiritual Strivings." Du Bois invites his reader to ask these questions: Does history, like biological evolution, unfold in random, chaotic patterns that don't add up to a coherent "story" or "plot"? Or does history have a deep logic, an order, a meaning, a final "destination" toward which it is moving? "Of the Dawn of Freedom," the second essay in *Souls* (about the Freedmen's Bureau), gives us some indication as to how Du Bois might reply. Consider the epigraph he chose for the essay—a passage adapted from James Russell Lowell's abolitionist poem "The Present Crisis," written in 1845 on the eve of the Mexican War:

> Careless seems the great Avenger;
> History's lessons but record
> One death-grapple in the darkness
> 'Twixt old systems and the Word;
> Truth forever on the scaffold,
> Wrong forever on the throne;
> Yet that scaffold sways the future,
> And behind the dim unknown
> Standeth God within the shadow
> Keeping watch above His own.[11]

In affixing these lines to an essay on the Freedmen's Bureau, Du Bois argues, in so many words, that the history of the Freedmen's Bureau is a special instance—a local example—of a general tendency in history whereby liberty realizes itself, gradually and often obscurely, over time. In the story of the Freedmen's Bureau we find (let us say) yet another of "History's lessons" in an ever-continuing "death-grapple in the darkness / 'Twixt old systems and the Word." The "old system" in this case is the system of bond slavery in America or, more broadly, the political economy of white supremacy. The "Word" is (by implication) the proposition at the heart of our civil religion: "all men are created equal." The "truth" of this "Word" will manifest itself in our institutions. Mankind will emancipate itself. But history shall take centuries—has already taken millennia—to make this emancipation real. Du Bois chooses his epigraphs well. Bear in mind, then, these three controversial ideas, all of which Du Bois subscribed to, as had Lowell before him: human history has a purpose, a direction, a destination toward which it is moving; we can discern this purpose as it unfolds; and that purpose is the ultimate emancipation of the "spirit" of man. These ideas are hardly unique to Du Bois (or to Lowell). They animate the philosophies of Hegel and Marx. In *The Souls of Black Folk* Du Bois doesn't wholeheartedly assent to this optimistic theory of history. But he does entertain it, as any close reader of the book must see. *Souls* tests our faith in the possibility of political and social progress.[12]

"Soul" and "spirit," then, are the ideals. Against them Du Bois sets the prison house, the immanence, of flesh. There is, in his thinking, an abiding idealist (or perhaps "dualist") notion that Self *cannot* be somehow identical with Body. This notion leads him (Simone de Beauvoir would understand the logic) to speak of the "unmanning" of men by the allure of the flesh, by which Du Bois means, in the farther reaches of his allegory, the allure of *all* things purely "material" (even in the pecuniary sense of the word). There is a patriarchal drift to the language in which *Souls* is written, notwithstanding that Du Bois was a feminist. The peculiar situation of African American men made this inevitable. Some anxious reassertion of masculinity had to be made against the predations of a culture that would assign the prerogatives of "manhood" to *white* men only—a culture that insisted, moreover, on articulating its power in gendered (and sexualized) terms. The aspiring self Du Bois imagines in *Souls* is implicitly masculine. The terms of the debate in which he engaged—and these he certainly didn't set—somehow required it. But if Du Bois's thinking is "patriarchal," it is so in a way well summarized by Beauvoir in *The Second Sex*. One can see here how the soul's aspiration becomes always a movement away from woman and from the body with which woman is identified: "Man is in revolt against his carnal state; he sees himself as a fallen god: his curse is to be fallen from a bright and ordered heaven into the chaotic shadows of his mother's womb. This fire, this pure and active exhalation in which he likes to recognize himself, is imprisoned by woman in the mud of the earth. He would like to be inevitable," says Beauvoir, "like a pure Idea, like the One, the All, the absolute Spirit; and he finds himself shut up in a body of limited powers, in a place and time he never chose, where he was not called for, useless, cumbersome, absurd" (146). Precisely this experience of "absurdity" "unmans" the upward-looking freedmen of whom Du Bois speaks in *Souls*, "befouling" them, as he puts it in a passage I will examine later, with the "dirt and dust" of the "low" life of the "slave" (527). White supremacy—white-supremacist *patriarchy*—exploits the sheer *givenness* of a "black" body to set an absolute limit on the "powers" black men can exercise. Every day, in a hundred ways, men are reminded, in the culture Du Bois writes about, that their horizons are bounded by the *fact* of their flesh. In *Souls* the "body" figures as a prison to which the "crime" of having a "black" skin sentences men without possibility of parole—until the moment of death, when the bond binding black "soul" to black "body" is cut. Black folk, as subject to the strictures of white supremacy, are, in this book, gendered feminine precisely to the extent that they remain so subjected. Why else would Du Bois call Booker T. Washington, whose policies he considered unduly conciliatory to white interests, an "emasculator" (*Souls* 404)? Man would "aspire to the sky, to the light," Beauvoir says, but "through the fact of his birth murderous Nature has a hold upon him" (146). The capital injustice of white supremacy, as Du Bois makes clear, is to apply this "law" asymmetrically. Black "selves" are bound to the "bodily" realm of the "Natural." White "selves" are not. Bear in mind, with Beauvoir, that in Western thought this fundamental "asymmetry" applies also to sex—that is, "female" selves dwell chiefly in the "bodily" sphere of the Natural, while "male" selves do not—and it is easy to see why Du Bois should be led to masculinize the "souls" of black folk, and to feminize their bodies. Having said as much, I shall look briefly into Du Bois's 1928 novel *Dark Princess*.

The opening paragraphs of the novel tell the story of how Matthew Towns, the black protagonist, is compelled to leave the Medical University of Manhattan in his junior year when he is refused admittance into the requisite course in obstetrics. The college dean (a new hire, and a Southerner) dismisses him with the curt declaration that no white woman should be expected to permit a "nigger doctor" to deliver her baby (4). The attendance of a black obstetrician on the delivery of a white baby is, within the terms set by white supremacy, unthinkable. Beauvoir has suggested that, at the moment of parturition, the body of a woman is, at least as patriarchy would have us see her, somehow most essentially a "body." ("Wherever life is in the making . . . it arouses disgust," she says in *The Second Sex* [146]. Hence the ancient taboos and proscriptions stigmatizing menstruation and childbirth and requiring purification from them. See Leviticus 12:1–8 and 15:18–25, for example.) In speaking of the "souls" of black folk, of course, Du Bois all along, and with force, shows how white supremacy thinks of colored bodies as more purely physical and sensual, and less "intellectual" and "spiritual," than white ones.[13] The attendance of a "nigger doctor" on a white birth is intolerable because he would de-spiritualize the parturition all the more. He would de-sanctify it, animalize it, biologize it—he would put the "white" mind in an unbearable relation to the prospect of its own reproduction (which it must necessarily view as not merely biological, not merely animal). The proscription is of course double because "black" fathering of "white" babies is both forbidden and hysterically feared. That route of insemination is radically "unspiritual," radically biological. It doesn't "tie a subtle knot" between spirit and body; it *reduces* spirit to body. Under white supremacy, blackness is everywhere a token of animality, of pure physicality. The racist assumptions of "social Darwinist" thinking make this clear, as does also the behavior of white colonizers in Africa and Asia. Du Bois would certainly have gotten the point of the London bank clerk's song in Kipling's "Mandalay" (quoted already in chapter 1): "Ship me somewheres east of Suez, where the best is like the worst, / Where there ain't no Ten Commandments an' a man can raise a thirst." The clerk is thinking of a "Burma girl" he once enjoyed—and thereby temporarily converted, or so he believed—while in the colonial service. "Plucky lot she cared for idols when I kissed 'er where she stud!" (5). To be sure, this white, imperious association of color and sexuality explains much about *Souls*. It explains why the book so often relies on metaphors of sensualist "decadence" to figure what had been done to the freedmen and their posterity (as in "Of the Wings of Atalanta"). It explains why Booker T. Washington should so consistently be stigmatized in the book as a kind of "feminizing" force, as a seducer who would "unman" African Americans (*Souls* 365), giving them over entirely to the fate of the body, and also to the abuse, if not of London bank clerks, then of the Northern financiers who helped fund his Tuskegee Institute. It explains why Du Bois takes pains to defend black Americans against the charge, urged constantly in those days, often on "scientific" grounds, of sexual immorality (*Souls* 368, 460). It explains why Du Bois sometimes sounds monkish and otherworldly, rather, in fact, like an ascetic—as when he quotes with approval Goethe's injunction in *Faust*, "Deny yourself, you must deny yourself" (*Souls* 420). To all of this I will return. For the moment, and to complete the picture, we need only add that, for Du Bois, the black American is a "colonized" subject, as were people of color everywhere on earth in 1903. A "colonial subject" is, as the vast enterprise of white-supremacist patriarchy positions him, "feminine."

DuBois and The Wizard

This brings me again to the Wizard of Tuskegee, Booker T. Washington, and to Du Bois's great debate with him about *The Souls of Black Folk*. In "Of Our Spiritual Strivings," Du Bois sketches out, in brief, the history of the postwar period for African Americans. There was Emancipation itself; then the granting of citizenship and suffrage; then what Du Bois bitterly calls "The Revolution of 1876" (the "Redemption" of which I earlier spoke); and, with that, the freedmen and their sons and daughters were left to wander like forsaken Israelites in a desert somewhere between Pharaoh and a nation they could rightly call home. In this "wilderness" appeared before the freedmen, like the Biblical "Pillar of Fire," what Du Bois calls "the ideal of 'book learning'; the curiosity, born of compulsory ignorance, to know and test the power of the cabalistic letters of the white man, the longing to know. Here at last seemed to have been discovered the mountain path to Canaan" (*Souls* 367). "Cabalistic" letters, says Du Bois, choosing his adjective carefully: one tradition associates the Kabbalah with the Oral Torah, given by God to Moses on Mt. Sinai and preserved in the Talmud. Du Bois sets up an exact allegory in *The Souls of Black Folk*: "ten thousand thousand" black Americans are adrift, and two men would be their Moses—Du Bois with his Kabbalah (all the "book learning" of the West), and Washington with his Tuskegee program of agricultural and industrial training. The one tends to the "souls" of black folk, the other chiefly to their "bodies."

The chief underwriters of black educational institutions in the South in the post-Reconstruction period were organizations whose funds came from Northern capitalists. The money was disbursed through two organizations: the Southern Education Board and the General Education Board. As David Levering Lewis points out, "a partial roster of the officers and trustees of the S.E.B. was a roll call of the arbiters of the Industrial North and the New South"—railroad money, money from the Wanamaker Department Store fortune, from Wall Street, from Standard Oil, and so on. The S.E.B. (founded in 1901) and the G.E.B. (1902) disbursed some $176 million to white colleges and universities and some $21 million to black colleges and universities between 1902 and 1930 (Lewis 267). The directors of the organizations sought reconciliation between North and South and the development of Southern labor and resources by Northern capital. These goals ultimately required that they defer to Southern opinion on The Negro Question. By 1876, "the rich and dominating North," Du Bois explains in *Souls*, "was not only weary of the race problem, but was investing largely in Southern enterprises, and welcomed any method of peaceful cooperation" (398). Booker T. Washington well-suited the purposes of "the rich and dominating North" after his celebrated 1895 speech, familiarly known as the "Atlanta Compromise" (touched upon already in the introduction). In it, he agreed to put off demands for political and civil rights in favor of modest economic development.

Washington reports in *Up From Slavery* that "one of the saddest things" he ever saw was a young black man "sitting down in a one-room cabin, with grease on his clothing, filth all around him, and weeds in the yard and garden, engaged in studying a French grammar" (122). The youth, Washington meant, would be better off, and happier, if he practiced a trade instead of studying "big books" with "high sounding subjects" (122–23). And recall his contention in his Atlanta Exposition address that "The opportunity to earn a dollar in a factory just now is worth infinitely more than the opportunity to spend a dollar in an opera-house" (141). To all of which Du Bois drily retorts in *Souls*: "One wonders what Socrates and St. Francis of Assisi would say to this" (393). What Northern capitalists had to say to it was plain. Washington on the merits of studying French grammar and visiting opera-houses was music to their ears. He soon became a salaried field agent for the S.E.B., with the result (among other things) that Du Bois's Atlanta University was ignored by Northern benefactors, while Tuskegee flourished. Du Bois later remarked of the period in *Dusk of Dawn*: "After a time, almost no Negro institution could collect funds without the recommendation or acquiescence of Mr. Washington. . . . The control [of the S.E.B. and G.E.B.] was to be drastic. The Negro intelligentsia was to be suppressed and hammered into conformity" (607–8). All of which explains why Du Bois's attack on Washington in *The Souls of Black Folk* is so devastating, despite the fact that Du Bois manages, throughout, to sustain a temperate, even cordial, tone. His iron fist is velvet-gloved.

The heart of his argument against Washington is this:

> Mr. Washington represents in Negro thought the old attitude of adjustment and submission; but adjustment at such a peculiar time as to make his programme unique. This is an age of unusual economic development, and Mr. Washington's programme naturally takes an economic cast, becoming a gospel of Work and Money to such an extent as apparently almost completely to overshadow the higher aims of life. Moreover, this

> is an age when the more advanced races are coming in closer contact with the less developed races [i.e., owing to imperialism], and the race-feeling is therefore intensified; and Mr. Washington's programme practically accepts the alleged inferiority of the Negro races. Again, in our own land, the reaction from the sentiment of war time has given impetus to race-prejudice against Negroes, and Mr. Washington withdraws many of the high demands of Negroes as men and American citizens. In other periods of intensified prejudice all the Negro's tendency to self-assertion has been called forth; at this period a policy of submission is advocated. In the history of nearly all other races and peoples the doctrine preached at such crises has been that manly self-respect is worth more than lands and houses, and that a people who voluntarily surrender such respect, or cease striving for it, are not worth civilizing. (*Souls* 398)

In the story Du Bois tells, Washington is an instrument in the hands of white supremacy and capital. Both institutions—the political and the economic—employ him for the purpose of re-enslaving the freedman, of "adjusting" him, more or less bloodlessly, to "submission" (the bloodier instruments of this adjustment were wielded chiefly by elements of the Southern white working class, under the protection of the Democratic Party). Du Bois associates Washington with the capitalist extremism of the Gilded Age, which, in its "astonishing commercial development," had grown "ashamed of having bestowed so much sentiment on Negroes," and which henceforth would be "concentrating its energies on Dollars," as Du Bois phrases it (*Souls* 392). This "unusual economic development"—the word "unusual" carries the considerable force of Du Boisian understatement—had also come to comprise the acquisition and administration of colonies in Hawaii, the Caribbean, Guam, and the Philippines (*Souls* 400). The reassertion of white supremacy at home, in the post-Reconstruction period, was part of a larger project: the consolidation of white authority over peoples of color everywhere in the world—by the United States, England, France, Germany, Italy, Holland, and Belgium.[14]

Du Bois would also argue, in *Black Reconstruction* (1935), that the failure to make American democracy real—the opportunity we squandered when we destroyed a nascent "industrial democracy" in the South in the early 1870s—had world-historical significance: "During the war, labor was resentful," he explains. Why? Because workers "were forced to fight in a strife between [Northern and Southern] capitalists in which they had no interest and they showed their resentment in the peculiarly human way of beating and murdering the innocent victims of it all, the black free Negroes of New York and other Northern cities; while in the South, five million non-slaveholding poor white farmers and laborers sent their manhood by the thousands to fight and die for a system that had degraded them equally with the black slave. Could," asks DuBois, "one imagine anything more paradoxical than this whole situation?" (28–29). When, during the Radical Reconstruction, that paradox appeared to resolve itself for a few years in such places as South Carolina (1868–76), America "stepped forward in the first blossoming of the modern age and added to the Art of Beauty, gift of the Renaissance, and to Freedom of Belief, gift of Martin Luther and Leo X, a vision of democratic self-government: the domination of political life by the intelligent decision of free and self-sustaining men." America might no longer have been an imaginary nation with real people living in it. "It was the Supreme Adventure, in the last Great Battle of the West, for that human freedom which would release the human spirit from lower lust for mere meat, and set it free to dream and sing." "And then," writes DuBois with his singular irony, "some unjust God leaned, laughing, over the ramparts of heaven and dropped a black man in the midst." The result? "It transformed the world. It turned democracy back to Roman Imperialism and Fascism; it restored caste and oligarchy; it replaced freedom with [neo]slavery and withdrew the name of humanity from the vast majority of human beings" (30)—and then followed the Scramble for Africa, the Boer Wars, two World Wars, and then the many wars of decolonization, whose consequences are with us yet. The story of the twentieth century *was* the story of the color line.

When he is set in this larger, global context, Washington emerges, under Du Bois's direction, as a veritable agent of colonial rule—as a figure who would sell out black "manhood," and who would, in fact, pander his race to a white ravisher. He had become, Du Bois implies, the Great Emasculator: he had "sapped the manhood" of the race (*Souls* 399), advocated a "policy of submission" (398), withdrawn the demands of Negroes "as men" (398), acquiesced in their relegation, again, to a "servile caste" (399), yielded up their "manhood rights" (397), and "overlooked certain elements of true manhood" (394). I could go on, but the point is made. It is exactly as Du Bois would have it in the epigraph, from Byron, that he chose for "Of Mr. Booker T. Washington and Others": "From birth to death enslaved; in word, in deed, *unmanned!*" The line occurs in canto 2, stanza 74, of *Childe Harold's Pilgrimage*. The canto is better known to readers of the nineteenth-century abolitionists for the often-quoted opening lines of stanza 76: "Hereditary bondsmen! Know ye not / Who would be free *themselves* must strike the blow?"[15] It is no accident that when Du Bois convened a 1906 meeting of the Niagara Movement, an organization dedicated to the fight for full and immediate political rights and out of which came the NAACP, he chose as the site Harpers Ferry, where John Brown—the "meteor of the war," as Melville put it (xi)—had struck *his* blow in 1859. It was "in significance if not in numbers," Du Bois says in *Dusk of Dawn*, "one of the greatest meetings that American Negroes have ever held. We made pilgrimage at dawn bare-footed to the scene of Brown's martyrdom and we talked some of the plainest English that has been given voice by black men in America." The battle that these "pilgrims" waged, as they explained in a public statement, was not for themselves alone, but for "all true Americans." It was and still remains a battle "for ideals, lest this, our common fatherland, false to its founding, become in truth [and again] the land of the Thief and the home of the Slave—a by-word and a hissing among nations for its sounding pretensions and pitiful accomplishment" (618–19). In America, Du Bois explains in *John Brown* (1909)—a biography of the man and a book too seldom read—"we had built a wonderful industrial machine," and had done it on the backs of colored labor. It was a machine "quickly rather than carefully built, formed of forcing rather than of growth, involving sinful and unnecessary expense" (236). His admonition to his countrymen—and here Du Bois only follows Brown as he would have *us* understand that martyr's legacy—is still as crystalline in its simplicity as it is revolutionary in its implications for capitalism: "Better smaller production and more equitable distribution," he says; "better fewer miles of railway and more honor, truth, and liberty; better fewer millionaires and more contentment" (236).

Finally, as for the origins of *John Brown*, there is this to say: in late 1903 Ellis Paxson Oberholtzer invited Du Bois to write a book about Frederick Douglass for the American Crisis Biographies series, of which Oberholtzer was the general editor. Du Bois readily agreed, only to have the invitation rescinded a few months later. Booker T. Washington, it turned out, wanted the volume on Douglass for himself, and, given Washington's fame, Oberholtzer yielded, offering an angered Du Bois the chance to choose another subject. Du Bois proposed a biography of Nat Turner, leader of a bloody slave insurrection in 1831. But when that, too, was denied him, Du Bois accepted Oberholtzer's suggestion that he write instead about John Brown. The reader should bear in mind these prickly negotiations because *John Brown* obliquely, but devastatingly, extends Du Bois's unforgiving critique of the accommodationist strategies he associates with Washington in *Souls*.[16] Indeed he is at pains, in *Souls*, to distinguish between the rebellious tradition to which Turner and Brown alike belonged and the tradition of compromise Washington had embraced (396–98). How must the latter have felt when he read, if he read it, Du Bois's remarkable declaration that Brown—not Douglass, let alone Washington—is "the man who of all Americans has perhaps come nearest to touching the real souls of black folk" (*John Brown* xxv)? Had Carnegie read that, he'd have—well, one can only imagine.

The Wings of Atalanta

Du Bois points out that "the hushing of the criticism of honest opponents" of Washington "is a dangerous thing. It leads some of the best of the critics to unfortunate silence and paralysis of effort, and others to burst into speech so passionately and intemperately as to lose listeners" (*Souls* 395). Du Bois's challenge in Souls is to criticize the Wizard of Tuskegee candidly and thoroughly, but to do so subtly, so as not to "lose listeners," or at least not many. He says he writes "in all sincerity and utter courtesy" (394). But surely the claim is disingenuous, coming as it does from a man who has just hailed Washington as "the most distinguished Southerner since Jefferson Davis" (393). Du Bois mastered the art of damning with faint praise. His solution to the problem of dealing with Washington in such a way as not to "lose listeners"—though Washington's loyalists would hardly have been persuaded—is to stage the most devastating phase of his attack allegorically, in a parable he tells of Atalanta, Hippomenes, and the Golden Apples, in (by my estimation) the richest essay in Souls: "Of the Wings of Atalanta" (from which the title of the present book is taken).

"Of the Wings of Atalanta" is many things. It is an essay about the "New South," whose unofficial capital was the city of Atlanta, a city which had risen, phoenix-like, from the ashes of the war, reinventing itself as a center of commerce and industry. It is an essay about America in the post-Reconstruction "Gilded Age," for which Atlanta serves as an epitomizing symbol. It is also an essay about education—about the fate of Du Bois's own Atlanta University in an era when the monies of a madly money-making nation were directed ever more exclusively, at least when it came to the education of black Americans, into schools of vocational training. And it is an essay about what sort of nation America should become in the century that, for Du Bois, loomed ominously ahead—the twentieth.

In the years after Reconstruction ended, "they of Atlanta," writes Du Bois, "turned resolutely toward the future; and that future held aloft vistas of purple and gold:—Atlanta, Queen of the cotton kingdom; Atlanta, Gateway to the Land of the Sun; Atlanta, the new Lachesis, spinner of web and woof for the world. So the city crowned her hundred hills with factories, and stored her shops with cunning handiwork, and stretched long iron ways to greet the busy Mercury in his coming. And the Nation talked of her striving" (416). Mercury is the god of commerce and the market, and Lachesis one of the Fates (here she spins out of Southern cotton a web of trade and finance that would bind to Atlanta the far-flung markets of the world). The questions Du Bois puts are simple. Shall the "fate" of the onlooking nation be to sell its "soul" for this great promise of "gold and purple"—of wealth and power? Shall it prostitute its Declaration of Independence in market-driven idolatry before the mercurial gods of "greed" and "lust," whose instrument at home is "Jim Crow" and whose instrument abroad is Empire? Du Bois continues (in a passage already quoted in the introduction):

> Perhaps Atlanta was not christened for the winged maiden of dull Boeotia; you know the tale,—how swarthy Atalanta, tall and wild, would marry only him who out-raced her; and how the wily Hippomenes laid three apples of gold in the way. She fled like a shadow, paused, startled over the first apple, but even as he stretched his hand, fled again; hovered over the second, then, slipping from his hot grasp, flew over river, vale, and hill; but as she lingered over the third, his arms fell round her, and looking on each other, the blazing passion of their love profaned the sanctuary of Love, and they were cursed. If Atlanta be not named for Atalanta, she ought to have been. (416)

Atalanta/Atlanta is "swarthy" and "wild." Her great energies, libidinal in their intensity, might issue in the downward-looking appetites of a "blazing passion," as perhaps would befit an immature daughter of "dull Boetia" (it was a proverbially backward sort of place); or else they might be sublimated, through aspiring self-discipline and sacrifice, into "high and generous ideals" (416). Greed and lust exist, for Du Bois, in an equation. Each is a species of materialism, of sensualism—a tendency to reduce humanity to bodiliness, to "defile the Temple of Love," and to "befoul" the chaste "Gospel of Work" (416). Slavery had done all of these things, degrading slave and master alike. Now, the new "slavery" of Empire and "Jim Crow" on which the United States seemed to Du Bois to have embarked in its Gilded Age promised to do it again. Will Atalanta/Atlanta be allowed—in fact encouraged—to grow out of the Boetian stupor into which her first slavery had driven her? Or will a "second slavery" now arise to replace the first, the better to keep her benighted—and, what is worse, to do it with her own connivance?[17] Hippomenes is "wily" (416).

Out of this strange allegory emerges the full force of Du Bois's decision to speak of the *souls* of black folk, and of their "*spiritual* striving." For Du Bois, as I have indicated, it is as if the "white" mind forever sexualizes the black body—forever sees in it something "swarthy" and "wild." With what he intimates is a "wanton license of fancy," post-Reconstruction-era sociologists "gleefully count [the freedmen's] bastards and prostitutes" (368). This lewd sociological imagination, which would reduce black souls to flesh, is but a refinement, a translation into more rarified quarters, of a will to power over black men and women that had, to be sure, *itself* impressed on those bodies, as a token of domination, what Du Bois calls "the red stain of bastardy": "two centuries of systematic legal defilement of Negro women" under slavery "meant not only the loss of ancient African chastity, but also the hereditary weight of a mass of corruption from white adulterers, threatening almost the obliteration of the Negro home" (368). Atalanta is vulnerable indeed. Her burden is not only to save herself, but to "save" her tempter also, because she is the last best hope of the nation—the "truest exponent of the human spirit of the Declaration of Independence," as we have seen. Her "chastity" is of great moment in *The Souls of Black Folk*. "Two figures," Du Bois says, "ever stand to typify" the epoch of slavery "to coming ages":

> A gray-haired gentleman, whose fathers had quit themselves like men, whose sons lay in nameless graves; who bowed to the evil of slavery because its abolition threatened untold ill to all; who stood at last, in the evening of life, a blighted, ruined form, with hate in his eyes;—and the other, a form hovering dark and mother-like, her awful face black with the mists of centuries, had aforetime quailed at that white master's command, had bent in love over the cradles of his sons and daughters, and closed in death the sunken eyes of his wife;—aye, too, at his behest had laid herself low to his lust, and borne a tawny man-child to the world, only to see her dark boy's limbs scattered to the winds by midnight marauders riding after "damned Niggers." (383)

The formula Du Bois develops in this "typifying" allegory goes like this: master is to slave as man is to woman, and as ravisher is to ravished. Bondage had "feminized" the slave, "unmanned" him. It had put him in a "feminine" position with respect to the "master class," as we have already seen (and as Du Bois so repeatedly suggests). And of course, the "mother-like" figure in the passage above is "representative": in her are comprehended both men and women. And "even today," Du Bois says, in an apostrophe to the "Southern Gentleman," "the masses of the Negroes see all too clearly the anomalies of their position and the moral crookedness of yours. . . . When you cry, deliver us from the vision of intermarriage, they answer that legal marriage is infinitely better than systematic concubinage and prostitution. And if in just fury you accuse their vagabonds of violating women, they also in fury quite as just may reply: The rape which your gentlemen have done against helpless black women in defiance of your own laws is written on the foreheads of two millions of mulattoes, and written in ineffaceable blood" (*Souls* 436). So much, then, for the decadent legacy of the planter. So much for his peculiar husbandry of Southern "institutions." We have now to address his successor in the "New South" that emerged after 1876—a successor whose good "husbandry" even of the "body" of the land itself is in doubt.

"The Wizard of the North—the Capitalist—had rushed down in the seventies to woo this coy dark soil," we are told (*Souls* 446). The land, to be sure, had been "raped" by the old regime of mono-crop slave-based agriculture (449).[18] Now, by the abusive system of tenancy that arose in slavery's wake, the land would be raped again, or at any rate "wooed" (the "new" slavery was a bit less forward). All of lower Georgia, Du Bois explains, was now being "ravished into a red waste" (451). The "soil" is described in such a way—"coy, dark"—as to suggest its affiliation, if not identity, with the dark, politically "unmanned" laborers who work it. Plainly, the relation of Northern capital to Southern labor—to labor everywhere, Du Bois believed—was abusive. Landlord is to land as white man is to black, as man is to woman (under patriarchy), and as rapist is to victim: that is the bleak equation. The decades-old tendency "born of slavery" had been "quickened to renewed life by the crazy imperialism" of the 1890s with the result that, now, as Du Bois says, "human beings" were ranged "among the material resources of a land to be trained with an eye single to future dividends" (428). No wonder, then, that when Du Bois takes his Gentle Reader down to what had been the "Egypt of the Confederacy," the Black Belt of Georgia, he finds there, and directs our attention to, a "pretty blue-eyed quadroon" (449). Thinking of the competition among the European nations for their place in the sun, and for cheap, colored labor, he writes: "Plain it is to us that what the world seeks through desert and wild we have within our threshold;—a stalwart laboring force, suited to the semi-tropics; if, deaf to the voice of the Zeitgeist, we refuse to use and develop these men, we risk poverty and loss. If, on the other hand, seized by the brutal afterthought, we debauch the race thus caught in our talons, selfishly sucking their blood and brains in the future as in the past, what shall save us from national decadence?" (425). Such is the tendency, and such the legacy, of a culture that "debauches" everything it touches, that everywhere turns "souls" into "bodies." Ours is a "a happy-go-lucky" nation, as Du Bois puts it, "which goes blundering along with its Reconstruction tragedies, its Spanish war interludes and Philippine matinees, just as though God really were dead" (466). In the midst of it all, Atalanta-Atlanta undertakes the race of her life. As she goes, so will the nation.

After the brief "democratic" experiment of 1867–76, some of whose good results I reviewed at the outset of this chapter, Americans set about (as I've indicated) to re-establish white supremacy: at home, through the establishment of the new "Jim Crow" apartheid, and abroad, through the suppression of Filipino republicans—men who had trusted the promise of self-government held out in our own Declaration of Independence when they took up arms, with our encouragement, against Spain. As Du Bois saw it, we were selling out nothing less than the "New World" promise of America itself. In the following passage, notice the metaphors of sexual encounter and of degeneracy, so characteristic of Du Bois's writing in *Souls*; and notice the quiet reminders of our forsaken American errand.

> In the Black World, the Preacher and Teacher embodied once the ideals of this people—the strife for another and a juster world, the vague dream of righteousness, the mystery of knowing; but today the danger is that these ideals, with their simple beauty and weird inspiration, will suddenly sink to a question of cash and a lust for gold. Here stands this black young Atalanta, girding herself for the race that must be run; and if her eyes be still toward the hills and sky as in the days of old, then we may look for noble running; but what if some ruthless or wily or even thoughtless Hippomenes lay golden apples before her? What if the Negro people be wooed from a strife for righteousness, from a love of knowing, to regard dollars as the be-all and end-all of life? What if to the Mammonism of America be added the rising Mammonism of the re-born South, and the Mammonism of this South be reinforced by the budding Mammonism of its half-wakened black millions? Whither, then, is the new-world quest of Goodness and Beauty and Truth gone glimmering? Must this, and that fair flower of Freedom which, despite the jeers of latter-day striplings, sprung from our fathers' blood, must that too degenerate into a dusty quest of gold;—into lawless lust with Hippomenes? (418–19)

Du Bois draws his allegory sharply. He warns his Gentle Readers lest black Americans—again, those truest exponents of the Declaration of Independence—bed down with the Golden Apple of "white" capital. The "defilement," the "lawless lust," would in this case be double, for it is, by the inexorable logic of the allegory, a figure for the most "rapacious" "husbandry" of our "natural" and of our "human" resources. It is the sort of husbandry, Du Bois makes clear in Souls, that antebellum white planters, post-1876 absentee landholders, and colonial bureaucrats alike indulged in, *mutatis mutandis*. All the while, the demagogic constabulary of the Democratic Party of an un-Reconstructed South seldom let slip an opportunity to get up lynching parties with whispers of fates worse than death visited on the White Magnolias of the South. Harsh words. But they are what Du Bois implies. Booker T. Washington's role in the whole gaudy pageant, at least as scripted in *Souls*, is hardly enviable. Du Bois's careful phrasing does allow for the possibility that Washington might merely be a "thoughtless" Hippomenes, rather than a "ruthless" or a "wily" one (the latter two, I suppose, stand in for his wealthy Northern backers) (419). But that is thin absolution.

What is to be done? Well, Du Bois suggests, after unwinding his devastating allegory of America in its Gilded Age "debauch," "the hundred hills of Atlanta are not *all* crowned with factories" (my emphasis):

> On one, toward the west, the setting sun throws three buildings in bold relief against the sky. The beauty of the group lies in its simple unity:—a broad lawn of green rising from the red street and mingled roses and peaches; north and south, two plain and stately halls; and in the midst, half hidden in ivy, a larger building, boldly graceful, sparingly decorated, and with one low spire. It is a restful group;—one never looks for more; it is all here, all intelligible. There I live, and there I hear from day to day the low hum of restful life. In winter's twilight, when the red sun glows, I can see the dark figures pass between the halls to the music of the night-bell. In the morning, when the sun is golden, the clang of the day-bell brings the hurry and laughter of three hundred young hearts from hall and street, and from the busy city below;—children all dark and heavy-haired;—to join their clear young voices in the music of the morning sacrifice. In a half-dozen classrooms they gather then;—here to follow the love-song of Dido, here to listen to the tale of Troy divine; there to wander among the stars, there to wander among men and nations,—and elsewhere other well-worn ways of knowing this queer world. Nothing new, no time-saving devices, simply old time-glorified methods of delving for Truth, and searching out the hidden beauties of life, and learning the good of living. The riddle of existence is the college curriculum that was laid before the Pharaohs, that was taught in the groves by Plato, that formed the *trivium* and *quadrivium*, and is today laid before the freedmen's sons by Atlanta University. And this course of study will not change; its methods will grow more deft and effectual, its content richer by toil of scholar and sight of seer; but the true college will ever have one

goal,—not to earn meat, but to know the end and aim of that life which meat nourishes.

The vision of life that rises before these dark eyes has in it nothing mean or selfish. Not at Oxford or at Leipsic, not at Yale or Columbia, is there an air of higher resolve or more unfettered striving; the determination to realize for men, both black and white, the broadest possibilities of life, to seek the better and the best, to spread with their own hands the Gospel of Sacrifice;—all this is the burden of their talk and dream. Here, amid a wide desert of caste and proscription, amid the heart-hurting slights and jars and vagaries of a deep race-dislike, lies this green oasis, where hot anger cools, and the bitterness of disappointment is sweetened by the springs and breezes of Parnassus; and here men may lie and listen, and learn of a future fuller than the past, and hear the voice of Time: "Entbehren sollst du, sollst entbehren." (*Souls* 419–20)

Even the architecture of the place is modest, chaste, and retiring: "plain," "half-hidden in ivy," "simply decorated," and conducive to rites of "morning sacrifice" (in fact to a "Gospel of Sacrifice"). Students at Atlanta University in 1903 would have recognized the German with which the passage concludes as a line from Goethe's *Faust*, a poem Du Bois no doubt studied at the University of Berlin, and which he here ascribes to "the voice of Time" itself: "Deny yourself, you must deny yourself." True, it is a monkish ideal—hardly the sort of thing marketing offices at universities now say to prospective students. But the unworldiness of this description of a college campus is precisely the point: "bodies" are of the world merely, and "spiritual strivings" are not. I've already quoted Du Bois's retort to Washington's easy dismissal of that young black man bent over a French grammar in a tumbledown hovel in Virginia. I am quoting, here, his answer. Deny yourself (he says, with Goethe). Chasten yourself. America—and, in an age of empire, all the world—is alive with "golden apples." Tend to *The Souls of Black Folk* more than to their bodies, shun Hippomenes, and you will help this nation realize, at last, its "errand into the wilderness":[19] to "reform" a world that "white" Europe, at its worst, had left reeling and debauched.

Let us spell it out. In the larger story Du Bois would tell, black America is Atalanta, the last best hope of the nation; Washington is her "thoughtless" Hippomenes; and the Golden Apple he holds out—his Tuskegee program of "industrial training," social "separation," and "humility"—is the poison of a Gilded Age. Mere bread-winning in the service of white supremacy. So, Du Bois implies, should Atalanta turn to whoring, and take all of America with her, we will know who pandered her off. Du Bois's assessment of his powerful rival—and, more important, of his rival's promoters on the G.E.B and the S.E.B., for they are the "ruthless" and "wily" ones—is just that unforgiving, no matter how suavely delivered.

But what of the *trivium* and *quadrivium*? What of the course pursued at Du Bois's own Atlanta University, as at the great universities of the Old World? This curriculum, of course, is but a token of a larger and decidedly political promise, which we can approach, by inference, from what Du Bois says below. "The Wings of Atalanta," he explains, "are the coming universities of the South" (to recur to a passage quoted in the introduction):

> They alone can bear the maiden past the temptation of golden fruit. They will not guide her flying feet away from the cotton and gold; for—ah, thoughtful Hippomenes!—do not the apples lie in the very Way of Life? But they will guide her over and beyond them, and leave her kneeling in the Sanctuary of Truth and Freedom and broad Humanity, virgin and undefiled. . . . Let us build the Southern university—William and Mary, Trinity, Georgia, Texas, Tulane, Vanderbilt, and the others—fit to live; let us build, too, the Negro universities:—Fisk, whose foundation was ever broad; Howard, at the heart of the Nation; Atlanta at Atlanta, whose ideal of scholarship has been held above the temptation of numbers. Why not here, and perhaps elsewhere, plant deeply and for all time centres of learning and living, colleges that yearly would send into the life of the South a few white men and a few black men of broad culture, catholic tolerance, and trained ability, joining their hands to other hands, and giving to this squabble of the Races a decent and dignified peace? (*Souls* 421–22)

Here, we have to do with no committee meeting wrangle as to whether young black men and women will, on the one hand, study Goethe, Hume, and French grammar, or, on the other, accounting, "hospitality," and "business"—or, as at many public universities today, some unsatisfying combination of them all. At stake for Du Bois, startling though it may seem, is nothing less than the fate of men everywhere in the twentieth century, for the history of slavery and empire—this great "squabble of the Races"—had, by 1903, made the debate unspeakably urgent in Alabama, in Georgia, in the Belgian Congo, in the Philippines, and on the veldts of southern Africa (it would only be the more urgent down through the 1930s, when white supremacy came to its head in the Nazi regime.[20]) Are we really to treat men and women of color as bodies alone—as Calibans? Who is to say what Caliban might become, and allow us to become in turn, if we supposed, at the outset, that he was a thing in apprehension like an angel? And are we, to seal the devil's bargain, to "ravish" the "body" of the earth in an economy of depletion such as had threatened, already by 1850, even the forgiving soil of the Cotton Belt? Shall we let the market's "golden apples" direct all the energies of our production? Is there no other end to the race? Every one of these questions is entailed in Du Bois's injunction that we "conserve our souls from sordid aims and petty passions" (*Souls* 422); never mistake his ascetic language for late-Victorian prudery. Only in light of these questions can we understand the force of his chastening allegory about the dubious fate, in 1903, of the body of this so thoroughly American Atalanta, and about her Tempter at the Cotton States Exposition in 1895, Booker T. Washington: "When night falls on the City of a Hundred Hills, a wind gathers itself from the seas and comes murmuring westward. And at its bidding, the smoke of the drowsy factories sweeps down upon the mighty city and covers it like a pall, while yonder at the University the stars twinkle above Stone Hall. And they say that yon gray mist is the tunic of Atalanta pausing over her golden apples. Fly, my maiden, fly, for yonder comes Hippomenes!" (423).

At the Opera House

Toward the end of *The Souls of Black Folk*, in its penultimate chapter, Du Bois tells an emblematic story of two young men named John. The two boys grow up "play-fellows" in the seacoast Georgia hamlet of Altamaha. One is white, the son of the local judge. The other is black and poor. In due course both put away childish things. White John heads to Princeton to become a "man" (523). Black John, the hope of Altamaha's African American residents, goes North—despite dark words of warning from his white townsmen (522)—to work his way through a small Negro college named Wells Institute (the tale is narrated by one of his teachers). At Wells, black John takes hard-won courses in Du Bois's *trivium* and *quadrivium*, pondering "long over every new Greek word," and wondering "how it must have felt to think all things in Greek" (524). Meanwhile, at Princeton, white John does what well-bred gentlemen of uncertain aspirations always do in college. Seven years pass. Then, one afternoon, quite by chance, the two Johns of Altamaha encounter one another in a queue at the box office of a New York City Opera house. White John has come with a lady on his arm; black John has come alone—and he is not at ease in this setting:

> He was pushed toward the ticket-office with the others, and felt in his pocket for the new five-dollar bill he had hoarded. There seemed really

no time for hesitation, so he drew it bravely out, passed it to the busy clerk, and received simply a ticket but no change. When at last he realized that he had paid five dollars to enter he knew not what, he stood stockstill amazed. "Be careful," said a low voice behind him; "you must not lynch the colored gentleman simply because he's in your way," and a girl looked up roguishly into the eyes of her fair-haired escort. A shade of annoyance passed over the escort's face. "You WILL not understand us at the South," he said half impatiently, as if continuing an argument. "With all your professions, one never sees in the North so cordial and intimate relations between white and black as are everyday occurrences with us. Why, I remember my closest playfellow in boyhood was a little Negro named after me, and surely no two,—WELL!" The man stopped short and flushed to the roots of his hair, for there directly beside his reserved orchestra chairs sat the Negro he had stumbled over in the hallway. He hesitated and grew pale with anger, called the usher and gave him his card, with a few peremptory words, and slowly sat down. The lady deftly changed the subject.

All this John did not see, for he sat in a half-daze minding the scene about him; the delicate beauty of the hall, the faint perfume, the moving myriad of men, the rich clothing and low hum of talking seemed all a part of a world so different from his, so strangely more beautiful than anything he had known, that he sat in dreamland, and started when, after a hush, rose high and clear the music of Lohengrin's swan. The infinite beauty of the wail lingered and swept through every muscle of his frame, and put it all a-tune. He closed his eyes and grasped the elbows of the chair, touching unwittingly the lady's arm. And the lady drew away. A deep longing swelled in all his heart to rise with that clear music out of the dirt and dust of that low life that held him prisoned and befouled. If he could only live up in the free air where birds sang and setting suns had no touch of blood! Who had called him to be the slave and butt of all? And if he had called, what right had he to call when a world like this lay open before men? (*Souls* 526–27)

All the post-Reconstruction American elements are here: the genteel hypocrisy of the South ("one never sees in the North so cordial and intimate relations between black and white as are everyday occurrences with us"); the complicit, indulgent, "roguish" winking of the North ("Be careful, you must not lynch the colored gentleman simply because he's in your way," a sentence uttered here in playful courtship); and then the inadvertent touch of the skin ("and the lady drew away"). This last is all it takes to bring John down, again, into the imprisoning immanence of his body, "befouled" by "dirt" and "dust." He would "rise high and clear," like Lohengrin's swan, as with the wings of Atalanta he assumed at Wells Institute; he would have a soul as well as a body. But to white eyes he is merely, and always, the flesh—alive, like Caliban, with a vivid animality. That is why his altogether accidental jostling of this Miranda, of this white lady on the arm of the Judge's John, is later re-imagined, in a way a thousand times replayed in the South Du Bois knew, as an act of "force": "Oh," white John says on encountering his black play-fellow again back home in Altamaha, "it's the darky that tried to force himself into a seat beside the lady I was escorting" (533).

The half-muted fantasy of rape, the almost religious certainty that in the presence of black John he simply must be in the presence of something fundamentally sensual in its (beastly) address: this is what *The Souls of Black Folk* tries to make its "gentle reader" understand, for it does seem inexplicable. The animating motive of white supremacy, as Du Bois understands it, is nothing less than this: a sensualizing will-to-power, everywhere fascinated by what it everywhere also detests, whereby black "souls" are reduced to bodies—in fact, to the "mortified flesh" *as such*. And that is why Du Bois simply had to write his book about the *souls* of black folk. The general situation also accounts, as he knew, for the ritually sexualized nature of so much of the violence directed against blacks in the period with which Du Bois here has to do: the whole brutal enterprise was an effort to "emasculate" a population (to adapt his metaphor for it)—an effort to reduce that population to a condition of "Boetian" subjection. James Baldwin, Du Bois's successor, would write in *The Fire Next Time*: "Yes, it does indeed mean something—something unspeakable—to be born, in a white country, an Anglo-Teutonic, antisexual country, black" (*Essays* 304). For Black John—the white folks in Altamaha all say so—it means a life of humble labor; and, if he really insists on going North to study his *trivium* and *quadrivium*, well, it means he must be made to agree, on returning to take charge of the local colored school, never to put "fool ideas of rising" into the heads of his black students (*Souls* 532); they must understand that they are bound to hew wood and haul water. And as for black Jennie, John's younger sister, the girl who cleans the Judge's kitchen: she is mere flesh too, when "measured by the tape of a world that looks on in amused contempt and pity." "Why," says white John, "I never noticed before what a trim little body she is. Hello, Jennie! Why, you haven't kissed me since I came home" (534).

In "The Forethought," Du Bois calls "The Coming of John" a tale "twice-told" but "seldom written" (*Souls* 359). To be sure, the plot has its weird familiarity. When a black body lays claim to its soul down South, there *must* be bloodshed. And, in due course, white John tackles Jennie in callous sport, "befouls" the "trim little body" that she simply *is* for him (she doesn't "have" a body; she *is* one); black John hears the cry, comes running, and strikes dead his white doppelganger—whose father, the Judge, had already marked out for him a lively career in post-Reconstruction Georgia politics—"with all the pent-up hatred of his great black arm" (534). All that remains, now, is for black John to take leave of his mother; she doesn't yet know what has happened. Telling her a truth that is also not a truth, he says: "Mammy, I'm going away,—I'm going to be free." With his eye not on the North, as she supposes, but on "the North Star pale above the waters," he heads for the breakers, there to await the lynching party. When it arrives, black John hums a strain of Wagner to himself (we are in the opera house again, *pace* Booker T. Washington on the merits of spending a dollar there). He sings the "Song of the Bride": "Joyfully led, pass along to that place . . ."—and lets "the storm burst round him." "And the world," Du Bois says, "whistled in his ears" (535).

If he has read with "patience" and "charity," the Gentle Reader—the reader on the other side of the color line—is perhaps left thinking again of the stanza from Fitzgerald's *Rubaiyat of Omar Khayyam* that Du Bois places at the head of his essay on "The Training of Black Men":

> Why, if the Soul can fling the Dust aside,
> And naked on the Air of Heaven ride,
> Were't not a Shame—were't not a Shame for him
> In this clay carcase crippled to abide? (*Souls* 424)

Banquo's Ghost

I began this chapter with a glance back at the Hamburg Massacre of 1876, an episode representative in too many ways of the "Redemption" of the South from Reconstruction. Here I will take a brief second glance at the episode and its bloody corollaries, because that Redemption is what *The Souls of Black Folk* was written in order to denounce, and also to explain.

Two months after the Hamburg Massacre, in September 1876, a band of armed white men gathered in Edgefield, South Carolina, twenty-odd miles northeast of Hamburg. At their head was Nathaniel Butler, a one-armed Confederate veteran and the brother of the attorney (Matthew Calbraith Butler) who was, in July, to have brought charges against Dock Adams—the black Union Army veteran who headed up the local militia in Hamburg. And, having gathered, Butler's mob went looking for one Simon Coker, a black man. Coker was, at the time, a Republican State Senator from nearby Barnwell County; he'd embarked on an investigation of white militancy in that part of South Carolina. Butler and his men seized Coker (he was already in the custody of local whites); they led him into the brush along a country road, and, after permitting him to pray, and agreeing to return the key to his corn-crib to his wife, they shot him dead where he knelt. Party to the business, again, was a young white farmer named Benjamin Tillman. Afterward, the record shows, Tillman enjoyed a meal of barbecued pig, corn pone, and coffee, and got himself home to Edgefield.

The bloody summer of 1876 marked Tillman's debut in South Carolina politics. He would eventually become governor, and, later still, would sit for several terms in the Senate of the United States. When Tillman died in 1918, W. E. B. Du Bois wrote an obituary and published it in *The Crisis*, which he then edited for the NAACP. We can see in it the influence of Marx, a figure increasingly important, in those days, to Du Bois. "It can hardly be expected that any Negro would regret the death of Benjamin Tillman," Du Bois wrote. "And yet it is our duty to understand this man in relation to his time. He represented the rebound of the unlettered white proletariat of the South from the oppression of slavery to new industrial and political freedom. The visible sign of their former degradation was the Negro. They kicked him because he was kickable and stood for what they hated; but they must as they grow in knowledge and power come to realize that the Negro far from being the cause of their former suffering was their co-sufferer with them. Some day a greater than Tillman," Du Bois continued, "will rise in the South to lead the white laborers and small farmer, and he will greet the Negro as a friend and helper and build with him and not on him" (*Writings* 1177). The "unlettered white proletariat of the South," the very men Ben Tillman represented, had themselves been "oppressed" by slavery. The insight is characteristic of Du Bois, as is also the promise he holds out of a *real* redemption—this vision of a class solidarity that would, at the end of the day, resolve the problem of the color line not only where it scarred the county of Edgefield, South Carolina, and not only where it divided the United States from itself, but where it had, by generations of Europeans, been etched across what we now call the Third World. It may be that only a man burdened by "double-consciousness" could have achieved just this insight, and entertained just this promise, in the last year of the First World War between the great colonial powers, and the first year of the Bolshevik Revolution. It is certainly the case that Du Bois was writing, as he penned his oddly inspiring obituary of a damned Redeemer, about the souls of *white* folk.

On March 29, 1900, Ben Tillman stood in the Senate Chamber to deliver a speech. In it he acknowledged—Du Bois would hardly have objected—that the "race question" had "been the cause of more sorrow, more misery, more loss of life, more expenditure of treasure than any and all questions which have confronted the American people from the foundation of the Government to the present day. Out of it grew the war, and after the war came the results of the war, and those results are with us now. The South has this question always with it. It cannot get rid of it. It is there. It is," he affirmed, unforgettably, "like Banquo's ghost, and will not down."[21] Had he read this, Du Bois might have said, *Give the unlettered old boy enough rope and he will hang even himself.* Here, to be sure, is an example of a man astonishingly unaware of what his words imply. Here is dramatic irony of a high order. But it may be better to imagine (again, as Du Bois might have) that Tillman is, in fact, *somehow* aware that his allusion to *Macbeth* constitutes the inadvertent confession of a ruthless politician—a politician who murdered another politician, Simon Coker, in 1876, in order to get his start. Surely it is fitting that Tillman, and the post-Reconstruction South he helped create, should be haunted, as Macbeth was, by the specter of a good man slaughtered along the king's highway in a drive for absolute power; and fitting, as well, that he (and it) should have been made sleepless by the fear that that good man's sons must someday inherit the kingdom. Fleance is always alive.

But however that may be, a shrewder, because more deliberate, evocation of the same unquiet banquet in Shakespeare's tragedy comes in *The Souls of Black Folk*, three years after Tillman strutted and fretted his hour upon the Senate stage with Banquo's ghost. It is as good a passage as any with which to close this chapter. "And yet," Du Bois says, thinking of Banquo's apparition, and quoting Macbeth's horrible importunity—"And yet the swarthy spectre sits in its accustomed place at the Nation's feast. In vain do we cry out to this our vastest social problem: 'Take any shape but that, and my firm nerves / Shall never tremble!' The Nation has not yet found peace in its sins; the freedman has not yet found in freedom his promised land" (366). That Tillman and Du Bois should alike have been enthralled by *Macbeth*—that they should both, in fact, have re-imagined our America as Macbeth's bloody Scotland—*this* is a telling irony of American literary history, and one not even the "weird sisters" could have arranged. It makes one wonder what William Dean Howells could possibly have had in mind when he famously said, in 1886, ten years after the sorry collapse of the Reconstruction, that "the more smiling aspects of life" are "the more American," that "the large, cheerful average of health and success and happy life" is "peculiarly American," and that the human race, in America, "has enjoyed conditions in which most of the ills that have darkened its annals might be averted by honest work and unselfish behavior" (128–29). Honest work and unselfish behavior hadn't gotten the freedmen anywhere, and the lynchings rolled on by the day. Howell's ability to ignore this fact is a characteristic American talent, and in it he is perfectly sincere.[22]

But terror, as Du Bois would have understood, was nothing new on our soil when, with Timothy McVeigh, it came to Oklahoma City in a rented van in 1995. Nor should we, in 1995, have been at all surprised—and this, too, Du Bois would have understood—that the terrorist carried in his car a copy of *The Turner Diaries*, a novel by a white supremacist devotee of *The Protocols of the Elders of Zion*. Nor should we fail to see the significance of the fact that McVeigh wore on his T-shirt a picture of Abraham Lincoln above the legend—they were the white supremacist John Wilkes Booth's words in Ford's Theatre—*Sic Semper Tyrannis*. In America, the problem of the twentieth century was indeed, all the way down to 1995, all the way down to Oklahoma City, the problem of the color line.

CHAPTER THREE

THE MEPHISTOPHELEAN SKEPTICISM OF STEPHEN CRANE

> ... this happy-go-lucky nation, which goes blundering along with its Reconstruction tragedies, its Spanish war interludes and Philippine matinees, just as though God really were dead.
>
> —W. E. B. Du Bois, *The Souls of Black Folk*

Crane, the Civil War, and the 1890s

I reprise at the head of this chapter a phrase quoted not very many pages back: I aim here to trace the happy-go-lucky moods of Stephen Crane's fiction to the national distemper so well diagnosed, as we have just seen, by Du Bois. The two authors are of an age, after all, and Crane's remarkable novel *The Red Badge of Courage* (1895) alerts us—as does *The Souls of Black Folk*—to what Du Bois calls the rapid passing away, in the 1890s, of the "ideals" for which the American Civil War had been waged, by the best of Radical Republicans anyway (*Souls* 392). He means, simply, the ideals of widening democracy and of emancipation: in short, the new birth of freedom of which Lincoln spoke in 1863, and for which men like Robert Gould Shaw, Joshua Lawrence Chamberlain, and a host of other "Radicals" (and thousands of black soldiers) believed themselves to be fighting and dying.

Du Bois and Crane register this passing away of war "ideals" in utterly different keys. The one is angry, elegiac, disturbed, indignant. The other is cool, irreverent, detached, whimsical, ironic. Du Bois would impress upon us the heroism of the men who fought, or who thought of themselves as fighting, for the better angels of our nature (in such books as *Black Reconstruction* [1935]). Crane satirizes heroism and courage, quarantines them in quotation marks. He seems highly skeptical that such things actually motivate men. The war, as we know it in his pages, has nothing to do with principles. Alfred Kazin gets Crane about right in *On Native Grounds* (1995): "The surest thing one can say about Crane is that he did not care which way the world went. No one was ever less the reforming mind" (68). And the surest thing one can say about Du Bois is that he did and was.

It is a nice bit of poetic justice that the most hostile review of *Red Badge*, on its publication in 1895, came from the pen of retired Union General Alexander McClurg, the man who would, eight years later, publish *The Souls of Black Folk*.[1] Some dismiss McClurg as a prude. But he understood how the novel treated the (to him) high theme of the war irreverently, "as if God really were dead," as if the still-fresh "Reconstruction tragedies" (*Souls* 466) had really been a farce. "Nowhere are seen," McClurg writes of *Red Badge*, "the quiet, manly, self-respecting, and patriotic men, influenced by the highest sense of duty, who in reality fought our battles" (54). His "in reality" doubtless overstates the matter, but of course it issues from the pen of a man with Radical Republican inclinations. Still, I aim to show the merit in McClurg's review. To borrow the remark an astonished John Ruskin made, as he considered American responses to the war, it is quite as if Crane were "washing his hands in blood and whistling."[2] So much anyway for the glory of the coming of the Lord. Crane's eyes had never seen it. One looks in vain in all his fiction of the war for any consideration of its causes, its political meaning, its bleak consequences in the 1890s. McClurg believed he understood what an ostentatiously ironic (and "antiheroic") treatment of the war amounted to in the political context of 1895: acquiescence to the general drift away, in America, from the principles that had, to a large extent anyway, guided the Lincoln administration after the autumn of 1862, and that had also informed the Reconstruction during the best phases of Grant's two administrations, when the Ku Klux Klan was effectively suppressed, and when voting rights for black Americans were protected to a degree we'd not see again until the late 1960s. *The Red Badge of Courage* is perfectly symptomatic of the 1890s, when, as Du Bois says, the nation was "a little ashamed of having bestowed so much sentiment on Negroes" (*Souls* 392), shadowy figures who make no appearance on the stage of *The Red Badge of Courage* (except, on its first page, as capering contraband, entertaining white soldiers). The passing away of the war ideals to which Du Bois refers in *Souls*, ideals to which both he and McClurg subscribed, was also the passing away of a particular dream of what America might mean to the rest of the onlooking world. It wasn't merely a matter of what Americans at the time inaptly called "the Negro Problem." In Crane it is as if America had no errand—into the wilderness, or into anyplace else. He is a scoffer at the American civil religion, a cavalier citizen in good standing of the "happy-go-lucky" nation to which Du Bois refers. In *Red Badge* he gives us, as McClurg points out, an "ignorant and stupid country lad" who enlists in the Army of the Potomac from "no definite motive" (53)—a fact as true of Henry Fleming as it is of every soldier we encounter in the pages of the novel. Crane would hardly disagree. More than once he calls his soldiers "yokels": "A contemptuous term" of nineteenth-century origin, as the *OED* has it, "for a (stupid or ignorant) countryman or rustic; a country bumpkin." These are the men who people *The Red Badge of Courage*. Crane regards them with the eye of a downtown New York bohemian.

William James, in that same mean decade of the 1890s, once suggested that "if your heart does not *want* a world of moral reality, your head will assuredly never make you believe in one." He might well have been addressing Stephen Crane, or at any rate young men like him, as when he continues in the same passage: "Mephistophelean skepticism, indeed, will satisfy the head's play-instincts much better than any vigorous idealism can. Some men (even at the student age) are so naturally cool-hearted that the moralistic hypothesis never has for them any pungent life, and in their supercilious presence the hot young moralist always feels strangely ill at ease. The appearance of knowingness is on their side, of *naiveté* and gullibility on his. Yet, in the inarticulate heart of him, he clings to it that he is not a dupe, and that there is a realm in which (as Emerson says) all their wit and intellectual superiority is no better than the cunning of a fox" (*Will to Believe* 23). Let's say that Crane—a writer of "the student age" in 1894—brings into American literature a Mephistophelean skepticism of the sort James has in mind. Let's further suppose that his prose is intended to satisfy the "head's play-instincts" alone, as against any "moral hypotheses." McClurg is correct to find in *Red Badge* what he calls a "riot of words." The point he misses is that the "unusual associations of words," the "forced and distorted use of adjectives," and the often "absurd similes" and queer grammar he condemns are, in fact, exactly what *ought* to draw our interest (and our praise) (54).

These aren't obstacles or embarrassments; they are the reason the book exists. They satisfy the head's play instincts very well.

Historian David Blight distinguishes three "visions," as he calls them, of the Civil War in American memory (*Race and Reunion* 2). There is the "reconciliationist" vision that developed in the years after Reconstruction was destroyed by Southern "Redeemers"—the era of, as Blight puts it, "Blue-Gray fraternalism" (199). Among the most consequential developments of this school was the program advanced by advocates of the "New South"—advocates, that is, of a South that accepted the verdicts of the war, in their mildest and most forgiving form. This was a South that embraced Northern capital and hoped to build a new political economy founded on industry and modern agriculture. It was a South that the Republican Party, purged of its Radical elements by 1890, could easily do business with. The new Republicans in due course proved themselves perfectly ready to resign the freedmen and their posterity to a resurgent (and avowedly white-supremacist) Southern Democratic Party. Reconciliationists, Blight explains, tended to speak of the war as having been a war of principles in which much might be said in favor of either side. The war, it was believed, simply settled in a bloody way the old debate about the proper relation of state to federal power; slavery, it was urged, had been an "incident" to the war, and not the chief cause of it. Associated with this vision of the war was the "plantation school" of literature, with its faithful slaves and beloved mammies, as we find it in the work of Thomas Nelson Page and, in a somewhat more complex form, in the work of Joel Chandler Harris (and, as we saw in the introduction, in Jefferson Davis's *Rise and Fall of the Confederate Government*).[3]

This "reconciliationist" vision of the war found its dark complement in what Blight calls the "white-supremacist" vision, which, in fact, is the vision most closely aligned with the expressed purposes of the founders of the Confederacy—men like Confederate Vice President Alexander H. Stephens, who announced in the February 1861 speech quoted at length in chapter 1 that "our new Government is founded upon . . . the great truth that the Negro is not equal to the white man." Stephens looked forward "with confidence to the ultimate universal acknowledgment of the truths upon which" the Southern system rested. In a sense, he got it right. By the 1890s—the era of rampant Anglo-Saxonism, and the high-water mark of European empire, in Africa, East Asia, and elsewhere—that "universal acknowledgment" seemed actually to have arrived. The South emerged from Reconstruction vindicated. One can almost feel General McClurg smarting at these developments as he condemns the British press for embracing

The Red Badge of Courage: "In October, 1861, *Blackwood Magazine* said exultantly," McClurg reminds us, that the "venerable Lincoln, the respectable Seward, the raving editors, the gibbering mob, and the swift-footed warriors of Bull's Run, are no malicious tricks of fortune, played off on an unwary nation, but are all of them the legitimate offspring of the Great Republic," whose end, the magazine added, with delight, would more likely "be ridiculous than terrible" (53). McClurg goes further still, associating the British response to *Red Badge* with its own imperial exploits: "We all know with what special vindictiveness 'The Saturday Review' always treats any book upon our late struggle written from the Northern standpoint. And so it is with all British periodicals and all British writers," who are, McClurg suggests, "puffed up with vain-glory over their own soldiers who seldom meet men of their own strength, but are used in every part of the world for attacking and butchering defenseless savages, who happen to possess some property that Englishmen covet." "Under such circumstances," he adds, "we cannot doubt that *The Red Badge of Courage* would be just such a book as the English would grow enthusiastic over" (53).

However that may be, against the "reconciliationist" and "white supremacist" styles of remembering the Civil War (with their implicit imperial adjuncts), there was a third: the "emancipationist" vision, as Blight calls it, which saw in the Civil War, and in the Constitutional amendments that followed in its wake, a struggle to make real and practical the promise that "all men are created equal." This is the vision of Lincoln's Gettysburg Address; of Frederick Douglass and Albion Tourgée; of the Radicals within the Republican Party (Sumner and Stevens chief among them); of the millions of African American voters—and thousands of African American politicians—who sought to create working multi-racial democracies during the Reconstruction, democracies superintended, in fact, by the working class;[4] it is the vision in Crane's own generation of William Vaughan Moody, Alexander McClurg, John Jay Chapman, Mark Twain, William James, Du Bois, and many others.

Where does Crane, in his fiction of the war, fit into this tripartite scheme? We can say without controversy—and here's where McClurg gets it right, by implication—that Crane's writing doesn't allow for an "emancipationist" vision. Crane's Union soldiers don't trample out the vineyards where the grapes of wrath are stored. (You would never know from *Red Badge* that some 180,000 black soldiers served in the Union Army.) *Red Badge* is more "reconciliationist" in its bearing, more in harmony with that element within the reconciliationist school that sought to get on with the unsentimental business of nation-building and untrammeled capitalism associated with the Gilded Age. Reconciliationists preferred to concentrate more on the individual soldiers' "devotion" to the opposed causes of Southern independence and Union than on the causes themselves. As Blight makes clear, the suffering, sacrifice, and heroism of individual soldiers muted any "moral" differences between Union and Confederate armies, Union and Confederate governments, and, finally, between Union and Confederate war aims. Men laid emphasis on what the narrator of *Red Badge* calls a "subtle battle brotherhood more potent even than the cause for which they were fighting" (33).[5] The war was a gentleman's bout of honor, the politics and legacy of which were beside the point (and bad form to mention in the parlor). Crane, in an oblique way, exemplifies these developments, with the difference that his soldiers, Confederate and Union alike, are unified less in their heroism than in their yokelish awkwardness—in their comical anti-heroism. The Civil War, insofar as it was "about" anything for Crane (and admittedly we can only work by inference here), was about the consolidation of a new nation so massive and overbearing in its machinery as to rob the little guy, the "grunt," of his dignity (a development about which Crane doesn't seem much to care, even as he registers it). The new Union is simply too big, too unanswerable. And if we can neither embrace nor protest the new Leviathan of the Gilded Age, what remains is the way Crane took: the way of detachment, irony, and disaffection—the "Mephistophelean skepticism" of which James speaks. With this comes an incuriosity about politics that McClurg thought he'd found in Crane. The writer is left with a sense of style alone. Crane's stylistic innovations—which McClurg simply couldn't understand—are unlike those of the notably innovative writers of the American Renaissance. They do not bring him into the main currents of a radically "American" democracy. They will, in fact, allow him to become, as Emerson, Thoreau, Whitman, Douglass, and Melville never did, a genuinely "secular" writer with respect to the American civil religion. In Crane—and here he differs utterly from Whitman and Douglass, and even Emerson—we have to do with the writer as "individual," not with the writer as "citizen."

But let us take the year 1863 as our touchstone, as our representative passage through the American Civil War, about which Crane would write so unforgettably. In November of that year, when he appeared at Gettysburg to dedicate the cemetery, Lincoln could see about him the open graves of thousands; the exhumation and reburial had fallen behind schedule. Here, to be sure, was evidence of a battle that to many seemed as wasteful and indecisive as the battle imagined in *The Red Badge of Courage* would later seem to Crane. And as for the battle at

Chancellorsville, which took place in May of the same year, and on which *Red Badge* is apparently based, Lee Clark Mitchell's assessment in an article on Crane is apt: "Twenty-seven thousand men died in a conflict whose immediate consequences seemed nil at best and at worst senseless; the North lost despite a decided superiority, the South won a merely Pyrrhic victory, and after two days both sides were left almost exactly where they had been" ("Introduction," *New Essays* 16). But despite all this, Lincoln was able, in his great speech at Gettysburg, to transfigure the ghastly scene about him, the battle, and the larger war itself, with a splendid new conception of the American errand, an enterprise in which, it seems safe to say, Crane had absolutely no interest in his response to the conflagration of the war. Lincoln gave us an America whole, at least in prospect. In it we looked "to gather paradise" (to borrow a phrase from Emily Dickinson [507]). It was an hour of great expansion, and of a most poetical union. We dwelt in possibility, a fairer house than prose.

However, what followed over the next few decades was the assembly of an America united in prosaic fact. Markets—literary markets included—were for the first time truly nationalized. (No better illustration of this exists than the fiction and reportage of the globe-trotting Stephen Crane, who wrote for the burgeoning newspaper syndicates.) The postwar amendments to the Constitution gave the Union a new consistency and integrity from state to state, from region to region (at least on paper, which is all most Americans cared about). Truly national, even continental, communication and transportation infrastructures were put into place—the sort of infrastructures that would allow Scratchy Wilson, Crane's slightly ridiculous West Texas outlaw in "The Bride Comes to Yellow Sky," to dress himself in clothes purchased "for purposes of decoration" and made "principally" (as Crane precisely says) by "some Jewish women on the east side of New York" (320).

In most every respect but an industrial one, the post-Reconstruction years were a period of diminishing possibility. The western frontier had been closed; the whole continent was more or less digested (with its Natives consigned to reservations); and the freedmen and their sons and daughters were disenfranchised, beaten, and murdered by the thousands during the lynching terror of the 1880s and 1890s. In Stephen Crane's America, geographical "expansion" and political "emancipation" alike seemed at an end. The Lincolnian "star of our liberty," as one Populist put it in 1894, the year *Red Badge* was serialized in the newspapers, had "sunk into night" (Pollack 10). These facts tell us much about the determinism of the new "naturalist" fiction, about the bleak "social Darwinism" of the Robber Barons, and about the ascendant *realpolitik* of imperialists in a new Republican Party—now dominated by men like Mark Hanna, William McKinley, and Theodore Roosevelt—hankering to take up the white man's burden in the Caribbean, the Philippines, Guam, and Hawaii. And there are, in the developments associated with literary "naturalism," important "vocational" consequences, at least for an innovative writer like Crane. Earlier writers than Crane—writers who dwelt in "possibility," as had Emerson—felt themselves to be intimately engaged in the national enterprise. The remarkable styles—the rhetorical extravagance—of the great writers of the American Renaissance took heart from the expanding energies of the nation. Literary composition was for them aligned with the composition of the nation itself. They felt as if they possessed America, and they were, in turn, most possessed by its spirit when writing. Examples include Whitman in the 1855 preface to *Leaves of Grass* ("The United States themselves are essentially the greatest poem" [iii]); Emerson in such works as "The Young American" (1844), *Nature* (1836), "The American Scholar" (1837), and "The Poet" (1844); and Frederick Douglass (as we have seen) in *My Bondage and My Freedom* (1855). Nowhere do we meet this energy, let alone this extravagance, in Crane. For him, style, and what it affords us, are (as I've said) private resources, not "public" ones; and style—again, for him—is nothing if not temperate (nobody ever set Crane boiling, as Emerson did Whitman). The discipline of writing does not carry him away with the nation; the discipline of writing is there to *prevent* his being carried away by the alienating drift of a nation so impersonal in its maneuvers as to admit no vital participation on the part of the "simple separate person" (as Whitman put it). Hence the stark naturalism of "The Open Boat" and "The Blue Hotel." With Crane, stylistic innovation is for good and all detached from the possibility of making the world new. That is what I mean in speaking of his as a "secular" vocation; writing isn't, for him, the "higher" calling that Whitman, Emerson, and Frederick Douglass answered to. In Crane we find consummated the developments of which Andrew Delbanco speaks in an essay on *The Red Badge of Courage*: "When the fighting [of 1861–65] was over and American writers undertook what Edmund Wilson has called the 'chastening of the American prose style'— the reduction of metaphoric density to the spare language of realism—the organ tones of union oratory became more often a subject for parody than for celebration" ("The American Stephen Crane" 50).

Having surveyed the 1890s, we may consider *The Red Badge of Courage* in detail. Much work has been undertaken to unearth Crane's sources for the novel. We know, among other things, that in the spring of 1893 Crane was absorbed in reading "Battles and Leaders of the Civil War," a series which had run in *Century* magazine in the middle 1880s, and which was subsequently published in a plush four-volume set in 1888. There Crane found, among other things, a detailed account of the battle of Chancellorsville, upon which most scholars believe his novel to have been loosely based (though its abstraction from any particular campaign is, to my mind, the more salient point). The *Century* series commissioned officers on both sides of the conflict to write narratives of the battles in which they had been engaged. As David Blight points out, the purpose of the series was "to use war recollections as a depoliticized vehicle of sectional reconciliation." "Why the war came," Blight explains, "and how it had transformed America were not the subjects of this prolonged soldiers' symposium; the issues of slavery and race were resoundingly silent" (*Race and Reunion* 175). The spirit of the series is well summed up in the letter John O. Casler, who had served under Stonewall Jackson, wrote to the editors about his own contribution. Casler assured the editors that his essay contained "nothing referring to the causes of the war or the right or wrong of it" and that it would be "interesting to all classes" (quoted in *Race and Reunion* 176).

The debt Crane owed or did not owe to the *Century* series, as to the particulars of the battle he described, is not really the point here. The point is that *The Red Badge of Courage*, in its reconciliationist tendency, in its "resounding silence" about the causes and consequences of the war (to borrow Blight's phrase), takes its place amongst a constellation of post-Reconstruction literary treatments of the war that includes, also, the *Century* series. The tendency of all these works is to level differences between North and South by concentrating our attention on the behavior of individual soldiers. Whether that behavior is heroic, cowardly, or comical hardly matters. What matters is the way these works harmonize the discord of the war by transforming the whole show into a theater for the testing of individual will, strength, and "character." Instead of a war about the destiny of the Union and the fate of the slave—as the war definitively was after the autumn of 1862—it becomes something like an arena in which even the losers win. The war no longer concerns politics. It concerns good sportsmanship—the possession of it, the lack of it, whatever. This is most evident in *The Red Badge of Courage*. Daniel Aaron is right: "Stephen Crane did not think of the War as a national tragedy," and "Negroes and Lincoln and hospitals and prisons are not to be found in [his] theatre" (211, 215). So much for the sacrifices of the 1860s.

But *The Red Badge of Courage* certainly bears witness to the history in which it took shape in the life of Crane's imagination. The structure of feeling peculiar to it is what makes it so thoroughly a document of the 1890s, and what makes Crane's Civil War so thoroughly a war of the post-Reconstruction era: there is not a thread in it of what in those days was called the "Bloody Shirt," which politicians who spoke too triumphantly, and piously, about the Grand Army of the Republic were inevitably accused of "waving." Andrew Delbanco's point is well taken: "If the sound and sight of the flapping flag—'sun-touched, resplendent'—are sometimes huge in Henry Fleming's consciousness, the socially inscribed meaning of that flag is an abstraction quite outside his understanding, and becomes equally so for us" as we read *Red Badge* ("The American Stephen Crane" 54). Let us turn, now, to the prose, where, if these effects are registered, we must trace them out.

Washing Your Hands in Blood and Whistling

One of Crane's best effects depends on a tonal polyphony that oddly harmonizes what would otherwise be discordant moods. The effect usually suggests the complexity, or the ironic objectivity, of Crane's point of view. A fine example occurs early in Red Badge of Courage:

> After complicated journeyings with many pauses, there had come months of monotonous life in a camp. [Henry Fleming] had had the belief that real war was a series of death struggles with small time in between for sleep and meals; but since the regiment had come to the field the army had done little but sit still and try to keep warm.
>
> He was brought then gradually back to his old ideas. Greeklike struggles would be no more. Men were better, or more timid. Secular and religious education had effaced the throat-grappling instinct, or else firm finance held in check the passions.
>
> He had grown to regard himself merely as a part of a vast blue demonstration. His province was to look out, as far as he could, for his personal comfort. For recreation he could twiddle his thumbs and speculate on the thoughts which must agitate the minds of the generals. Also, he was drilled and drilled and reviewed, and drilled and drilled and reviewed. (8–9)

The rhetoric of the first paragraph is uncomplicated. It merely gives us to understand that army life and army myth are not the same. The second paragraph is a repetition, almost verbatim, of an earlier passage describing the content of Henry's "ideas." Crane often resorts to repetition of this sort. Here, it suggests (somewhat condescendingly) the poverty of Henry's mentation, and also its wavering incoherence: men no longer fight because they are "better"; men no longer fight because they are too "timid"; men no longer fight because they have been educated out of the instinct; men no longer fight because the lords of the land find it unprofitable to allow them to. The alternatives in each case exclude one another, and should a single mind contemplate them all simultaneously, it would be an incoherent mind indeed. But as I say, no single mind is before us here. Crane's mind—the mind of his ironic narrator, if I may speak of a narrator as having a mind—overlaps and circumscribes the more limited mind of his protagonist. I suspect we are to understand that Henry sees no irony in his "old ideas," that he regards the pairs of alternatives as in each case live, whereas for Crane the second in each pair pretty clearly undercuts the first, with the final irony being, simply, that timidity, prudence, decency, and altruism are insufficient, even in combination, to moderate our "throat-grappling instinct." The third paragraph quoted also revives the uncomplicated mode of the first, with a flourish of repetition in the last sentence registering the tedium of camp life. We are getting a fair picture of the alienation of the common infantryman who learns to regard himself as "part of a vast blue demonstration" (9).

That much seems to me more or less unremarkable, though fine. The next two paragraphs of the passage, however, are pure Crane:

> The only foes [Henry] had seen were some pickets along the river bank. They were a sun-tanned, philosophical lot, who sometimes shot reflectively at the blue pickets. When reproached for this afterward, they usually expressed sorrow, and swore by their gods that the guns had exploded without their permission. The youth, on guard duty one night, conversed across the stream with one of them. He was a slightly ragged man, who spat skillfully between his shoes and possessed a great fund of bland and infantile assurance. The youth liked him personally.
>
> "Yank," the other had informed him, "yer a right dum good feller." This sentiment, floating to him upon the still air, had made him temporarily regret war. (9)

Here, Crane wryly bullies his characters. Notice how he narrates at once from inside and outside his hero's sensibility. Henry might well see the rebel pickets as "sun-tanned," of course, and also as "philosophical" in the colloquial sense of "mature" and "steady of nerve." But Henry would not think of their pot-shots as "reflective"—an adjective motivated by the term "philosophy," but ironically so, in that the idle shooting is almost certainly thoughtless and cruel.[6] To say that the offending pickets are "reproached" by their targets is to speak as if their musketry is essentially a show of bad form—"barbarously abrupt," as the difficult breakers are said to be in "The Open Boat" (277). It might be regarded as such either by (let us say) a cavalier Virginia officer or by the grunts in his command, though the two parties would resent the sniping for different reasons: the first as a sin against honorable combat, the second as a sin against the fellowship that ought to bind together, in solidarity against the conceit of the officer corps, the poor grunts on both sides of the skirmish—a solidarity which is, in fact, a theme in this passage.

But what is Crane's investment in the affair? It is the amused "investment" of an onlooker who sees little sense in the whole display—whether on the grunts' part or the officers'. In any case, to speak of "reproaches" and the "expression of sorrow" is ironically to pretend that the business is more dignified and politic than it really is. But that is precisely what the soldiers themselves sometimes do. The youth, for example, appears to believe that his rebel picket possesses an admirable assurance; that is the pretense. But in fact, his "great fund" of assurance is said to be "bland and infantile"—two terms that Henry would neither contemplate nor apply in this situation, their complexity of implication (and their ironic affect) clearly being beyond him. W. M. Frohock has noticed this technique of Crane's: Crane will often lay into the "free indirect discourse" associated with Fleming—that is, into language originating in, and loosely inhabiting, Fleming's mind—words and phrases that Fleming himself would neither use nor entirely understand (144–46). A typical example occurs in this passage: "He had no rifle; he could not fight with his hands, said he resentfully to his plan. Well, rifles could be had for the picking. They were extraordinarily profuse. Also, he continued, it would be a miracle if he found his regiment" (62). The phrasing of the second sentence ("Well, rifles could be had for the picking") is conditioned by Henry's mind, while that of the third, which merely restates the idea in whimsically high diction ("They were extraordinarily profuse"), is conditioned by Crane's. The phrases "said he" and "he continued" disingenuously specify the "habitat" (so to speak) of all these reflections as interior to Henry. But in fact, there is, in this passage, a seamless blending of two trains of thought—the character's and the narrator's—just as when the adjectives "bland and infantile," which reflect the view Crane takes, are dropped in to qualify and vitiate the impressive "assurance" Henry credits the Confederate soldier with. The effect is to make us always feel that Crane exercises a kind of leverage against his yokel hero—that he has mirthfully colonized his mind and built a playground in it. In any event, we understand, in the longer passage quoted above, the impression the rebel picket makes on Henry, and are also given to understand that he is a little foolish to be so impressed: "'Yank,' the other had informed him, 'yer a right dum good feller.' This sentiment, floating to him upon the still air, had made him temporarily regret war." Crane, too, may "regret" war, but not because it has no respect for the dignity of encounters like this one. Crane himself allows for no dignity in it.[7] Henry is a fool for "regretting" war and a fool (a moment before) for not "regretting" it. Crane simply will not let him alone.

Notice that the vernacular is here employed not for the neutral purpose of verisimilitude but for the tendentious purpose of comical stereotype. Crane's humor is that of a city slick, or of a literary naturalist who, like Mencken after him, merrily exposes what Marx and Engels called (in the *Communist Manifesto*) "the idiocy of rural life" (208). It is certainly true that Crane never allows his more bumpkinish characters to speak as well as he does himself. The language they speak is tightly circumscribed by his, and as far as may be from the nuanced vernacular of (say) a book like Frost's *North of Boston* (1914). Circumscription of this kind is, in fact, something of a naturalist technique: the naturalist sets bounds to men—*diminishes* men. Crane deploys his vernacular to stereotype his characters, a point made perfectly clear if we compare his handling of dialect to, say, Twain's handling of it in *Huckleberry Finn*. In the latter book (white) vernacular voices are given a subtlety of implication, and a real purchase on experience, that we simply do not hear in Crane. In fact, Twain wrote his first-person narrative partly for the purpose of emancipating the vernacular—poor, rural white vernacular—from "yokeldom."

A fair example of what Crane does with dialect is to be found late in *Red Badge*, in a passage that has, for all the world, a *Hee Haw* corniness:

> "O Flem, yeh jest oughta heard!" cried one, eagerly.
> "Heard what?" said the youth.
> "Yeh jest oughta heard!" repeated the other, and he arranged himself to tell his tidings. The others made an excited circle. "Well, sir, th' colonel met your lieutenant right by us—it was damnedest thing I ever heard—an' he ses: 'Ahem! ahem!' he ses. 'Mr. Hasbrouck!' he ses, 'by th' way, who was that lad what carried th' flag?' he ses. There, Flemin', what d' yeh think 'a that? 'Who was th' lad what carried th' flag?' he ses, an' th' lieutenant, he speaks up right away: 'That's Flemin', an' he's a jimhickey,' he ses, right away. What? I say he did. 'A jimhickey,' he ses—those 'r his words. He did, too. I say he did. If you kin tell this story better than I kin, go ahead an' tell it. Well, then, keep yer mouth shet. Th' lieutenant, he ses: 'He's

a jimhickey,' and th' colonel, he ses: 'Ahem! ahem! he is, indeed, a very good man t' have, ahem! He kep' th' flag 'way t' th' front. I saw 'im. He's a good un,' ses th' colonel. 'You bet,' ses th' lieutenant, 'he an' a feller named Wilson was at th' head 'a th' charge, an' howlin' like Indians all th' time,' he ses. 'Head 'a th' charge all th' time,' he ses. 'A feller named Wilson,' he ses. There, Wilson, m'boy, put that in a letter an' send it hum t' yer mother, hay? 'A feller named Wilson,' he ses. An' th' colonel, he ses: 'Were they, indeed? Ahem! ahem! My sakes!' he ses. 'At th' head 'a th' reg'ment?' he ses. 'They were,' ses th' lieutenant. 'My sakes!' ses th' colonel. He ses: 'Well, well, well,' he ses. 'They deserve t' be major-generals.'" (112)

The vernacular, here, doesn't "characterize" the soldier celebrating Henry Fleming; it caricatures him in a cracker-barrel way. For such reasons, Crane's characters lack real "interiority"—and this notwithstanding that Henry Fleming's every thought is made available to us. Any revelation we have of what might be called Henry's "inner life" somehow makes him seem the more superficial—especially given that Crane so often laces Henry's thoughts, as rendered in a free indirect discourse, with phrases that puncture their dignity (as we have already seen). Henry, with all the other soldiers, is manifestly a "type." That type, of course, is the "rustic," as W. H. Frohock and others have pointed out (the "ignorant and stupid country lads" General McClurg speaks of). And more than simply "rustics"—who might claim an agrarian sort of dignity, especially at a time of populist agitation, with all its rhetoric about the essential decency and nobility of "the man with the hoe"—Crane's men are "yokels."

Here is a description of poor Jim Conklin ("the tall one") making a meal of hardtack and salt pork as his regiment marches toward the conflagration in which he will horribly die: "The tall one, red-faced, swallowed another sandwich as if taking poison in despair. But gradually, as he chewed, his face became again quiet and contented. He could not rage in fierce argument in the presence of such sandwiches. During his meals he always wore an air of blissful contemplation of the food he had swallowed" (26). The yokel, here, lapses into a kind of stupor when he *feeds* (we don't feel quite licensed to say that he "eats"). And then there is the point at which Crane himself first deploys the diminishing epithet "yokel." It comes in a passage one might have expected would be allowed to work itself out without a punch line. Henry has fallen in with a group of wounded and dying men:

> The youth joined this crowd and marched along with it. The torn bodies expressed the awful machinery in which the men had been entangled.

> Orderlies and couriers occasionally broke through the throng in the roadway, scattering wounded men right and left, galloping on followed by howls. The melancholy march was continually disturbed by the messengers, and sometimes by bustling batteries that came swinging and thumping down upon them, the officers shouting orders to clear the way.
>
> There was a tattered man, fouled with dust, blood and powder stain from hair to shoes, who trudged quietly at the youth's side. He was listening with eagerness and much humility to the lurid descriptions of a bearded sergeant. His lean features wore an expression of awe and admiration. He was like a listener in a country store to wondrous tales told among the sugar barrels. He eyed the story-teller with unspeakable wonder. His mouth was agape in yokel fashion. (49–50)

This is meant to be funny, as is also the gratuitous observation, during the charge in which Henry ultimately "distinguishes" himself, that the enlisted men "stare" up at their commanding lieutenant with "blank and yokel-like eyes" (100). "Yokel" isn't a descriptive epithet; it is the kind of epithet that relieves one of the obligation to describe. And this sort of comedy is, I would wager, quite specific to the 1890s, or to the post-Reconstruction period. Owing to the new mobility, the cosmopolitan "center" was ever more often venturing, both "for real" and merely "imaginatively," out into the provinces. The Long Depression of the 1890s had done nothing to make the rural districts, and the provinces, appear any less backward or any more sophisticated to East Coast urbanites like Crane. Of course, the political interests (and cultural affiliations) of the provinces were increasingly at odds with those of the more cosmopolitan East Coast centers. There was real antagonism, which, on the one hand, could take the form of suspicion and hatred (of the provinces toward the center), or, on the other hand, of contempt and condescension (from the center toward the provinces). I am reminded of our current Red State / Blue State divide. As Richard Hofstadter has pointed out, farmers were themselves well attuned to the sort of condescension I have in mind. He quotes a writer who anticipated the problem already in 1835 (it was a long time coming): "A certain class of individuals [has] grown up in our land who treat the cultivators of the soil as an inferior caste . . . whose utmost abilities are confined to the merit of being able to discuss a boiled potato and a rasher of bacon" (34). As Crane sees him—and no matter what our readerly sympathies may be—Jim Conklin, in the presence of Army-issue salt-pork, is just such a character as that.

Crane's sense of humor consistently involves an awareness of rural America and its quaint inhabitants as backward and gauche. As Mencken would be after him, Crane is a dissenter from the American religion of the common man—of the religion that contemplates "plain" folks "down on the farm," and that subscribes wholeheartedly to what Hofstadter calls "the agrarian myth" (24). This myth, much drawn upon in populist oratory of the 1890s, celebrated "the special virtues of the farmer and the special values of rural life," and held that the yeoman farmer was "the incarnation of the simple, honest, independent, healthy, happy human being." And "because he lived in close communion with beneficent nature," the farmer's life "was believed to have a wholesomeness and integrity impossible for the depraved populations of cities. His well-being was not merely physical, it was moral" (24). The "agrarian myth" is what gives comic point to a November 1896 letter Crane wrote to Catherine Harris. Harris had queried him (by mail) about *Maggie: A Girl of the Streets*. In his reply, Crane says this of the miserable denizens of the Bowery: "In a story of mine called 'An Experiment in Misery' I tried to make plain that the root of Bowery life is a sort of cowardice. Perhaps I mean a lack of ambition or to willingly be knocked flat and accept the licking. The missions for children are another thing and if you will have Mr. Rockefeller give me a hundred street cars and some money I will load all the babes off to some pink world where cows can lick their noses and they will never see their families any more" (*Letters* 133). Crane is making fun partly of philanthropic schemes, partly of slum-reformers, and partly of the rural prophet who, on behalf of the "pink world where cows" might lick the poor kids' noses, rails against the sins of the Big City. He likely also refers sarcastically to programs, common at the time, whereby children were separated from their parents in poorhouses and shipped off to the countryside to do agricultural labor at cut rates (or for no pay at all).[8] In any case, Crane's "pink world," with its nose-licking cows, is, of course, the American "heartland." Crane's vaguely flippant invocation of it suggests a mind as little vulnerable to Nebraska-born populist William Jennings Bryan as it is to the labor organizer Samuel Gompers. And of course, we are still in the grip of the agrarian myth: all our campaigns start in Iowa—whose caucus, were he to rise from the dead and run for president, Crane would surely skip.

But I want to return now to the passage in which Henry and the Confederate picket have their moment of tenderness in the still night air. Immediately following that passage occurs the best part of this, the first chapter of the novel.

> Various veterans had told him tales. Some talked of gray, bewhiskered hordes, who were advancing with relentless curses and chewing tobacco

> with unspeakable valor; tremendous bodies of fierce soldiery who were sweeping along like the Huns. Others spoke of tattered and eternally hungry men who fired despondent powders. "They'll charge through hell's fire an' brimstone t' git a holt on a haversack, an' sech stomachs ain't a' lastin' long," he was told. From the stories, the youth imagined the red, live bones sticking out through slits in the faded uniforms. (9)

The insertion of the phrase "chewing tobacco" does the deflationary trick. The irony, of course, depends on the way the "advance" of the fierce soldiery and the "chewing" they do somehow seem alike to share in this "unspeakable valor." The parallelism is comically false. And it is as if Crane chose precisely the wrong adjective to modify "valor": "inexpressible valor" appears to be the phrase around which Crane allusively orbits, here. But of course, "unspeakable," his arch substitution, means something more like "reprehensible"—a nuance motivated by the sense of affronted outrage the green Yankee soldiers feel. As they experience them, the Confederate attacks are a capital rudeness, a breach of good decorum, as much deserving a "reproach" as a counterattack. Crane's diction slyly evokes, in a parodying way, the gentlemanly cult of good breeding that some still liked to believe, especially in the post-Reconstruction era of the Lost Cause, had governed the combat at least of the "Cavalier" rebels. And Red Badge is nothing if not a satire of chivalry. As for choosing precisely the "wrong" word, another example is "bewhiskered" in the phrase "gray, bewhiskered hordes." The adjective might more commonly be applied to a face one finds attractive in a quaint sort of way. "Grizzled" is what one expects to find in the martial context before us here. The "bewhiskered" alternative sets a slight ironic distance between the narrator and the men he describes. In characterizing their views of the situation confronting them he never quite adopts their language. Or say: the language Crane uses swings unsteadily between their discourse and his own. Finally, there is the transference of the mood of the soldiers to the "powders" they fire: "despondent." Throughout, Crane plays with adjectives in ways to which General McClurg objected in his review. "Notice the violent straining after effect in the mere unusual association of words," he complained, "in the forced and distorted use of adjectives" (54).

But let's attend still more closely to Crane's manner, which, as I see it, persistently suggests that he regards himself as existing above, and outside of, the situations with which he has to do. And this is precisely why readers have never comfortably been able to assimilate *The Red Badge of Courage* to conventionally "heroic" modes. It explains also why readers whose cultural/political orientation sets them apart from Crane's cocky mode of urbanity find his writing unsettling and vaguely offensive, as did McClurg for one reason, and as did the members of the Port Jervis, New York, V.F.W. for another. In 1983 they demanded that "Stephen Crane Memorial Park" be renamed "Veterans Memorial Park at Orange Square." Why? They regarded *Red Badge* as a standing insult to our men and women in uniform.[9]

The tonal complexity of passages like the ones we've just examined can at once explain and settle the most important and long-standing controversy surrounding the novel: Is Henry Fleming a "hero"? Does he, or does he not, "mature" as the novel progresses? Does the conclusion of the novel mark a turn, an upward development, in his character? Or is he, all the way through to the bitter end, regarded with ironic condescension by the narrator (and by Crane)? Related to this is another important controversy. Do we encounter in Crane the acid irony, the inexhaustible impiety, of a writer like H. L. Mencken? (Alfred Kazin offers the best account of him in these terms in *An American Procession* and elsewhere.) Or instead of a cynical ironist do we encounter in Crane a writer genuinely in search of the providential sense of national and individual purpose that we Americans lost in the Gilded Age? The best reading of Crane along these lines is Andrew Delbanco's in "The American Stephen Crane." In this debate, I favor Kazin, who seems more in harmony with Crane's sense of style—with the work Crane really did do *as a writer*.

To be sure, the novel does, as Delbanco suggests elsewhere, lend itself inevitably to readings of it as a bildungsroman: "It has long been an English teacher's favorite, because it has a conveniently interrogatory form: What, it obliges us to ask, does Henry Fleming learn?" (*Required Reading* 104). This question has been variously answered by critics. Henry learns (we are sometimes told) to accept mortality. Or he learns to become a soldier—to subordinate his private interests to the imperatives of the larger social body to which he belongs, the army. Or Henry learns how to be a man: he faces his fears, disciplines and manages them, and in the end recognizes that honor (for example) is a higher principle than survival. Arguing along these lines, R. W. Stallman contends that "Henry progresses upward toward manhood and moral triumph."[10] I find none of these answers compelling, chiefly because I think the question "What does Henry learn?" is itself impertinent. Henry, in fact, learns nothing.

To an extent, the controversies to which I refer here are explained by a simple historical fact: the text of *The Red Badge of Courage* has been difficult to establish. The first text to appear was a severely truncated version that ran in several newspapers late in 1894. The second was a much longer text published in book form in 1895 by D. Appleton and Company of New York. For decades readers assumed that this latter text was the most authoritative available, and it was upon the basis of it that the debate as to Henry Fleming's "heroism" arose. But beginning in the 1950s more documentary evidence came to light, and, as the textual scholar Hershel Parker demonstrated in a masterful 1986 essay, the Appleton text is not, in fact, reliable—or even coherent. Crane's editor at Appleton, Ripley Hitchcock, caused Crane, however indirectly, to cancel a number of passages from the novel, and an entire chapter (this would have been chapter twelve in the original, swelling the total to twenty-five chapters). The effect of the excisions—which total several thousand words—is to mute the severity of Crane's ironic treatment of Henry, with the result that it becomes possible to see, in the broad outline of the plot (and if you squint), a story of his redemption. The *reductio ad absurdum* to which this reading of the novel may be taken is best illustrated by Stallman's interpretation of it as a *Christian* allegory of redemption: "The theme is that man's salvation lies in change, in spiritual growth. . . . Henry Fleming recognizes the necessity for change and development but wars against it. But man must lose his soul in order to save it. The youth develops into a veteran: 'So it came to pass . . . his soul changed.' Significantly enough," suggests Stallman, "in stating what the book is about Crane intones Biblical phrasing" (*Omnibus* 193). In due course Stallman concludes that, as he witnesses Jim Conklin's death, Henry figuratively "partakes of the sacramental blood and body of Christ [Stallman makes much of the dead soldier's initials, J. C.], and the process of his spiritual rebirth begins at the moment when the wafer-like sun appears in the sky. It is a symbol of salvation through death" (200). This is a far cry from the usual reading of Crane as an insouciant rebel against his parents' strict Methodism. It is a reading that finds the father and the mother in the son, and, withal, the Son of the Father Himself in that most famous "sun" in late nineteenth-century American literature, the one Crane "pastes" in the sky "like a wafer"—a communion wafer, if Stallman is to be believed (200).

I suppose there is a sense in which this reading has its integrity. And it has been an influential reading owing to the fact that Stallman's richly detailed biography of Crane, which recapitulates it, remains *something* of a standard.[11] But this "redemptive" reading ought to make any reader wary, if only because its solemnity, its gravity, sorts so uncomfortably with Crane's playfully sardonic prose (and then there are always the textual problems any Christian/Redemptive reading of the novel must overcome, as Hershel Parker makes clear). My suspicion is that the network of "ecclesiastical" metaphors with which Stallman is concerned—and they are there to be dealt with—is motivated less by any aspiration of Crane's to probe matters eschatological than by a more or less opportunistic tendency on his part to follow out, dutifully, the implications of the figurative language available to him. So, when, early on in *Red Badge*, we find a reference to the "cathedral light of the forest," we ought not think of it as anything other than an extension of what is, after all, a commonplace and centuries-old figure (i.e., the forest as "cathedral," whether with "bare ruined choirs where late the sweet birds sang" or not). Nor should we be either surprised or put on our guard for Deep Meaning when the youth stumbles into a grove "where the high, arching boughs made a chapel," which, as chapels tend to do, also has "portals" and "doors" (in this case, green), and a "carpet" (in this case, of pine needles). What else would one expect to find in the "chapel" of a forest "cathedral" than "religious half light"? Why would not the wind-swayed trees be said, there, to "sing a hymn of twilight" in "chorus," and the "insects," their own song abating, be said to "bow their beaks" and make a "devotional pause" (45–46)? Crane's habit—call it his hobby, his avocation—is to follow out even the most commonplace of metaphors in careful, at times ludicrous, detail. His real interest is precisely in what critics used to call the "vehicles" of his metaphors, more than in their "tenor," or cargo, which explains the characteristic fastidiousness with which he so often develops them, though they are certainly not without their odd, even careless, flourishes. Can insects, for example, be said to have "beaks"? It is as if the metaphor whimsically confuses birds and insects. Crane's prose everywhere has the effect of arresting our movement from "vehicle" to "tenor": the "vehicles" are, for Crane, simply too much fun to toy with; they satisfy the head's play instincts too well. In the passage before us here, for example, Crane's mind is chiefly on the fact that "cathedrals" imply "chapels," and that "chapels" imply "portals" and "carpets"; and on the fact that all of these things imply "hymns," "bowing," and "devotion." Nothing in a religious allegory, if that is what we had here, would require him to lay it on so thick. All of which is merely to say: Stephen Crane is not the later T. S. Eliot, no matter how much the New Criticism—and, here, R. W. Stallman is representative of the school—may have needed him to be. Stallman so needs to find in Crane the model of a "serious" artist that at one point he writes: "[Crane] brooded over his germinal ideas the same as Brahms and Yeats and Conrad" (*Omnibus* 211). Whatever else he may have been, Crane was not, as we experience him on the page, a "brooder" or a Brahms. I find in the famous "chapel" scene in chapter 7 of the novel, whose verbal details I have been considering, neither a particularly *Christian* inquiry into the fact of mortality—notwithstanding that a corpse is among the furnishings of this "chapel"—nor a seriously Christian crisis in the "spiritual growth" of Henry Fleming. The corpse in the copse may be a *memento mori*. But nothing about this scene really inspires us gravely to say, as with George Herbert in "Church Monuments": "how tame these ashes are, how free from lust."

And as for this question of growth and development, consider in some detail the famous conclusion to the novel:

> So it came to pass that as he trudged from the place of blood and wrath his soul changed. He came from hot plowshares to prospects of clover tranquility, and it was as if hot plowshares were not. Scars faded as flowers.
>
> It rained. The procession of weary soldiers became a bedraggled train, despondent and muttering, marching with churning effort in a trough of liquid brown mud under a low, wretched sky. Yet the youth smiled, for he saw that the world was a world for him, though many discovered it to be made of oaths and walking sticks. He had rid himself of the red sickness of battle. The sultry nightmare was in the past. He had been an animal blistered and sweating in the heat and pain of war. He turned now with a lover's thirst to images of tranquil skies, fresh meadows, cool brooks—an existence of soft and eternal peace.
>
> Over the river a golden ray of sun came through the hosts of leaden rain clouds. (125–26)

We are told, here, that the world is now a world "for" Henry Fleming, "though many discovered it to be made of oaths and walking sticks." What degree of vanity should inspire in him so proprietary a sentiment? In the first place, the world can be "for" Henry Fleming only in the absurd sense in which, say, the Pullman Palace Car is "for" Sheriff Potter and his new wife in Crane's "The Bride Comes to Yellow Sky" (as we shall soon see). The Pullman car is, Crane tells us, "the environment of their new estate," and Potter gazes upon it with "the pride of an owner" (314). In the same way, Henry Fleming looks on his new estate of manhood with proprietary satisfaction, as a thing achieved. But we know, and are never allowed to forget, that his lush Gilded Age "environment" rather owns the yokelish Sheriff Potter: it foreshortens him; it makes him and his dish-washing bride appear ridiculous to the upper-crust passengers bound for southern California—passengers for whom, after all, Texas is but a tedious obstacle to be endured. As the Populist "Omaha Platform" of 1892 puts it: "The time has come when the railroad corporations will either own the people or the people must own the railroads" (Pollack 63). And plainly, Sheriff Potter and his bride are now owned.

As for the "oaths and walking sticks" of which too many discover, it seems, the world to be "made": what can be the meaning of *these*? We are invited, it appears, to suppose that Henry is no longer "hobbled" by the world—that on the serene plateau to which he thinks he has ascended no more vexations will elicit from him "oaths," nor any constitutional weakness send him reaching for his "walking stick." But the reader simply must conclude—Crane's arch tone leaves him little choice—that for Henry the world will always be, as it is for every other character in Crane, made *precisely* of oaths and walking sticks; and that he is "a coxcomb not to die in it" (to borrow a phrase from an oft-quoted passage in Crane's "The Blue Hotel" [348]). The mastery, the sheer *fluency*, that Henry here supposes himself to have achieved—the thought of it is introduced, I take it, in free indirect discourse—is an illusion. Again: "So it came to pass," we are told, "that as he trudged from the place of blood and wrath his soul changed. He came from hot plowshares to prospects of clover tranquility, and it was as if hot plowshares were not. Scars faded as flowers" (125). The "place of blood and wrath," "hot plowshares" (as opposed to "cool swords"?), and "clover tranquility": the phrases are either a bit too stereotypical or a bit too odd to be taken seriously. Anyway, the postcard pastoral of the scene here evoked, with its tranquil skies and fresh meadows, is but the emanation of Henry's still naively "youthful" state of mind. He has recovered what Crane earlier calls (archly) an ability "to see himself in a heroic light" (62). He has acquired adequate breathing space, as Crane says after the first of the two climactic charges is done, "in which to appreciate himself"; and he does just that—with "much satisfaction" (109). The successful charge against the enemy color guard only leaves him "preparing to resent some new monstrosity in the way of dins and smashes" (122).

It would be hard to demonstrate that the following late passage is any less ironic in tone than those toward the beginning of the book, where, clearly, we are to regard Henry's self-knowledge as faulty in the extreme: "He found that he could look back upon the brass and bombast of his earlier gospels and see them truly. He was gleeful when he discovered that he now despised them. With this conviction came a store of assurance. He felt a quiet manhood, non-assertive but of sturdy and strong blood. He knew that he would no more quail before his guides wherever they should point. He had been to touch the great death, and found that, after all, it was but the great death. He was a man" (125). For my part, I feel invited here to suppose that Henry's "store of assurance" is like that of our old friend the Confederate picket: "bland and infantile." And what of the last sentence in the novel, the one so often quoted? "Over the river a golden ray of sun came through the hosts of leaden rain clouds." Readers who find in *Red Badge* an intricate pattern of contrasts—for example, light/dark, haze/translucence, confusion/insight—regard this conclusion as the capstone to the whole symbolic edifice of the novel: Henry has at last emerged from the tempest of his youthful ordeal into something like a harbor. It is as if the weather of the novel exteriorizes Henry's state of mind. "That Crane plotted the entire novel by images and situations evoking contradictory moods of despair and hope is evidenced not only in this terminal image of the book," writes R. W. Stallman, "but in the opening image of chapter one" (*Omnibus* 370n3), in which the fog clears from the land. Yet this terminal image, so integral to the pattern of the book as Stallman understands it, is not present in the surviving manuscript of *Red Badge*, and there is some controversy as to whether it "belongs" in the book at all. As Hershel Parker sees it—and the evidence is strong—Crane's editor Ripley Hitchcock

> prevailed upon [him] to compose a new and upbeat final paragraph: "Over the river a golden ray of sun came through the hosts of leaden rain clouds." As John T. Winterich said in 1951, this sentence "bears the unmistakable spoor of the editor" and "sounds like a concession to the send-the-audience-home-feeling-good school." With these last changes—maybe the little decisively placed addition was the last of all—Hitchcock had engineered disproportionately great changes in the apparent meaning of crucial passages. In the first stage of expurgation, he had purged the book of passages likely to prove most objectionable, those where Henry Fleming indulged in vaingloriously adolescent ontological heroics; in the second, the mopping up stage, he had purged it of those where Fleming displayed a heartlessly triumphant egotism. (40–41)

In short, the passages missing from the published text and present in the manuscripts, or else present in the published text and missing from the manuscripts, strongly suggest, when taken all together, that the novel, as Crane "really" wrote it, is unremitting in its irony: Fleming is a youth who never comes into his majority. He remains perpetually a minor, in what Crane at one point calls "an ecstasy of self-satisfaction" (37). Never does he attain what Stallman calls his "own bright serenity, his own tranquility of mind"; never is his "conscience reborn and purified" (*Omnibus* 195–97).

I see no "education" worthy of the name as having taken place, nor any profound "development" in Henry's character. The elements of the bildungsroman are certainly there, but so are the elements of a Wild-West tale "there" in "The Bride Comes to Yellow Sky": in both cases—and the point is hardly a new one, with respect to the latter story—the effect is parody. I am suggesting, then, that the "coming-of-age tale" is at work only *stereotypically* in *Red Badge*. It is present in such a way as to stimulate in a certain sort of reader the impression that he has in fact read a "coming-of-age story." But this is an illusion—an illusion of the sort Crane was particularly good at exploiting. *The Monster*, we might say, exploits late-nineteenth-century social protest writing in similar ways, just as *Maggie* exploits the muckraking literature of the slum for its chiefly comic effects (more furniture is destroyed in that short book than would fill an IKEA). In all of these cases, Crane's relation to genre is parasitic. His books feed off of genres—in the case of *Red Badge*, the battle-scarred bildungsroman—to which we can never precisely assimilate them. And they are filled with matter of the most "conventional" sort, from Irish apes, to country bumpkins, to minstrel show dudes, to small-town philistines. Sometimes the conventions are allowed to exist unmolested, as it were. But as often as not they are there to make us feel them as "conventional," in the way of parody generally.

For example, at one point in *Red Badge* Henry resolves to lose himself in death: "He had concluded that it would be better to get killed directly and end his troubles. Regarding death thus out of the corner of his eye, he conceived it to be nothing but rest, and he was filled with a momentary astonishment that he should have made an extraordinary commotion over the mere matter of getting killed. He would die; he would go to some place where he would be understood. It was useless to expect appreciation of his profound and fine sense from such men as the lieutenant. He must look to the grave for comprehension" (27). What could be more childish in its "you'll-miss-me-when-I'm-gone" posturing? But the oncoming racket of the battle turns him about, whereupon we are treated to another "tender" scene, in which this time Henry's mouth is the one yokelishly agape (mouth-breather that he apparently is):

> The youth, forgetting his neat plan of getting killed, gazed spell bound. His eyes grew wide and busy with the action of the scene. His mouth was a little ways open.
> Of a sudden he felt a heavy and sad hand laid upon his shoulder. Awakening from his trance of observation he turned and beheld the loud soldier.
> "It's my first and last battle, old boy," said the latter, with intense gloom. He was quite pale and his girlish lip was trembling.
> "Eh?" murmured the youth in great astonishment.
> "It's my first and last battle, old boy," continued the loud soldier. "Something tells me"—
> "What?"

> "I'm a gone coon this first time and—and I w-want you to take these here things—to—to—my—folks." He ended in a quavering sob of pity for himself. He handed the youth a little packet done up in a yellow envelope.
> "Why, what the devil"—began the youth again.
> But the other gave him a glance as from the depths of a tomb, and raised his limp hand in a prophetic manner and turned away. (28)

What reader—and, now, what movie-goer—has not witnessed a score of such scenes? By all appearances the "loud soldier" had himself witnessed a few too many, and so acted the "Greeklike" part—complete with the melodramatic touch of a limp hand raised in prophecy—so that all might be fulfilled: nothing is missing from this soldier's story. Crane's wry relationship to stock scenes like this one resembles his relation to the coming-of-age tale as a whole.

But if Crane is not *really* writing about the progress of a boy into manhood, or about the redemption of a boy from fear, or about "spiritual" growth, or about the sacramental blood of Christ, or even about the making of a veteran soldier, what is the "subject" of the novel, the "theme"? We can best answer the question by attending, again, to the prose. Crane's fiction is forever chiefly concerned with, or chiefly captivated by, *writing*. Most remarkable about Crane's style is the character and integrity of his metaphors, which are, at times, extended over a great many pages. As Frederick Crews has noted: "In pursuing his elegant and sometimes strained metaphors, Crane verges on self-conscious dandyism—another trait common to many writers of the nineties."[12] No doubt Crane was a fine craftsman, and a genius of sorts. But he is not as much concerned with "design," in (say) Stallman's pompously august sense, as he is with "style" more generally—with style as a way of cutting a figure in the world; with style as charisma; with style as a mode of address; with style as a thing cultivated not for the purpose of realizing any *particular* work of art, but for the purpose of creating, of making vividly real, a "literary" and "cool" personality. So, by all means attend to what Stallman calls the "surface" of Crane's prose. But do so with the idea that the surface is all there really needs to be. I'm not concerned with the patterns of darkness or smoke, and light or sunshine, that respectively (and implausibly) "symbolize," for Stallman, "concealment and deception" on the one hand, and "spiritual insight and rebirth" on the other (*Omnibus* 187). Nor do I suppose that the "retiring fogs" in the opening phrases of the novel really anticipate, and symbolize, the "mental awakening" Henry is said by some to achieve at the novel's end (*Omnibus* 193). I am instead concerned with Crane's words as very concrete things-in-themselves, as "vehicles" without much heavy cargo, since that is the way—or so the writing suggests—Crane himself experienced them. R. G. Vosburgh, with whom Crane shared a room in 1893–94, published a brief memoir of Crane in 1901. "In revising his work," Vosburgh recalls, Crane "would rewrite a whole sheet when a correction was necessary rather than make an erasure, if only to change one word." So captivated was he by his own turns of phrase, and by his metaphors, that he "studied them out with much care, and after they had been trimmed and turned to final form he would repeat them aloud and dwell on them lovingly" (338–39). That strikes me as about right.

A good place to extend our inquiry along these lines is chapter 1, which opens as follows:

> The cold passed reluctantly from the earth, and the retiring fogs revealed an army stretched out on the hills, resting. As the landscape changed from brown to green, the army awakened, and began to tremble with eagerness at the noise of rumors. It cast its eyes upon the roads, which were growing from long troughs of liquid mud to proper thoroughfares. A river, amber-tinted in the shadow of its banks, purled at the army's feet; and at night, when the stream had become of a sorrowful blackness, one could see across it the red, eyelike gleam of hostile camp-fires set in the low brows of distant hills. (3)

Informing these sentences is a simple equation: the army is like a single man; the army is in fact a man, which might, as men do, "stretch out on the hills, resting," and which might "awaken," and "cast its eyes upon the roads." Nothing seems out of the ordinary here, and the personification is, in certain respects, conventional—so conventional as not to be strongly felt "as a metaphor." But Crane, I believe, is doing something new with this familiar metaphor, which, as he reminds us, is always implicit in military terminology: an army is a "corps," a body. This is confused when the "distant hills" are said to have "brows" with campfires for eyes: that makes it seem like the land, and not the "corps" of men upon it, is the "body" with which we have to do, or perhaps that one "body" is laid upon another. But that confusion is no matter. What does matter here is the idea that two "corps," two bodies, are facing one another across a river. And as the novel unfolds we see just how "literal" Crane takes this metaphor to be. If the army is a "body," a "corps," then the individual soldiers themselves must be its "cells" or "corpuscles." And, lo, later we find Crane developing precisely this idea: "A small procession of wounded men were going drearily toward the rear. It was a flow of blood from the torn body of the brigade" (36). The "corps" is here in danger of becoming a "corpse"; and, to be sure, at one point on its march the great body divides to clear the way for exactly that, a "corpse," in which it no doubt sees itself mirrored (36). The metaphor latent in phrases like "a great body of troops" has been worn away through their sheer familiarity. Crane's achievement is to make old metaphors feel like metaphors again, as he does with another phrase in the following sentence: "At nightfall the column broke into regimental pieces, and the fragments went into the fields to camp" (17). Crane takes what is usually not felt as a metaphor—the column "broke"—and follows it out scrupulously as if it were one; he makes the metaphor live again. There is something in him of the mischievous pedant who forever points out, with delight, the strangeness of ordinary speech (as when we say the sun "rises"). Though no one instance of this mischief much matters, there is, to be sure, a cumulative effect as the play recurs page after page. Even the most unadorned English—for Crane's prose is hardly purple—comes to seem peculiar again, and fresh.

More complex is Crane's handling of a more or less conventional metaphor first introduced in chapter 18 of *The Red Badge of Courage*, in which Henry Fleming overhears two officers discussing tactics. This is the passage in which the officers dismissively call the infantrymen "mule drivers." It is a revelation to Henry: "New eyes were given to him. And the most startling thing was to learn suddenly that he was very insignificant. The officer spoke of the regiment as if he referred to a broom. Some part of the woods needed sweeping, perhaps, and he merely indicated a broom in a tone properly indifferent to its fate. It was war, no doubt, but it appeared strange" (96). What "startles" Henry is the idea, forced upon him many times during the course of the novel, that he is simply an instrument in "a vast blue demonstration"—that he is not a "real" agent at all. He is a broom, or, what is worse (and more accurate), a single straw in the homely regimental brush of a broom. The broom is first brought out of the closet by another soldier, and to another purpose, in a remark about the Confederate dead: "Lost a piler men, they did. If an' ol' woman swep' up the woods she'd git a dustpanful" (93). He imagines his and Henry's regiment wreaking havoc and an old woman cleaning up after them; it is a satisfying thought, and "sweeping" or "mopping up" is commonplace military slang. But on hearing the officers confer, Henry reworks the regiment's relation to the "broom" along humiliating lines. In any case, he now feels that a broom is no implement to carry into battle, let alone to *be* in battle; brooms are for women's work and dustpans. It is a double indignity (Henry feels) for a soldier to think of himself as one; it unmans him. And soon after, a grunt along the line prophesies to Henry, as they contemplate the opposing Confederates: "We'll git swallowed" (97).

The ideas of the broom and of the swallowing coalesce to absurd effect some ten pages later, in chapter 20: "As [Henry] noted the vicious, wolf-like temper of his comrades he had a sweet thought that if the enemy was about to swallow the regimental broom as a large prisoner, it could at least have the consolation of going down with bristles forward" (107). The thought is "sweet" not least because it redeems the figure of the regimental broom, here oddly imagined as a "large prisoner" of war. If the soldiers are but a broom, in the eyes of haughty commanders, they may as well fight dirty. So, the "bristling" gunfire mentioned by the narrator a handful of sentences back becomes the porcupine "bristles" of a "broom" reluctant to be "swallowed" by the enemy, as if in some terrible (and terribly undignified) kitchen brawl. It is not clear whether Henry himself appreciates the ludic quality of the metaphor as much, and in the same way, as does the narrator: defeating a hostile and tenacious regiment is like swallowing a broom, bristles forward. True, in what is for him an impressive show of intellection, Henry himself draws together the broom and the swallowing; we are given access to his thoughts, as so often, through the medium of free indirect discourse. But I doubt whether Crane ascribes to him the full ironic purchase on his commander's disdain that this "sweet," "bristling" thought would allow. In any case the figure of the "bristle" is used to different purpose by the narrator, who first employs it ("their curving front bristled with flashes"), than it is by Henry Fleming. Here is an odd example of the discourse of a character coalescing with that of his narrator, almost as if Fleming "overheard" his author and troped him (as one of the mowers in Andrew Marvell's "Upon Appleton House" overhears Marvell allegorizing about him in Biblical tones, and tropes *him*: "He called us Israelites!" the mower exclaims in astonishment, with reference to the speaker of the poem [88]). The transaction usually goes the other way, of course, with Crane troping the speech of his characters. But however that may be, the refreshing thing about the passage before us here is the way it recalls, and fuses, two distinct metaphors from two chapters back in the novel—the broom and the swallowing—and adds to them the lucky flourish of those equivocal "bristles." The facility with which Crane performs the maneuver argues a spirited but leisurely sort of play carried on superfluously above the narrative and hard to associate with the business of war, let alone with the *gravitas* of much popular discourse about the Grand Army of the Republic. And the effect is entirely characteristic of him.

Earlier in the novel, in chapter sixteen, Crane says in the midst of a passage describing the clamor of battle: "At last the guns stopped, and among the men in the rifle pits rumors again flew, like birds, but they were now for the most part black creatures who flapped their wings drearily near to the ground and refused to rise on any wings of hope" (85). Here Crane takes up a figure laid down first at the start of chapter 4: "[The soldiers] mouthed rumors that had flown like birds out of the unknown" (28). And in this second example, from chapter 16, the simile is developed with almost pedantic deliberation, as if Crane's interest, again, were more in the "vehicle" than in the "tenor" of the figure. Crane's technique, in passages like this, is to take more seriously than is usual the implications of commonplace figures of speech like "the rumors flew" or "the wings of hope."

And then there is the queer comedy of this passage: "Bullets began to whistle among the branches and nip at the trees. Twigs and leaves were sailing down. It was as if a thousand axes, wee and invisible, were being wielded" (29). Bullets as "wee axes"? The technique, here, involves a well-managed incongruity of adjective and noun: "wee" belongs to an effete, infantile—or perhaps just quaintly "Scotch-Irish" or "leprechaunish"—lexicon; its association with axes is a bit startling. We are asked to imagine, if only for an instant, a welter of tiny elves chipping away at the trees. To similar effect is this passage from the same page: "There was rustling and muttering among the men. They displayed a feverish desire to have every possible cartridge ready to their hands. The boxes were pulled around into various positions, and adjusted with great care. It was as if seven hundred new bonnets were being tried on" (31). Again, the joke involves an apt incongruity, which here brings together a stereotypically feminine preening (as with the bonnets), and the panic of men preparing to receive an enemy charge; what the two things apparently have in common is a striking fastidiousness. And what of the peculiar quality of phrases such as the following? "Strange gods were addressed in condemnation of the early hours necessary to correct war" (79), where the phrase "to correct" seems by turns to mean "to conduct war correctly," or to "put war aright," or "to admonish war," and yet can be reduced to none of these; its grammatical ambiguity, its suspension, is precise and perfect (the grammatical ambiguity has to do with whether or not "to correct" is an infinitive, or whether "correct" is an adjective modifying "war").

Next, consider this description of Henry, as he readies himself to panic: "His hands," we are told, "seemed large and awkward as if he was wearing invisible mittens. And there was a great uncertainty about his knee joints" (39). What is the difference between saying "as if he were wearing mittens" and saying "as if he were wearing *invisible* mittens"? The "as if" makes the "invisible" oddly redundant, at least for the purposes of the figure. A little strangely, we imagine Fleming not so much wearing *mittens* as wearing (indeed) *invisible* mittens. Better still is the preposition "about" in "there was a great uncertainty about his knee joints." Here, Crane neatly allows the secondary sense of "about" ("in the vicinity of") to infect the primary sense ("concerning"), quite as if the "great uncertainty" were something Henry might shoo away from his knee joints, as he would a fly. As a last example, consider what he does with the expression "stir the fire," in the chapter where the ignominiously wounded Henry—who gets his "red badge" of a wound when a fellow soldier pistol-whips him to make him shut his pie-hole—at last returns to his regiment. A kind soldier prepares to nurse him, and to that end gets the fire going: "He fussed around the fire and stirred the sticks to brilliant exertions" (75). "Exertions" brings out the figurative sense of "stir." The soldier is imagined to *inspire* the sticks, to *move* and *exhort* them, which is of course what "stirring" can mean, though we usually treat it, in this context, as a reference to physical movement.

In the aggregate, as they accumulate page after page—and one might cite many other instances—these tricks and devices dislodge us, a bit, from our customary habits of attention to words. That dislodging, I suspect, is what Crane's work is somehow always "about." He is much more interested in the texture of what he says than in the "weight" of it. His concern is levity, not gravity. I think this helps us understand why he should treat the Civil War as he does in *The Red Badge of Courage*—that is, with no sense at all of the ideological or political dimensions of the catastrophe. Crane isn't really writing *about* war, certainly not about the *American Civil War*; he is writing, and writing playfully, in the *vicinity* of "war." Crane simply cannot forget that he is *writing*, nor be persuaded that the writing isn't always the main thing. Crane's general preoccupation with style, as against polemics or politics or ideological crises, is what, in my view, makes untenable Andrew Delbanco's suggestion—and he is otherwise a fine reader of Crane—that "if the character and destiny of American nationhood eluded him as the issues at stake in the Civil War, then, in the end, he felt their absence not as a means to taunt naive believers, but as the loss of an immensely valuable act of mind" ("The American Stephen Crane" 57). In my view, Crane did not write *Red Badge* so much "out of and about a crisis of faith—both about God and about God's instrument, the American nation," as Delbanco goes on to say. He wrote it out of the complacent assumption that "faith," whether in God or in America as God's instrument, was the sort of thing about which only a certain sort of politician—Democrat *or* Republican: it would hardly matter in 1896—made "heartfelt" appeals to a certain sort of constituency (the constituency, in fact, that Mencken, a sympathetic reader of Crane if ever there was one, was later to denominate *boobus Americanus*).

"Dry up!"

To better understand Crane's treatment of the war, I turn now to Thomas Beer's *Stephen Crane* (published first in 1903). This was the first book-length study of Crane, and it is still among the most provocative responses to him, despite its many (likely mischievous) inaccuracies about the details of Crane's life, and despite the many embellishments that have led some to dismiss it as an interesting fabrication. "As heroic legend," Beer says, the history of the Civil War "has been curious and remains unwritten because of that spiritual censorship which strictly forbids the telling of truth about any American record until the material of such an essay is scattered and gone."

> How did the men who scorched their youth and scarred their bodies think of those four years, before the easy sentiment of senility clouded down? One knows that in 1868 General Custer's wife noted: "My husband's troopers seem to have absolutely no unkind feeling toward the Secessionists at all and they never talk about their triumphs and exploits. They are always teasing each other about how badly they fought and how many times they ran away. It is distressing to see and hear how little exalted their views are." And one knows that in 1869 at a banquet of the Grand Army a man lifted his glass and toasted: "Everyone that ran at Shiloh, like I did!"
>
> The distress of Mrs. Custer [supplies] a conjecture. . . . The common man's attitude toward the myth of a pure, courageous host bent on the Lord's work was truly shocking. The swift cynicism of the American which is the basis of our popular thought rounded promptly on romantic views of the Rebellion. Duval, the leading ballad singer of New York, was hissed from the stage in June of 1865 when he tried to please an audience speckled with soldiers by chanting: Home Have Come Our Boys in Blue. The gunbearing animals shouted: "Dry up!" and "Sing something funny!" . . . There were songs current attributing mistresses to the popular Northern generals, doubtless due to an adolescent habit of making heroes in all things strenuous, and a New York publisher found that John Esten Cooke's frankly Southern novels, *Surry of Eagle's Nest* and *Mahon* sold most readily in the North although Cooke had not one flattering word to say of the Union forces, and the Virginian himself wrote that "I am surprised by the number of handsome letters that come to hand from former soldiers of the enemy." (242–42)

The wonderful details of Beer's report may be partly invented. But there can be no doubt about the parable he deploys them in order to tell, which is both suggestive and acute. The popularity of the forthrightly "Southern" novels of J. E. Cooke is what literary historians have in mind when they speak of an epoch of reconciliation and romance—the vogue for sentimental fiction about the Antebellum South and the Lost Cause. And I am suggesting that we imagine *The Red Badge of Courage* as a toast proposed to the nation along precisely these lines: "Everyone that ran at Shiloh, like I did!" It is certainly a book to disconcert Rotarian pieties, as General McClurg's denunciation of it implies. That is satisfying, so far as it goes, in a Falstaffian sort of way, to correct the excesses of the Ancient Pistols among us (especially those who had, as many did have, political aspirations). In Crane's army there is always what he, at one point, calls "a singular absence of heroic poses"—a singular "neglect" of "picturesque attitudes" (34). And in that sense his novel is "anti-heroic," and satirical in its relation to the literature of war. Honor (it tells us) is a mere scutcheon.

But if we are to take Beer's hypothetical soldier's toast as "representative" in emphasis, as if the Grand Army itself were speaking; if we are to give way "cynically" to the trampling of "exalted" ideals, as Beer admirably does (he learned much from Crane); if we are altogether to explode the "myth" of the Lord's good work—well, that is perhaps another thing. I say this because it was necessary in the 1890s to repudiate "exalted" views of the Union Army and its political leadership if the Republican Party, and the capitalists it now represented, were to consummate their *rapprochement* with a New South ready to draw Northern investments into its cheap labor markets. It was ideologically necessary (so to speak) to deflate anyone breaking out with "Home Have Come Our Boys in Blue." After the sorry bargain that ended Reconstruction, the Bloody Shirt was no longer in good form at the North, not even among firm Republicans (as is clear from the decisive defeat in the Senate of the 1890 "Force Bill," which would have provided for supervision of Federal elections in the South, with the aim of enforcing the 14th and 15th amendments; it died of a Southern filibuster). *Red Badge* perfectly serves the turn: "Dry up!" Crane's novel re-describes the Civil War—or at least a representative part of it—in such a way as to make impossible a "heroic" reading of it. *The Red Badge of Courage*, we might say, is written expressly to make ridiculously untenable all talk about the Glory of the Coming of the Lord, which, as every serious-minded Unionist had at one time or another felt (especially after the Emancipation Proclamation was issued), was what the Civil War amounted to. Thousands of Union soldiers didn't sing "John Brown's Body" for naught.

Coincident with the demolition of romantic views about the Grand Army of the Republic was the cultivation of decidedly romantic views about the Southern *ancien régime*, as in the novels not only of J. E. Cooke but of Thomas Nelson Page and others like them. For the 1880s and 1890s saw the perfection of the so-called plantation myth, with its happy darkies, its mammies, and its "paternal" institutions—a mythic sort of fiction so unlike Crane's work in character and tone, but so like it (truth be told) in at least *one* tendency: to wit, in its tendency to consign what Beer archly calls "the Lord's work" to the dustbin of history. So, it is worth considering whether or not a general deflation of the Union cause in the war *did* help facilitate a reconciliation, which, in due course, allowed—as historians of the period have long maintained—for a businesslike re-institution of white supremacy in the Southern states, the better to facilitate capital investments therein.[13] The nation, as with one set of eyes, simply looked the other way—much to the chagrin of a dying Frederick Douglass. The cynicism of which Beer speaks in the passage quoted above doubtless *was* associated with the new order of things in the 1890s, though that was not its only significance. And an appreciation of its possible political resonance—which is what I've tried to lay the groundwork for here—helps us see both how and why, as Andrew Delbanco puts it, "reading *Red Badge* relieves us of our ideology" ("Stephen Crane's America" 54). In this connection, it is, yet again (and worth mentioning yet again), perfectly fitting that the most hostile response to *Red Badge* should have come, immediately on its publication, from the pen of the Union general who would soon print W. E. B. Du Bois's *Souls*.

I have already quoted at some length the review in which General McClurg waves the Bloody Shirt at Crane, accusing him of having done little more than gratify the cynicism of men who never had "correct" ideas about the Grand Army of the Republic anyway. McClurg is simply voicing the Radical Republican line, which had, since 1890 (and even before), fallen afoul of polite opinion, and which we might summarize as follows: a) We must never forget that the Union cause was just; b) we must never accede to the sort of moral "equalitarianism" that had, after 1877, allowed for a reinterpretation of the war as a struggle between two "noble" but "incompatible" ideals, either one of which might appeal to men of integrity; c) we must never tolerate the nostalgic haze that the cult of the Lost Cause had thrown over the Old South to sanitize slavery (and to shore up the neo-slavery into which the freedmen's children had been thrown); and d) we must hold fast to the idea that American institutions—especially the army—must never be put at the disposal of imperialist wags, who would have our nation enter into the business of Empire. All of these tenets are to be discerned, for example, in William Vaughan Moody's Radical

Republican and anti-imperialist "Ode in a Time of Hesitation" (1900), in Twain's anti-imperialist writings, and in William James's denunciations of American policies in the Philippines. Of course, anyone holding to all these tenets, as McClurg did, would find little to like in Stephen Crane, who must have seemed, in this context, a fin-de-siècle aesthete.

But there is much to be said in defense of *Red Badge*. The novel is a thoroughly disenchanting devaluation of that problematic word "courage." The hitch, of course, is that Henry Fleming is praised for actions that were, as Crane portrays them, incontinent and undignified. He'd been utterly out of control when he made his "heroic" charge, to the point where another soldier felt compelled to inquire into his sanity. Indiscretion of an almost disturbing sort is the better part of his valor. In the midst of the last great charge, his lieutenant finds it necessary to seize Henry by the arm and to grapple with him "as if he planned to drag the youth by the ear on to the assault" (101). Earlier in the same engagement, and much to his embarrassment, Henry finds himself firing away at a deserted field: "He was recalled by a hoarse laugh and sentence that came to his ears in a voice of contempt and amazement. 'Yeh infernal fool, don't you know enough t' quit when there ain't anything t' shoot at? Good Gawd!'" Crane can't resist adding to this reproach his own rather more highbrow condescension: "[Henry] looked bewildered for a moment. Then there appeared upon the glazed vacancy of his eyes a diamond point of intelligence. 'Oh,' he said, comprehending" (91). Well, even a yokel has his epiphanies, so long as he can crank up what Crane later (and archly) calls the "usual machines" of his "reflection" (123). But those "diamond points of intelligence" are sheer mockery.

And as for his "courage" in carrying forward the flag after the color sergeant is felled by a bullet: this is hardly what it is later made to seem when Henry "marshal[s] all his acts," "gilds" the "images of memory," "sees" that "he was good," and decisively puts his earlier "sin" of desertion "at a distance" (123–25). In point of fact, Henry half-heartedly contends with another private for the right to make himself conspicuous with the flag: "Each felt satisfied with the other's possession of it, but each felt bound to declare, by an offer to carry the emblem, his willingness to further risk himself" (103). The passage puts me in mind of the Earl of Rochester's quip: "All men would be cowards if they durst." In his great moment, Henry Fleming, Crane lets us know, is thinking about "reputation" (104). In short, it is not at all easy to see how the details of Henry's conduct during the charge, as Crane presents them, can be assimilated to a meaningfully "heroic" story, nor easy to see how he might be said to "redeem" himself through battle, as R. W. Stallman, and ten thousand high-school teachers, maintain that he does.

It is as if Crane everywhere suggests that the names whereby we dignify our conduct and our beliefs are always, in the last instance, misleading. He develops, in this debunking enterprise, a certain tactically useful engine of rhetorical analysis. His habits of expression, his ironic style, are inimical to all sorts of highly eulogistic talk about "nation," "justice," "responsibility," "self-sacrifice," and so on. He really needn't write against the prosecution of the Spanish-American War, as Moody and Twain and James did, because his writing is already a critique of the hyperinflated terms in which that war, and its sequel in the Philippines, was often sanctified. He seems to have understood that even the most eloquent of the old Radical Republicans were often (as we now say) "in denial" about American purposes. It might well be that Crane's fiction "opts out" of "the good fight." But his sense of style, his craft, entails a self-cultivation by irony that does (if followed through) help foster a healthily independent sort of thinking. We need not suppose his resolutely "private" aims as a writer altogether incompatible with the more "social" responsibilities.

I do not mean to get high-handed with Stephen Crane. I do not mean, in other words, to wave the Bloody Shirt at him, as if, when speaking of the Civil War, he should have looked to the higher commitments, with McClurg and William Vaughan Moody and Du Bois. His Civil War fiction may do nothing to keep the jeremiad fires of the great American mission burning. It may give up the Lincolnian national errand—the "new birth of freedom"—with a shrug. It may even have no use for the American religion of "possibility" and "optimism." But at least it refused to countenance any hypocrisy about the redemptive legacy of the Civil War—hypocrisy that still often colored the sentiments of a nation falling all over itself, in the 1890s, to abandon its "dedication," as Lincoln put it at Gettysburg, to "the proposition" that "all men are created equal." Crane—we might experimentally say—puts the whole "Columbian" enterprise in quotation marks. Alfred Kazin suggests that Crane sought "to puncture some overgrown pieties about American 'idealism' in fighting the Civil War" (quoted in Mitchell 59). That seems good enough to me, though I'd rather say Crane's *writing* somehow punctures those pieties. One wonders just how deliberate he was about all this; like many writers who strike it young, he seems instinctive about his work, as if he builded better than he knew.

Contrast Crane's war novel to the Civil War stories of Ambrose Bierce. Bierce is often associated with Crane. Both are sardonic, ironic, and rigorously unsentimental; and we know that Crane read Bierce with interest.

Bierce, for his part, initially praised *Red Badge*, but soon dismissed its author as "the Crane freak."[14] Percival Pollard, in a review of *Red Badge*, remarked that Crane had "merely done crudely what Mr. Bierce did most admirably" (Monteiro 60). Bierce was a much older man, of course. He fought in the war from beginning to end, and had been reared in an Ohio abolitionist family in which John Brown was admired. (Daniel Aaron reports the rumor that the swords Brown and his men used at Pottawatomie had been bought with funds supplied by Bierce's uncle [182].) A shrewd political sense always shapes Bierce's accounts of battle. For example, take this brief aside, from the beginning of "What I Saw of Shiloh." Bierce describes his Union Army camp: "Little negroes of not very clearly defined status and function lolled on their stomachs, kicking their long, bare heels in the sunshine, or slumbered peacefully, unaware of the practical waggery prepared by white hands for their undoing" (1). No one would liken this to the single passage in which an African American makes an appearance in *Red Badge*, early in the novel. Jim Conklin has just startled his comrades with rumors of the coming battle: "A negro teamster who had been dancing upon a cracker box with the hilarious encouragement of two score soldiers was deserted. He sat mournfully down." A world of difference separates these two evocations of "frolicking" Negroes. *Not very clearly defined status and function*: as of April 1962, when the Battle of Shiloh was fought, neither the War Department nor Lincoln had arrived at a consistent policy with regard to the fugitives that gathered behind their lines every time the armies moved South. In August 1861 General John C. Frémont declared martial law in Missouri (which had adopted a policy of armed neutrality) and emancipated the slaves therein. Lincoln countermanded the order, relieved Frémont of command, and directed that fugitives be returned to their masters (a policy adopted partly to prevent Missouri from seceding). In the same month (August 1861) the designation "contraband of war" was first applied (in official documents) to fugitive slaves at Fort Monroe, Virginia, then under the command of General Benjamin Butler. Fugitives were given quarter and set to labor; soon, thousands sought refuge behind Union lines. But the status of fugitives elsewhere remained ambiguous during the first eighteen months or so of the war. Some commanders, following Frémont's example, declared the fugitives free, only to find their decrees reversed by the White House: the fugitives, it appeared, were now legally the property of the United States government; no officer subordinate to the Commander in Chief could emancipate them (and it wasn't yet clear that he could or would). An Act Prohibiting the Return of Slaves passed Congress on March 13, 1862, a few weeks before Shiloh: "All officers or persons in the military or naval service of the United States," the law stated, "are prohibited from employing any of the forces under their respective commands for the purpose of returning fugitives from service or labor, who may have escaped from any persons to whom such service or labor is claimed to be due, and any officer who shall be found guilty by a court-martial of violating this article shall be dismissed from the service." So things stood in April 1862 when one of the things Bierce "saw of Shiloh" involved "little negroes of not very clearly defined status and function" (within a year, black refugees would be armed and mustered in). Bierce's remark at first seems incidental, but it is duly informed, and rich with implication, whereas in Crane we have little more than minstrelsy (a teamster dancing on a cracker box).

And consider the acute (if subtly arrived at) satire of the cult of Anglo-Saxonism—the form white supremacist thinking assumed in the years after Reconstruction—in the opening paragraph of Bierce's "Chickamauga." It describes a deaf and dumb white child, son of a Georgia slaveholder: "One sunny autumn afternoon a child strayed away from its rude home in a small field and entered a forest unobserved. It was happy in a new sense of freedom from control, happy in the opportunity of exploration and adventure; for this child's spirit, in bodies of its ancestors, had for thousands of years been trained to memorable feats of discovery and conquest—victories in battles whose critical moments were centuries, whose victors' camps were cities hewn of stone. From the cradle of its race it had conquered its way through two continents and passing a great sea had penetrated a third, there to be born to war and dominion as a heritage" (41). What follows in "Chickamauga" is a ghastly account of Anglo-Saxon self-slaughter in an episode (Bierce seems to suggest) that is but an event in the "memorable" history of white conquest in the westering course of empire: "practical waggery" at the expense of innocent Negroes indeed. In "Chickamauga," Bierce is gunning for the likes of Josiah Strong, whose *Our Country: Its Possible Future and Its Present Crisis* (1885) had been a runaway bestseller. Strong foresaw a "final competition of races, for which the Anglo-Saxon is being schooled": "This race of unequalled energy, with all the majesty of numbers and the might of wealth behind it—the representative, let us hope, of the largest liberty, the purest Christianity, the highest civilization—having developed peculiarly aggressive traits calculated to impress its institutions upon mankind, will spread itself over the earth. If I read not amiss, this powerful race will move down upon Mexico, down upon Central and South America, out upon the islands of the sea, over upon Africa and beyond. And can any one doubt that the result of this competition of the races will be 'the survival of the fittest'?" (175). Doubtless Crane found this sort of thing ridiculous. But nowhere in his writing about the Civil War do I find evidence that he cared about the politics of race. Again, this is not a card to play against Stephen Crane; it's a hint of where his real interests as a writer always lay—in *style*. His calling is belletristic, a thing I'd never say of Bierce.

Scratchy Wilson, Sheriff Potter, and *The Monster*

Crane is especially good at effects arrived at by dislocating the reader's point of view, and this habit of his is not without its philosophical and even political significance. A fine example occurs in "The Bride Comes to Yellow Sky" in the passage describing the rounds Scratchy Wilson fires at a dog in front of the Weary Gentleman Saloon:

> The dog . . . had not appreciated the advance of events. He yet lay dozing in front of his master's door. At sight of the dog, the man paused and raised his revolver humorously. At sight of the man, the dog sprang up and walked diagonally away, with a sullen head, and growling. The man yelled, and the dog broke into a gallop. As it was about to enter an alley, there was a loud noise, a whistling, and something spat the ground directly before it. The dog screamed, and, wheeling in terror, galloped headlong in a new direction. Again there was a noise, a whistling, and sand was kicked viciously before it. Fear-stricken, the dog turned and flurried like an animal in a pen. The man stood laughing, his weapons at his hips. (321)

The gunshots are, of course, described from the dog's point of view. His way of making sense of the world simply doesn't include the equipment he needs in order to understand the connections linking the report of a gun, the whistling sound of a bullet in the air, and a burst of sand where the bullet strikes the ground. It is worth pointing out further that as the narrator, in what Crane allows him to know, becomes more "canine," the dog himself is subtly (and whimsically) humanized: he is said to "scream," to be unable to "appreciate the advance of events," and so on. The comic personifications only point up the pathos of his real situation.

We might take this analysis of the dog's situation a step or two further, the better to understand the "naturalism" of which I spoke earlier in connection with *The Red Badge of Courage*. Imagine for a moment that Crane shows us by exaggeration what he believes to be true about our plight, not simply about the dog's. In his fiction, Crane suggests that we lack the conceptual and intellectual equipment we need in order to make good sense alike of the social and natural worlds we inhabit. There are some things, and some connections between things, that simply do not "register" in our minds, and some things of which we remain aware in wrong or inappropriate ways. The difference between us and Crane's dog is that our limitations are culturally determined and can be changed, while his are natural or biological and cannot. You can't talk a dog into understanding drunken banditry.

In "The Open Boat" and "The Blue Hotel," Crane places us in a world that makes little sense, that is indifferent to us, and in which we cut a fairly ridiculous figure; it is the same world in which he places Henry Fleming. Crane did not, it turns out, regard his late-nineteenth-century compatriots as occupying a position very much superior to the dog's in "The Bride Comes to Yellow Sky." It is certainly true that, in this story, Jack Potter and his wife feel themselves, however dimly, to be the butt of some great joke at their expense, quite as if the new America in which they find themselves—and which is epitomized by the Pullman train that conveys them across Texas—is so large and alienating as to beggar description. They flurry like animals in a pen. The new couple hear the report of the Gun of History, note a Whistling Sound about their ears, and feel the Sand in their Eyes. But they cannot put it all together. They can only achieve the vague feeling of having *somehow* been affronted, of having struck their fellow passengers as ridiculous in ways they can't quite understand ("a number of travelers [cover] them with stares of derisive enjoyment" [314]). Theirs is a world turned upside down, whose social relations are unreadable, opaque. "Historically," we are told, "there was supposed to be something infinitely humorous in their situation" (314). Even the African American porter finds them ridiculous: "This individual at times surveyed them from afar with an amused and superior grin. On other occasions he bullied them with skill in ways that did not make it exactly plain to them that they were being bullied. He subtly used all the manners of the most unconquerable kind of snobbery. He oppressed them, but of this oppression they had small knowledge" (314). Potter and his bride are like Henry Fleming when he overhears the officer speaking of his fellow grunts as if they were "mule drivers," or as if they were merely some sort of regimental "broom" with which to sweep the woods of rebels. This is much more than idle social comedy about a bumpkin and his bride, of whom it is said that "it was quite apparent that she had cooked, and that she expected to cook, dutifully" (313). Apparent to whom? Well, to the same person who might "suppose" there to be something "infinitely humorous" about her "historical situation"—not to other men and women *like* her, who would, of course, not take note of such a thing ("dutiful" cooking being natural to their station). Potter regards his new suit with an air of intimidation; it alienates as much as clothes him ("a direct result of his new black clothes was that his brick-colored hands were constantly performing in a most conscious fashion. From time to time he looked down respectfully at his attire" [313]). Popping off his rounds, Crane makes Jack Potter and his new bride dance, as it were, just as surely as Wilson makes the dog "flurry" before the Weary Gentleman Saloon; the tactic is typical of him. His narration is cocksure and gets the better of his characters. ("The Open Boat" is a salient exception, but then Crane *himself* had been in that boat.) Yet, there is a naturalist sense in this story, as elsewhere in Crane, that we are all the dupes of History, as even Crane's imperious African American porter must feel the minute he steps off the Pullman parlor car in the post-Reconstruction Jim Crow Texas and Louisiana of 1896 (the year of *Plessy v. Ferguson*). There was more than enough "oppression" to go around in America in those years.

"The great Pullman" emerges as the sole unanswerable force in "Yellow Sky." From its vantage, Texas itself, that gloriously indigestible old republic, is shown to be simply swept eastward, swallowed up: "The great Pullman was whirling onward with such dignity of motion that a glance from the window seemed simply to prove that the plains of Texas were pouring eastward. Vast flats of green grass, dull-hued spaces of mesquite and cactus, little groups of frame houses, woods of light and tender trees, all were sweeping into the east, sweeping over the horizon, a precipice" (313). The America into which the Pullman Palace car ushers Jack Potter and his bride is simply what William Graham Sumner, in his apologia for plutocrats like George Pullman, calls "inevitable." He writes, in "The Absurd Effort to Make the World Over" (1894): "The movement of industry has been all the time toward promptitude, punctuality, and reliability. It has been attended all the way by lamentations about the good old times; about the decline of small industries; about the lost spirit of comradeship between employer and employee; about the narrowing of the interests of the workman; about his conversion into a machine or into a 'ware,' and about industrial war" (101). But let no one suppose that Sumner mourns. "These lamentations have all had reference to unquestionable phenomena attendant on advancing organization," he concedes, but, he insists, organization "is to go on faster than ever, now that . . . the intensification of industry has begun. The great inventions both make the intension of the organization possible and make it inevitable, with all its consequences, whatever they may be.

I must expect to be told here, according to the current fashions of thinking," he adds, scorning Progressives, "that we ought to control the development of the organization. The first instinct of the modern man is to get a law passed to forbid or prevent what, in his wisdom, he disapproves," Sumner adds, as if he were a member in good standing of Americans For Prosperity (the Koch brothers' Super PAC) (101). "A thing which is inevitable, however, is one which we cannot control. We have to make up our minds to it, adjust ourselves to it, and sit down to live with it" (101) What is "The Bride Comes to Yellow Sky" about? It is about how Jack Potter, his wife, and the outlaw Scratchy Wilson, do precisely this: acknowledge that the post-Reconstruction era, the Robber Baron, Gilded Age era—with all the new imperatives of industry, "advancing organization," and nationalized markets—are inevitable; and that they must make up their minds to sit down and live with it all; and that it would indeed be absurd to make it over. And so, they resign themselves to their new condition. The last of the outlaws—himself now seeking a role in the new economy—is done: "He picked up his starboard revolver, and placing both weapons in their holsters, he went away. His feet made funnel-shaped tracks in the heavy sand" (324). There are no frontiers anymore. The charismatic sort of irony Crane developed in his fiction equips his reader to perfect this sort of resignation. He turns to the cultivation of a private (and privatized) literary style that is remarkably "cool"—in several senses of the word, including the one now current. The guiding principle here is (and you can detect it too in William Graham Sumner's essay): *Never be a chump.*[15] Crane was to the Gilded Age what David Letterman has been to the *New* Gilded Age (before he resigned his show to Stephen Colbert, whose relentlessly political comedy differs markedly from the Hoosier surrealism of his predecessor). A sense of humor, like a sense of style, can't develop unaffected by, or unadjusted to, larger economies of exchange. Crane and Letterman charm us with a certain detachment from anything outside the studio (so to speak). Not, of course, that I don't read the one and didn't watch the other. I must acknowledge this scholarly quietism mine—a failing the benefit of which (I hope) is a keener eye and ear for Crane's performances.

The Pullman Palace Car Company is the real motive "character" in "The Bride Comes to Yellow Sky." The gaudy decor of the Pullman constitutes "the environment" of Jack Potter's "new estate," as Crane puts it. Potter may survey "the dazzling fittings" of the coach with "the pride of an owner" (314). But it is perfectly clear to us—to adapt a celebrated line of Emerson's—that things are in the saddle and ride *him*. The sorry truth is that Potter and his bride are "owned" by their new environment ("All organization implies restriction of liberty," writes Sumner [101]). And theirs is an America in which none of us ever really feels at home, because in Crane's fiction "home"—whether Yellow Sky, Texas, or, as in "The Blue Hotel," Fort Romper, Nebraska—is a thing we may no longer be said to "possess": it moves about us, as it moves about Scully in his blue hotel, like an oncoming mirage of "ilictric streetcars" (332). "Yellow Sky" and "The Blue Hotel" are stories about the ridiculously dispossessed—tell-tale parables of the age of the Standard Oil Trust, whose rail, mining and petroleum operations were consuming America, and, as the populists had it, making short work of the little guy, and of local industry and culture alike. "We picture the world as thick with conquering and elate humanity," writes Crane in "The Blue Hotel," "but here [in Nebraska], with the bugles of the tempest pealing, it was hard to imagine a peopled earth. One viewed the existence of man then as a marvel, and conceded a glamour of wonder to these lice which were caused to cling to a whirling, fire-smote, ice-locked, disease-stricken, space-lost bulb" (348). "When it occurs to a man that nature does not regard him as important," he writes in "The Open Boat," "and that she feels she would not maim the universe by disposing of him, he at first wishes to throw bricks at the temple, and he hates deeply the fact that there are no bricks and no temples. Any visible expression of nature would surely be pelleted with his jeers. Then, if there be no tangible thing to hoot, he feels, perhaps, the desire to confront a personification and indulge in pleas, bowed to one knee, and with hands supplicant, saying: 'Yes, but I love myself.' A high cold star on a winter's night is the word he feels that she says to him. Thereafter he knows the pathos of his situation" (294).

"The Unwinking Eye"

I have spoken already, in connection with a passage in "The Bride Comes to Yellow Sky," of Crane's dislocation of the reader's point of view. Related to this technique is another that might be called the achievement of perspective by inappropriate affect, a technique much on display in *The Monster* (1898). The technique signals the dislocation of the narrator from what we might take to be "ordinary" ways of responding to the situations he narrates, and *The Monster* is full of such local effects. These are of importance to me here in that they indicate something larger than the dislocation merely of the narrator from "ordinary" structures of feeling; the novel itself achieves precisely such a dislocation. It concerns the persecution of a black man in a small white town, and this at the height of the lynching terror, when the civil and political rights tentatively secured for black Americans were everywhere being assailed and rolled back (as the introduction and chapters 1 and 2 have shown). I will proceed here from consideration of local stylistic matters to larger questions about Crane's sympathies and dispositions—to questions, that is, about Crane's commitments, which here again, despite the extraordinary political significance of his themes in the post-Reconstruction era, are to matters chiefly aesthetic.

The plot of the novella is simple. Dr. Trescott, one of the worthies of Whilomville, the small, notably suburban town in which the story is laid, employs a black hostler named Henry Johnson. Henry is a slightly ridiculous figure, compacted of a handful of very recognizable clichés borrowed from the minstrel-show stage and from popular late-nineteenth-century caricatures of black Americans. He is vain in a way that white men find oddly appealing. He struts in his finery, in the fashion of Zip Coon (the urbanite counterpart to the rural Jim Crow). And he is childlike in his devotion and in his thinking. The Trescott house is a comfortable domicile with an impeccably tended lawn. Dr. Trescott doesn't so much mow his lawn as sacramentally "shave" it, as if it were "a priest's chin" (190). And when fire destroys the house, Henry, at great risk to himself, storms the burning building alone to rescue the Trescott's little boy Jimmie, with whom he has a special bond (himself being, as Crane imagines him, an overgrown child). The boy, with his help, escapes unharmed, but Henry is badly burned by the blaze; his face is disfigured horribly by chemicals after he collapses in the laboratory the doctor maintains on the lower floor. The injuries leave Henry feeble-minded, and the townspeople vacillate wildly from condemning him as a coward to celebrating him as a hero and savior to quietly suggesting to the doctor, who has taken charge of the injured man, that it would be better if the self-sacrificing Negro would simply be allowed—or even caused—to die. Those who favor the latter course we might range with Dr. Paul B. Barringer—chairman of the faculty at the University of Virginia (1895–1903) and president of Virginia Tech (1907–13)—in his *The Sacrifice of a Race* (1900): "When it comes to a fight, industrial or otherwise, between white and black, the whites are for the whites. What then? Compassion, charity and mercy; missionaries, churches and hospitals—i.e., euthanasia" (4). To the white citizens of Whilomville, Henry is an embarrassment, a thing better remembered than actually dealt with; and, what is more, Henry's mangled face terrifies the local white kids, with the result that the townsfolk find themselves burdened with what used, in those days, to be called a "Negro Problem." Dr. Trescott refuses to abandon Henry; he takes up the white man's burden; he will not stoop to less. And for this he is ostracized. His medical practice suffers, no one attends his wife's teas, and that is where the story ends. *The Monster* is, to be sure, an indictment of small-town intolerance and nastiness (it looks forward to Sinclair Lewis and Sherwood Anderson). But the questions I'll be asking are these: Is it anything *more* than an indictment of small-town nastiness? And does it really matter that Henry Johnson is black? Once again, let's turn to the prose.

Crane's metaphors often startle and disorient us, at times to surreal effect, as when the fire that consumes the Trescott house in *The Monster* is said to roar "like a winter wind among the pines" (202). The metaphor combines the ideas of extreme heat and extreme cold, and of the outdoors (a forest) and the indoors (a living room). A more startling example of the same technique occurs earlier in the same passage: "A wisp of smoke came from one of the windows at the end of the house and drifted quietly into the branches of a cherry tree. Its companions followed it in slowly increasing numbers, and finally there was a current controlled by invisible banks which poured into the fruit-laden boughs of the cherry tree. It was no more to be noted than if a troop of dim and silent gray monkeys had been climbing a grapevine into the clouds" (201). Several things strike me. The first is the comparison of the smoke to water—a happy confusion of elements. This works by paradox, in the way that the comparison of the fire to the winter wind does. Then there is the idea that wisps of smoke are *companionable*. But the odd feature of the passage is the suggestion in the last sentence that the progress of the smoke is "no more to be noted than if a troop of dim and silent gray monkeys had been climbing a grapevine into the clouds." *No more to be noted*? By whom? How may we understand such a remark? Most observers would "take note" if they saw a troop of dim and silent gray monkeys climbing a grapevine into the clouds, even if they saw it in a place called Whilomville. And why a *grapevine*, among all other vines seldom associated with monkeys? The metaphor works by visual analogy on the basis of color: a rising column of smoke is compared to a troop of *gray* monkeys—to *something* gray, anyway. But the monkeys, the "troop," and the grapevine are sheer extravagances, as is also the disclaimer that there might be nothing at all unusual in the prospect they afford.

But what interests me is less the startling quality of particular metaphors in Crane than the general tone of detached irony to which they give rise, as they appear, page after page, in his fiction. The effect, again, is impressively cumulative. Which brings me to a discussion of what I have called the technique of *inappropriate affect*. In *The Monster* the structure of feelings that might be said to characterize Crane's narrator often seems oddly out of place. The fire is for him an occasion for play of a notably whimsical (if not Mephistophelean) sort. There is little gravity in the narration. The tone always alerts us to the fact that Crane is an *observer* but never, sympathetically speaking, a *participant-observer* in the scenes he describes. He is a god paring his nails who hardly deigns to notice when a troop of gray monkeys climbs a grapevine into the clouds. This is why he can describe Mrs. Trescott, in her alarm for the safety of her son Jimmie, in language that leans toward ridicule. She is incontinent in her emotions. And Crane—always cool, no matter what the situation—disdains her. She is said to wave her skinny arms about "as if they were two reeds." He makes a straw woman of her. She is "maniacal." She "babbles" (202–3). She is as much a spectacle as an object of sympathy. Crane's art often works in this region between spectacle and sympathy.

The interest of the narrator is more in the fire itself than in anything the fire might destroy. The fire is to him a lovely thing. Little Jimmie Trescott's room, we are told, "had no smoke in it at all. It was faintly illuminated by a beautiful rosy light reflected circuitously from the flames that were consuming the house. The boy had just been aroused by the noise. He sat in his bed, his lips apart, his eyes wide, while upon his little white-robed figure played caressingly the light from the fire" (203). The narrator misses not the smallest effect of grace in this tableau. His investment in the scene is that of a connoisseur, as when he reports that Jimmie, having been seized by Henry Johnson, the man who will save him, "let out a *gorgeous* bawl" (204). It is a bawl to be appreciated on its own terms, not simply a cry of distress. The narrator's interest in the scene is set apart from the interest the characters *themselves* take in it; his affect is to that degree dislocated.

But the best awaits us in Dr. Trescott's laboratory. "At the entrance to the laboratory," Crane writes, Henry Johnson and the boy he carries meet "a strange spectacle. The room was like a garden in the region where might be burning flowers. Flames of violet, crimson, green, blue, orange, and purple were blooming everywhere. There was one blaze that was precisely the hue of a delicate coral. In another place was a mass that lay merely in phosphorescent inaction like a pile of emeralds" (205). Crane has already run through three metaphors—this fire is like a flower garden (terrestrial), or like undersea coral (submarine), or like a heap of jewels (commercial). He continues, animating the fire and its effects: "There was an explosion at one side, and suddenly before [Henry] there reared a delicate, trembling sapphire shape like a fairy lady. With a quiet smile she blocked his path and doomed him and Jimmie" (205). Henry is able, in his last exertion, to lay Jimmie down near a window. But he himself collapses onto the floor beneath a table on which sit beakers and jars of various chemicals, one of which seems "to hold a scintillant and writhing serpent. Suddenly the glass splintered, and a ruby-red snake-like thing poured its thick length out upon the top of the old desk" (205). And now, not only are the fire and its results animated; they are endowed with sinister motive: "It coiled and hesitated, and then began to swim a languorous way down the mahogany slant. At the angle it waved its sizzling molten head to and fro over the closed eyes of the man beneath it. Then, in a moment, with a mystic impulse, it moved again, and the red snake flowed directly down into Johnson's upturned face. Afterward the trail of this creature seemed to reek, and amid flames and low explosions drops like red-hot jewels pattered softly down at leisurely intervals" (205–6).

In connection with this remarkable passage, I want to ask a question about point of view that is also a question about the narrator's mood. What sort of mind could imagine this particular fire in this particular way? It must be a mind utterly unaffected and unsentimental, a mind capable of seeing in the fire a show of light, color, and form; a mind provisionally indifferent—Olympian, even—to the appalling suffering the fire causes the men and women immediately touched by it. They are, the possessor of such a mind must feel, a little selfish in seeing the fire only in terms of what it can do to them. They are little people. Crane writes *about* his characters, but not *for* them. He veers from satire to ridicule to something like contempt. His manner, if I may say so, allies him with the "high cold star" that looks on the suffering men in the open boat with such sublime indifference. Crane's narrator is like the Universe in his best-known poem: when reminded that men exist, the Universe replies that the fact creates in it no "sense of obligation" (*War Is Kind* 56). That is the indifferent force with which Crane would affiliate himself, or so the evidence of his cool prose suggests. Crane's narrator is like George Pullman himself. He is a Robber Baron, a *generalissimo*. And his fiction is the environment of the new (and notably unsentimental) American estate, circa 1898. *The Monster* may be about a black man, defaced and compelled to live behind a veil. But no one, I think, would find in it any real exception to the drift of things in a nation that was (again, as Du Bois said) "a little ashamed," in the 1890s, "at having bestowed so much sentiment on Negroes" (*Souls* 392). This will become clear when we consider, in a moment, a crucial passage describing Henry Johnson and his sweetheart Bella Farragut.

William James points out in *Pragmatism* that, from our point of view, the astonishing "fitness" of the woodpecker's beak to get at the grubs hiding beneath the bark of a tree appears beautiful and perfect (535). It argues "design" in the universe of a remarkably harmonious and symbiotic sort. From the point of view of the grubs, of course, it is evidence of something else altogether: a diabolical sort of "design." Everything depends on perspective. One sometimes hears epidemiologists speak of the "elegance" or "beauty" of a particularly nefarious virus. It is possible to regard Ebola Zaire, for example, with a certain aesthetic detachment—to regard it as Ebola Zaire itself might wish to be regarded: as a strand of RNA ideally suited to painting a room with human blood. When we think that way we are interested only in power, only in force; we have transcended merely "human" interests. We are in any case well beyond jeremiads, and the interest they always take in the "human" significance of History. And this is the direction in which Crane's fiction usually tends.

A cultivated detachment, combined with often startlingly incongruous metaphors, is what accounts for the peculiar feeling of disorientation we feel in reading Crane's most characteristic prose. In *The Monster*, the fire that disfigures Henry Johnson is described precisely as a fire might like to be described. The fire is done justice to. The fire is flattered. It has good reason to deploy its flames like "flags" "joyfully" waving in the wind, as Crane puts it. No wonder the townspeople look up with eyes that "shine" with "awe," as Crane says they do (210). For they, too, are *pyrophiliac*, and can appreciate a fire. To *appreciate* it—as theater, as a spectacle, as a thing of force and beauty—is in fact what they came to the Trescott's burning house to do. They are, so far as their moral investment in the scene is concerned, like the narrator himself: indifferent, and, as the story soon permits them to show, incapable of empathy. They would as soon kill the disfigured Henry Johnson as look at him—if they could do so by taking thought. The local boys, as boys will, hurry to the fire as to a circus: they are "deeply moved" by the "whole affair," and take special pleasure in it (after all, "it was fine to see the gathering of the companies," and the lads display an "impish joy" at the sight of the flames [208]). One might write this off as childish insouciance, which is what it is. But the adults are the same. The men are at their best when describing the affair to their fellows in a theatrical, self-dramatizing way (209). The whole business takes on the holiday air of a parade (210). And lest we ascribe this to a forgivably human weakness for excitement and sensation, Crane soon shows us that the townsfolk care nothing at all for the suffering Henry Johnson. The judge speaks for them all: "Somehow," he says, "I think that that poor fellow ought to die" (213). It is "one of the blunders of virtue," he suggests, to care for him any longer (213), and this, very plainly, because to care for him is a nuisance. So much for the white man's burden Kipling admonished us to take up in 1899, the year after *The Monster* was published. *The Monster* might be a satire of the bad faith with which that "burden" was everywhere assumed. But to imply that it *ought* to be assumed (Kipling-wise) is itself an act of paternalism.

Now, clearly, we are invited to condemn the townspeople for their detachment: they cut Dr. Trescott off when he refuses to turn Henry out to die. But we are never invited to judge the narrator, and I shall attempt to make the implications of this fact clear. The reason we condemn the townsfolk is that, under the circumstances, they *ought* to be committed to seeing the fire in terms chiefly of what it can do to them, and to their fellows; they ought to be humanists. That is to say, they *ought* to be humanly self-centered, as the grubs in James's analogy are self-centered in a grubbish way, for that would be the beginning of a grubby empathy. No time out to admire the woodpecker's plumage. They are not writers describing imaginary events, as is Crane; they are characters in a story behaving like writers describing imaginary events. And that is the moral problem to which Crane's novella alerts us: at the end of the day, Henry Johnson is not, for the good white people of Whilomville, *real*. He is not one of their fellows. They see him, if they see him at all, as through a veil of unreality. In fact, Crane has Henry wear a veil, as if anticipating Du Bois's great metaphor in *The Souls of Black Folk*. The white townsfolk indeed look on Henry, veiled as he is, with "amused contempt and pity" (to borrow Du Bois's phrase in *Souls*, 364). This explains their verdict: it would have been much more convenient if Henry Johnson had simply been allowed to die. Had little Jimmie Trescott's savior been white, would the townsfolk have felt the same way? Many would answer no, but the story hardly insists on the point, and I suspect it wasn't uppermost in Crane's mind.

No sooner do we follow out this train of thought than we board another one headed in a direction even less auspicious: for Crane himself, Henry Johnson is, in an important sense, unreal. As presented by the *narrator*, not by the characters in the story, Henry is drawn out of the worst clichés of the minstrel-show stage, as I've suggested. He is a cartoon man—a caricature. He is—as many readers have felt—Zip Coon. And having been educated by the story into condemnation of the townsfolk for their callous indifference to Henry's humanity, should we condemn the narrator for *his*, and, after the narrator, should we chide Crane himself? Is Crane's condescending and hollowed-out portrait of a black man somehow bound up with the retreat from the Reconstruction-era commitment to civil and political equality for black Americans? It wasn't as though writers such as Frederick Douglass, Ida B. Wells, Frances E. W. Harper, Paul Laurence Dunbar, and Charles Chesnutt were unavailable to him as resources to complicate and augment his imagination in this regard. Had he really wanted to know the lives of his black countrymen, he could have. The evidence is that he chose not to—in his fiction in any case. He simply doesn't know what to make of them; this allies him not only with his white countrymen, but with the white folk who people his novella.

Consider the scene describing the visit Henry makes to his girlfriend Bella Farragut at her home in Watermelon Alley: "The duty of receiving Mr. Johnson fell upon Mrs. Farragut, because Bella, in another room, was scrambling wildly into her best gown. The fat old woman met him with a great ivory smile, sweeping back with the door, and bowing low. . . . After a great deal of kowtow," we are told, "they were planted in two chairs opposite each other in the living-room" (197). They aren't allowed simply to *sit*, or even to "plant" *themselves* (why the passive voice?). "Here they exchanged the most tremendous civilities, until Miss Bella swept into the room, when there was more kowtow on all sides, and a smiling show of teeth that was like an illumination. The cooking-stove was of course in this drawing room, and on the fire was some kind of a long-winded stew. Mrs. Farragut was obliged to arise and attend to it from time to time. Also young Sim came in and went to bed on his pallet in the corner. But to all these domesticities the three maintained an absolute dumbness" (197). We might first suppose that Crane expects us to admire the studied dignity with which these three conduct themselves in their impoverished circumstances, as they politely ignore the fact that a single room serves for a parlor, bedroom, and kitchen. But Crane expects nothing of the kind, no more than he expects us to be moved to sympathy by Maggie's embattled sense of honor in *Maggie: A Girl of the Streets* (1893). Bella is not vouchsafed much dignity in her "wild scramble" to make herself lovely after she sights her dandified beau on his approach to "Watermelon Alley" (197) (the literary ghetto in which Crane places his back folk): she leaves off "gossiping at long range" (that is, shouting in an unseemly manner) only to "gallop like a horse" into the house (which is less a domicile than a stable) (196). There, we learn, the cooking stove is "of course" in the drawing room (197), and the force of this insertion is equivocal, in that it involves neither sympathy for, nor smiling at, the poverty of the family: "of course" their rooms are cramped and few; "of course" they cook in the parlor. What of it? And are we to chuckle at the family's culinary efforts—at the fact that their "long-winded stew" huffs and puffs its way toward its conclusion? Or at the "tremendousness" of their civilities? (197).

There can be no doubt that this scene is *meant* to be funny, but with laughs at whose expense, and at what social cost, so to speak? To whom does this comedy pay its "psychological wage" (the term Du Bois coined in *Black Reconstruction* [700])? Not, I am certain, to Du Bois, had he read it. This is *white* fiction for a *white* reader, and it pays a *white* wage: the peculiar benefit of mocking a man you are also invited to find sympathetic. In any case, Crane continues: "They bowed and smiled and ignored and imitated until a late hour, and if they had been the occupants of the most gorgeous salon in the world they could not have been more like three monkeys" (197). Plainly, this is an example of what we might call "inappropriate affect" on the part of the narrator, though in this case we have to do with an impropriety of which Crane is not a conscious manipulator. The Farraguts and Henry Johnson are minstrel show darkies—what with all their white teeth, their monkeying imitation of white manners, and their comical pretensions (Crane all but animalizes them). You can take a darky out of Watermelon Alley and put her in the finest salon in the world; but you can't take Watermelon Alley out of the darky. Crane is himself talking like one of the less generous characters in his own story (we can't distinguish him, here, from the narrator). He is a citizen of Whilomville in good standing (as he would likely acknowledge with a shrug). A continuity links the general mode of the comedy in this novella—what I have been calling the narrator's inappropriate affect—to the sort of minstrel-show stereotype we find in this scene, with its monkeyshines; and it is a stereotype that marks the story as very comfortably belonging in the 1890s, when the lynching terror neared its peak, and when the nation, under Republican leadership, cast the freedmen and their children (and children's children) most callously aside. That is why Crane's satire in *The Monster*, if satire is the right word for it, never rises into indignation. Crane isn't indignant at all. He isn't writing any jeremiads about the broken promises of Reconstruction and the Republican Party in the 1890s. As often as not, he is simply amusing himself with observations about long-winded stews. Crane's story about a persecuted black man is not a story about a man persecuted *because* he is black; in fact, the significance of his being black is more than a little obscure to me. It is a story about a much more generalized, historically non-specific sort of intolerance—to the extent that it is *really* about intolerance at all. Also to the point, here, are the shifting rhetorical and aesthetic strategies of *The Monster*. Part farce, part satire, part minstrel show, and part exposé of small-town American pettiness of the sort we find in Twain's "The Man That Corrupted Hadleyburg" (1899), the novella never assumes coherent shape, until it becomes quite impossible to say whether or not, and even why, it should *really* matter to the reader that Henry Johnson is black. The reader might object that we can say of *Huckleberry Finn* that it too, shifts rhetorical and aesthetic modes: it is by turns satire, farce, and idyll; and in it, too, the main black character appears before us now as a figure of sympathy, and now as one of ridicule. But we never doubt that *Huck Finn* is a politically committed book, whatever its defects; that novel, written by the reconstructed Southern spouse of a Yankee abolitionist, does, in fact, wave the Bloody Shirt, if we think of it, as we should, as a document in the history of the post-Reconstruction years when it was written (1876–84). To the extent that a latent white supremacy infects the novel there is in it as well a self-loathing—a fierce self-recrimination: the book is everywhere an inquiry into the poverty of its own imaginative resources, which is the poverty of the white imagination. Never do we encounter any such thing in the only novel Crane was ever to write on anything remotely calling to mind "The Negro Question": *The Monster*. Crane—to put it plainly—simply didn't care which way the world went (as Alfred Kazin rightly said). His interest was always in style.

There is very little in *The Monster*, or anywhere else in Crane's fiction, to suggest that the suffering to which he bears witness ought to, or can be very much, alleviated—which may be simply to point out the obvious: he isn't Ida B. Wells (just as he isn't the later T. S. Eliot). Against Crane's abortive foray into the sorry plight of a black American—and against his novel about the war that ended slavery—I would set, again, William Vaughan Moody's "Ode in a Time of Hesitation," with its demand that Americans take up anew what Thomas Beer dismissively calls "the Lord's work," and to make good on Lincoln's, Charles Sumner's, Frederick Douglass's, and Thaddeus Stevens's great promise. The implication of Crane's work seems to be that the best we who do not suffer like Henry Johnson, or who suffer less than him, can do is adopt a satisfying attitude with respect to bad conditions; we certainly can't propose to "make the world over," as William Graham Sumner says, or as the Radical Republicans had most certainly attempted to do circa 1866–76. The result for the reader of Crane is a kind of muddle—a mode of irresolution, which is, as I've been attempting to show, symptomatic of the 1890s, and of a piece with the political economy of that decade.

After the smoke has cleared over the ruins of Dr. Trescott's well-manicured home, and after the extent of Henry's injuries is plain to all, the Judge pays the doctor a visit. "He arose and entered the house," we read, "his brow still furrowed in a thoughtful frown. His stick thumped solemnly in regular beats. On the second floor he entered a room where Dr. Trescott was working about the bedside of Henry Johnson. The bandages on the negro's head allowed only one thing to appear, an eye, which unwinkingly stared at the judge. The latter spoke to Trescott on the condition of the patient. Afterward he evidently had something further to say, but he seemed to be kept from it by the scrutiny of the unwinking eye, at which he furtively glanced from time to time" (212). Henry's unwinking eye: this is what the Judge and the townsfolk wish to extinguish. That eye is a standing reproach. Under the gaze of this black figure the white citizenry simply cannot get a good night's sleep. Henry is like Banquo's ghost (or like Ben Tillman's evocation of Banquo's ghost, discussed at the close of chapter 2). His eye is a witness against them all, and for this reason it is unbearable. The Judge simply must turn away from it, lest he be forced to confront the horrible importunities of Henry and his suffering kind. The question I would ask is this: does Crane, too, shrink from that unwinking eye? Does all the minstrel-show mischief at Henry's expense amount to a turning away, to a denial of (literary) quarter to this representative of an outraged, persecuted and (in the 1890s) abandoned people? Does the comedy of *The Monster* really sort well with its half-hearted moralism, at least so far as this moralism has to do with the very vexing problem of race (as opposed to the easier problem of small-town pettiness)? This is a book of no genre. Crane *does* shrink from that unwinking eye, though the fact that he sets that eye a-gazing in the midst of his novella may indicate that he (like Twain in *Huck Finn*) somehow wishes to be found out. It is a tell-tale eye, and its silent, sullen gaze weighs white gods and white men alike (to borrow yet another phrase from Kipling's "The White Man's Burden"). It is a gaze *The Monster* neither controls nor contains—nor rightly understands.

Toward a Conclusion

What, then, is missing in Crane's world? "Truth with a big 'T,'" as William James might say (*Pragmatism* 588). In certain respects, his thinking is what we would now call "anti-foundational," or, in American contexts, "pragmatist." But his is the anti-foundationalism, the suave "irony," that many writers on the left complain of in certain strains of postmodern theory on the grounds that it simply cannot support, let alone offer, a program of political reform. I have in mind particularly the Marxist literary critic Terry Eagleton, whose objection to Richard Rorty and to neo-pragmatism falls out along these lines. See, for example, Eagleton's remarks in the afterword to the second edition of his widely read *Literary Theory: An Introduction*: "For American neo-pragmatists like Rorty and [Stanley] Fish, the collapse of transcendental viewpoints signals, in effect, the collapse of the possibility of full-blooded political critique. Such a critique, the argument runs, could only be launched from some metaphysical vantage-point completely beyond our current life-forms; and since there is self-evidently no such place to stand—or since, even if there were, it would be irrelevant and unintelligible to us—even our most apparently revolutionary claims must always be in collusion with the discourses of the present" (203). This is a bad reading of Rorty. But it might well apply to Crane.

In any case, we know that the battle described in *The Red Badge of Courage* was, "in real life," many things: an episode in a struggle to abolish slavery; an episode in a national-Providential story about the Glory of the Coming of the Lord; an episode in the extension of politics by other means to settle a question about the nature of Federal power, and to resolve for good and all the future of labor in the American west (free or slave, or both?); an exercise in military strategy, in which warfare, particularly under Grant and Sherman, was decisively "modernized"; a "vast blue demonstration"; a theater for the staging of adolescent crises; or, as for interpreters like W. E. B. Du Bois, an episode in a centuries-old conflict over the right relations of whites to non-whites everywhere in the world (that is to say, a local episode in a global struggle [*Souls* 372]). The battle is all of these things at once: but not one of them, for Crane, is ever allowed to characterize it. He lacks commitment. He had, in fact, *perfected* the art of lacking commitment. It isn't merely whimsical to say that he anticipated a new vein of American humor, which issued, among other things, in the ironic comedy of David Letterman (who might have authored one of Ring Lardner's short plays). Crane is our first great "hip" writer, as I've suggested; he is cool, but never "woke" (as we now say). For him there is no master narrative in terms of which we might understand the motives and aims of the men involved in making the Civil War, which is precisely why, it seems to me, Andrew Delbanco is mistaken to find in Crane some notable vestige of "the appetite for the very idea of divine superintendence that the Civil War had thrown into doubt, and, more seriously, into disrepute" ("American Stephen Crane" 63). On the contrary, Crane resists altogether—it never seems to occur to him even to consider—the priority of the master narrative of "emancipation" that a writer like Moody takes for granted in his "Ode in a Time of Hesitation." Crane isn't writing any jeremiads. He isn't recalling us, as Americans, to our forgotten covenant. He never even addresses his reader *as an American*; he addresses us as *readers*. He discredits (it seems) the very idea of American jeremiads.[16]

So, for Crane, the Civil War is determined by nothing much at all. The war assumes what emancipationist accounts of it never do: an air of the absurd, of the anti-heroic, of the farcical. In fact, his decision to approach the war as he does indicates a lack of interest in the larger, more comprehensive view that "emancipationists" take. The fighting we witness in *Red Badge* is invested with no meaning at all. The incoherence of the experience of war in *Red Badge* is symptomatic of an incoherence everywhere encountered in Crane, who was not (whatever else he was) an especially original or consequential thinker so far as political, historical, and ideological matters are concerned. Joseph Conrad may well have had this in mind when he observed that Crane's thinking was "never very deep": "My enthusiasm withers as soon as I close the book," he wrote of Crane's work. "While one reads, of course, he is not to be questioned. He is the master of his reader to the very last line—then—apparently for no reason at all—he seems to let go his hold. It is as if he had gripped you with greased fingers. His grip is strong but while you feel the pressure on your flesh you slip out from his hand—much to your own surprise" (235).

The implication in *The Red Badge of Courage* is that Henry Fleming's alienated situation is representative. It is pure egotism to think of yourself or of your nation as having a special claim to make on the sympathies of the onlooking world. The life of each one of us is, to each one of us, fraught with significance and interest. We love ourselves. But to others we may be but an anecdote, a part of the scenery—what the Union officer whom Henry Fleming overhears contemptuously refers to as "mule drivers" (95). We may be the butt of a grand joke somehow effected by George Pullman and his Palace Car Company, as Potter and his dish-washing belle dimly know themselves to be in "The Bride Comes to Yellow Sky." We may be culturally quarantined in some "Watermelon Alley" of the Jim Crow American 1890s, with Henry Johnson and Bella Farragut in *The Monster*. Like Billie the oiler in "The Open Boat," we may be dead on the beaches of Florida, having made it that far, and no further—as Crane's astute contemporary readers would have known—from a sinking cache of weapons illegally bound for Cuba (the voyage had been a filibuster). Or we may be, as the ravages of American history are in *The Red Badge of Courage*, simply invisible. To know these things as Crane did is to dwell in a nation of diminished possibility: a house of prose, with chain gangs in the South and strike-breaking Pinkerton agents in the North. The sorry prospect, and the sense of loss, is enough to break anyone's heart. But it never broke Stephen Crane's.

CHAPTER FOUR

CHARLES CHESNUTT: NOWHERE TO TURN

On March 14, 1862, Federal forces captured the inlet port city of New Bern, North Carolina, which they would hold through the rest of the Civil War. Slaves soon gathered behind Union lines; local white landholders fled; and a chaplain in one of the Massachusetts regiments occupying the city, a man named Horace James, undertook to organize the "contraband," as the dislocated slaves were then called (as we saw in the foregoing chapter). He arranged for them to settle along the Trent River on plots of abandoned land. To honor their benefactor, the now-freed slaves named their settlement James City.[1] The freedmen prospered and, according to James, by 1865 most of them had laid up considerable property, in the form of livestock, carts, and the like, and a number had succeeded as merchants. And there they lived for twenty-eight years until, in 1893, Governor Elias Carr dispatched a regiment of the First North Carolina Militia to evict the men and women of James City. Title to the land had long been in dispute in the courts—that is, until a decision was made, in 1891, to transfer the land to its antebellum owners so as to make enforceable certain deeds possessed by the white family who had, at the end of a long series of exchanges, most recently purchased the "bad paper"—as the merchants of debt now call it—from them (or rather, from their successors). In 1893, when the eviction orders were put into effect, the black men of James City had no choice but to sign three-year leases to work the land they had owned, or so they believed, for thirty years (quite as if they'd been victims of sub-prime mortgages and predatory lenders). They had nowhere to turn. They had had a taste of an America made real, but soon enough the "swarthy specter" of slavery took "its accustomed seat" at the nation's post-Reconstruction feast (*Souls* 366). America was again what Du Bois said it had always been: an "armed camp for [the intimidation of] black folks," and for the abuse of their labor (*Souls* 436).[2]

The James City farmers' predicament, however sensational its details, was not unusual in the North Carolina that Charles Chesnutt knew. Something about the tenuous hold that black farmers always had on the land is subtly communicated in "The Goophered Grapevine" (1887), the first story in Chesnutt's first book, *The Conjure Woman* (1899). In that story, we are told of how Uncle Julius, who had, since 1865, been making a "respectable revenue" on the land he once worked as a slave, is displaced in 1877 by a new white owner—in fact, by an Ohioan named John, who had been seduced southward into North Carolina by the promise of cheap land (17).[3] In short order, John secures a legally binding deed to Uncle Julius's old estate, the title to which had been in dispute, amongst Old Master's heirs, since the war. Uncle Julius might as well have been living in James City.

What, then, was life like in North Carolina for men and women like Uncle Julius—of whom there were some 330,000 in 1865? They were, of course, subject to the same uncertainties, as to political and economic arrangements, that affected white folk when the Confederacy collapsed, with one of its last significant battles fought on North Carolina soil (The Battle of Bentonville, March 19–21, 1865, in which W. T. Sherman defeated Joseph E. Johnston). But the situation of the freedmen was unique, and new laws were enacted (and old ones retained) that specifically limited their freedom of movement and their ability to seek employment on fair terms. The new Black codes, passed immediately after the war, allowed for $500 fines to be levied "from time to time" against blacks who entered North Carolina from other states; a native North Carolinian freedman, on leaving the state for six months, was liable to the same sanctions. Black girls were to be bound out as apprentices until the age of twenty-one, whereas white girls achieved their majority at eighteen. County courts could hire out the children of any black parents who were, in the eyes of the court, not profitably engaged in "some honest, industrious occupation"; no such provision existed in the case of white parents. And in all cases former masters were to be granted first right to apprentice men and women whom they had previously owned. Vagrancy laws, while artfully written to avoid mention of race, were clearly intended to apply disproportionately to black men, and of course they did. White employers were allowed, under the law, to pay black laborers in kind (i.e., in clothing, food, etc.) rather than in cash;

and marriage between whites and blacks was a criminal offense, as Roberta S. Alexander points out in *North Carolina Faces the Freedmen* (45–49). In short, when Chesnutt's fictional Ohio couple, John and Annie, stroll onto the old plantation in 1877 with an eye single toward turning it, again, to profit, Uncle Julius has little choice but to charm them, by whatever wiles he has, into a relationship of patronage: on his own, and without white protectors, he would indeed be insecure. His sole asset—and his friends and family alike depend on him to use it well—is his wit. He must "wear the mask" and sing for his supper, to adapt Paul Laurence Dunbar's phrase. *The Conjure Woman* tells the story of how he set about to do exactly that.

Dunbar's "mask" is no mere metaphor; neither are Julius's wiles ungrounded in history and tradition. For example, Peter H. Wood, in *Black Majority: Negroes in Colonial South Carolina* (1974), finds ample evidence of disguise, dissembling, mask-wearing (of several kinds) in advertisements placed by masters, in colonial South Carolina, whose slaves had run away: "It was understood among whites that captured runaways were never to be fully trusted in giving their owner's name, much less in their other statements." "Some absentees," Wood adds, "sought to preserve their autonomy by literally playing 'dumb,' feigning ignorance, inarticulateness, or deafness." Slave-holder Richard Wright "offered a £10 reward for a mustee slave named Nedd: 'about 20 Years old, he is a short well set Lad, full faced, short curl'd Hair, but not woolly, thick lip'd, small Eyes, speaks very plain, *and is very artful in making a Story to get off*, upon any examination'" (my emphasis; 259). But let us cross the border back into North Carolina (and into 1877), toward which the *South* Carolina incidents on record in *Black Majority* inevitably led. If deceit—or "artful" story-telling—might aid a fugitive slave, it also afforded freedmen like Uncle Julius a certain liberty, a certain purchase on themselves, even as they were dispossessed with the close of Reconstruction. In *The Sellout*, Paul Beatty—or Beatty's narrator—sums the matter up: "Back in the day, to avoid the succession of booby traps laid by the white man, black people had to constantly be thinking on their feet. You had to be ready with an impromptu quip or a down-home bromide that would disarm and humble a white provocateur. Maybe if your sense of humor reminded him there was a semblance of humanity underneath that burrhead, you might avoid a beating, get some of that back pay you were owed. Shit, one day of being black in the [1940s] was equal to three hundred years of improv training with the Groundlings and Second City" (243). That last remark is telling. Out of this history developed the sensibilities unique to African American comedy from Bert Williams to Richard Pryor to Dave Chapelle.[4]

"The Performance Was No New Thing"

"The Goophered Grapevine" appeared first in 1887 in the *Atlantic Monthly*, and, in that text, Chesnutt makes clear at once when the action of the story takes place: "ten years ago"—or 1877. That year, of course, saw the collapse of the last of the Reconstruction-era Republican state governments. John and Annie, the white couple who have come south from Ohio to buy some land "for a mere song" (5), typify certain post-Reconstruction developments (of which we have already made a survey): the influx of Northern investments in the New South (in fact, John flatters himself that his own operations are "often referred to by the local press as a striking illustration of the opportunities open to Northern capital in the development of Southern industries" [17]). Chesnutt has so arranged things as to represent, in this engagement between John and Uncle Julius, the new regime whereby Southern blacks often answered not to Southern white "owners," as they had before the war, but to white capitalists from the North. In this connection, consider John's account of his first impression of the plantation he ultimately buys:

> I went several times to look at a place that I thought might suit me. It was a plantation of considerable extent, that had formerly belonged to a wealthy man by the name of McAdoo. The estate had been for years involved in litigation between disputing heirs, during which period shiftless cultivation had well-nigh exhausted the soil. There had been a vineyard of some extent on the place, but it had not been attended to since the war, and had lapsed into utter neglect. The vines—here partly supported by decayed and broken-down trellises, there twining themselves among the branches of the slender saplings which had sprung up among them—grew in wild and unpruned luxuriance, and the few scattered grapes they bore were the undisputed prey of the first comer. (6)

John's eye is naturally proprietary. As we soon learn, and as John himself admits, the vineyard had not at all been "neglected" (17): Uncle Julius has been farming it, if on a modest scale, for twelve years—from 1865 to 1877, in fact, precisely the years of the Reconstruction (both presidential and Congressional). But John sees the land with a "white" gaze: a thing not used by a white man is, for him, simply a thing not genuinely "used." John's sense of entitlement is manifest—as manifest as had been the entitlement of white folks, in the late nineteenth century, to the western lands that had so long been "neglected" by Native Americans. So there is inevitably a note of finger-wagging, if indulgent, disapproval in John's voice—as if he had caught a child nicking a bit of candy—when he first lays eyes on Uncle Julius: "Upon Annie's complaining of weariness I led the way back to the yard, where a pine log, lying under a spreading elm, afforded a shady though somewhat hard seat. One end of the log was already occupied by a venerable looking colored man. He held on his knees a hat full of grapes, over which he was smacking his lips with great gusto, and a pile of grape-skins near him indicated that the performance was no new thing" (8).

John wastes no time in sizing Julius up, in an ethnological sort of way: "He was not entirely black, and this fact, together with the quality of his hair, which was about six inches long and very bushy, except on the top of his head, where he was quite bald, suggested a slight strain of other than negro blood. There was a shrewdness in his eyes, too, which was not altogether African, and which, as we afterwards learned from experience was indicative of a corresponding shrewdness in his character" (8). John makes race and intelligence a question of blood, and in this he is a man of his day. In the 1870s, there was much interest of a pseudo-scientific nature in character traits associated with Anglo-Saxon blood, Gallic blood, Teutonic blood, Negro blood, etc. Indeed, John speaks as if he is *au courant*—a reader, say, of Francis Galton's influential *Hereditary Genius: An Inquiry into Its Laws and Consequences* (1869). Galton—a pioneer in the infamous field of eugenics—there opines that "the average ability of the [ancient] Athenian race [that produced Plato] is, on the lowest possible estimate, very nearly two grades higher than our own—that is, about as much as our race is above that of the African negro. This estimate, which may seem prodigious to some, is confirmed by the quick intelligence and high culture of the Athenian commonalty, before whom literary works were recited, and works of art exhibited, of a far more severe character than could possibly be appreciated by the average of our race, the calibre of whose intellect is easily gauged by a glance at the contents of a railway book-stall" (342).[5] Any cunning, or "shrewdness," Julius might display must, of course, derive from white blood of some sort. (As for Julius's authentic *Negro* blood: some indication of what its legacy means to John may be gleaned from his later report that Julius "was a marvelous hand in the management of horses and dogs, with whose mental processes he manifested a greater familiarity than mere use would seem to account for" [30].) But all the while, in this story, Chesnutt lets us see that "race" (*pace* Galton) is more a role we learn to perform than an identity we are born into. Julius is a consummate performer, shrewd in ways that John's facile theories leave him unable to understand. Julius always wears the mask. He puts John and Annie at ease by playing the deferential, self-deprecating "darky": "But ef you en young miss dere doan' min' lis'nin' ter a ole nigger run on a minute er two w'ile you er restin', I kin 'splain to you how it all happen," he says, in introducing his tale of the "goophered," or bewitched, grapevine (9). He evokes, when it suits his purposes, nothing so much as the minstrel stage: "Now, ef dey's an'thing a nigger lub, nex' ter 'possum, en chick'n, en watermillyums, it's scuppernon's. Dey ain' nuffin dat kin stan' up side'n de scuppernon' for sweetness; sugar ain't a suckumstance ter scuppernon'. W'en de season is nigh 'bout ober, en de grapes begin ter swivel up des a little wid de wrinkles er ole age,—w'en de skin git sot' en brown,—den de scuppernon' make you smack yo' lip en roll yo' eye en wush fer mo'; so I reckon it ain' very stonishin' 'dat niggers lub scuppernon'" (9). And he doesn't so much affect naiveté as affect an *affected* naiveté, a thing sure to delight the more paternalistic instincts of a man like John: "Nex' spring, w'en de sap commence' ter rise in de scuppernon' vime, Henry"—another former slave—"tuk a ham one night. Whar'd he git de ham? *I* doan know; dey wa'n't no hams on de plantation 'cep'n' w'at 'uz in de smoke-house, but *I* never see Henry 'bout de smoke-house. But ez I wuz a-sayin', he tuk de ham ober ter Aun' Peggy's . . ." (12). Surely this is calculated. Otherwise, why all this coyness over a theft that happened decades earlier, if it happened at all? Does Julius simply mean to assure the white couple of his honesty? I doubt that; Julius is playing out the script of the darky who "professes too much"—which has the paradoxical effect of putting his auditors at ease. Notice also that Julius exercises great tact when criticizing—mocking, really—his old white master: "So atter a w'ile Mars Dugal' begin ter miss his scuppernon's." Parties unknown have been appropriating them. "Co'se he 'cuse' de niggers er it, but dey all 'nied it ter de las'. Mars Dugal' sot spring guns en steel traps, en he en de oberseah sot up nights once't er twice't, tel one night Mars Dugal'—he 'uz a monst'us keerless man—got his leg shot full er cow-peas. But somehow er nudder dey couldn' nebber ketch none er de niggers. I dunner how it happen, but it happen des like I tell you, en de grapes kep' on a-goin' des de same" (10). Julius knows perfectly well how it happened: Old Massa was an idiot. To call him a "monst'us keerless" man understates things in an artful fashion—all the more artful, given that the story allows us to suppose, without ever quite specifying the matter, that Julius is making most of this up on the spot. His portrait of Mars Dugal' is ingeniously satirical.

What does Julius intend to accomplish with the conjure tales that so delight his white auditors? First, of course, Julius hopes to dissuade John from buying the old plantation (which Julius might claim by right of long labor, if not by legal title). And this is precisely what John thinks he is up to: "I found, when I bought the vineyard, that Uncle Julius had occupied a cabin on the place for many years, and derived a respectable revenue from the product of the neglected grapevines. This, doubtless, accounted for his advice to me not to buy the vineyard, though whether it inspired the goopher story I am unable to state" (17–18). Notable first of all is the incoherence only a white man would fail to notice in his own remarks: *neglected* grapevines do not yield "a respectable revenue." But the reader has also to ask: is Julius really naive enough to suppose that a conjure story might frighten a calculating, up-to-date, Ohio white man like John out of buying a likely spread of land—a white man who amuses himself, as we later learn, by reading Herbert Spencer's hyper-rationalist *First Principles* (1860)?[6] Hardly. Julius's motives must be more complicated. Telling the stories gives him a sort of "mastery." At times he can, of course, affect John's behavior in ways beneficial to him; he gets a stipend out of John, and more. But he also exercises a certain moral and intellectual authority over John. The stories Julius tells are sophisticated parables about slavery, and also about post-Reconstruction race relations. For example, in "The Goophered Grapevine" the slave Henry is bewitched or "conjured" in a special way: when the sap rises in the vines each spring, old Henry grows spry and energetic (even to the point of "cuttin' up didos" with the women [13]); his hair grows back and curls up "in little balls, des like dis yer reg'lar grapy ha'r, en by de time de grapes got ripe his head look des like a bunch er grapes." When the sap falls in autumn the transformation runs in reverse: Henry's hair falls out, and he begins to get "ole and stiff in de j'ints ag'in" (13). Master McAdoo soon enough cashes in—it has to be "a monst'us cloudy night when a dollar git by him in de dahkness," Uncle Julius tells us (13)—by selling Henry dear in the spring and buying him back cheap in the fall, and in this way makes $5,000 in five years. The parable couldn't be plainer: the body of the slave is identified with the crop and with the land; the slave's body, like the land, is harrowed, plowed, inseminated, harvested.[7] Master McAdoo's exploitation of the slave's body perfectly complements his exploitation of the body of the land, which he exhausts and impoverishes out of greed to the point where, by the time the war breaks out, it yields him nothing.

But does Julius really believe in all this "conjure" business? Likely he does not. His interest in the tales he spins is moral, political, and even, by all appearances, "literary." Such tales as "Po' Sandy," "Hot-Foot Hannibal" and "The Gray Wolf's H'ant" seem made to order, as John comes to believe. These and other tales so perfectly suit Julius's ulterior motives that it is hard to believe he hasn't designed them expressly for the purpose of realizing those motives. So, it is not accurate to say that Julius "believes" in the conjure stories in quite the way that he pretends to, though this is not to say that his relation to the folk-culture of the slaves (or to their syncretic religious practices) is purely instrumental and artful. In the stories he tells, Julius sees how "conjuring" was itself a politically interested enterprise: almost always in these tales, conjuring is a way for slaves to exercise some kind of power over their masters. So, Chesnutt, through his mouthpiece Julius, offers up a penetrating analysis of the folklore of the slaves: he shows us how that folk-culture arose from specific material conditions, and how it was in fact a way of managing those conditions, both literarily (that is, symbolically), and also practically. The old folk tales Julius draws on, then, are complex in their motivation and social function—every bit as complex as the goopher stories Julius himself makes up (for we must conclude that a good deal of what he relates is improvised or concocted, as John himself surmises on a number of occasions [18, 29, 72, 82]). For this reason, the issue of whether or not Julius "believes in" the "truth" of these tales is doubly complicated: the tales surely do, as he feels, have a mythic "truth," quite apart from any "factual" truths about the fate of Henry, or Tenie and Sandy, they may propose to set forth. The stories he tells also adjust, ever so slightly, the relations of production—or the economy—of the plantation. Julius gets out of his tales a durable living as a chauffeur, a building for his congregation, clothes for a poor relation, and more. He makes John pay.

"We will find ourselves in their midst before they think it"

The Conjure Woman, as many scholars have pointed out, belongs alike to the postwar genres of "local-color fiction" and the "plantation tale." The development of both these genres is intimately linked to the social, economic, and cultural transformation of America in the post-Reconstruction years. These years saw the nationalization of markets for industrial and consumer goods, as intercontinental transportation and communication became a fait accompli; and, in a sense, the nationalization also of a common American "culture," as disseminated through magazines such as *The Atlantic Monthly*, for example, which now enjoyed a truly national readership, and in which a number of Chesnutt's stories first appeared. The effect of these developments was, almost inevitably, a gradual attenuation of radical "regional" differences, though this took a good many years to work itself out.[8] "Local-color" fiction, evolving out of this cultural matrix, and existing against its background, performed what the critic Richard Brodhead calls the work of "mourning" (introduction to *The Conjure Woman and Other*

Conjure Tales, 3): precisely at the moment when authentic regional differences were vanishing, these same differences became a literary fetish. Much local-color writing is therefore marked by nostalgia, and at times it tends, when it turns its attentions to the past, to clothe the antebellum years in an idyllic dress.

The "plantation tale" was a specific subgenre in the local-color tradition, and, as historians and literary critics have shown, its cultural function was complex: it arose just as Reconstruction ended—that is to say, just as the last Federal troops withdrew from the last of the Southern capitals to harbor them, and as political and economic "reconciliation" became a fact of American life (as I've suggested in chapters 2 and 3). Against this backdrop, it becomes clear that plantation tales, such as those published by Joel Chandler Harris (author of the Uncle Remus series) and Thomas Nelson Page, had, as Brodhead explains, "the more or less overt function of excusing the North's withdrawal from the plight of the freed southern slave" (5); they thereby had also, I'd add, "the more or less overt function" of restoring the relations of production peculiar to white supremacy (notwithstanding the *adjustments* to them that such men of wile as Uncle Julius made). Freed slaves in these stories seem to have little but nostalgia for the old days, and remain with their former owners as "faithful retainers." The appetite for this new fiction was insatiable; it sold like hotcakes. A complementary development in historiography attended and abetted this literary revolution. Scholars such as William Dunning (at Columbia University) began to produce a prodigious number of books about the Reconstruction, the tendency of which Du Bois characterizes in "The Propaganda of History," the last chapter in *Black Reconstruction* (touched on already). "Herein lies more than mere omission and difference of emphasis," says Du Bois. "The treatment of the period of Reconstruction reflects small credit upon American historians as scientists. We have too often a deliberate attempt so to change the facts of history that the story will make pleasant reading for Americans" (713)—and, as he indicates in every chapter of *Black Reconstruction*, so as also to *adjust* Americans to the new forms industry and commerce assumed in the late nineteenth and early twentieth centuries, whose issue for black folk, and more especially *poor* black folk, was ruin. Ruin for many white folks, too, of course. But they could always count—in the South especially, where their poverty was often at its worst—on the "psychological wage" (as Du Bois reminds us) that white supremacy paid them: "It must be remembered that the white group of laborers, while they received a low wage, were compensated in part by a sort of public and psychological wage. They were given public deference and titles of courtesy because they were white. They were admitted freely with all classes of white people to public functions, public parks, and the best schools. The police were drawn from their ranks, and the courts, dependent upon their votes, treated them with such leniency as to encourage lawlessness. Their vote selected public officials, and while this had small effect upon the economic situation, it had great effect upon their personal treatment and the deference shown them. White schoolhouses were the best in the community, and conspicuously placed, and they cost anywhere from twice to ten times as much per capita as the colored schools. The newspapers specialized on news that flattered the poor whites and almost utterly ignored the Negro except in crime and ridicule" (*Black Reconstruction* 700). So much for the political function that the new literature and historiography alike performed.

A typical statement of the "plantation" ideal is given by Colonel Owen in Chesnutt's story "The Passing of Grandison," collected in his second book, *The Wife of His Youth and Other Stories of the Color Line* and discussed at some length below. The Colonel has just elicited from one of his slaves an expression of devotion, which, unbeknownst to him (so caught up in the myth is he), will prove to have been terrifically disingenuous: "The colonel was beaming. This was true gratitude, and his feudal heart thrilled at such appreciative homage. What cold-blooded, heartless monsters they were who would break up this blissful relationship of kindly protection on the one hand, of wise subordination and loyal dependence on the other! The colonel always became indignant at the mere thought of such wickedness" (193). If the real Col. Owenses of the South had lived long enough to read Jefferson Davis's *Rise and Fall of the Confederate Government* they'd have been deeply gratified. In the "plantation tales"—to which genre Davis's book has a specific relation—black men and women seem perfectly content with their condition, and the stories in which they appear seem devoted to the purpose of assuring Northern readers (and Southern ones) that things in the South aren't so bad at all, and that labor relations between former slaves and former owners are essentially cordial, productive, and healthy. Chesnutt himself was well aware that "plantation tales," together with other, cognate media—from minstrelsy to popular novels to history and, later, to film (*Birth of a Nation*)—fulfilled precisely this political-economic function.[9]

In any case, it was into these combined literary and economic circumstances that Chesnutt introduced his complex and subtler (even countercultural) version of the "local-color" "plantation tale." There is an analogy to be drawn between the "conjures" described in Uncle Julius's stories and the stories themselves: both are exercised—partly effectively, partly not—against "white" authority. And we can regard *The Conjure Woman* itself in this light: as a partly effective, though not completely satisfactory, effort on Chesnutt's part to subvert "white" literary authority. The antagonism here is played out even in the history of the book's composition and publication. It was Chesnutt's first book, and its contents were arrived at though a compromise on Chesnutt's part with his (white) establishment publisher, Houghton Mifflin and Company, of Boston. Chesnutt felt that the plantation tale genre was too constricting. It didn't allow for a broad range of representation of African American life, and he had determined to abandon it. Houghton Mifflin, however, declined at first to publish the non-plantation fiction he had begun to write, and asked him instead to submit a number of new "conjure" stories, together with those he had already published; out of these, Houghton selected what became *The Conjure Woman*. Julius's position as a storyteller addressing, and being constrained by, an exclusively white audience, matches, in certain respects, Chesnutt's position as an African American author writing within an almost exclusively white literary establishment (one wonders whether his editors at Houghton "got" that analogy): he is able to do remarkable things, many of them subtly and ironically subversive, but there is something unsatisfactory about the fact that he, like Julius, never really has his liberty.[10]

It is worth asking now what Chesnutt intended to accomplish in the *Conjure Woman*. We have seen that he essentially "dramatizes" his relation to his white audience in the relationship between Julius and the white Northerner, John. The stories perform, for Chesnutt, a certain ironic, educative role. He is (like Julius) at once charming his readers and criticizing and admonishing them; and he does this in ways that no doubt remain unknown to some of his white readers (for that matter, many of his early readers assumed he was white). Chesnutt also engages in indirect literary criticism: he is revising and critiquing the "plantation tale" genre, and the "plantation myth" itself (as he does in "The Passing of Grandison")—and doing so, moreover, in astonishingly ingratiating ways. Citing Chesnutt's aspiration, as expressed in an 1890 entry in his journal, to "elevate" his white readers, Joseph McElrath and Robert Leitz speak tellingly of Chesnutt's effort to "mask his condescension toward unregenerate white readers," the better to win their confidence. McElrath and Leitz continue, again quoting from Chesnutt's journal: "The 'trumpet tones' used by the abolitionists would not work: 'the subtle almost undefinable feeling of repulsion toward the negro, which is common to most Americans—and easily enough accounted for—cannot be stormed and taken by assault; the garrison will not capitulate: so their position must be mined [as, say, the Confederate position was at Petersburg], and we will find ourselves in their midst before they think it.' [Chesnutt] would win 'social recognition and equality' for the African American by accustoming 'the public mind to the idea; and while amusing them . . . lead them on imperceptibly, unconsciously step by step to the desired state of feeling'" (19). This Chesnutt accomplishes, insofar as anyone can, in *The Conjure Woman*. In the years to come he would rely increasingly on the trumpet tones of the abolitionists, in novels of protest like *The Marrow of Tradition* and *The Colonel's Dream*. But first there would come *The Wife of His Youth and Other Stories of the Color Line* (1900), which is, like its predecessor, a landmark of turn-of-the-century American letters, and a masterpiece in its genre.

"The Wife of His Youth"

The conjure stories are brilliant. But Chesnutt could not long remain satisfied mining a vein adulterated by, or under-mining a position fortified by the white-defined conventions of the dialect tale. In fact, already in 1889, ten years before *The Conjure Woman* appeared, we find him writing the novelist and lawyer Albion Tourgée to the following effect: "I think I have about used up the old Negro who serves as mouthpiece, and I shall drop him in future stories, as well as much of the dialect" (*To Be an Author* 44). The problem was that plantation tales particularly, and dialect tales more generally, narrowed a writer's range. "All of the good negroes," Chesnutt observed in a letter to George Washington Cable, "whose virtues have been given to the world through the columns of the *Century* [a popular literary magazine], have been blacks, full-blooded, and their chief virtues have been their dog-like fidelity and devotion to their old masters. Such characters exist," he added, "but I don't care to write about these people" (*To Be an Author* 65). He wanted, he explained, to write about lawyers, judges, doctors, botanists, and musicians—about the full range of African American experience as he had come to know it in Cleveland and elsewhere. "The Wife of His Youth," the title story of his second volume, achieves precisely this, while at the same time obliquely registering the difficult relations that often obtain between "vernacular" and "mainstream" cultures in African American writing.

"Mr. Ryder was going to give a ball" (101). So begins this story of the color line. Mr. Ryder, Chesnutt's narrator tells us, is the "dean" of the Blue Vein Society of Groveland (a fictional city based on Chesnutt's native Cleveland) (101). The Blue Veins are a society of colored folk established to "maintain correct social standards," and to foster the general appreciation of finer things (for example, the poetry of Tennyson). "By accident, combined perhaps with some natural affinity," we are told, with dry understatement that at times approaches sarcasm, "the society consisted of individuals who were, generally speaking, more white than black. Some envious outsider made the suggestion that no one was eligible for membership who was not white enough to show blue veins. The suggestion was readily adopted by those who were not of the favored few, and since that time the society, though possessing a longer and more pretentious name, had been known far and wide as the 'Blue Vein Society,' and its members as the 'Blue Veins'" (101). There is a nice equivocation here: the affiliation in question is grounded partly on what might be called "biological," and partly on "cultural," criteria. The Blue Vein Society is compromised by the late-nineteenth-century American tendency to make social distinctions a matter of "color." It might well be said that we find practiced, amongst the Blue Veins, a kind of intraracial racism; and that, for this reason, the Blue Vein Society is an ideological adjunct of white supremacy, whereby men and women of color are taught to despise (or anyway to distrust) those aspects of themselves that the culture as a whole deems "colored." Instill in African Americans (or colonial subjects) habits of self-doubt, and the work of white supremacy, in its political and economic dimensions, is well advanced. Men wait upon false promise; capital sits at ease. It is as fine a mechanism as a Reagan or a Paul Ryan budget.

The problem is well illustrated in the following passage, where Mr. Ryder is allowed to speak for himself: "'I have no race prejudice,' he would say, 'but we people of mixed blood are ground between the upper and the nether millstone. Our fate lies between absorption by the white race and extinction in the black. The one doesn't want us yet, but may take us in time. The other would welcome us, but it would be for us a backward step. 'With malice towards none, with charity for all,' we must do the best we can for ourselves and those who are to follow us. Self-preservation is the first law of nature'" (104). The white supremacist Devil is in the details—in, for example, the asymmetry in terms that ought to be parallel: "*absorption* by the white race and *extinction* in the black." And in appealing to "the first law of nature," "self-preservation," Mr. Ryder engages one of the most powerful of late-nineteenth-century racist metaphors—the metaphor, borrowed from Darwin and associated with "social Darwinism," of a "struggle for existence." Mr. Ryder's thinking is not unaffected by these ideas, which incidentally include the corollary idea in Eurocentric anthropology that "black" is to "white" as "primitive" is to "advanced" (hence the "*backward* step" of which Mr. Ryder speaks). The sad confusion of it all is manifest: this social Darwinian talk of "laws of nature" and "extinction" sorts very uncomfortably, and not a little ironically, with the democratic sentiment of Lincoln's Second Inaugural Address, which Mr. Ryder echoes: "With malice toward none, with charity for all, with firmness in the right as God gives us to see the right, let us strive to finish the work we are in, to bind up the nation's wounds, to care for him who shall have borne the battle and for his widow and orphan, to do all which may achieve and cherish a just and lasting peace among ourselves and with all nations" (361). Mr. Ryder's invocation of Lincoln in 1890 (the date of the story's action) only reminds the reader how far the nation in general, and the Republican Party in particular, had moved from the proposition that all men are created equal: disenfranchisement was well under way, and the working class in the South had been thoroughly divided (and therefore weakened) through the deft cultivation of racial animosity and anti-unionism. "The Wife of His Youth" is manifestly a story about the legacy of the war that had, by the time Lincoln spoke in 1865, become a war *for* enfranchisement (a prospect Lincoln entertained in the last speech he ever gave [*Speeches* 365]). In fact, making its unsettling way into the Blue Vein Society is precisely what our narrator calls "a bit of the old plantation life," and a genuine relic of the antebellum years (105): the illiterate former slave with whom Mr. Ryder had lived in Missouri, as husband, before the war, and from whom he has been separated since 1861.

Mr. Ryder, it happens, is in love with a Mrs. Molly Dixon, a young widow who had been born into the highest circles of Washington's Reconstruction-era colored society, and who now, having relocated to Groveland after her husband's death, is the most accomplished, sought-after (and light-skinned) of the Blue Veins. And on the afternoon of the evening of the ball that was to have afforded Mr. Ryder the perfect opportunity to propose to her, he receives a visit from Liza Jane, the wife of his youth alluded to above: "She was very black—so black that her toothless gums, revealed when she opened her mouth to speak, were not red, but blue." Here and there, from underneath her bonnet, protrude tufts of "short gray wool" (105). And her speech, as rendered here, and by contrast to the other black voices in the story, is thick with the plantation dialect spoken by Uncle Julius in *The Conjure Woman*. Mr. Ryder has long ago abandoned his antebellum name, Sam Taylor, and the changes of twenty-five years, together with a marked elevation in social class, have made him unrecognizable. Liza Jane appeals to him simply because he is a man of consequence in the black community of Groveland. Can he, she wonders, help her find her long-lost husband?[11] She relates the story of her quarter-century quest, which took her through every major city in the South, and in due course she produces an old daguerreotype. Mr. Ryder gazes "intently at the portrait," we are told: "It was faded with time, but the features were still distinct, and it was easy to see what manner of man it had represented" (108). Into that last, quietly bitter clause are folded the regrets, the guilt, and the ambivalence of a lifetime of self-invention—all the shameful fears of suffering "extinction" in a blackness so complete as to show "blue gums" instead of "blue veins." When Liza Jane takes her leave—and as she unwittingly makes herself the occasion for the "kindly amusement" of passers-by on the street outside—Mr. Ryder retires to his bedroom and stands "for a long time before the mirror of his dressing-case, gazing thoughtfully at the reflection of his own face" (109). What manner of man had he become? Could he somehow bring this reflection into the same frame with that image in the old daguerreotype? Must he always, when gazing in the mirror, see double? Must he always see there something dubious, or even duplicitous? Must he forever see either a black body, or a man, either "wool," or hair, either "black skin," or skin, and never both at once?

As it happens, of course, he acknowledges this thing of darkness his. After hypothetically putting the case of such a man as himself to the Blue Veins, who have gathered in his house for the ball, he asks them all: what should a man in this situation do—acknowledge his first wife and bind himself to her, or marry the woman of his later aspirations? Mrs. Dixon herself makes the answer: "She had listened, with parted lips and streaming eyes. She was the first to speak: 'He should have acknowledged her'" (112). When all the company agrees, as Mr. Ryder expected they would, he turns toward "the closed door of an adjoining room, while every eye followed him in wondering curiosity": "He came back in a moment, leading by the hand his visitor of the afternoon, who stood startled and trembling at the sudden plunge into this scene of brilliant gayety." "'Ladies and gentlemen,'" he says, "'this is the woman, and I am the man, whose story I have told you. Permit me to introduce you to the wife of my youth'" (112). To an extent, the story concerns the relation of vernacular black culture to the white standards against which it was invidiously judged. Chesnutt hopes to achieve here a kind of "triple" solidarity: a solidarity of the black working class and the black middle class, upon which basis only, he felt, real progress in civil and political rights could be made; a solidarity of "vernacular" and "literary" cultures, upon which basis only genuine literary art could be produced; and, of course, a solidarity, or fusion, of "blackness" and "whiteness," upon which basis only will the color line ever be transcended.

And it may well be that, in this restrained and affecting story, Chesnutt confronts some vestigial measure of self-hatred that the culture of white supremacy had left even him with: the imperfectly subdued note of disgust that attaches to the description of Liza Jane, with her toothless blue gums and white wool, may be telling (though it likely attaches only to Mr. Ryder, not to his author).

"The Passing of Grandison"

Eric Sundquist, in a fine reading of "The Wife of His Youth," expresses its complexities well: "Ryder's choice operates on [several] levels . . . Included within his recognition of Liza Jane are several implicit indications of Chesnutt's own cultural obligations: to join with the lower classes in the struggle for rights; to put the good of the community before the advance of the few who were able to enter directly into the white social and cultural mainstream; and to take control of the popular conceptions of 'the old plantation life' that are being generated by racist commentary and unscrupulous artistry" (300). Nowhere does Chesnutt better achieve this latter end than in "The Passing of Grandison," a brilliant satire of "popular conceptions" of the old plantation life collected first in *The Wife of His Youth*. Set in the early 1850s, when the passage of the Fugitive Slave Bill had much agitated the slavery question, the story concerns the undistinguished (and spoiled) first son of a Kentucky slave-holding family of marked aristocratic pretensions—the Owens. Charity Lomax, the girl of Dick Owen's dreams, refuses to entertain his advances until such time as he proves himself a man. As an example of what she has in mind—and, incidentally, congratulating herself on her own Quaker ancestry—she points to the actions of a man who went to prison for attempting to help a fugitive slave escape. Not that Charity is herself a serious abolitionist; she admires the Yankee for his courage more than for his convictions. In response to the challenge, young Dick conspires to free a slave himself: "I'll run off one of the old man's," this model Cavalier says to Charity, "we've got too many anyway" (190). The only problem is how to do it. Dick decides on a trip North, with a slave, Grandison, as a servant. The Colonel, needless to say, has no idea what his frivolous son intends to do. In New York and Boston, Dick so arranges things that Grandison has every opportunity to escape; he even notifies—anonymously, of course—the local abolitionists in Boston, and, sure enough, they seek Grandison out. But to Dick's utter vexation the slave never once takes the bait. "'Mars Dick,' he says," wearing the mask, "dese yer abolitioners is jes' pesterin' de life out er me tryin' ter git me ter run away. I don' pay no 'tention ter 'em, but dey riles me so sometimes dat I'm feared I'll hit some of 'em some er dese days, an' dat mought git me inter trouble. I ain' said nuffin' ter you 'bout it, Mars Dick, fer I did n' wanter 'sturb yo' min'; but I don' like it, suh; no, suh, I don'! Is we gwine back home 'fo' long, Mars Dick?'" (197). Dick has a good mind to scold him, and yet, on reflection, he has to concede the point: "How could he, indeed, find fault with one who so sensibly recognized his true place in the economy of civilization, and kept it with such touching fidelity?" (198).

No doubt Grandison acts and speaks (and even gestures) so as to flatter every instinct toward mastery that can animate a white man's heart. When, in an interview designed to determine his trustworthiness for the trip North, Grandison is asked whether he envies the "poor free negroes down by the plank road, with no kind master to look after them and no mistress to give them medicine when they're sick," he heartily replies: "'Well, I sh'd jes' reckon I is better off, suh, dan dem low-down free niggers, suh! Ef anybody ax 'em who dey b'long ter, dey has ter say nobody, er e'se lie erbout it. Anybody ax me who I b'longs ter, I ain' got no 'casion ter be shame' ter tell 'em, no, suh, 'deed I ain', suh!'" (193). At this, the Colonel "beams"—and then we read (in a passage quoted earlier to different purposes): "This was true gratitude, and his feudal heart thrilled at such appreciative homage" (193). Colonel Owen, of course, has persuaded himself that Grandison really is contented: he doesn't own a plantation so much as a "plantation myth," and the circumstance has placed him out of touch with reality. Grandison, like Uncle Julius, wears a mask; and to men like the Colonel and Dick he is utterly opaque, completely invisible. They simply fail to see him—which is precisely what Grandison wants, for he is up to something subversive of all good slave-holding order and of "his true place in the *economy* of civilization," to adapt Dick's phrase.[12] Never once does it occur to Dick that Grandison may not wish to flee without first securing the freedom of his family and of his fiancée, who of course remain at his old Kentucky home. Grandison, though very much on the scene, is invisible *as a husband, son, nephew, etc.* Dick Owen's blindness was epidemic. Peter H. Wood observes: "Dwelling at length upon aspects of white involvement seriously distorts the actual experience of black runaways. It lends misleading support to the traditional assumption of white interpreters that slaves, stripped of initiative in so many ways, were incapable of independent thought and action. Even in the act of running away, when they quite literally and obviously took their lives in their own hands, these individuals have been misrepresented as passive objects, 'forced,' 'urged,' 'allowed,' or 'provoked' to escape by various whites. This bias began among the early slaveowners themselves, who refused to acknowledge among runaways signs of rationality, emotion, and independence, which they hoped to both ignore and suppress." "The drive to sustain family connections was a significant motivation of which white owners," Wood adds, "were only occasionally aware" (248).

At his wit's end, Dick Owen resorts to a remarkable stratagem. He takes Grandison across the border into Canada, on the other side of Niagara Falls. "'You are now in Canada, Grandison,'" Dick says on their arrival, "'where your people go when they run away from their masters. If you wished, Grandison, you might walk away from me this very minute, and I could not lay my hand upon you to take you back.'" But the mask remains in place: "'Let's go back ober de ribber, Mars Dick,'" Grandison replies. "'I's feared I'll lose you ovuh heah, an' den I won' hab no marster, an' won't nebber be able to git back home no mo'" (199). And at this point Chesnutt does something very peculiar with the narrative: he briefly changes its point of view. Dick leaves Grandison alone, drops into a nearby inn for lunch (where a young lady serves him), and then returns, irritated, to find his faithful servant sound asleep, waiting. Whereupon we read:

> Dick retraced his footsteps towards the inn. The young woman chanced to look out of the window and saw the handsome young gentleman she had waited on a few minutes before, standing in the road a short distance away, apparently engaged in earnest conversation with a colored man employed as hostler for the inn. She thought she saw something pass from the white man to the other, but at that moment her duties called her away from the window, and when she looked out again the young gentleman had disappeared, and the hostler, with two other young men of the neighborhood, one white and one colored, were walking rapidly towards the Falls. (201)

This is a curious maneuver. Throughout the rest of the story the narrator is closely attached to the mind of Dick Owen. What Dick knows, we know; all his motives and machinations are laid bare. But here we witness the scene from the point of view of the waitress at the inn, a woman entirely unknown to us—a walk-on. Chesnutt hides from us, just as he does from her, the details of what passes between Dick and the colored hostler, and this is by no means without consequence. For, some weeks later, after Dick has gone home, and after he has married Charity Lomax, Grandison reappears on the old plantation, telling a story of abduction and torture, the truth of which the reader has no means accurately to assess (though good reason to doubt in large measure). Here is the story, as refracted through the "feudal heart" of Colonel Owen:

> It's astounding, the depths of depravity the human heart is capable of! I was coming along the road three miles away, when I heard some one call me from the roadside. I pulled up the mare, and who should come out of the woods but Grandison. The poor nigger could hardly crawl along, with the help of a broken limb. I was never more astonished in my life. You could have knocked me down with a feather. He seemed pretty far gone,—he could hardly talk above a whisper,—and I had to give him a mouthful of whiskey to brace him up so he could tell his story. It's just as I thought from the beginning, Dick; Grandison had no notion of running away; he knew when he was well off, and where his friends were. All the persuasions of abolition liars and runaway niggers did not move him. But the desperation of those fanatics knew no bounds; their guilty consciences gave them no rest. They got the notion somehow that Grandison belonged to a nigger-catcher, and had been brought North as a spy to help capture ungrateful runaway servants. They actually kidnaped him— just think of it!—and gagged him and bound him and threw him rudely into a wagon, and carried him into the gloomy depths of a Canadian forest, and locked him in a lonely hut, and fed him on bread and water for three weeks. One of the scoundrels wanted to kill him, and persuaded the others that it ought to be done; but they got to quarrelling about how they should do it, and before they had their minds made up Grandison escaped, and, keeping his back steadily to the North Star, made his way, after suffering incredible hardships, back to the old plantation, back to his master, his friends, and his home. Why, it's as good as one of Scott's novels! Mr. Simms or some other one of our Southern authors ought to write it up. (203)

It is a story as good as one of Walter Scott's novels, and one, in addition, altogether worthy of the pen of that pro-slavery apologist from South Carolina, William Gilmore Simms.[13] But is it the truth, the whole truth, and nothing but the truth? Dick, of course, is in no position to contradict Grandison in front of the Colonel, to whom he lied about his misadventures in the North. He does, it is true, wonder aloud whether "the yarn sounds a little improbable," if only as a hint to Charity that he hadn't acted completely ignobly (203). But Chesnutt leaves the reader in doubt. Has Grandison fabricated this tale, the better to gladden the feudal heart of the Colonel, who, predictably, is reduced to tears at its recital, and who, in gratitude, "kills the fatted calf" for Grandison, and relaxes his customary vigilance (204)? Is Grandison—having somehow smoked Dick out—making things hot for his young master by allowing his bride to conclude that he is both cruel and foolish? Has Grandison simply embellished a tale that conveys the truth? What exactly did pass between Dick Owen and that hostler, and what followed up in Canada? The reader cannot say; the narrative never allows Grandison to emerge from behind his mask—that is, until the last paragraph. And even then, when he stands and unfolds himself, all the capital in Kentucky couldn't fetch him.

Grandison, it turns out, has returned to Kentucky for one purpose only: to free his family and fiancée. "About three weeks after Grandison's return," we learn, "the Colonel's faith in sable humanity was rudely shaken, and its foundations almost broke up."

> One Monday morning Grandison was missing. And not only Grandison, but his wife, Betty the maid; his mother, aunt Eunice; his father, uncle Ike; his brothers, Tom and John, and his little sister Elsie, were likewise absent from the plantation; and a hurried search and inquiry in the neighborhood resulted in no information as to their whereabouts. So much valuable property could not be lost without an effort to recover it, and the wholesale nature of the transaction carried consternation to the hearts of those whose ledgers were chiefly bound in black. Extremely energetic measures were taken by the colonel and his friends. The fugitives were traced, and followed from point to point, on their northward run through Ohio. Several times the hunters were close upon their heels, but the magnitude of the escaping party begot unusual vigilance on the part of those who sympathized with the fugitives, and strangely enough, the underground railroad seemed to have had its tracks cleared and signals set for this particular train. Once, twice, the colonel thought he had them, but they slipped through his fingers.
>
> One last glimpse he caught of his vanishing property, as he stood, accompanied by a United States marshal, on a wharf at a port on the south shore of Lake Erie. On the stern of a small steamboat which was receding rapidly from the wharf, with her nose pointing toward Canada, there stood a group of familiar dark faces, and the look they cast backward was not one of longing for the fleshpots of Egypt. The colonel saw Grandison point him out to one of the crew of the vessel, who waved his hand derisively toward the colonel. The latter shook his fist impotently—and the incident was closed. (204–5)

The Colonel's power comes to nothing, and the Fugitive Slave Law of 1850 is made a very dead letter. He's been outfoxed by a man who understands much better than he ever will the illusions under which the nation he now leaves in his wake labors, and who understands as well how to exploit those illusions for subversive purposes. The point is plain: Grandison is everywhere inaccessible to the Colonel. The Colonel owns him, supposes himself on intimate terms with him; but in fact, Grandison is something less to him even than a stranger.[14] And a certain suspicion that his readers stood on the other side of the color line from him led Charles Chesnutt to shield a little of Grandison from their scrutiny as well. The reader sees him always as from a distance, and his backward look, with its derisive jocularity, is as unsettling as *Brown v. Board of Education* to the pretensions and institutions of white supremacy. The fleshpots of Egypt indeed.

"The Passing of Grandison" suggests many things, among them that the "plantation myth" didn't merely allow whites to misrecognize their real relations to people of color in such a way as happily, and in all good conscience, to oppress them and thereby secure cheap labor (and degrade laborers of all races). It also dialectically allowed for a certain impenetrability, a certain privacy, a certain space within the veil, as Du Bois might say—of which black Americans could at times avail themselves. It is quite as if the "plantation myth" were a one-way mirror. On the one side of it stand white men who see in it (though of this they remain unaware) only the reflection of their own fantasies; on the other side stand black men for whom that mirror is in fact a window into the darkest recesses of the white man's heart. America is the station-house interrogation room in which white and black stand separated by that one-way mirror so favored by directors of cop shows. For a man such as Grandison, Colonel Owen and his kind are perfectly transparent (as the Staten Island police are to men like Eric Garner). Men such as Grandison know all the codes. And when Chesnutt's art achieves its ends—and it often does much more than merely achieve them—it inverts the mirror, lays bare the codes, and begins the work of disencumbering white American readers of their chief embarrassment: the color-consciousness that blinds them to their own heart of darkness. "The object of my writings," Chesnutt once wrote in his journal, "would be not so much the elevation of the colored people as the elevation of the whites" (19).

The House Behind the Cedars

Chesnutt's first novel, *The House Behind the Cedars*, appeared in 1900. The plot follows the contours of what literary critics sometimes call the novel of "the tragic mulatto." Rena Walden and her brother John are born, out of wedlock, to a light-skinned "colored" mother and a white father. Though known in their native town of Patesville, North Carolina, as "black," they are light enough in complexion to pass for white. And this they do in neighboring South Carolina in the fading plantation town of Clarence, to which John had removed just before the Civil War began, and in which he has been living, for ten years, as a "white" man. As the action of the novel opens, he is a distinguished lawyer and moves at the highest levels of white society, to which he had gained admittance, in part, by marriage into a prominent white family (he is now a widower). Rena, a young woman of remarkable beauty, attracts the attention of George Tryon, a highborn white man from eastern North Carolina who has retained the services of John to settle various legal affairs in South Carolina. Tryon proposes marriage, and, after an anguished week during which she wonders whether or not she should reveal that she is "black," Rena decides to accept, and a date is set for the wedding. A series of accidents worthy of a novel by Thomas Hardy shortly brings out the novel's tragic dimension: Tryon, a proud white supremacist in the post-Reconstruction mode, discovers the "truth" about Rena; repudiates her; is beset by doubts about his convictions; resolves to marry her anyway, but is too late: the lingering shock of his disavowal, and the predatory attentions of an unscrupulous man named Wain, drive Rena to despair and break her health. She dies of exposure after trying to make her way home, on foot, to rejoin her aging mother, who waits back in Patesville, in the house behind the cedars where Rena was born.

What distinguishes this novel is its psychological complexity. *The House Behind the Cedars* is best read, in fact, as an investigation of the psychosexual problem of the color line; it concerns "white" America's relationship to "blackness," which, in turn, concerns nothing less than white Americans relationship to the body as such, and to sexuality. At one point in the novel, before he has discovered the truth about Rena's parentage, Tryon visits Patesville to see his mother's cousin, Dr. Green. The doctor is out and, while awaiting his return, Tryon idly peruses a medical journal, which contains an article on ethnology. "The writer maintained," the narrator tells us, "that owing to a special tendency of the negro blood, however diluted, to revert to the African type, any future amalgamation of the white and black races, which foolish and wicked Northern negrophiles predicted as the ultimate result of the new conditions confronting the South, would therefore be an ethnological impossibility; for the smallest trace of negro blood would inevitably drag down the superior race to the inferior level, and reduce the fair Southland, already devastated by the hand of the invader, to the frightful level of Hayti, the awful example of negro incapacity" (338).[15] Chesnutt directs our attention to a singular white panic. Nothing less than a fear of falling into animality motivates this article, whose argument is, in fact, conventional to the 1890s. The white imagination—the imagination of what the article in question here calls "the all-pervading, all-conquering" Anglo-Saxon race (338)—felt itself everywhere confronting a "savagery" that had at once to be disciplined, repressed, and, where possible, sublimated into "useful" enterprise (in agricultural and industrial labor—a labor force debased in wages, imperiled by the trap of convict-leasing, and denied the right to unionize or vote). It is savagery of this sort that Tryon imagines he can detect beneath the thin "veneer" of civilization with which Rena has bedecked herself. Having (temporarily) resolved to go through with the marriage (after first backing out of it), he approaches the house behind the cedars, to which, some weeks earlier, Rena had returned to visit her mother. It so happens that on the night of Tryon's arrival in Patesville, Rena's family had arranged a party to receive a visiting cousin. Tryon arrives, approaches the house, peers through its windows, and spies Rena dancing: "To-night his eyes had been opened—he had seen her with the mask thrown off, a true daughter of a race in which the sensuous enjoyment of the moment took precedence of taste or sentiment or any of the higher emotions. Her few months of boarding-school, her brief association with white people, had evidently been a mere veneer over the underlying negro, and their effects had slipped away as soon as the intercourse had ceased. With the monkey-like imitativeness of the negro she had copied the manners of white people while she lived among them, and had dropped them with equal facility when they ceased to serve a purpose" (416). Several things bear mentioning. First, note the association, inevitable in the discourse of white supremacy, of "color" with the flesh—with the senses. To be "colored" is to have a uniquely intense relation to the body (here, to "sensuous enjoyment" [416]). White is to black as mind is to body, or as soul is to body. Given that in the Christian, patriarchal culture of which Tryon is a representative, the flesh is always to be disciplined, always to be subordinated to "higher" purposes and emotions, any people thought to be peculiarly "sensual" were regarded with wariness, and were, in the post-Reconstruction South, subject to severe repression (the castrations that often accompanied lynchings and the white hysteria about "black rape" are the worst symptoms of this disease). A pathological anxiety about the body and sexuality afflicts men like Tryon, and here he projects it outward onto a racial "Other": what Tryon would repress in himself he oppresses in the culture as a whole. Ask your typical American white man what he thinks of parti-colored humanity, set whirling on the savannas of Africa half a million years ago yesterday, and he tells you instead about himself, whether he knows it or not.

The most vicious expression of the ideas animating Tryon is to be found in the Christian, scriptural argument for a "polygenetic" order of creation, whereby the "negro" was brought into being along with the beasts over whom God gave (white) mankind dominion. The idea had a certain vogue in pro-slavery propaganda of the 1840s and 1850s. But its fullest expression dates to the post-Reconstruction era, when Negrophobia reached its height, and Galtonian eugenics began its long slouch toward Nuremberg. Charles Carroll revived, and refined to spectacularly odious degree, the pre-Adamite arguments of earlier writers such as Samuel Cartwright (1793–1863).[16] In *The Negro a Beast*, Carroll writes, speaking of mankind and "Negroes" as if they belong to different species (the former category cannot include the latter):

> Thus, while but two creations—matter and mind—combine to perfect the Negro, three creations—matter, mind and soul—combine to perfect man. While these two creations—matter and mind—exist in an imperfect state in the germs [i.e., the sperm and ovum] of the male and female Negro, as mutually dependent sides or parts of the life system of the animal, three creations—matter, mind and spiritual life—exist in an imperfect state in the germs of the male and female man, as mutually dependent sides or parts of the life system of man; and such is the attraction between matter and mind as they exist in their imperfect state in the germs of man and the Negro that sexual intercourse between the two will unite and perfect these two creations. But the soul creation in its imperfect and dependent state in the germ of the man, finds no corresponding side or part in the negress. Hence, this creation having no attraction remains passive, and if conception ensues from the union of the germs and the consequent perfecting of the matter and mind creations of man and the Negro, this passive creation forms no part of the offspring of this unnatural union. Thus, it is impossible for either side or part of the life system of man—the male or the female—to transmit these three creations—matter, mind and soul to their offspring by the Negro, in whom matter and mind alone exists. In other words, the male and the female can only transmit to their offspring such creations as are common to both. (133–34)

Not all white Southerners held this belief, of course, or proclaimed it; but hundreds of thousands certainly acted as if they did. No other conclusion is possible for any reader of Douglas Blackmon's *Slavery by Another Name: The Re-Enslavement of Black Americans from the Civil War to World War II* (2008); or *Without Sanctuary: Lynching Photography in America* (2000), by James Allen et al.; or *At the Hands of Persons Unknown: The Lynching of Black America* (2003), by Philip Dray; or *Blood in the Water: The Attica*

Uprising of 1971 and Its Legacy (2017), by Heather Ann Thompson; or *I Can't Breathe: A Killing On Bay Street* (2017) by Matt Taibbi. Chesnutt's Tryon has his literary home somewhere in the neighborhood of Carroll's *The Negro a Beast*. As George Frederickson points out in *The Black Image in the White Mind*, Carroll argues that "the apelike Negro was the actual 'tempter of Eve,' and miscegenation was the greatest of all sins—the true reason for God's destruction of slavery. As for the mulatto, the offspring of an unnatural relationship, he did not have the 'right to live'; for it was the mulattoes, Carroll contended, who were the rapists and criminals of the present time" (277). Rena Walden is the product of this original sin; should he sleep with her, Tyron would not only participate in it, but in some sense commend it. Frederickson cites, as evidence that Carroll's phobia was shared, an often-quoted document: "A Southern Woman's View," by the Georgia-born novelist Corra Mae Harris. The lynching of Sam Hose outside Atlanta on April 23, 1899 occasioned the article, which Harris sent for publication to the *Independent* (based in New York). She meant to rebuke and instruct its editor, William Hayes Ward, who had lately condemned the lynching in the *Independent*, an eminent journal of liberal opinion. Harris excused the murder, which hundreds of Atlantans had boarded special trains to witness as if on holiday. The lynch mob hung Sam Hose from a tree and burned him alive, mutilating his body for trophies. Du Bois lived and worked in Atlanta at the time and reported that Hose's knuckles had been displayed in a white-owned grocery store (*Dusk of Dawn* 603). Harris, later a celebrated novelist, defended the lynching with arguments that echo *The Negro a Beast*:

> The pioneer in colonial days protected his wife and child from the wild beasts with his gun and knife; but to-day in the South every white woman lives next door to a savage brute who grows more intelligent and more insolent in his outrages every year, against whom the dilettante laws of Georgia and other Southern States offer no protection. . . . Nothing can be more truly said of the ordinary negro than that he is a spiritual hypocrite. The most prominent women in their religious enthusiasms are oftenest public prostitutes. Only yesterday I passed one of them "preaching" to a crowd of men on a street corner, and I assure you her ethics were high, while her gestures were lewd and blasphemous. Out of this cesspool of vice rises that hideous monster, a possible menace to every home in the South. He has the savage nature and the murderous instincts of the wild beast, plus the cunning and lust of a fiend. . . . To him liberty has always meant license of one sort or another. Is it any wonder North Carolina, Mississippi and Louisiana have passed laws virtually disfranchising him?[17]

It is telling that Ward, an enlightened man by American standards, felt obligated to publish the letter—presumably in a spirit of fair play. Whatever the case, Tryon acts on each of the assumptions Harris makes, which come, here, with a complementary defense of disfranchisement, the political counterpart to extrajudicial violence. The economic aims of these programs, as we have seen, were clear: to discipline and degrade black labor (and thereby discipline labor more generally, all to the benefit of capital). The startling satisfaction white men and women took in such spectacles as the lynching of Sam Hose, and in the circulation of postcard photographs of other lynchings like it (a common practice at the time), was among the "psychological" wages paid them under white supremacy. Even the most degraded of white laborers might feel his station rise at the thought and sight of Sam Hose—if only because the example reminded him that the rights to due process, to trial by jury, and to protection by the police, were his and his alone. The "animalization" of black bodies elevated and "spiritualized" white ones.

The impulse to degrade the body, and to disassociate the "self" from it, as John Dewey suggests in *The Quest for Certainty*, dates to the earliest moments in human history. At some point in this unrecoverable past it occurred to us, horrified at the prospect of change, instability, mortality, and of a life in Time, to draw a distinction between body and soul, and to say of the body, with St. Paul: *This is not me*.[18] Was it 100,000 years ago in the cave of Qafzeh? Is that where the trouble began? Whatever the case, Dewey lays his finger on the main point:

> Men have been glad enough to enjoy the fruits of such arts as they possess, and in recent centuries have increasingly devoted themselves to their multiplication. But this effort has been conjoined with a profound distrust of the arts as a method of dealing with the serious perils of life. Doubt as to the truth of this statement will be dispelled if one considers the disesteem in which the idea of practice has been held. Philosophers have celebrated the method of change in personal ideas, and religious teachers that of change in the affections of the heart. These conversions have been prized on their own account, and only incidentally because of a change in action which would ensue. The latter has been esteemed as an evidence of the change in thought and sentiment, not as a method of transforming the scene of life. The places in which the use of the arts has effected actual objective transformation have been regarded as inferior, if not base, and the activities connected with them as menial. The disparagement attending the idea of the material has seized upon them. The honorable quality associated with the idea of the 'spiritual' has been

reserved for change in inner attitudes. The depreciation of action, of doing and making, has been cultivated by philosophers. But while philosophers have perpetuated the derogation by formulating and justifying it, they did not originate it. They glorified their own office without doubt in placing theory so much above practice. But independently of their attitude, many things conspired to the same effect. Work has been onerous, toilsome, associated with a primeval curse. It has been done under compulsion and the pressure of necessity, while intellectual activity is associated with leisure. On account of the unpleasantness of practical activity, as much of it as possible has been put upon slaves and serfs. Thus the social dishonor in which this class was held was extended to the work they do.[19] There is also the age-long association of knowing and thinking with immaterial and spiritual principles, and of the arts, of all practical activity in doing and making, with matter. For work is done with the body, by means of mechanical appliances, and is directed upon material things. The disrepute which has attended the thought of material things in comparison with immaterial thought has been transferred to everything associated with practice. (8–9)

The classic formula of this disposition to degrade the body occurs in Romans 7: "For we know that the law is spiritual: but I am carnal, sold under sin. For that which I do I allow not: for what I would, that do I not; but what I hate, that do I. If then I do that which I would not, I consent unto the law that it is good. Now then it is no more I that do it, but sin that dwelleth in me. For I know that in me (that is, in my flesh,) dwelleth no good thing. . . ." These ideas so permeate Western philosophy and theology—Paul, in Hellenizing Christianity, brought Plato into it—as to make them the sine qua non of metaphysics. That they should have come to shape our ideas about race and sexuality—as they do for the "white" characters who people *The House Behind the Cedars*, and for the likes of Charles Carroll—was inevitable. Dewey traces these habits of thought directly back to the origins, in antiquity, of slavery, serfdom, and class/caste, and also to the degradation of physical labor. As for the "age-long association of knowing and thinking with immaterial and spiritual principles," and of everything else with the "body" and with other "material things": evidence of these tendencies abounds. Consider Raphael's address to Adam in Book V of *Paradise Lost*:

> O Adam, one Almightie is, from whom
> All things proceed, and up to him return,
> If not deprav'd from good, created all
> Such to perfection, one first matter all,

> Indu'd with various forms, various degrees
> Of substance, and in things that live, of life;
> But more refin'd, more spiritous, and pure,
> As neerer to him plac't or neerer tending
> Each in thir several active Sphears assignd,
> Till body up to spirit work, in bounds
> Proportiond to each kind. So from the root
> Springs lighter the green stalk, from thence the leaves
> More aerie, last the bright consummate floure
> Spirits odorous breathes . . . (150)

On the night of the party, as he gazes in through the windows of the house behind the cedars, Tryon believes he witnesses in Rena a de-sublimation from spirit to corporeality, from "aerie" leaves and flowers, to the dust of earth and matter, as she becomes again "a true daughter of a race in which the *sensuous enjoyment* of the moment took precedence of taste or sentiment or any of the *higher* emotions" (my emphasis). She lacks the capacity Raphael assigns to Adam and Eve (as if she were, in fact, descended from some separate creation); she cannot be "improved by tract of time," or by "obedience" to reason (as Milton puts it later in the same passage [151]), or by the discipline of education: "Her few months of boarding-school, her brief association with white people, had evidently been a mere veneer over the underlying negro"—the metaphor is duly hierarchical—"and their effects had slipped away as soon as the intercourse had ceased." Later in *Paradise Lost*, when Adam asks whether or not angels make love, and how, Raphael replies:

> Let it suffice thee that thou know'st
> Us happie, and without Love no happiness.
> Whatever pure thou in the body enjoy'st
> (And pure thou wert created) we enjoy
> In eminence, and obstacle find none
> Of membrane, joynt, or limb, exclusive barrs:
> Easier then Air with Air, if Spirits embrace,
> Total they mix, Union of Pure with Pure
> Desiring; nor restrain'd conveyance need
> As Flesh to mix with Flesh, or Soul with Soul. (245)

Tyron certainly "obstacle" finds "of membrane, joynt, or limb." Should he bed down with Rena, he would fall—in fact, "plunge"—from grace. He recoils at the thought of making love to her: "he, a son of the ruling race, had been miserable for six weeks about a girl who had so far forgotten him as already to plunge headlong into the childish amusements of her own ignorant and degraded people. What more, indeed, he asked himself savagely,—what more could be expected of *the base-born child of the plaything of a gentleman's idle hour*"—a product of lust, not love—"who to this ignoble origin *added the blood of a servile race*? And he, George Tryon, had honored her with his love; he had very nearly linked his fate and *joined his blood* to hers by the solemn sanctions of church and state" (my emphasis; 416).

As for the metaphor of a "mask," or of a "veneer": "civilization," Tryon believes, attaches to people of color only in the most contingent and superficial way (a belief in accord with Corra Mae Harris and the lynch mobs she defends). So went the argument with which reactionaries in the post-Reconstruction South defended segregation, disenfranchisement, and racist homicide; and with which they also sought (as if with Dewey's philosophizing class) to divert funds that might have supported *liberal* education for blacks into *industrial* training programs (merely physical creatures, it was thought, were best suited for merely physical labor; such was the ideal the white South sought in its relations of production).[20] In any case, at the bottom of it all lies panic: Tryon's panicked refusal ever to think of himself as, in fact, a "body," as a thing that must someday go the way of all flesh. White racism, as Chesnutt reveals it (and as we find it laid bare in Douglass and Du Bois), is in fact a hatred of the human condition—a hatred of the brute fact of mortality, and an unwillingness to acknowledge this thing of clay we simply *are*. In the passage from *Apology for Raimond Sebond* that may have inspired Shakespeare to pen Hamlet's "What a piece of work is a man?" speech, Montaigne acknowledges the Pauline/Platonic ardor that so early seized us, even as he qualifies it with wit and skepticism:

> Presumption is our natural and original disease. The most wretched and frail of all creatures is man, and withal the proudest. He feels and sees himself lodged here in the dirt and filth of the world, nailed and riveted to the worst and deadest part of the universe, in the lowest story of the house, the most remote from the heavenly arch, with animals . . . and yet in his imagination will be placing himself above the circle of the moon, and bringing the heavens under his feet. 'Tis by the same vanity of imagination that he equals himself to God, attributes to himself divine qualities, withdraws and separates himself from the crowd of other creatures, cuts out the shares of the animals, his fellows and companions, and distributes to them portions of faculties and force, as himself thinks fit. (232)

What we do to animals, and to the "animal" portion of ourselves, white supremacy does to any class of persons it regards as more thoroughly "animal" than white folk. It takes but a short leap forward to see how white supremacy entails, as a kind of codicil, what Peter Singer calls "speciesism"—hence polygenetic theories of human origin, for example; hence also Charles Carroll's disturbed theo-psychology. We have to do, here (as in the hearts of men like George Tryon), with a hatred that our roots should lie in earth and not in heaven, and with a hatred of change and mortality. We have to do with what Dewey calls "the age-long association of knowing and thinking with immaterial and spiritual principles," and also with "the disparagement" that attends "the idea of the material." Or, as James Baldwin would later say in *The Fire Next Time*: "What Americans do not face when they regard a Negro" is nothing less than "reality—the fact that life is tragic. Life is tragic," he explains, "simply because the earth turns and the sun inexorably rises and sets, and one day, for each of us, the sun will go down for the last, last time. Perhaps the whole root of our trouble, the human trouble, is that we will sacrifice all the beauty of our lives, will imprison ourselves in totems, taboos, crosses, blood sacrifices, steeples, mosques, races, armies, flags, nations, in order to deny the fact of death, which is the only fact we have" (*Essays* 339).[21] To be of African descent in the West, Baldwin once said in a letter, "is to be the 'flesh' of white people—endlessly mortified."[22] George Tryon certainly imprisons himself in totems and taboos: he forfeits the only love (for Rena Walden) he ever really felt, or would feel. He's a resident alien in the country of his own heart and mind. Insofar as he represents white America in the post-Reconstruction years—and in many ways he surely does—the meaning of his alienation is plain: America had yet to discover itself—had yet to yield to the better angels of its nature. And now, as I write (in 2018), a man somewhat of George Tryon's disposition occupies the White House and almost weekly finds ways to "animalize" persons of color; at the rallies he regularly holds, something sinister is whipping up.

The Marrow of Tradition

Chesnutt's *The Marrow of Tradition* (1901) merits Eric Sundquist's placement of it among the most remarkable historical novels written by an American. The novel, Chesnutt's second, presents in a fictionalized form the Wilmington, North Carolina riot of November 1898. The riot had its origins in a conspiracy on the part of disaffected white Democrats to wrest control of the city away from a "Fusion" coalition, as it was then called, of Republicans and Populists who had won the state elections of 1894 and 1896. Blacks were in the majority in Wilmington and the surrounding area (New Bern and James City), and for that reason the Democratic conspirators—who included Alfred Moore Waddell, the model for Chesnutt's General Belmont; Mike Dowling, the model for his Captain McBane; and Thomas Clawson, the model for his Major Carteret—found it necessary to resort to intimidation and violence to secure a victory for "white supremacy," as they forthrightly put it, in the 1898 elections. As the date of the election drew nigh, white men armed themselves (in part with weapons and ammunition shipped in from other states); and the terrorist wing of the Democratic party (known popularly in South Carolina as the "Red Shirts") poisoned the air with racist propaganda. The conspiracy succeeded; the elections went to the Democrats. But nonetheless, as if a blood sacrifice simply had to attend this "redemption" of the city, whites rioted a few days after the election. They torched the building that housed the local black newspaper, ordered a number of prominent black citizens to leave town, murdered at least a dozen black citizens (the exact number has never been determined), assaulted scores of men and women, and destroyed thousands of dollars' worth of black-owned property. The victory was complete—on the ballot also had been a provision to disenfranchise blacks—and North Carolina would not recover from it for more than sixty years.[23]

Chesnutt artfully weaves the riots, and the events leading up to them, into a story about two families related by ties of blood but separated by the color line: the Carterets and the Millers. Major Carteret has married Olivia Merkell, the daughter of a white man who, in the antebellum years, stood at the absolute peak of Wellington society (Wellington is the name Chesnutt gives to his fictional Wilmington). As the novel opens, Olivia, a frail and delicate woman, is giving birth to the son that will redeem, as the Major sees it, the legacy of his own illustrious family, whom the Civil War had ruined. The reader soon learns that Mr. Merkell had, after Olivia's mother died, taken as his mistress the family's black house-servant, Julia. By her he fathered another daughter, named Janet, who is fair-skinned and who, for all the world, looks like Olivia's twin. Janet, though cast out of the house at Mr. Merkell's death, secures for herself a liberal education, travels widely, and marries Adam Miller, a physician. The son of a black entrepreneur—who, after buying himself out of slavery, had established a respectable business on the wharfs in Wellington—Dr. Miller establishes a local hospital to serve the black community, and wins the respect of the more liberal elements of white Wellington. He settles in the house formerly occupied by the Carterets, and the dignity and consequence of his family—indeed, their very existence—is a constant humiliation to Olivia and the Major.

The Major, an ardent Democrat, uses the editorial page of the paper he owns to foment a popular movement to reinstate white supremacy and to purge from Wellington and from the state as a whole any vestiges of the Radical Reconstruction. In this endeavor, he recruits General Belmont, a calculating politician with designs on statewide office, and Captain McBane, a low-born white man who heads up the local Red Shirt faction, and who'd been a Ku Kluxer during its heyday in the late 1860s. The plot of the novel moves inexorably toward the riot, which Chesnutt fixes, in a slight departure from the historical record, on the eve of the 1898 election. What emerges is a devastating and politically shrewd portrait of North Carolina, which may certainly stand in, as Chesnutt no doubt intends it to do, for the New South in the post-Reconstruction period. The success of the novel lies in its precision and economy: Chesnutt manages to personify in a small cast of characters virtually every development in late-nineteenth-century Southern politics. All the figures are here: the fading but worthy aristocrat—a man who'd never liked slavery and who now strives in good faith to overcome its legacy, and in whose eyes the agitation for white supremacy is as vulgar as it is dishonest (old Mr. Delamere); the men Du Bois once called "the 'cracker' Third Estate" (*Souls* 417), who filled the ranks of the Klan and the Red Shirts, and who, having sprung from poor white origins, resented equally the freedmen and the planter class that dominated antebellum Southern politics (Captain McBane); the New South breed of Democrat, who sought to lure Northern capital into the states of the former Confederacy to rebuild its infrastructure on an industrial, "modern" basis (General Belmont and Major Carteret); the rising black middle class, who wished to cooperate with the better sort of white folk, and who favored compromise and patience rather than violence in their dealings with whites (Dr. Miller); the "New Negro," who, having come of age during Reconstruction, saw no good reason why he shouldn't be entitled to what the Constitution now guaranteed him—full citizenship, voting rights, and equal protection under the law—and who is prepared to meet white violence with violence of his own (Josh Green, a character who anticipates such later figures as Bigger Thomas, the hero of Richard Wright's 1940 novel *Native Son*); and, finally, the "tragic mulatto," caught between the black and white worlds, and never quite at ease in either (Janet).

As the novel reaches its denouement, any close reader of it cannot help but believe that, though there is, perhaps, "time enough" to recover American democracy at the turn of the twentieth century, there is certainly "none to spare" (718): the hope of the "white" South, in the person of the infant son of the Carterets (a white family who, in the wake of the riot, stands in horror at what they wrought in Wellington), now lies on his deathbed, racked with fever. The only doctor who can come to his aid is the same black man, Dr. Miller, whose own cherished son lies dead from the bullet of a white rioter, and whose presence in the Carteret house would, only a day before, have been thought a pollution. In the *The Marrow of Tradition* Chesnutt hopes to find some way out of the great American impasse: in a note on the novel published in 1901, he confessed his faith "that the forces of progress will in the end prevail, and that in time a remedy may be found for every social ill" (873). But the logic of white supremacy, as *The Marrow of Tradition* reveals it, operates with the grim force of a Fate from which the nation may never emancipate itself. An atmosphere of anxiety, even of doom, shades the novel. No doubt its *realpolitik* bleakness accounts for the fact that *The Marrow of Tradition* sold as poorly as it did on its publication in 1901—a development that eventually put an end to Chesnutt's aspiration to support himself by writing. In an era of the plantation tale, with its mammies, faithful retainers, cakewalks, and darkies; in a period when the Republican Party, playing the part of Pilate, said, *What is truth?* and would not stay for an answer; with the freedmen's sons and daughters consigned to the machinery of a resurgent Democratic Party; in a season when American soldiers were fighting to put down a war for independence in the Philippines—at exactly this point, white American readers preferred not to listen to the story Chesnutt had to tell. His work stands awkwardly "post-bellum" and "pre-Harlem," as he himself once put it an essay (906–12)—that is to say, in a literary-historical wilderness, caught between the Egypt of slavery and the Canaan of what would aptly be called the Harlem (or "New Negro") Renaissance, during which, at last, black writers began to secure a reliable (and autonomous) market for serious literary writing. On the other side of the Harlem Renaissance, of course, lie such authors as Wright, James Baldwin, Ralph Ellison, and Gwendolyn Brooks, whose work Chesnutt helped make possible.

A brilliant scene occurs in a chapter of *The Marrow* titled "The Cakewalk." "A party of Northern visitors had been staying for several days at the St. James Hotel [in Wellington]. The gentlemen of the party were concerned in a projected cotton mill, while the ladies were much interested in the study of social conditions, and especially the negro problem" (555). Notable here is the conventional Victorian division of gender roles, whereby practical affairs were reserved for men, sentiment and uplift for women. The vaguely humanitarian interests of the women cloak their families' business enterprise in a certain gentility, as if to suggest: Northern capital really does care about the Negro. But as Chesnutt intimates, this is a pretense, in which North and South alike conspire. Every encounter these philanthropic Northern visitors have with black folk is mediated by Southern whites, who, at "elaborate luncheons," expound upon the "disappearance of the good old negro of before the war," and who congratulate themselves on the money the South has poured into black education (555). Chesnutt's narrator explains the result:

> The visitors were naturally much impressed by what they learned from their courteous hosts, and felt inclined to sympathize with the Southern people, for the negro is not counted as a Southerner, except to fix the basis of congressional representation. There might of course be things to criticise here and there, certain customs for which they did not exactly see the necessity, and which seemed in conflict with the highest ideals of liberty: but surely these courteous, soft-spoken ladies and gentlemen, entirely familiar with local conditions, who descanted so earnestly and at times pathetically upon the grave problems confronting them, must know more about it than people in the distant North, without their means of information. The negroes who waited on them at the hotel seemed happy enough, and the teachers whom they had met at the mission school had been well-dressed, well-mannered, and apparently content with their position in life. Surely a people who made no complaints could not be very much oppressed. (556)

The satire is rich. Exposed here is the unacknowledged tendency, even at the late date in which the novel is set, to think of the black population as somehow "foreign" to the culture of the South: "The negro is not counted as a Southerner," we are told, "except to fix the basis of congressional representation." The South relies on the freedmen's sons and daughters to augment its power in congress, but only such that the South may, with the indulgence of the North, more efficiently oppress them as laborers—and not in violation of section 2 of the Fourteenth Amendment:

> Representatives shall be apportioned among the several States according to their respective numbers, counting the whole number of persons in each State, excluding Indians not taxed. But when the right to vote at any election for the choice of electors for President and Vice President of the United States, Representatives in Congress, the Executive and Judicial officers of a State, or the members of the Legislature thereof, is denied to any of the male inhabitants of such State, being twenty-one years of age, and citizens of the United States, or in any way abridged, except

> for participation in rebellion, *or other crime*, the basis of representation therein shall be reduced in the proportion which the number of such male citizens shall bear to the whole number of male citizens twenty-one years of age in such State. (my emphasis)

As Chesnutt knew, and likely expected his readers to recall, the Lodge "Force Bill" (introduced in 1890), which would have allowed for Federal intervention to secure adherence to the letter of section 2, never came to a vote (I mentioned this bill in chapter 3 in a similar connection). To Charles Sumner's dauntless anger, the text of section 2—the result of considerable compromise in the so-called Committee of Fifteen, led by Thaddeus Stevens—failed explicitly to bar proscription of the franchise based on race or color. And the insertion of the "crime" clause—the right to vote shall not be abridged "except for participation in rebellion, or other crime"—would, in time, allow Southern states to criminalize African American mores (with "vagrancy laws," and other instruments), and on that basis deny the ballot to millions, while (as Chesnutt indicates) relying on the disenfranchised to increase their power in the House. Sumner's condemnation of an earlier draft of the amendment, in a remarkable speech given on February 6, 1865, applied as well to the amendment as adopted: "There are tricks and evasions possible, and the cunning slave-master will drive his coach and six through your amendment stuffed with all his representatives" (quoted in *Black Reconstruction* 295). And the cunning slave master did, as *The Marrow of Tradition* shows; and when he wished, he drove his coach and six armed to the teeth.[24] Of course, the "crime" clause warps American politics still: millions of ex-convicts and parolees—disproportionately African American—are, as of this writing, denied the right to vote, and all fifty states bar inmates from voting.[25]

Most important, though, is the way the passage quoted above (from *Marrow*) typifies the post-Reconstruction rapprochement between North and South: as I have already suggested, this reconciliation, for the purposes of capital investment, was accompanied by a romantic idealization of plantation life that excused the North of its responsibilities to the freedmen. If things weren't all that terrible (so went the argument), why continue the costly Reconstruction program of the Radicals? ("Surely a people who made no complaints could not be very much oppressed," say Chesnutt's Northern visitors.) Weren't the resources of the Federal government and of the US Army needed out West to secure it for white settlers in quest of golden apples? And wouldn't it be better simply to let the Southerners handle the Negro problem on their own ("surely these courteous, soft-spoken ladies and gentlemen . . . must know more about [the race question] than people in the distant North")? The better to enforce the point, these "courteous" North Carolina hosts stage a "genuine negro cakewalk" for their Northern guests. Here (they assure the visitors) shall be exemplified "the joyous, happy-go-lucky disposition of the Southern darky and his entire contentment with existing conditions" (556). But the winner of the cakewalk, as it happens, is not a black man at all, but a white man— Tom Delamere, the dissolute grandson of old Mr. Delamere—dressed up in blackface and impersonating his grandfather's faithful retainer, Sandy. The "genuine negro cakewalk" is in fact a fraud; the "Southern darky" on exhibit is in a very real sense a white man's Negro. He is an imposter, a fiction; he is the artificial "darky" of plantation tales and the minstrel-show stage. The astonishing thing is that no one notices the fraud—least of all the Southerners who claim so intimate a knowledge of black folk, and who ought to be able to detect the ruse: they dwell so entirely within the horizons of white supremacy as to mistake their own fantasy of black lives for the "real" thing. (Plainly, *they* inhabit an imaginary nation with real people in it.) Tom Delamere, on being awarded the cake, returns his thanks in a speech which sends the white onlookers into "spasms of delight at the quaintness of the darky dialect and the darky wit" (557). In fact, only one man—Ellis, Major Carteret's protege at the newspaper office—senses that things might be amiss, and even he can't put his finger on it. "There was a vague suggestion of unreality about this performance" which Ellis "did not attempt to analyze" (558). He finds it passing strange that Sandy—for that, again, is whom Tom Delamere impersonates—would abandon his usual courtly demeanor to take part in so undignified a spectacle. No white man, he reflects, could "possess two so widely varying phases of character" as Sandy did: "but as to negroes, they were as yet a crude and undeveloped race, and it was not safe to make predictions concerning them. No one could tell at what moment the thin veneer of civilization might peel off and reveal the underlying savage" (558). We have seen it time and again in these pages: to the white mind, black was to white as "savage" was to "civil" (the rule applied as well in North Carolina as in the Belgian Congo). And Chesnutt's novel—together, of course, with the facts of the case in the South—shows that this formula turns things upside down. Blackness is simply the name whites give to their own savagery, as this is projected outward onto men and women they oppress (again, as much in the Carolinas as in the Congo). Whites are themselves "double"—like Tom Delamere in black face, or like Robert Louis Stevenson's Dr. Jekyll/Mr. Hyde (to whom, in fact, the rampaging white mob in *The Marrow of Tradition* is compared [645]).

For Tom, to put on the mask of color is to cross a boundary into lawlessness and anarchy, not merely into a cakewalk: later in the novel, he corks up his face again, and again borrows Sandy's distinctive clothes, and burglarizes Carteret's aunt, Mrs. Ochiltree (he needs the money to meet a gambling debt). Suspicion falls on Sandy, as of course Tom intends, and the fellow barely escapes lynching, in giddy anticipation of which the local railroads schedule special "excursion" trains, so all in the outlying countryside could enjoy the spectacle. (For this latter detail, Chesnutt likely relies on the case of Sam Hose, already alluded to. When Hose was lynched near Atlanta in 1897, the city ran special trains to accommodate the enraptured crowds.) The charge of rape had, of course, fantastically been added to that of burglary (the white imagination sensualizes black motives). The sorry episode aggravates the racial tensions Major Carteret has deliberately inflamed in the columns of his newspaper (in anticipation of the coming elections). In due course, the rioting follows in a terrifying display of white savagery, which, as I indicated, Chesnutt carefully models on the Wilmington riots of 1898. Old Mr. Delamere, devastated that a descendant of his—Tom—could have behaved so despicably, and shocked at the epidemic of lynchings then sweeping the South, bitterly observes: "I have lived to hear of white men, the most favored of races, the heirs of civilization, the conservators of liberty, howling like red Indians around a human being slowly roasting at the stake." The white population, he adds, has been turned into a "mob of primitive savages," well capable, as we know, of mutilating the bodies of their victims, and carrying away an ear, or worse, for souvenir (628). The delusion of color, in this devastating novel, confuses all efforts to understand, and therefore overcome, what must be called our innate depravity as a republic. Within its pages, one can hardly imagine *any* wings of Atalanta sufficient to raise that republic's spirit.

Dreams Deferred

Chesnutt published only one more novel in his lifetime, *The Colonel's Dream* in 1905. The character who gives the book its title, Colonel Henry French, is a quixotic white Southerner, who, after making his fortune in the North, returns on what he supposes will be a short summer visit to his native town of Clarendon, North Carolina in the post-Reconstruction years. But he finds himself enlivened by opportunities he sees there, and, a widower with a young son, falls in love with Laura Treadwell (whom he had known before the war); and he determines to help his native state—for which he fought in the Confederate Army—recover from the damage slavery had done. He invests in an abandoned cotton mill in Clarendon, which he aims to rebuild and operate under enlightened and color-blind labor policies. For this he eventually draws the ire of white reactionaries, chief among whom is a local man aptly named William Fetters—an abusive landlord, chief stockholder in a rival cotton mill in nearby Carthage, and a dealer in convict labor (one of the most infamous systems of labor relations ever to degrade the post-bellum South). "Fetters had begun to worry the colonel," we read. "He had never seen the man, and yet his influence was everywhere. He seemed to brood over the country round about like a great vampire bat, sucking the life-blood of the people. His touch meant blight. As soon as a Fetters mortgage rested on a place, the property began to run down; for why should the nominal owner keep up a place which was destined in the end to go to Fetters? The colonel had heard grewsome tales of Fetters's convict labour plantation; he had seen the operation of Fetters's cotton-mill, where white humanity, in its fairest and tenderest form [i.e., in children], was stunted and blighted and destroyed."[26] The Colonel aspires to right these wrongs—to unfetter at least his cherished precinct of North Carolina. After visiting the mill in Carthage, he gives an impassioned account of what he saw there to a judge he's befriended in Clarendon, and then unfolds his dream:

> I've been in business for twenty years, but I have never sought to make money by trading on the souls and bodies of women and children. I saw the little darkies running about the streets down there at Carthage; they were poor and ragged and dirty, but they were out in the air and the sunshine; they have a chance to get their growth; to go to school and learn something. The white children are worked worse than slaves, and are growing up dulled and stunted, physically and mentally. Our folks down here are mighty short-sighted, judge. We'll wake them up. We'll build a model cotton mill, and run it with decent hours and decent wages, and treat the operatives like human beings with bodies to nourish, minds to develop; and souls to save. Fetters and his crowd will have to come up to our standard, or else we'll take their hands away. (120)

The judge says little in reply to this vision of social democracy, but we are told that he "was not altogether happy" (120)—and this is ominous. Still, the Colonel's dream for Clarendon broadens by the week: he plans to build a public library, open to black and white alike, and a new industrial school (162, 292). He pays good wages to the men in the integrated workforce he employs to lay the new foundations at his mill, and he elevates a black mason to foreman (190–91). But here he takes a step too far: white men refuse to work under a black foreman, and so begins in earnest the turn against him. The town and the state are in the midst of a bitter gubernatorial campaign, and the forces of reaction—deliberately following the example set by neighboring South Carolina, where white supremacy had been firmly reinstituted (by means touched on above, in chapter 2)—are on the move. Misfortune, as if in service to this general menace, quickly follows. Peter French, the Colonel's former slave, and now his employee, is killed in a trainyard while attempting to save the Colonel's young son Phil (who had wandered idly onto the tracks, chasing after a cat); Phil himself soon dies of injuries sustained during the incident; the local white folk heatedly object when the Colonel proposes to bury both in his family plot (it is in a "white" cemetery); he defies them, allowing Peter's family and friends to attend the dual burial; in reprisal, a gang of white men dig up Peter's coffin under cover of night, and deliver it to the Colonel's dooryard after nailing to it a crude note: "Take notis. Berry yore ole nigger somewhar else" (281). He takes notice indeed, and retreats—alone, and before his mill ever nears completion—to his adopted city of New York, abandoning his native Clarendon to segregationists who would dominate the South long after Chesnutt's own death in 1932—in fact, well into my own generation. *The Colonel's Dream* is perhaps the least hopeful of Chesnutt's novels (notwithstanding his attempt to hearten readers with an allusion, in the book's penultimate paragraph, to the Roosevelt administration's 1903 attempt to check peonage in the South). "White men go their way, and black men theirs, and these ways grow wider apart, and no one knows the outcome," we read on the closing page (294). The book sold even more poorly than had *The Marrow of Tradition*. Chesnutt found himself compelled to abandon his aspiration to support himself as an author (as the Colonel had been forced to abandon his "dream" of enlightened democracy in North Carolina). He turned instead to the legal stenography business he had launched in Cleveland; he had nowhere else to turn. True, he scattered short stories and essays in various periodicals from time to time (including the NAACP's Crisis); and he wrote at least two more novels, *Paul Marchand, F.M.C.* (i.e., "Free Man of Color") and *The Quarry*. But he secured publication for neither.[27]

The best coda to Chesnutt's literary career is a curious story titled "Baxter's Procrustes," which appeared in the *Atlantic Monthly* in 1904.[28] Baxter, a poet of sorts, belongs to a society of bibliophiles pretentiously styled The Bodleian Club. Now and then, the club publishes literary works in fine bindings as collector's items. And when the club's publications committee learns of Baxter's poem-in-progress, titled "Procrustes," they offer to print it in a plush "limited" edition. Baxter accepts the offer with a sardonic gleam that fails to arouse suspicion—until, too late, and caught entirely by surprise, the club is taken in. Baxter, it turns out, has submitted a ream of blank paper to the printer, and the resulting book, complete with its hand-tooled binding and rich linen paper, is entirely empty: no one on the editorial committee bothered to examine the manuscript before dispatching it to the printer; no one on the review committee—tasked with introducing the volume at a dinner celebrating its appearance—bothered to read the finished book (they were, to a man, loath to cut the pages, for fear of reducing the value of the volume as a specimen of fine bookmaking). "Baxter's Procrustes" mocks the American literary marketplace, with its "Procrustean" demands for a standardized product, and its readership of fools and unoriginal minds. A fitting envoi for a subtle writer whose brilliance the white literary establishment would fail to recognize until some fifty years after his death, when, even as the academy canonized him, the Reagan administration (and the entire GOP) began its project of dismantling such Great Society programs as had been designed to mitigate the twinned evils of racism and poverty.

CHAPTER FIVE

RICHARD WRIGHT: EXILE AS NATIVE SON

> *I tell you frankly that there is more freedom in one square block of Paris than there is in the entire United States of America.*
>
> —Wright, "I Chose Exile" (1951)

Words and Weapons

It all began with a fire: the one Richard Wright himself set when he was four years old. He had wondered, he tells us at the start of his autobiography, *Black Boy (American Hunger)*, "just how the long fluffy white curtains would look if I lit a bunch of straws and held it under them" (5).[1] They looked splendid; it is a wonder no one was killed. As it turned out, the little boy Wright still was at the time came closer to death than anyone, and not from the fire itself, but from the beating his mother gave him in the aftermath. "I was lashed so hard and long that I lost consciousness," he recalls. For years he was "chastened," as he puts it, when he remembered that his mother "had come close to killing" him (8–9).

At about that time, his father abandoned the family, and Wright, the oldest child, underwent an ordeal of initiation. When some local Memphis boys beat him and stole the money his mother sent with him to market, she simply gave him more money, a heavy stick, and then locked him out of the house: "I am going to teach you this night to stand up and fight for yourself," she said. And so he went back out, paralyzed with fear: "I was alone upon the dark, hostile streets and gangs were after me. I had the choice of being beaten at home or away from home." When the gang set upon him, he "let the stick fly, feeling it crack against a boy's skull," lashing out again and again. His fury horrified the boys. "They had never seen such frenzy" (18–19). There were many more beatings, but now they only came from Wright's guardians: his mother, his grandmother, his grandfather.

There were mystifying events, too, as when the young boy awoke once to a commotion in the next room: his aunt's lover had stolen money from a woman—Wright never learned exactly who—knocked her unconscious and set her house ablaze. He fled in the night with Wright's aunt and a pistol; white men were after him. Another aunt, Maggie, had been married to Silas Hoskins, with whom the family briefly lived in Elaine, Arkansas, when Richard Wright was nine—that is, until Hoskins was killed by whites who "coveted his flourishing liquor business" (53). This time the whole family fled. "Why had we not fought back?" Wright asked his mother. But "the fear that was in her made her slap [him] into silence" (53). The little boy was learning what it meant to "limp through days lived under the threat of violence" (72). Later, he heard a tale about a black woman who shot four white men to death—they'd murdered her husband—and the story "gave form and meaning" to feelings that had long been "sleeping" in him: violent "fantasies," as he puts it, were no longer merely "a reflection of his reaction" to the ominous white world beyond; these fantasies had become for him "a culture, a creed, a religion" (71). And when a young schoolmistress whispered to him the bloody story of *Bluebeard*, who married seven women and murdered them all, Wright was enchanted. Hearing that story was the first experience in his life, he reports, to elicit from him "a total emotional response": "I vowed that as soon as I was old enough I would buy all the novels there were and read them to feed that thirst for violence that was in me, for intrigue, for plotting, for secrecy, for bloody murders" (38–39). Bought them he did, when he was old enough and had the money; but, what is more important, he composed novels himself, all of them written about, and out of, his experience of violence. Wright would show his readers what it felt like to live in a nation foreclosed by fear. He dwelt in *impossibility*. Hazel Rowley is certainly right: "His fictional landscape is a nightmare" (410). James Baldwin also gets it right: "When in Wright's pages a Negro male is found hacking a white woman to death, the very gusto with which this is done, and the great attention paid to details of physical destruction reveal a terrible attempt to break out of the cage in which the American imagination has imprisoned him" (*Essays* 251). The only things constant in the lives of the men Wright writes about are fear and the ever-present threat of violence—a violence that might break out at any time, without provocation, and which always promises to tear the lives of black men apart.

    A catalog: There was the time his mother beat him with a barrel stave until he ran a fever of 102, imparting to him, all the while, little gems of Jim Crow wisdom ("Ethics of Living Jim Crow" 226). Or the morning he watched two white men (a father and son) kick a black woman to the back room of their store, where they assaulted her. Later Wright saw them washing their hands at the sink, "chuckling"; the bloody floor was "strewn with wisps of hair and clothing," and the men slapped Wright on the back and grinned ("Ethics" 230). Omitting to say "Sir" to a white man got him an empty whiskey bottle between the eyes; he fell backward, stars in his eyes and bloody, feet tangled in the spokes of his bicycle. The white men comforted him: He was a lucky bastard; had he spoken that way to any other white man, he'd be a "dead nigger" now ("Ethics" 231). He took a job in a disreputable hotel and saw a black bellboy castrated for sleeping with a white whore ("Ethics" 234). In "Big Boy Leaves Home," from Wright's first book, *Uncle Tom's Children* (a collection of novellas), a white man shoots Buck and Lester, only to find himself shot, in turn, by Bobo—who, in short order, finds himself lynched, his body dismembered into macabre "souvenirs" (271). In "Down by the Riverside," Mann guns down the white bigot—he has no choice but to do it—who tries to stop him from taking his wife to the hospital (292). In "Long Black Song," Silas bullwhips his wife for having been raped, murders the white man who raped her, and then drags his body to the middle of the road (343–49). In "Bright and Morning Star," a mother is made to watch as white men stretch her son across a log, shatter his bones with a crow-bar and burst his eardrums with a well-placed blow to the head; she carries a gun, hidden, and she shoots one of the white men dead, but fails when she tries to relieve her son with a bullet; and so the white men shoot the both of them (440–41). *Uncle Tom's Children* is a record of beatings, torture, rape, castration, homicide, and murder. But notice this: Wright, as he developed, favored plots in which his black protagonists are *forced by circumstance* to kill white men and women. There is a logic, here: it allows for the symbolic expression of violent impulses while redeeming, always, the motive. There is another logic, too: Wright so arranges the plots of his novels as to suggest that white folk have so arranged American affairs as to compel *themselves* into acts of self-destruction. White supremacy is as suicidal as it is homicidal; Wright's bloody novels make this perfectly clear.

What sort of a man was Wright? Those who knew him speak always of his mild manners. He was a gentle man, full of mirth. Richard Wright had a light heart. The sublimation of violent impulses into his art was perfect. Reading and writing offered him a way to redeem his violent "fantasies," a way to redirect them toward socially useful ends. Acts of violence are always, in Wright's books, creative, expressive, or transformative. That is why his protagonists—Bigger Thomas chief among them—inevitably decide to "own" their violent acts, even when these seem a product of circumstance or chance. And if violent acts can be "expressive," then expressive acts can, in some sense, be "violent": words do hurt. Obscenity fascinated Wright for exactly this reason, well before he was old enough really to understand why. For this reason, too, he was electrified when he first read that most pugilistic of American critics, H. L. Mencken. "This man was fighting, fighting with words," Wright felt at once when he peeked into *A Book of Prefaces*, a book he had obtained with a forged library pass at the "whites only" public library in Memphis ("Dear Madam: Will you please let this nigger boy have some books by H. L. Mencken?" it had read). Wright was "jarred and shocked by the style, the clear, clean, sweeping sentences." He "pictured the man as a raging demon"—and here the book became, for Wright, a kind of prospective mirror—"slashing with his pen, consumed with hate, denouncing everything American," and "mocking God, authority" (*Black Boy* 237). Mencken "was using words as a weapon, using them as one would use a club" (237). Richard Wright had found his calling. Writing emancipated him, as in a somewhat different way it had emancipated Frederick Douglass; and what is more, writing laid before him an instrument of retribution against a world that seemed unwilling to allow him even to exist. In the novel of violence Wright would find redemption from the violence that had, since earliest youth, laid claim to him, when it had all begun with a fire.

Richard Wright was born in 1908 on a farm near Roxie, Mississippi, the son of an illiterate sharecropper and a sometime-schoolteacher. The following year Du Bois would help found the NAACP. Five years earlier, in *The Souls of Black Folk*, he'd documented the conditions under which men like Wright's father labored: "In considerable parts of all the Gulf States, and especially in Mississippi, Louisiana, and Arkansas, the Negroes on the plantations in the back-country districts are still held at forced labor practically without wages.... Such a system is impossible in the more civilized parts of the South, or near the large towns and cities; but in those vast stretches of land beyond the telegraph and the newspaper the spirit of the Thirteenth Amendment [ending slavery] is sadly broken" (*Souls* 467). The parents of Wright's parents had, of course, been born in slavery, though one of them, his maternal grandfather, had served in the Union Navy during the war, after the Mississippi River fell under Union control. By 1908, when Wright was born, Mississippi had been sitting in darkness for some twenty years: the state was among the first to disenfranchise African Americans. The methods the state Democratic Party used to achieve this end became a model for the rest of the South ("the Mississippi Plan"), with such results as we have already surveyed. Reconstruction was destroyed there with savage ferocity. "In Mississippi, the White League began organized work in 1874. Seven organized armed groups were formed in Vicksburg to control the city election," writes Du Bois in *Black Reconstruction* (1935). "The charge here was extravagance in building school-houses and 'too many niggers in office.' Armed companies patrolled the city, and yet there was perfect order at the polls. Voters were thus intimidated and kept at home while in the surrounding counties some 200 Negroes were killed. At Clinton, in 1875, another blow was struck when a mass meeting and barbecue was being held by the colored people. Five hundred armed white men assembled, food and wagons were destroyed, mules and horses stolen, hundreds of Negro homes searched, and fugitives driven away" (685). Wright's extended family would have known most of these events intimately. White supremacy seized Mississippi, and would hold it until at least the late 1960s, by which time Wright, for years an expatriate, lay buried in a cemetery in Paris.

When Wright was five his father deserted the family, and there began a period of drifting. He lived in Natchez and Jackson, Mississippi; in Elaine and West Helena, Arkansas; in Jackson again; in Greenwood, Mississippi; in Jackson a third time; and in Memphis: this was all by the time he was sixteen. Most of the time Wright lived with his mother, but at one point he was consigned to an orphanage, and for a while he lived with relatives. When he was ten, his mother suffered an incapacitating stroke, whereupon his grandmother, a strict Seventh Day Adventist, took charge of the impoverished family. In schools in a number of towns Wright managed an itinerant sort of education, attending, in the end, Smith Robertson Junior High in Jackson, from which he graduated valedictorian. For two years thereafter, he worked in Memphis doing odd jobs at an optical company and washing dishes; it was at this time that he discovered H. L. Mencken, and, through Mencken, introduced himself to novels by Theodore Dreiser, Sinclair Lewis, Sherwood Anderson, and Alexandre Dumas. In 1927 he moved to Chicago, following the path many southern-born African Americans took during the period of the Great Migration and afterwards.

He took work in a delicatessen, sent for his mother and brother, and, eventually, landed a job at the Central Post Office. During his early months in Chicago, Wright continued his self-education, reading voraciously. By 1930 he had begun a novel of his own, tentatively titled "Cesspool," which appeared posthumously in 1961 under the title *Lawd Today!*

Lawd Today! chronicles one long day in the life of Jake Jackson, a hapless black employee of the Central Post Office in Chicago. In it, Wright adopts certain elements of the "documentary" style developed by John Dos Passos in his *U.S.A.* trilogy. The novel is set on Lincoln's birthday, and extracts from a patriotic commentary on the life of the Great Emancipator and on the Civil War, taken from a radio broadcast, punctuate the narrative, in the manner of Dos Passos's "newsreels." The counterpoint is of course ironic. Some sixty years after the war, Wright's black protagonist runs out the course of his life in what Wright figures as a "squirrel cage" (the subtitle of one section of the novel): the meaning of "emancipation" remained, in 1935, obscure.

The plot of the novel is simple: we follow Jake from dawn to deep midnight, as he argues with his wife, plays the numbers, cuts up with his friends, reports for work, struggles to keep his job, and has his pocket picked at a midnight party. The novel ends with a bitter, drunken, bloody fight between Jake and his wife Lil. "Lawd, I wish I was dead," she says to herself, weeping, while outside "an icy wind" sweeps around the corner of the building, "whining and moaning like an idiot in a deep black pit" (219). The echo in that last phrase of the passage in *Macbeth* from which William Faulkner takes the title of his 1929 novel *The Sound and the Fury* is deliberate, as is also the echo of T. S. Eliot's *The Waste Land* in the subtitle of the concluding section of *Lawd, Today!*, "Rats' Alley." Wright's novel adapts both the techniques and the characteristic themes of the high modernists to new purposes: a study of the alienation—economic and otherwise—peculiar to American blacks in the great American cities of the twentieth century. The novel succeeds admirably in this ambitious project, but it is also, more immediately, an indispensable record of African American life in the Depression era: here Wright captures better than he ever would again the idioms, the vitality, and the great range of black American English. The long, rambling conversation of Jake and his friends over a casual game of bridge is a tour de force in vernacular writing. Wright easily surpasses Chesnutt in this regard (Langston Hughes, too, for that matter). And among other things, *Lawd Today!* shows us how far African American writers had come since Douglass made his uneasy compromise with the speech of that "genuine African," Sandy Jenkins.

Wright had, in 1931, become interested in Communism—the party was active in Chicago, especially among blacks—and in 1933 he joined the local chapter of the John Reed Club, a national organization of left-wing writers and artists associated with the Communist Party; the following year he joined the party itself. His poetry began to appear in *Left Front*, in *Anvil*, and in *New Masses*—the leading organs of the literary left, which was, in those days, a formidable element in American intellectual life. In 1937, Wright moved to New York City, and there he began to distance himself from the party, which now seemed to him quite possibly inimical to his interests as a writer, and, although he continued to publish in its journals and to endorse its general aims, he never submitted to its discipline again. (He officially withdrew from the party in 1944 and later published a bitter essay about his experiences there titled "I Tried to be a Communist.")[2]

Lawd Today! is a novel of Wright's apprenticeship to writers like Dos Passos, Faulkner, Eliot, and Joyce. His second book, *Uncle Tom's Children*, published by Harper and Brothers in 1938, reflects his engagement with the Communist Party. It is an experiment in socialist realism. With intoxicating optimism, and despite its often bleak and violent content, the book points toward a resolution of racial conflict in class solidarity—the goal toward which Radical Republicans had worked in South Carolina in 1870, and which would bring Martin Luther King, Jr., to Memphis in late March 1968 to support striking sanitation workers (he never left the city alive). As the last of the four novellas, "Fire and Cloud," concludes, a black preacher named Taylor leads a march of poor white and black folks on city hall, demanding fair distribution of food to the Depression-starved masses: "A baptism of clean joy swept over Taylor," we read. "He kept his eyes on the sea of black and white faces. The song swelled louder and vibrated through him. This is the way! he thought. Gawd ain no lie! He ain no lie! His eyes grew wet with tears, blurring his vision: the sky trembled; the buildings wavered as if about to topple; and the earth shook . . . He mumbled out loud, exultingly: '*Freedom belongs t the strong!*'" (406). As the title "Fire and Cloud" suggests, the novella, and the book as a whole, is a powerful reworking of the Mosaic story of the Exodus, which of course African Americans had long made use of in their literature and song (as we've seen in chapters 1 and 2): the passage of the Israelites out of the wilderness of bondage and exile, and their crossing into the Promised Land, are here adapted to the transracial (and secular) dream of a socialist revolution.

Uncle Tom's Children was a commercial success; a second edition, to which a fifth story and a searing essay titled "The Ethics of Living Jim Crow" were added, appeared in 1940. Yet the book left Wright unsatisfied;

its warm reception troubled him. "I found that I had written," he confesses in an essay titled "How Bigger Was Born," "a book which even bankers' daughters could read and weep over and feel good about. I swore to myself that if I ever wrote another book, no one would weep over it; that it would be so hard and deep that they would have to face it without the consolation of tears. It was this that made me get to work in dead earnest" (874). The book he produced is *Native Son*, and in it we can see what I have already called a sublimation, a redemption, of the aggressive motive that underlay its composition—the desire to deal his readers a blow so hard as to deny them the consolation of tears. He would at last realize his ambition to make weapons out of words, and words out of weapons. And as for sentimental "bankers' daughters": his need to hurt them, to make them feel the pain of the dispossessed—insofar as they were able, and insofar as novels suffice to do the job—finds expression in symbolic action. For it is a banker's daughter of sorts—a naively leftist young woman who surely would have wept over *Uncle Tom's Children*—that Bigger Thomas kills: Mary Dalton, daughter of one of the wealthiest men (and largest landowners) in Chicago.

It is hard now rightly to estimate the force of *Native Son*, though the book retains the power to shock us. In 1940 it was utterly unprecedented: in its terrifying violence (two killings, the first horribly brutal in its aftermath, the second singularly brutal in its execution); in its embrace of a wounded and sociopathic hero; and in its candid exploration of sexuality, a feature of the novel muted in the somewhat bowdlerized first edition. (I will return to this matter shortly, but for details of the novel's textual history, see the "Note on the Texts" in volume 1 of the Library of America's edition of Wright: *Early Works: Lawd, Today!, Uncle Tom's Children, and Native Son*.)

The plot of the novel is brisk and has something of the momentum of a thriller. The opening section immerses us in Bigger Thomas's milieu, in the environment that produced him, and of which he is, in certain respects, the perfect expression: the poverty-stricken South Side of Chicago. We follow him next into the home of Mr. Dalton, to whom Bigger has been recommended as a chauffeur by a relief organization. Dalton is the type of the robber baron turned liberal philanthropist, and his daughter, Mary, is a fellow traveler in Chicago Communist Party circles and the lover of a Party organizer, Jan Erlone. Mary and Jan embrace Bigger with a solicitude that is at once condescending and oppressive, and which the novel satirizes effectively. They are like the white radicals who irritated Frederick Douglass when he entered the embrace of the Garrisonian abolitionists. They want Bigger Thomas to have a little more of the plantation in his speech. They want to hear "Swing Low, Sweet Chariot" (517). They want their sorrow songs. The Daltons—and in his differing way, Jan Erlone—are like the "lovers of the poor" in Gwendolyn Brooks's poem of the same name (discussed in chapter 2). What the family dispenses is "loathe-love largesse" (92) and it is an "investment" (to borrow terms from Brooks's poem) on which they expect a return: gratitude (the only black man they can understand is a grateful one, a forgiving one). This entire transaction, mingling, as Brooks would have it, "mercy and murder" (90), baffles Bigger Thomas, but he rightly perceives in Jan and Mary's gestures—as when they ask him to join them at Ernie's Kitchen Shack on the South Side—a threat of which even they remain unaware.

The killing itself is an accident: Mary drinks herself into semi-consciousness during a date with Jan, on this, Bigger's first night as the family chauffeur. On their return to the Dalton house, Bigger faces a dilemma: how can he get Mary into her bedroom without waking Mr. and Mrs. Dalton, who would then discover that Mary has not been, as she was supposed to be, attending a lecture? He can't simply leave her in the car; but neither can he wake the Daltons and reveal that he had ignored their instructions—even if he did so at Mary's insistence—to drive her to the lecture. So he hauls Mary upstairs on his own—a tantalizing, painful ordeal during which, as the un-bowdlerized text makes clear, Mary clumsily comes on to Bigger.[3] As he attempts to tuck her into bed—whether or not he intends to respond to her drunken sexual advances is not clear, though he is tempted—Mrs. Dalton appears in the doorway like an apparition. She is blind and cannot see Bigger, who, in desperation, covers Mary's face with a pillow to prevent her from answering her mother's call. (Wright adapts the family's surname from "Daltonism," a form of color-blindness [deuteranopia].) Should Bigger be found at Mary's bedside, no account he might give of how he got there would prevent his being fired; or so he fears—and with good reason. Before he realizes it, Mary is dead from suffocation; her mother, approaching the bed, gets a whiff of whiskey and cigarette smoke, concludes that the girl is drunk, and leaves her to sleep it off. Bigger stuffs the body into the basement furnace—he has to sever the head in order to make it fit—and cooks up a scheme to mislead police into believing that Mary has been kidnapped by local Communists. When a reporter, quite by chance, discovers fragments of bone in the ashes, Bigger flees, brutally murders his black girlfriend, Bessie Mears, out of fear that she'll betray him, and hides out among the dilapidated buildings of Chicago's South Side—the very buildings that absentee landlords like Mr. Dalton leave undeveloped so as artificially to inflate the rents they charge black tenants. (Wright had written about the practice for the *Daily Worker* during his days in the Party.) Bigger is captured, charged with capital murder and rape (a crime he did not, in fact, commit) and tried. The Communist Party provides Bigger with an attorney, Boris Max, who, in the course of a long argument before the jury, offers an analysis of American racism that he hopes will account for Bigger's actions in such a way as to mitigate his responsibility and thereby save him from execution. But the effort fails: Bigger is convicted and sentenced to die.

In "How Bigger Was Born," his account of the writing of the novel, Wright sets out a theory of authorship: the novelist's imagination, as he sees it, is an intersection of the "public" and "private"—by which he means an intersection of the "socially" determined and the "personally" directed. "An imaginative novel," Wright explains, "represents the merging of two extremes; it is an intensely intimate expression on the part of a consciousness couched in terms of the most objective and commonly known events" (505). Associated with this idea is Wright's acknowledgement that much of the meaning of *Native Son* simply seemed to "happen" to him as he wrote; he didn't "intend" so much as "discover" the meaning of the book. "I say frankly that there are phases of *Native Son* which I shall make no attempt to account for. There are meanings in my book of which I was not aware until they literally spilled onto the paper. I shall sketch the outline of how I *consciously* came into possession of the materials that went into *Native Son*, but there will be many things I shall omit, not because I want to, but simply because I don't know them" (506). It is through the action of forces beyond the management of the author—Wright calls these "public" as opposed to "private" materials—that his "internal" and "personal" motives actually unfold. Writing is the experience both of acting (in language) and of being acted upon (by language); it is in fact the experience of being *unable to distinguish* between acting and being acted upon.

Once we set the terms of the matter this way, it becomes apparent that Bigger Thomas in some sense "represents" the situation of his author—just as Uncle Julius "represents" Chesnutt's situation—and not merely because Wright "identifies" with his violent rebellion (though, in "How Bigger Was Born," he says that he does). *Native Son* situates Bigger precisely at the intersection of "external" compulsion and "internal" motivation, of "necessity" and "free will." Nowhere is this better achieved than in the first murder scene.[4] Wright constructs a scene wherein his protagonist is compelled to commit a crime: circumstance, not Bigger's own volition, is the agent here. Bigger seems to have no true agency—no genuinely personal motivation—in committing this crime. But though the killing is, in fact, an accident, the novel shows how it is also what the critic Kenneth Burke, in another connection, has called a *"representative* accident" (*Grammar of Motives* 307). The act may be "motivated" by necessity. But it unfolds, or allows to emerge, what Bigger himself comes to recognize as his own "true" motivation, his own will: he *did* have murder in his heart; he had the *mens rea*. Bigger discovered himself in the killing. "What I killed for, I *am*," he says to his lawyer, Max. "What I killed for must've been good!," at which Max recoils, marking his divergence from Wright, who never once recoils from his protagonist. "I didn't know I was really alive in this world," Bigger adds, "until I felt things hard enough to kill for 'em." At this point we read: "Max's eyes were full of terror" (849). In taking responsibility for the act—even to the point of acknowledging to his lawyer that he had been, with Mary Dalton, party to the erotic flirtation that preceded it—he makes his existence meaningful; he *creates* himself in the act. For the first time, he realizes that he is himself an agent—a "person acting," not merely "a thing in motion" buffeted about by forces he cannot control.[5] In short, in *Native Son*, Wright depicts an act that is at once "accidental" *and* a "murder," something that our legal code, nuanced though it may be, is unable to recognize. This is Boris Max's argument in his plea on behalf of Bigger: the occurrence at the Dalton home that night *did* in fact somehow *represent* Bigger's character, which had been hardened and tempered by oppression. Yet that occurrence was also pre-determined, and Bigger's role in it cast long ago. Because our culture is organized by assumptions of white supremacy, and because white supremacy had for generations been so violent and brutal in its operations, the killing of Mary Dalton had about it an air of inevitability (one hears a whisper: *this is what America does to—sets out to do, requires of—its native black sons and white daughters; this is the novel America was destined to produce; this is the novel America can't put down; this is our page-turner*).

The whole interest of the novel is in how Wright plays through the paradoxical implications of Bigger's situation. In killing Mary Dalton, Bigger was both "volunteer" and "draftee," both "actor" and "pawn." To what extent did he "act" that night? To what extent was he only "acted upon"? *Native Son* brilliantly explores these questions. And in so doing, it uniquely equips the reader to understand Wright's remarks about "authorship" in "How Bigger Was Born." In suffering the happy "accidents" of authorship, the novelist comes more deeply to feel his own, strictly "private" powers. And that, finally, is the situation Bigger Thomas finds himself in: his own purposes, his own meaning, are revealed by "accident." The moment of the killing is the moment where he seems least in control of his fate, and most a mere cipher compelled by circumstance; but that moment precisely marks the point at which, for the first time in his bewildered life, he becomes meaningfully *creative*, the first time he ever comes into "possession" of himself. Bigger begins to acquire what "this American world," as Du Bois phrases it, had for centuries denied black folk: "true self-consciousness" (*Souls* 364). The killing, in fact, marks the moment of Bigger Thomas's "birth"; and we may take it, in light of what Wright says in "How Bigger Was Born," as peculiarly emblematic of the new "birth" of freedom any author undergoes in risking so transgressive and original a novel as *Native Son*. In a fashion altogether uncanny, the novel is also an autobiography, or a confession.

The worst ravages of racism divide Bigger against himself. Racism has robbed him of "motive"; it has reduced his "agency" to degree zero. But it has also given him all too abundant "motive" in the sense of "cause" or "reason" to act. And it has left him unable to understand, or in any event to confront, his own emotions; they are alienated from him. We see this in his conversation with Gus before the planned robbery of Blum's Delicatessen. "'Sometimes I feel like something awful's going to happen to me,' Bigger spoke *with a tinge of bitter pride* in his voice" (my emphasis). He quickly clarifies the point: "Every time I get to thinking about me being black and they being white, me being here [on the south side of Chicago] and they being there [on the north], I feel like something awful's going to happen to me...." (463). A moment passes as a plane flies overhead, and Bigger puts a telling question to Gus: "You know where the white folks live?" (464). When Gus answers prosaically ("'Over across the 'line'"), Bigger corrects him with a gesture:

> "Naw; they don't," Bigger said.
> "What you mean?" Gus asked, puzzled. "Then, where do they live?"
> Bigger doubled his fist and struck his solar plexus.
> "Right down here in my stomach," he said.
> Gus looked at Bigger searchingly, then away, as though ashamed.
> "Yeah; I know what you mean," he whispered.
> "Every time I think of 'em, I feel 'em," Bigger said.
> "Yeah; and in your chest and throat, too," Gus said.
> "It's like fire."
> "And sometimes you can't hardly breathe...."
> Bigger's eyes were wide and placid, gazing into space.
> "That's when I feel like something awful's going to happen to me...."
> Bigger paused, narrowed his eyes. "Naw; it ain't like something going to happen to me. It's.... It's like I was going to do something I can't help...."

> "Yeah!" Gus said with uneasy eagerness. His eyes were full of a look compounded of fear and admiration for Bigger. (464–65)

Bigger confesses that he is proud that he will be compelled to do something, or proud that something will "happen to him." But how can a man take "pride" in Fate—in sheer Necessity—which affects him as the moon affects the tide? The tide can take no "pride" in its motions, because they are exactly that: motions, not actions. Notice how Wright develops the planned robbery. Bigger arranges it so that he will be compelled to commit an act that he in fact dreads doing: he frightens Gus into promising to participate, even as he fears the likelihood that his stratagem will succeed:

> Even though Bigger had asked Gus to be with him in the robbery, the fear that Gus would really go made the muscles of Bigger's stomach tighten; he was hot all over. . . . He hated Gus because he knew that Gus was afraid, as even he was; and he feared Gus because he felt that Gus would consent and then he would be compelled to go through with the robbery. Like a man about to shoot himself and dreading to shoot and yet knowing that he has to shoot and feeling it at once and powerfully, he watched Gus and waited for him to say yes. (468)

Bigger's motive is self-destructive, or at the very least paradoxical: he takes actions to limit his own choice, his own ability to at; he acts so as to leave himself no exit. But then, once things are set in motion, once the robbery is on, he acts—all the while not permitting himself to acknowledge his real motives—so as to prevent that robbery from ever occurring. He picks a fight with Gus in the pool hall, the hour to strike Blum's comes and goes, and the heist is off. "'You done spoiled things now,' G. H. [another member of the crew] said. 'I reckon that was what you wanted. . .' 'You go to hell!' Bigger shouted, drowning out G. H.'s voice" (482).

The novel everywhere studies the morality of action and passion, of doing and suffering: Bigger may indeed be a tragic character, despite his "naturalist" heritage, because for him doing and suffering coincide, action and reaction merge. Wright's world is not a world in which "individual will"—free will—has no meaning; he is hardly a determinist (this explains why he would later find the French existentialists so appealing). The moral problem with which Wright confronts us is fascinating: in order to make Bigger Thomas a "heroic" figure, as opposed to a merely shocking one, Wright must assign him some responsibility for his own actions, some degree of real agency. Otherwise, we might pity him, but we could never *identify* with him (or, to put it another way, *respect* him, even in fear). It is as Frederick Douglass says: "A man, without force, is without the essential dignity of humanity. Human nature is so constituted, that it cannot *honor* a helpless man, although it can *pity* him; and even this it cannot do long, if the signs of power do not arise" (*A* 286). At the same time, to the extent that Bigger is made responsible, culpable—that is to say, to the extent that he transcends the condition of being a "thing in motion," and thereby "owns" the killings—he becomes repugnant to us, a kind of monster. There is, of course, real danger in a novelist's allowing violent protagonists to become attractive, charismatic, and compelling. This unsettles readers who are, and not entirely without reason, disturbed by the "charismatic" qualities of violent acts. But were Bigger Thomas altogether bereft of power, the novel would be nihilistic, which it certainly is not. Bigger's appeal in fact depends upon his having power, twisted though its expressions may be. Deny him all responsibility for his actions, deny him the *right* to pay for his "sins," and you deny him his humanity, his agency: again, he becomes a "thing in motion," not a "person acting." Allow Bigger Thomas responsibility, allow him to "sin," to "act," and although this makes him in some sense "monstrous"—as when he deliberately murders his girlfriend Bessie, once he fears she'll betray him—it also makes possible our identification with him; his plight becomes meaningful only to the extent that his choices seem real. So long as "choice" is a reality in the novel, so long as the will is in some sense "free," there is hope. The novel makes Bigger into something truly terrible, the better that we might see in him something human—in order that we might see in him ourselves. Had Wright denied Bigger Thomas his agency, his will, the result would have been a fiction of resignation and despair (and a book that banker's daughters could weep over; as it is, the novel unsettles *that* peculiar relation of production). Men with no agency—men who cannot "sin" any more than a pit viper can—are unreclaimable, and, it is to be hoped, unimaginable. And at last, this is the ethical problem of the novel: in compelling us to accept Bigger Thomas as a real agent, Wright challenges our capacity for forgiveness.

Black Boy, the Book of the Month Club, and *Native Son*

The publication of *Native Son* was a landmark; it brought to discussions of American race relations a candor as refreshing as it was unnerving. Perhaps this was only possible in 1940 (and through the mediating buffer of the Book of the Month Club), given the changes the New Deal (and the Great

Depression) had wrought in the political economy: capital and plutocracy, after a decade of crisis, had made accommodation, even if from motives of self-preservation, with the redistributionist policies of the Roosevelt administration. Soon, wartime imperatives—and pressure from civil rights activist A. Philip Randolph—would compel FDR to issue Executive Order 8802 (June 1941), which created the Fair Employment Practice Committee, desegregated labor in the defense industry, and bettered the wages of black workers. Whatever the case, in the first three weeks of its release in 1940, *Native Son* sold more than 200,000 copies and made Wright a literary star (a successful stage adaptation, directed by Orson Welles, ran in New York through 1943). For the first time in his life Wright felt financially secure, and his private affairs, too, began to fall into order. In 1941, after his first brief marriage to Dhima Rose Meadman ended unhappily, Wright married Ellen Poplar, a Communist Party organizer of Polish-Jewish extraction. The couple would remain together—despite occasional troubles—bearing two daughters, Julia and Rachel.

On April 9, 1943, Wright delivered a lecture at Fisk University—Du Bois's old haunt—taking as his subject, as he put it later, "what I felt and thought about the world; what I remembered about my life, about being a Negro."[6] In this experience lay the impetus to begin his autobiography, and its complicated textual history bears looking into not simply for what it reveals about Wright's purposes, but for what it can tell us about the economic situation of the African American writer in the mid-twentieth century—something about his relation to the *market* (and something about the marketability of black lives). As for the difficult situation of African American writers at the turn of the century, we have seen what Chesnutt faced. And as to requests that he retain the "plantation manner" in his performances on the platform, we have seen what Frederick Douglass did.

In December 1943 Wright was able to deliver the manuscript of "American Hunger," as it was called, to his agent in New York. As it then stood, the book was divided into two sections: "Southern Night," which treats Wright's experiences in the South, up until he fled Memphis for Chicago in 1927; and "The Horror and the Glory," which for the most part concerns Wright's experiences as a member of the Communist Party in Chicago, and which brings the narrative up to 1937, when he moved to New York City. The book was accepted in January 1944 by Edward Aswell, Wright's editor at Harper and Brothers. Within a month, the revised typescript was at the manufacturing department, and by May, Aswell was sending out bound galleys of "American Hunger" to other authors for statements he could use in advertising. But in July, the Book of the Month

Club—still as formidable a force in American publishing as it had been in 1939–40 when it took on *Native Son*—expressed interest in the memoir, and thus began the exchange that ultimately led to the publication of only section 1 of the book, the section titled "Southern Night," and known ever since as *Black Boy*. The rest of the autobiography, about one third again the length of *Black Boy*, remained unpublished (in its entirety) until 1977, when Harper and Row released it as *American Hunger*, the title Wright had originally chosen for the work as a whole.

Correspondence in the Harper and Brothers archive at Princeton's Firestone Library makes clear that the book club requested that only the first part of the memoir be published.[7] The book now was to end as Wright fled to Chicago, with the stark summary that closes section 1 of "American Hunger": "This was the culture from which I sprang. This was the terror from which I fled." Wright supplied, also at the suggestion of the book club, several pages of new material to round out this conclusion; these followed the two sentences just quoted, after a type-break. The distinguished author Dorothy Canfield Fisher—a New England liberal, and one of the club's officials—acted as liaison between the club and Wright, working with the author on these final revisions, sometimes suggesting changes, which Wright followed or ignored as he saw fit. At one point, Fisher suggested a new way to end the book, putting it to Wright in the form of a question.

> From what other source than from the basic tradition of our country could the soul of an American have been filled with the "hazy notion" that life could be lived with dignity? Could it be that even from inside the prison of injustice, through the barred windows of that Bastille of racial oppression, Richard Wright had caught a glimpse of the American flag? The briefest recognition in our nation of this long-held aspiration, reaching you, valid enough to help keep alive in your heart that "consciousness of possibilities" which has continually led you up into wider and finer development—what a benediction that would be![8]

Canfield Fisher knew France; she'd worked in the ambulance corps during World War I. How she failed to see the irony in her Gallic overture to Wright is a feature of her white, New England liberalism. Her point is that, as the Revolution was to the Bastille, so the North (which she confuses with an America that has yet to exist) was to the South. Wright was no such easy believer in American "possibilities." He didn't go to his grave believing that we could build the New Jerusalem if we would; he knew the "Bastille of racial oppression" was a national and not a sectional matter. And he closed *Black Boy* without a patriotic "benediction." Still, it is only fair to

Fisher to add that she was not suggesting this particular change as a condition of the book's acceptance by the Committee. Instead, she was asking Wright, as one who should know, to confirm her belief in the democratic promise of America, a promise that simply must, she supposed, transcend cultural, racial, and geographical boundaries. She could not abandon her own Columbian ideals, not, especially, as the war against fascism was in progress. When Canfield Fisher wrote this letter, the Normandy invasion was in its third week; she simply had to believe that the white supremacists were chiefly on the Nazi side of the lines, even if that meant turning her eyes away from certain sordid American realities. Wright knew better, and he could not offer her this consolation; he had grown up amongst Uncle Tom's children. (He did, however, pen an appeal to readers—printed on the dust jacket of *Black Boy*—to buy war bonds.) Wright sent to Aswell this simple, straight remark: "I don't think I could relate myself any better—and keep within the facts—to the American scene."[9] Our Bastille didn't stop at the Ohio River, never had, and still does not. Canfield Fisher already had in hand a novel that made the general point better than any other ever had: *Native Son*. The book concerns (as I have indicated) the daughter of an American capitalist, killed, accidentally-on-purpose, by a member of the black lumpenproletariat, himself imperfectly understood by a Communist lawyer—and it ends on Death Row. How could Richard Wright have "[related] himself any better to the American scene" than he had there? Nevertheless, from 1945 until 1991 readers knew Wright's autobiography as *Black Boy* and read the text that reflected his compromise with the Book of the Month Club. In 1991, however, the Library of America published *Black Boy (American Hunger)* in the form it would have taken had the book club never intervened; that text is now the standard.

Black Boy (American Hunger) is a narrative of captivity and of escape; it is, like Douglass's great autobiographies, the narrative of a fugitive. And there is always something rootless, something restless, about Wright's life and work; we can see this even in the constantly changing style of his prose. The modernist experiment of *Lawd, Today!*, his first book, gave way to an exercise in socialist-realism, *Uncle Tom's Children*. After that came *Native Son*, an almost "sociological" novel undertaken in the tradition of Dreiser's great works of literary naturalism. Then came the autobiography; an existentialist novel, *The Outsider*, written in France; travel books; books on politics; his last novel, *The Long Dream*, which owes much to psychoanalysis, and which is set, as are no other of Wright's published novels, in his native Mississippi; and, perhaps most startling of all, a series of some 4,000 haiku, written toward the end of his life. Wright never once settled into a style, into a form, or even into a "language": his diction, from book to book, is unsure and eclectic. Doubtless this has something to do with the fact that Wright was an autodidact, but it is associated as well with a fugitive quality in his temperament and experience alike. But from what is he a fugitive—from what is he always in flight? What disallowed him from ever settling into a recognizable, into an *available*, "literary" and "social" space?

The best answer to the question lies in a description Wright gives, in *Black Boy (American Hunger)*, of his father, Nathan Wright (1880–1940)—the son of former slaves—as Wright saw him for the last time, after a separation of twenty-five years. The year was 1940, and the aged man—he was then sixty—stood "alone upon the red clay of a Mississippi plantation, a sharecropper, clad in ragged overalls, holding a muddy hoe in his gnarled, veined hands." "My mind and consciousness had become so greatly and violently altered," says Wright, "that when I tried to talk to him I realized that, though ties of blood made us kin . . . we were forever strangers": "I was overwhelmed to realize that he could never understand me or the scalding experiences that had swept me beyond his life and into an area of living that he could never know. I stood before him, poised, my mind aching as it embraced the simple nakedness of his life, feeling how completely his soul was imprisoned by the slow flow of the seasons, by wind and rain and sun, how fastened were his memories to a crude and raw past, how chained were his actions and emotions to the direct, animalistic impulses of his withering body" (34–35). His father was, and would always remain, a "creature of the earth," a "peasant" held back from what Wright calls the "alien and undreamed of shores of knowing" (35) (what Du Bois, of course, calls "the wings of Atalanta"). The logic underlying this remarkable passage is binary: animality/humanity, past/future, rawness/refinement, nature/culture, body/mind, nakedness/civility, peasantry/cosmopolitanism, and so on; and the terms of each pair are opposed to one another as father is to son. Wright sees in his father a man locked in what the existentialists he would soon be living amongst might call a life of "immanence": as Wright presents him to us, he is bound down by the fate of the body, and by the inhuman claim of "nature" (by the seasons, by the weather, by physical appetites—all regulated, of course, by the *cultural* system of debt peonage and sharecropping). His father dwells on the plane of what Wright later calls mere "physical living," a level at which, in fact, there can be no existence "worthy of being called human" (*Black Boy* 302). In him we see the face of disenfranchised black labor in the South. (I should add that the 1910 census, taken when Richard was two years old, indicates that his father could read and write, and worked, at the time, selling tobacco; this was four years before he abandoned his wife and son.)

As we have seen already, slavery and its aftermath had inculcated in white folks—and colonialism tended to do the same everywhere white Europeans undertook it—a habit of assimilating the opposition black/white to the oppositions body/mind, savagery/civility, and animality/humanity. We have seen also how this assimilation accounts for the often-morbid fascination with which white men and women contemplate the sexuality of people of color: color, in this context, comes to mean sexuality as such, or pure *embodiedness*. A life devoted to sensualism of a sort, a life led, as had been his father's, according to "direct, animalistic impulses," always haunts Wright as the terrible possibility somehow marked out for him by Mississippi and white supremacy. Fate seldom affords a man a hard look at what he *really* might have been, such as Wright had in that Mississippi cotton field in 1940. Toward the end of his time in the south, when he was living in Memphis (1925–27), educating himself, often by subterfuge, Wright considered giving up the struggle to transcend the merely "physical" plane of existence on which his father had lived. "I could, of course, forget what I had read," he writes, "thrust the whites out of my mind, forget them; and find release from anxiety and longing in sex and alcohol. But the memory of how my father had conducted himself made that course repugnant. If I did not want others to violate my life, how could I voluntarily violate it myself?" (241). There is something chaste in this line of reasoning, something a little ascetic: violation and self-violation are (as the phrase has it) fates worse than death.

Above all—like his predecessors Douglass, Du Bois, and Chesnutt—Wright resisted the reduction of men to bodies, or of persons to things, as the foregoing discussion of *Native Son* shows. This humiliating reduction clearly underlies a "violation" Wright recalls having suffered from a white co-worker in the following passage from *Black Boy (American Hunger)*:

> "Richard, how long is your thing?" he asked me.
> "What thing?" I asked.
> "You know what I mean," he said. "The thing the bull uses on the cow."
> I turned away from him; I had heard that whites regarded Negroes as animals in sex matters and his words made me angry.
> "I heard that a nigger can stick his prick in the ground and spin around on it like a top," he said, chuckling. "I'd like to see you do that. I'd give you a dime if you did it." (180)

At the request of the Book of the Month Club, who worried that it might be judged obscene, Wright cut this passage from *Black Boy*.[10] Obscene it surely is, but the obscenity is intrinsic to white supremacy: this is the characteristic gesture of a regime that would, and at the cost of much more than a dime, lock more than half of humanity into the "crude," "raw," "naked," "animalistic" prison house of the body. What is this but degraded white labor enjoying, by degrading black labor, its "psychological wage"—and all at the cost of a dime unspent? Who is to say that the Book of the Month Club did not, in a sense, pay its (chiefly white) readers a "psychological wage"? True, the club would give its constituents books like *Native Son* and *Black Boy*. But it would also spare Northern readers—by careful bowdlerization in *Native Son*, and by closing *Black Boy* with a train heading north out of Memphis—certain possibilities for uneasy self-reflection. The psychological wage would have risen to premium rates had Dorothy Canfield Fisher prevailed upon Wright to sweeten the tea for patriotic white readers in the midst of World War II: "Could it be that even from inside the prison of injustice, through the barred windows of that Bastille of racial oppression, Richard Wright had caught a glimpse of the American flag? . . . what a benediction that would be!" Fisher's exclamation adds a note of piety to this appeal to our civil religion; but as to that, Wright was no congregant. Whatever the case, he certainly had set about to withhold from white readers any "psychological wages" his books might pay them once he determined, after reckoning the reception accorded *Uncle Tom's Children*, that, in any further books he might write, he would deny "bankers' daughters" the "consolation of tears."

As for the prison house of the body: *Black Boy (American Hunger)* is a record of Wright's flight from precisely this fate, and the image of his broken father stands behind the narrative like an admonition; it is an unsettling, ambivalent experience when Wright sees "the shadow of his own face" in his father's, as he puts it, and when he hears in his father's voice "an echo of his own." This flight would soon lead Wright, together with his new family, into exile. *Black Boy* rose to the top of the bestseller list—in no small part owing to the marketing strategies of the Book of the Month Club—and earnings from its sales allowed Wright to resettle in Paris in 1947, where he hoped to put behind him for good the Bastille of racism he daily faced even in New York City. The "coming universities of the South" may have been, for Du Bois, the "wings" that would lift black Atalanta safely above the humiliating fate of the body. For the autodidact Wright, the wings were his own good books.

But as for this double question of sexuality and the body: having inquired into *Black Boy*, we should consider again the revisions the Book of the Month Club asked Wright to make to *Native Son*. The Book Club became interested in the novel in August of 1939, by which time its text had already gone into page proofs, a bound set of which Wright's editor, Edward Aswell, sent the club for review. (But for their intervention, the novel would have been published in 1939, coincident with the outbreak of war in Europe.) Aswell reports to Wright in an August 22 letter:

> And incidentally the Book Club wants to know whether, if they do choose *Native Son*, you would be willing to make some changes in that scene early in the book where Bigger and his friends are sitting in the moving picture theatre. I think you will recognize the scene I mean and will understand why the Book Club finds it objectionable. They are not a particularly squeamish crowd, but that scene, after all, is a bit on the raw side. I daresay you could revise it in a way to suggest what happens rather than to tell it explicitly.[11]

The Beinecke Library at Yale University holds the bound set of proofs Aswell sent to the club for their review, and I have examined it. The scene in question begins at page 25, line 9 of the first edition of *Native Son*. On the afternoon of Bigger's interview at the Dalton's (and therefore only a matter of hours before he commits the "murder"), he and Jack stop in at the Regal Theatre to see a movie. Here is the scene as it originally read, and as it again reads in the Library of America edition of the novel published in 1991:

> They walked six blocks in silence. It was eleven-thirty when they reached Forty-seventh Street and South Parkway and the Regal was just opening. They bought tickets and walked into the darkened movie and took seats. The picture had not yet started and they sat listening to the pipe organ playing low and soft. Bigger moved restlessly and his breath quickened; he looked round in the shadows to see if any attendant was near, then slouched far down in his seat. He glanced at Jack and saw that Jack was watching him out of the corners of his eyes. They both laughed.
> "You at it again?" he asked.
> "I'm polishing my nightstick," Bigger said.
> They giggled.
> "I'll beat you," Jack said.
> "Go to hell."
> The organ played for a long moment on a single note, then died away.
> "I'll bet you ain't even hard yet," Jack whispered.
> "I'm getting hard."
> "Mine's like a rod," Jack said with intense pride.
> "I wished I had Bessie here now," Bigger said.

"I could make old Clara moan now."
They sighed.
"I believe that woman who passed saw us."
"So what?"
"If she comes back I'll throw it in her."
"You a killer."
"If she saw it she'd faint."
"Or grab it, maybe."
"Yeah."
Bigger saw Jack lean forward and stretch out his legs, rigidly.
"You gone?"
"Yee-eeah..."
"You pull off fast..."
Again they were silent. Then Bigger leaned forward, breathing hard.
"I'm gone...God...damn..."
They sat still for five minutes, slumped back down in their seats. Finally, they straightened.
"I don't know where to put my feet now," Bigger said, laughing. "Let's take another seat."
"O.K."
They moved to other seats. (473)

In satisfying the book club, Wright removed all references to masturbation. But he also made a number of other changes in this scene, many of them designed to bring the new text back into alignment with the original plates so as to disturb as little of the type as possible (resetting type was costly). The result is a number of differences between the 1939 and 1940 texts, the most interesting of which is this: instead of *The Gay Woman*, the first movie of a double-feature in the 1940 text, in the 1939 text Bigger and Jack watch a newsreel, in the "Lifestyles of the Rich and Famous" vein, about none other than Mary Dalton, whom Bigger is later that night to kill. And it is from this newsreel that Bigger first discovers who the Daltons actually are (until now they have just been a name to him). The screen shows a rowdy gathering of women and men on a Florida beach ("This little collection of debutantes represents over four billion dollars of America's wealth," says the voice-over), and then zooms in on Mary: "Mary Dalton, daughter of Chicago's Henry Dalton, 4605 Drexel Boulevard, shocks society by spurning the boys of La Salle Street and the Gold Coast and accepting the attentions of a well-known radical [i.e., Jan Erlone] while on her recent winter vacation in Florida" (474). Bigger recognizes the address as the one to which he is to report that afternoon for an interview, and he mentions this fact to Jack. The rest of the scene more or less stands as it does in the text published in 1940: *Trader Horn* (1931), starring Harry Carey, and set in Africa amongst a "savage" people, follows the newsreel.

I compared the page-endings of the bound page-proofs (1939) to those of the first edition (1940), through to the end of the text, and was able to spot all revisions extensive enough to throw the type out of alignment. The next such revision occurs at page 95, line nineteen, of the 1940 text, where Wright has excised a reference to the newsreel (no longer present in the novel) by one of Bigger's friends. And it becomes clear later in the original text that this newsreel and the "objectionable" masturbation scene which precedes it are in fact intertwined in the novel as originally written, which is doubtless why, in the 1940 first edition, Wright replaced the newsreel with *The Gay Woman*; removing the masturbation scene meant he *had* to remove the newsreel. (The book club saw no problem with the newsreel; Aswell makes no direct reference to it in this connection in his letters.) From page 323 to the end Wright removed about 5–6 pages of material, throwing the published text out of alignment with the proof for most of the novel's final thirty pages. Max's speech is shortened.[12] But more interesting is Wright's revision of the prosecutor's speech, where, for the 1940 text, he once again excised reference to the newsreel. In the 1939 text, the prosecutor alleges that Bigger performed lewd acts *while watching* Mary Dalton on screen, all the time knowing that she was the daughter of the man who was soon to employ him. This makes Bigger's crime seem pre-meditated, which is exactly as the prosecutor wants it: Bigger is charged with the rape (as well as the murder) of Mary Dalton. The rape is the prosecutor's racist delusion, of course; none was committed. But as a consequence of this delusion, and to make the charge plausible, he conflates two episodes that are, in the original text, distinct: the masturbation scene (the manager of the theater told the DA about this) and the newsreel. It may well be that the book club's objection to the masturbation scene caused this other important alteration of the novel—that is, the removal of the prosecutor's allegation that Bigger masturbated while looking at images of Mary Dalton. But I cannot state definitely that this is the case. Wright may have had second thoughts about the newsreel, quite independently of any questions raised by the book club (it does seem implausible that the Dalton's street address would be so freely given out). He might readily have omitted the "objectionable" passage and yet left the newsreel and the prosecutor's speech alone: the prosecutor alludes to the incident euphemistically, and in any event distorts it broadly to support a rape charge that the reader knows full well is spurious.

Wright did make several other small but very important excisions at this time, almost certainly at the request of the book club, and all of them have to do with Bigger's sexuality. He cut a few phrases from the end of the passage describing the drive around "The Loop" which make it clear that Jan and Mary are making love in the back seat of the car, and that Bigger knows it and is aroused. Further, it is clear in the pre-book club text—as I've indicated—that Mary drunkenly comes on to Bigger as he carries her up the stairs, and that he responds: "He tightened his arms as his lips pressed tightly against hers and he felt her body moving strongly. The thought and conviction that Jan had had her a lot flashed through his mind. He kissed her again and felt the sharp bones of her hips move in a hard and veritable grind. Her mouth was open and her breath came slow and deep" (524). In fact, later, when Bigger makes love to his girlfriend Bessie Mears, he imagines (in an act of pseudo-necrophilia) that she *is* Mary Dalton. All of this Wright cut. No direct mention of these revisions is made in the correspondence held in the archives at Yale and Princeton; but they certainly were done when Wright made the revisions explicitly requested by the book club, and since they are consistent in character with those changes (all of them having to do with the controversial matter of Bigger's sexuality), there is good reason to believe that Wright undertook all of them to satisfy the book club.[13]

So, why rehearse the matter of the Book of the Month Club's interventions in such detail? *Native Son* brings to light the sinister, oppressive side of a way of thinking about "race" in America that often presents itself to us as generosity and admiration, as in a novel like *On the Road*, as I argue in chapter 6. I refer to the ready way in which District Attorney Buckley and the newspaper reporters who cover Bigger's story construct "blackness" as the region of uninhibited sexuality, license, barbarism, and so on; and to the easy way in which they imagine "blackness" as that which resists civility. For this reason, the only alternative is to oppress (and to repress): the result is a segregated city, with "black" life forced to inhabit one small corner of it. The result is also a kind of parasitic relation of white to black, as this novel makes clear: white capitalists and landowners profit by the exploitation. Such men as Mr. Dalton acquire dilapidated buildings for a song, neglect to renovate them, compel men and women to live in them at rents artificially inflated due to segregation (that is, when black men and women are prohibited from living in other areas of the city, competition for apartments in the Black Belt becomes artificially intense: Bigger's family sometimes has to wait months for the privilege of renting a one-room, rat-infested tenement).[14] Once Dalton secures his profits, he salves his conscience (and masks the real nature of his relation to families like the Thomases) through philanthropy: he donates money and ping-pong tables to the South Side

Boy's Club. Wright shows us how duplicitous Dalton's relationship to the Thomases actually is: one the one hand, Dalton flatters himself that he is benevolent—he funds the Boy's Club, he gives Bigger a job, etc. But on the other hand, his relation to them, the relation through which he makes his fortune, is hygienically abstracted through the fictions of capitalist ownership. Dalton owns stock in a company that owns the South Side Real Estate Company; this permits him to say, disingenuously, that the Thomases do not pay him rent, when in fact they do, as Max points out in interrogating Dalton at the coroner's inquest. In sum: we have a rigorously segregated city; we have a parasitic relation of white capital to black labor (and black lives); and we have a construction of "blackness" that finds in it the very essence of lawless sexual vitality (for D. A. Buckley and his confederates), but also of "soul" and "authenticity" on the other (for Jan and Mary). How *amenable* to white motives the disenfranchised black body is: get rich off it, launch a political career on its back, weep or swoon at the thought of it, just as occasion requires—but never confer on it the wings of Atalanta; that way lies not only democracy, but self-knowledge of a kind the white imagination may not be willing to tolerate. Into all of this tangled mess stepped the Book of the Month Club. True, they were not an especially "squeamish" lot, as Aswell says in his letter to Wright, and there is real courage in their decision to take *Native Son* on, even in its bowdlerized form. But their discomfort with Wright's portrayal of Bigger as a sexually mature man indicates something about the troubled location, in the culture, of the "black" body, and something also about what the white literary market would bear.[15]

One of the truly peculiar features of *Native Son* is Max's long speech in defense of Bigger Thomas, because in it Wright offers a reading of his own novel; that is, *Native Son* is at once fiction and literary criticism. The model is this: the lawyer as literary critic, and the novelist as social analyst and also as *advocate*. In other words, literary art (or so this novel seems to argue) can and should be a form of *advocacy* (that is to say, advocacy of political struggle and action). What Wright does is quite ingenious: he stages a crime, with his readers as witnesses, and then proceeds to put the criminal on trial, with readers as judge and jury. We hear two radically divergent accounts of the meaning of the crimes we witness—that of the District Attorney, and that of the Communist lawyer. And it seems fair to say that while Max, here, is speaking in large part for Wright, there are certain points at which Max and Wright do not speak with a single voice (as when Max recoils in "terror" when Bigger says, as we've seen already, that what he killed for "must've been good"—a claim Wright would understand). Of course, Wright has explained himself twice—once in Max's speech, and once in "How Bigger Was Born": for what is Max's speech if not an account of how Bigger was born?

At one point, Max argues: "We must deal here with a dislocation of life involving millions of people, a dislocation so vast as to stagger the imagination; so fraught with tragic consequences as to make us rather not want to look at it or think of it; so old that we would rather try to view it as an order of nature.... When situations like this arise, instead of men feeling that they are facing other men, they feel that they are facing mountains, floods, seas: forces of nature whose size and strength focus the minds and emotions to a degree of tension unusual in the quiet routine of urban life" (450). Max's remarks incidentally provide a useful commentary on the symbolism of race as a "natural force" in part two of the novel: the whiteness of the snowstorm, the winter, the cold. These "objectify" Bigger's antagonist. But they do more than this. Wright shows us how "race" is socially produced, how it is anything but a part of "nature." We created "race" and then "fetishized" it, alienated it: it came to dominate and control us (its makers), quite as if it were a natural rather than a social force. This is what Max argues, in any event, and he is compelling. Later, he says, referring to Bigger: "I beg you to recognize human life draped in a form and guise alien to ours, but springing from a soil plowed and sown by all our hands" (451). The metaphor is agricultural, and what does it imply? That this particular form of human life (that is, Bigger Thomas) is not of a "natural" kind, as is, say, an oak tree; instead, it is of an *"agri-cultural"* kind, as are the crops we sow and reap. This "form" of "life" is (again) socially produced, however "natural" and immutable its operations may seem. Notice the vast difference between Buckley's arguments and Max's appeal. Buckley ascribes everything to "nature": to him, Bigger is little better than an animal—something less than fully human. (His arguments recall the polygenetic theorist Charles Carroll, whom I discussed in chapter 4.) It is simply in Bigger's *nature* to brutalize women. Buckley's language draws on the vocabulary of social Darwinism, a mystifying way to think of social and racial relations. Buckley's crude Darwinism—in which Bigger is made out to be something atavistic, a sort of uncivilizable missing link—inevitably casts social relations as natural ones; it rationalizes oppression by dehumanizing the racial other. Max, by contrast, appeals to social and historical contexts; his arguments derive from a Marxist tradition whose chief aim is to demystify such habits of thought as Buckley depends upon (and to encourage such habits of "reading" as I try, in this book, to do some justice). When Max speaks of Bigger Thomas as "alien" to white America (805), he uses the term advisedly: whites have "alienated" a part of themselves onto their racial "other," where they refuse to recognize it as *intrinsic* to themselves. White folk produced and refined "race" (including the one they assign to themselves) in legal codes and through oppressive social, political, and economic relations; they made "whiteness" and "blackness"—they didn't "discover" or "describe" them. And now, their creation affects them as an "alien" force, a "natural" force in response to which they can only cower in fear or strike back in violence.[16]

Max speaks of Bigger's "masturbatory" relation to the entire world that white America has created: "Was not Bigger Thomas's relation to this girl a masturbatory one? Was not his relation to the whole world on the same plane? His entire existence was one long craving for satisfaction, with the objects of satisfaction denied; and we regulated every part of the world he touched. Through the instrument of fear, we determined the mode and the quality of his consciousness" (468). Max has already spoken of how a consumer-capitalist culture depends upon consumption and requires that we fashion and re-fashion ourselves through further acts of consumption. If we deny twelve million people[17] full access to the economy (which is also an "economy" of selfhood), and at the same time subject them to invitations to join it pitched at a ferocious intensity, then we deny them the form of "selfhood" and of "becoming" on which our culture rests. In other words, we constantly arouse desire in these men and women and at the same time deny them the objects that would satisfy that desire; this is what puts them, as Max says, in a "masturbatory" and fantastic relation to America and its economies (their America is imaginary, and dwell in it they do). In the only terms our culture seems able to understand, we turn these twelve million people into "non-entities"—into men and women whose desires may never be consummated, even though these desires are constantly aroused; in other words, in an economy that depends upon the "eroticism" of exchange and commerce, we have reduced twelve million souls to a kind of stultifying "auto-eroticism," which is too much to ask, as Max contends. This argument amounts to a "reading" of the novel, and, more specifically, of the scene in the movie theater. (For this reason, the Book of the Month Club's request that this scene be removed was particularly damaging: it cut right to the heart of Wright's argument about the erotics of commerce and exchange.) In other words, the scene emerges as a kind of paradigm for Bigger's relation to the world as a whole: he is invited to watch that world, to be thrilled and excited by it, but he is never allowed to participate in it—to become a part of it, to step into its frame. For this reason, the world of men and women like the Daltons is in a very meaningful sense *unreal* to him: Mary Dalton doesn't "exist" for Bigger

Thomas; she is an apparition—a creature of the screen and of Hollywood. As Max explains: "Jan and Mary were not human beings to Bigger Thomas. Social custom had shoved him so far away from them that they were not real to him" (816). And we are invited to recognize that Bigger Thomas is as unreal to Mary and Jan as they are to him. We may live among one another as black and white; but there is an unbridgeable chasm between us—a chasm figured in *Native Son* as the distance between audience and movie screen.

Exile

By the time it was published, in 1953, Richard Wright had been working on *The Outsider* for some years. The Beinecke Library at Yale holds a sheaf of "Notes Toward a Novel" with plot outlines, sketches, and miscellaneous fragments, some dating from as early as 1947. The book was a hard one for him to write, and, as was immediately recognized, marked a sharp turn away from *Uncle Tom's Children*, *Native Son*, and *Black Boy*—the books which had earned him both a reputation and the money he needed to emigrate. *The Outsider* was, in fact, Wright's first major work in eight years (*Black Boy* had appeared in the spring of 1945); it was the first of his books to register his engagement with French existentialism (though Dostoevsky is another important influence); and it was the first novel he'd written as an expatriate (he'd been living in Paris since 1947). *The Outsider* broke new ground in Wright's art, as it necessarily did in his working habits. This latter, more practical point is not without significance: *The Outsider* was written and revised in London and Paris for publication in New York, and it was the first of Wright's major works to be edited by Jack Fischer (his friend and longtime editor Edward Aswell had moved to Doubleday). The knotty, strange prose of the novel, with its highly eccentric diction, troubled Fischer, as did also the many (often quite long) passages of philosophical speculation. It was a novel written as if by a man unsure of his literary footing—or so its New York editor, and the readers he consulted, assumed. What these men could not see is that the novel's odd style and diction is an index of Wright's cultural and historical dislocations, an index of his own life as an "outsider" in his "native" land (as a quasi-compulsory expatriate).

Wright began work on *The Outsider* in 1948. He had moved with his family into apartments on the Rue de Lille in Paris, had embarked on extensive readings in Continental philosophy, and had formed close relationships with Jean-Paul Sartre and Simone de Beauvoir, the two leading exponents of French existentialism. *The Outsider* is a forthrightly philosophical novel, built upon the existentialist proposition, as its hero explains, that "man is nothing in particular" (484). The novel opens in Chicago, where Cross Damon, a black postal worker of a bookish turn of mind, finds himself trapped: his estranged wife demands child-support payments he can barely manage; his pregnant lover insists that he obtain a divorce and marry her, and, for leverage, hatches a plot to accuse him of statutory rape (she had lied to him about her age). When his wife, on discovering this new entanglement, reports his behavior to the Chicago postmaster, Damon's job is put in peril. Depressed, and drinking almost constantly, he considers suicide, finds himself unable to commit the deed, and descends into despair—only to be presented with a way out, entirely by chance: a subway accident leaves him shaken, but alive, and when the body of a man who had been riding next to him is found mutilated beyond recognition with Cross's coat tangled about his body—it had gotten hung up as Cross made his escape from the wreck, and his wallet was still in it—the police conclude that he is dead. He assumes a false identity, resolves to recreate himself, murders a friend who could expose him, and then moves to New York. There he is drawn into the intrigues of a group of Communist Party activists and commits three more murders, partly to protect himself, but partly out of contempt for what the Communists represent (two of his victims are members of the party, the third a racist landlord against whom they'd hoped to bring legal action).

The novel's "philosophical" argument emerges from lengthy conversations between Cross Damon and Ely Houston, the Manhattan District Attorney who uncovers his true identity, and from a protracted exchange between Damon and an official of the Communist Party who is suspicious of his intentions. The argument has two phases. First, Wright advances the Nietzschean view that behind all of the esteemed institutions that constitute Western culture—the Church, political parties, enlightened colonialism, and so on—lies a blind struggle of will. Self-sacrifice, altruism, the good of humanity, the white man's burden, the emancipation of the working class: these ideals are masks, impostures—instruments by means of which men, acting always in bad faith, dominate the lives of other men. Working through everything is a will-to-power that is itself amoral. This truth is hateful, which is why we have succeeded so splendidly in deceiving ourselves about the nature of some of our most cherished institutions: we do not want to think of ourselves as mere animals struggling for domination. However—and here is the second phase of Wright's argument—capitalist-industrial development had, in the nineteenth and twentieth centuries, eroded the authority and prestige of religious, political, and philosophical institutions to the point that man will soon be compelled to confront himself as he "really" is. The "sentimental illusions" that used to "bind man to man," as Marx and Engels put it in the *Communist Manifesto*, had, one by one, been drowned in the "icy waters" of cold, calculating power (206), as the West consolidated its grip on the productive capabilities (and also the markets) of the entire globe. Man had been stripped bare. As Wright sees it, this is at once a curse and an opportunity: it is a curse because man has been set adrift, has come unmoored from the ideals that used to anchor his enterprises, and now finds himself disoriented; it is an opportunity because man has for the first time acceded to the responsibility, which can be terrifying, to define himself honestly. *The Outsider* is well suited to examine these problems: when he is mistakenly identified as among the dead in the subway wreck, Cross Damon stumbles upon precisely the opportunity, and also the burden, of self-creation—a burdensome opportunity that Frederick Douglass had met when he escaped from bondage and bestowed a new name on himself, and which Wright, too, had struggled to meet, in undertaking his twofold escape (first from the South, and then from America). And what Cross Damon discovers both exhilarates and horrifies him: namely, as we have seen, that "man is nothing in particular."

The Outsider, on its appearance in 1953, confused some of Wright's readers, and disappointed others; reviews were ambivalent. His years abroad, his readings in philosophy, his fascination with Parisian intellectual life—all this had caused him to lose touch, it was claimed, with his "real" subject matter; all of this had led him to attempt a kind of novel for which he was unprepared. Even Wright's agent, Paul Reynolds, felt this way. On April 30, 1953, shortly after the book was published, he wrote to Jack Fischer: "I have been worried for a long while as to what Wright should do. He told his story in fiction in *Native Son* and in non-fiction in *Black Boy*. It seemed to me clear that he couldn't live in Paris and write about the Negro Problem in America. *The Outsider* showed evidence of a man out of touch" (Richard Wright Papers). Reynolds, it seems, couldn't imagine Wright taking on subjects other than "the Negro problem in America"—as if his "race" somehow determined his themes. To be sure, the writing in *The Outsider* is often awkward, so much so that it strikes many as pretentious. Wright's editor, Jack Fischer, required that he make extensive revisions to the manuscript; he and his consultants struck scores of phrases, sentences, and even entire paragraphs, from the typescript as it went into production.[18] And Wright does appear to have lost the sure-footedness that kept the diction of *Black Boy (American Hunger)* so forceful and clear. One encounters in *The Outsider* hundreds of such ungainly sentences as this: "His face was the living personification of stupefied surprise" (430). Or: "Imprisoned he was in a state of consciousness that was so infatuated by its own condition that it could not dominate itself; so swamped was he by himself with himself that he could not break forth from behind the bars of that self to claim himself" (488). Or: "The assumptive promises he had welched on were not materially anchored, yet they were indubitably the things of this world, comprising as they did the veritable axis of daily existence" (774). The colloquial vigor of "welched" blends uncomfortably with such starched, bookish phrases as "assumptive promises," "veritable axis," and with words like "indubitably"; the counterpoint seems neither intentional nor controlled. And why, one wonders, should Wright favor inversions like "imprisoned he was," which one usually encounters in poetry, and then only when necessities of meter and rhyme require the distortion? Still, the strange language in which *The Outsider* is written is fitting: it is, as I've suggested, an index of Wright's own restlessness as a man and as a writer—the restlessness that led him to reinvent himself with every new book, and which drew him, at last, into exile. This is certainly the prose of an "outsider," the prose of a man who never felt quite at home, of a man who was forever a resident alien. *The Outsider*, precisely because it is a tortured and awkward book, is central to Wright's career. It is perfectly natural that he should compare Cross Damon's struggle to reinvent himself to the work of authorship: Cross, we are told, "would have to imagine this thing out, dream it out, invent it, like a writer constructing a tale" (456). And neither Cross in *The Outsider*, nor Wright in his life and work, would ever find a language quite adequate to this purpose. It is a problem with which American writers have often found themselves saddled. Hence the queer, often hermetic diction and the often-unprecedented styles of some of the most important figures in our tradition, from Emerson, Whitman, and Melville to Dickinson, Stevens, Stein, and (especially) Hart Crane.

The difficulty of Wright's style in *The Outsider* is that of a man who is never entirely master of the language he uses. And his situation is realized allegorically in the situation of Cross Damon—a figure who, more than any other character in Wright's fiction, speaks for his author. Damon tries to stand apart from the fates that would determine him—the fates of the past, of family, and of race. But neither he nor Wright nor any of us can really stand as though a man were author of himself and knew no other kin. No man can ever truly possess himself, or so *The Outsider* seems to argue. And the matter was of particular interest to Richard Wright, owing to his own effort to emancipate himself from the past—from the nightmare of American history—and to reinvent himself through writing. This was an effort to transcend the "animalistic" fate to which his father had been consigned by a racist culture he could neither combat nor ignore; this was a struggle to outrun the fate of the body itself—the fate of lapsing from "personhood" into mere "thing-ness." Cross, we are told, "was despairingly aware of his body as an alien and despised object over which he had no power, a burden that was always cheating him of the fruits of his thought, mocking him with its stubborn and supine solidity" (381). His appetites ruin him and are in the end untameable. To the extent that he thinks of himself as a "body," to the extent that he allows his "body" to determine him—especially in a white-supremacist culture that sees in the "black" body the flesh *as such*—to that extent precisely he has ceased to be a "person." To that extent precisely he has been "chained," as Wright's own father had been, at least to hear the son tell the tale, to the "direct, animalistic impulses" of the body (*Black Boy* 35). Wright had nothing less than this great problem in mind when he dedicated *Black Power* (1954), his book about the West African nation of Ghana, which was, at the time, emerging from British colonial domination, to "the unknown African who, because of his primal and poetic humanity, was regarded by white men as a 'thing' to be bought, sold, and used as an instrument of production; and who, alone in the forests of West Africa, created a vision of life so simple as to be terrifying, yet a vision that was irreducibly human" (n.p.). This "unknown African" is the father he would remember in all his life's work—the father America had denied him, as it had, in another way, denied a father to Frederick Douglass. And at last, *The Outsider* sets before us a challenge: how can we, now that all our illusions about "humanity" have been shattered by slavery, war, and empire, begin at last to create a mode of living that deserves to be called "human"?

In the last moments of *The Outsider*, Ely Houston asks Cross Damon a question: "How was it with you?" (840). Some indication as to how Wright himself might answer this question if it were put to him is to be found in the Book of Job. It is hardly insignificant that Wright should have set passages from Job, that great and most baffling of meditations on suffering, as epigraphs at the head of no fewer than four of his books. *Native Son*: "Even today is my complaint rebellious, and my stroke is heavier than my groaning." *Black Boy*: "His strength shall be hunger-bitten, and destruction shall be ready at his side." *The Outsider*: "Mark me, and be astonished, and lay your hand upon your mouth." *Savage Holiday*: "And, behold, there came a great wind from the wilderness and smote the four corners of the house."

So, how *was* it with Richard Wright? Apparently as it had been with Job in the midst of his own ordeal. The world seemed to him a place of inscrutable suffering—a place where punishment is administered without regard to justice, and prosperity bestowed without regard to merit. The Communist Party, at least as Wright knew it, attempted a nuanced and redemptive account of this suffering: they gave it meaning, and indicated how it all might someday end. Evil was to the communists no mystery, and neither was it a permanent fixture of human nature, in all conceivable places and at all conceivable times. But for Wright evil appears to have remained precisely a fixture—which may be one reason why he could not, at the end of the day, remain satisfied with the utopian rationalism of Communism (any more than could Ralph Ellison and his "invisible man"). He had, in the "southern night" of which he speaks in *Black Boy*, seen too much of motiveless malignity ever to suppose it might really be overcome: his American books are a chronicle of savage beatings, sadistic laughter, and acts that chill the blood.

Wright's work, especially the fiction, suggests that he had seen something unspeakable in his fellow men. And as he aged, he found his satisfactions where he could, and expected little from the world—much less than he expected when he concluded the first edition of *Uncle Tom's Children* with an exhilarating promise of revolution. Out of his later years come the ephemeral, often whimsical, pleasures of haiku, a form hardly suited to the ambitious, totalizing analyses of political problems he had attempted in *Native Son* and *The Outsider*. These—and they are quite good—have now been published by his daughter Julia Wright as *Haiku: This Other World* (2011). And out of the same years come such scenes as the one in *Pagan Spain* (1957) that tells the charming though melancholy story of a meal he once shared with a Spanish family in Madrid, laughing into the dawn, cutting up, singing, and staging a mock bullfight (201–5). These are the good hours, Wright seems to suggest, when the world is somehow redeemed: a fugitive from Mississippi; a Spanish family left fatherless and widowed by Franco and the Fascists; an hour or two of mirth set against a Job-like world of torment; and a promise on Wright's part—for this is what he gave his new Spanish friends as he parted from them at the station—to tell what he had seen.

Still, from the time he published *The Outsider* until his death seven years later Wright would never again find an audience like the one that bought copies of *Native Son* and *Black Boy* by the hundreds of thousands. Several nonfiction books followed over the next few years: *Black Power: A Record of Reactions in a Land of Pathos* (1954), about the Gold Coast—now

Ghana, where Du Bois is buried—which Wright visited in 1953; *The Color Curtain* (1956), a book about the 1955 conference of nonaligned nations in Bandung, Indonesia, which Wright had attended; *Pagan Spain* (1957), the study of Spanish culture to which I have just referred; and *White Man, Listen!* (1957), a collection of essays. Wright's last major novel, *The Long Dream* (1958), which revisits his native Mississippi, appeared in 1958 to bad reviews. The following year, the Wrights began preparations to resettle in London; Wright had grown estranged from the literary culture of his adopted Paris and was an outsider once again. But the move was never completed. Wright suffered a series of illnesses and died of heart failure in a Paris clinic on November 28, 1960, at the young age of fifty-two—leaving the rest of us to mark him, lay our hands upon our mouths, and be astonished.

In 1942, J. Edgar Hoover's FBI opened a file on Richard Wright and never closed it. He figured also in the files of the CIA. Thirty-nine years after Wright's death, Ollie Harrington, an old family friend, gave a speech in Detroit. He'd never met a black person, he said, who did not believe Richard Wright had been murdered. Murdered by whom? As to that, Harrington didn't know. "There were so many possibilities," he said (Rowley 525). Every one of Wright's biographers has addressed the theory. None has signed on to it. But the facts of the death are not, to me, material (at least not here). What matters more is the wariness of the survivors. America had dispossessed millions of its native sons while they lived. Why not dispossess them also of quiet in death?

Imaginary graveyards with real people buried in them.

CHAPTER SIX

PEASANT DREAMS: READING *ON THE ROAD*

"We can learn something about the naive artist," Nietzsche writes in *The Birth of Tragedy*, "through the analogy of dream. We can imagine the dreamer as he calls out to himself, still caught in the illusion of his dream and without disturbing it, 'This is a dream, and I want to go on dreaming,' and we can infer, on the one hand, that he takes deep delight in the contemplation of his dream, and, on the other, that he must have forgotten the day, with its horrible importunity, so to enjoy his dream" (32). Its Dionysian ecstasies notwithstanding, Jack Kerouac's *On the Road* (1957) belongs to the tradition of Apollonian art that Nietzsche conceives of here: an art of willful illusion sustained against the encroachments (as Nietzsche later puts it) of "a whole world of torment" (33). Kerouac's is the work of forgetting (as is Stephen Crane's, in its differing ways). But what intrigues me are precisely the residues of memory, the shafts of daylight, that trouble this dreamer's sleep.

I am interested in whether or not *On the Road* finally believes, and in what sense it believes, in the mythology of America on which it depends— whether or not, by Kerouac's lights, the America he gives us forthrightly remains an imaginary realm. At times Kerouac seems directly to question the faith his narrator Sal Paradise has in all Dean Moriarty comes to represent: a peculiarly intense and charismatic masculinity, a vital relation to the body, cultural and spiritual authenticity, the promise of America itself. *On the Road* achieves, it may be, a certain distance from its own enabling myths, quite as if it were holding them up for scrutiny even as it plays them out. This has the effect of putting us and the novel itself in a strangely abstract relation to its ideological basis, which is why the problem of faith is crucial. *On the Road* constantly tests the limits of its own creed, but refuses, often poignantly, to abandon it. Kerouac's road novel outruns its own horizon and at the same time always fails to achieve escape velocity. Its dawning, at times anxious, awareness of this fact makes *On the Road* an Emersonian fiction, an affiliation that provides a clue about the origins of another characteristic of the book: its exuberant, frustrated optimism. *On the Road* is a book that refuses to be jaded, no matter how canny, ironic, and self-aware it becomes.

Digging Everything

On the Road involves a familiar American idea about belief: the act of believing in Dean actually brings Dean about—makes him, renews him, creates him. We do not believe in Dean; we believe Dean in, to adapt a phrase Robert Frost once used about God and the future (727–28).[1] Dean Moriarty cannot exist apart from our fictions of him, which is why even Neal Cassady, upon whom the character is based, isn't real. He had a legendary kind of existence as the "cocksman and Adonis of Denver," as Allen Ginsberg put it in *Howl*. Kerouac, Ginsberg, and Cassady himself were always inventing and reinventing "Neal Cassady," who, as Ginsberg says in the dedication to *Howl and Other Poems*, had published several books in heaven. Neal is too fine a creation for this world; his genius can never be embodied. And the same goes for America, with which Dean Moriarty is mythically identified. (When Carlo Marx addresses America in the person of Dean, he only makes explicit what Kerouac always implies: "Whither goest thou, America, in thy shiny car in the night?"[2])

On the Road tells a Young Goodman Brown sort of story. We look out on America and see double: promise and piety on the one hand, wickedness and fraud on the other. Dean Moriarty, in all his dubiety, simply *is* America: "tumbledown holy America," Sal equivocally says, catching the seediness and the grace (135). On the whole, his fidelity, his affection for Dean, makes *On the Road* an optimistic work in the tradition of Whitman. It says Yes to America in the way Mark Twain's "road" novel, *Huckleberry Finn*, says No—and this despite the fact that *On the Road* entertains dystopian possibilities. Kerouac's is another in a long line of American fictions (and nonfictions) in which utopian and dystopian modes weirdly cooperate. The dubiety of *On the Road* is easy enough to see: it records a long, postadolescent drunken odyssey that *also* purports to be a spiritual journey of personal and national dimensions. Those with no faith—for example, the copywriters who marketed early paperback editions of the book as a salacious, lurid tale—see only the orgy and the drunkenness, only the kicks. The faithful see something else altogether: Dean Moriarty, new American Saint, as Sal Paradise puts it (35). Of course, nothing can fulfil the promise of Dean Moriarty. Sal's faith at times seems a deliberately naive refusal to face the truth. His gee-whiz doggedness, taken to an extreme level of piety, marks him as a childlike character, a Forrest Gump, whose vast appeal for American audiences isn't hard to explain. He flatters our fidelity to the nation and our optimism about it. In *On the Road*, as in *Forrest Gump*, we are invited to admire a faithful, forward-looking hero and discouraged from ever regarding his faith and goodwill as a gullibility we could not respect. *On the Road* is tragically optimistic—a fine figure for the 1950s, a haunted, hopeful, doomed decade.

Kerouac's novel emerged as a new sense of American national identity was consolidating itself: both internally with respect to the possible full Americanness of black men and women, and externally with respect to its conflict with the USSR. Kerouac went west in 1947, *On the Road* appeared in 1957: the novel imaginatively spans the first decade of the American national security state and of the civil rights struggle. The Internal Security Act became law in 1950, to be followed in 1954 by the Communist Control Act. 1954 also brought the decision in *Brown v. Board of Education*. In 1949, eleven American Communist leaders were convicted under the Smith Act of 1940. Ethel and Julius Rosenberg were executed in 1953. During the same period, many states considered, and some passed, laws requiring oaths of loyalty for government employees. The US detonated the first hydrogen bomb at Eniwetok Atoll in November 1952. Between 1950 and 1953 defense spending quadrupled as the peacetime economy was militarized. By the end of 1950, US soldiers were fighting the Chinese in Korea. In 1955, Emmett Till was murdered in Mississippi, and Rosa Parks arrested in Montgomery, Alabama.

On the Road never refers directly to these events, but they are, in a nebulous sort of way, everywhere felt. Dean and Sal pass through Washington on the day of Truman's inauguration in 1949: "Great displays of war might," Sal says, "were lined up along Pennsylvania Avenue as we rolled by in our battered boat. There were B-29s, PT boats, artillery, all kinds of war material that looked murderous in the snowy grass" (121).[3] The next two paragraphs tell how the Virginia police harassed Dean just for the hell of it.

Sal points the moral: "The American police are involved in psychological warfare against those Americans who don't frighten them with imposing papers and threats. It's a Victorian police force; it peers out of musty windows and wants to inquire about everything, and can make crimes if the crimes don't exist to its satisfaction" (122). In a more paranoid vein, Old Bull Lee—the character based on William S. Burroughs—rants about predatory "bureaucracies" and what he calls "the big grab" going on "in Washington and Moscow" (134). *On the Road* plainly belongs to the era of containment: containment of the USSR without, containment of un-American elements within. All the essential Cold War questions trouble Kerouac's novel: What is America? Who are Americans? Are we the chosen or the damned? Kerouac need hardly address these questions directly, because the structure of feeling of *On the Road* is itself tempered by the Cold War, with its restless anxiety, its troubled optimism, its delirium and depression. Kerouac has Sal say, at a crucial moment late in the novel, when Sal and Dean are in Mexico: "Strange crossroad towns on top of the world rolled by, with shawled Indians watching us from under hatbrims and *rebozos*. . . . They had come down from the black mountains and higher places to hold forth their hands for something they thought civilization could offer, and they never dreamed the sadness and the poor broken delusion of it. They didn't know that a bomb had come that could crack all our bridges and roads and reduce them to jumbles, and we would be as poor as they someday, and stretching out our hands in the same, same way. Our broken Ford, old thirties upgoing America Ford, rattled through them and vanished in the dust" (269–70). Sal's peculiar optimism—his "*upgoing* America"—always has a haggard air of defeat about it.

"Everything was dead," Sal tells us in the first paragraph of the novel. What follows is a story of rebirth—an Emersonian story of the agitation always to redraw the outer boundaries of the soul's horizon. To Sal, Dean appears as "a western kinsman of the sun" (10). Sal speaks of "the coming of Dean" as if it were an advent, saying: "I could hear a new call and see a new horizon, and believe in it at my young age" (10). Dean is a Christ-like, vernal figure, and *On the Road* a gospel of his life and works.

But after sounding an overture to Dean, *On the Road* presents him to us in equivocal terms. His talk is a hipster-intellectual-comical patois. (Here is how he asks his girlfriend to fix breakfast and clean up their apartment: "In other words we've got to get on the ball, darling, what I'm saying, otherwise it'll be fluctuating and lack true knowledge or crystallization of our plans" [4].) His relations with women are so abusive and obtuse as to occasion wonder. We cannot discredit the judgment of Sal's aunt that Dean is a "madman." And there is no lack of suggestion that Dean is an evangelical fraud. Sal Paradise admits it at the outset: "[Dean] was simply a youth tremendously excited with life, and though he was a con-man, he was only conning because he wanted so much to live and to get involved with people who would otherwise pay no attention to him. He was conning me and I knew it (for room and board and 'how-to-write,' etc.), and he knew I knew (this has been the basis of our relationship), but I didn't care and we got along fine" (6). This perfectly expresses the complexity of the novel: its ambivalence about Dean and its happy, good-humored candor about its own mythology.[4]

It would be hard-hearted of us to debunk Sal's faith. Such is the conciliatory position *On the Road* forces us into if we are at all susceptible. Everyone else but Sal is a Philistine, we say without being able to decide; to lack faith is actually worse than to invest it in a fraud or fiction. All truly valuable things, this novel suggests, only come about through the creative and deceitful agency of belief—through yea-saying, not skepticism and denial. There are those in *On the Road* who lack faith, but they are always made to seem petty. Sal says early in the novel: "All my other friends [besides Dean] were 'intellectuals'—Chad the Nietzschean anthropologist, Carlo Marx and his nutty surrealist low-voiced serious staring talk, Old Bull Lee and his critical anti-everything drawl." He adds by way of summary that these men "were in the negative, nightmare position of putting society down" (9). All our sympathies lie instead with Dean, whose "criminality," as Sal says, was "a wild yea-saying overburst of American joy" (9). In this book it is *un-American* not to believe. And belief in Dean becomes belief in the possibility of the mythic "lost America of love" with which he is always identified.

America, Kerouac seems to say, has always been a beautiful fiction believing itself into existence as it unfolds west. Sal gets ready for his first trip west by reading books about "the pioneers." He gives himself over fully to what he calls "hearthside" ideas about America (12). Once on the road he subsists on apple pie and ice cream: "That's practically all I ate all the way across the country, I knew it was nutritious and it was delicious, of course" (14). Such is the patriotism of *On the Road*, which was a pretty good advertisement for America. Kerouac's novel chooses the West, as the saying used to go, and how different a document it is in this respect from *Howl and Other Poems*—published, as was *On the Road*, in 1957—with its tormented, cagey animosities.

In any case, Carlo Marx and Dean, we read in chapter 1, "rushed down the street together, digging everything in the early way they had, which later became so much sadder and perceptive and blank" (7). Kerouac is saying that to see "perceptively" is to be "sad" and "blank." He leaves us to infer that to be "digging everything," to live in faith and goodwill, is also to labor under a fortunate illusion—under the dominating power of belief; to be digging everything is somehow willingly to be subject to a con, willingly to turn away from the "whole world of torment" that "naive artists" like Kerouac can't bear to contemplate. The association of disillusion with perception, and of illusion with belief, has great consequence in a novel that in certain respects cannot imperil its belief in its most central and enabling American cultural illusions—illusions that have, it happens, chiefly to do with race. On the other side of the color line lies the world of "horrible importunity" that *On the Road* will not allow itself to register. That is the subject of the balance of this chapter.

Among the Fellahin

To be "beat" is to be among what Sal Paradise calls "the Fellahin peoples of the world." This explains Sal's feeling of solidarity—even of identity—with his Mexican-American lover Terry in part 1 of the novel. "Fellahin," as Kerouac uses the word, can refer either to peasants, or more specifically to peasants (and other persons) of color. (The word is of Arabic origin.[5]) In the passages describing Sal's life with Terry, Kerouac crosses the color line, as by an act of sophisticated minstrelsy: he puts on a mask of color.[6] But minstrelsy is only one generic category in play here. The second is pastoral, and the most remarkable thing about this interlude is the idyllic cast Kerouac gives to the lives of the Mexican and African American migrant farm laborers.

> We bent down and began picking cotton. It was beautiful. Across the field were the tents, and beyond them the sere brown cottonfields that stretched out of sight to the brown arroyo foothills and then the snow-capped Sierras in the blue morning air. This was so much better than washing dishes on South Main Street [in Los Angeles]. But I knew nothing about picking cotton. I spent too much time disengaging the white ball from its crackly bed; the others did it in one flick. Moreover, my fingertips began to bleed; I needed gloves, or more experience. There was an old Negro couple in the field with us. They picked cotton with the same God-blessed patience their grandfathers had practiced in ante-bellum Alabama; they moved right along their rows, bent and blue, and their bags increased.[7] My back began to ache. But it was beautiful kneeling and

hiding in that earth. If I felt like resting I did, with my face on the pillow of brown moist earth. Birds sang an accompaniment. I thought I had found my life's work. (87)

Sal's pastoral eye is hardly the eye of a migrant worker, whose felt relation to the cotton field is doubtless more economic in character than literary and romantic. His phrases are deeply evocative; they carry him away. "Kneeling" catches the piety of the scene, as Sal describes it; "hiding," the sense that he has managed among these (as he sees them) simple folk something like an escape. The "pillow" of earth on which Sal lays his head alerts us to the fact that his ruminations are oddly like a dream—a "peasant" dream, we might say. Sal is composing a "plantation tale": "antebellum Alabama" is as keenly felt here as post-World War II California. All of this encourages Sal, more and more sanguine by the hour, to believe he has found his "life's work" picking cotton. He says: "I was a man of the earth, precisely as I had dreamed I would be" (88).

The latter remark opens up a crucial chain of associations affiliating "earthiness" with "the Fellahin" and with "the primitive." To become a man of the earth is to take on color—to shed the over-civil skin of white cultivation in order to bring to life the essential man (and masculinity) that lie beneath. By this logic, to put on the mask of the Fellahin people of the world is really to take off the mask of the white bourgeois. Movement across lines of color and class leads Sal Paradise to conclude that the primitive and the (to him) Other are actually what is *essentially* human: it was with him all along, though whiteness had alienated him from it. *On the Road* is a fantasy of the sort Emerson entertains in "Self-Reliance": "What a contrast between the well-clad, reading, writing, thinking American, with a watch, a pencil, and a bill of exchange in his pocket, and the naked New Zealander, whose property is a club, a spear, a mat, and an undivided twentieth of a shed to sleep under! But compare the health of the two men, and you shall see that the white man has lost his aboriginal strength. If the traveller tell us truly, strike the savage with a broad axe, and in a day or two the flesh shall unite and heal as if you struck the blow into soft pitch, and the same blow shall the send the white to his grave" (*Essays* 279). *If the traveler tell us truly!* Right there you know what you're dealing with: a man too ready to believe; attribution is beside the point. "Fake news" and "alternative facts" as to black lives have always passed current in America; they're no novelty of the Trump era. In any case, if *this* Brahmin reader of an unnamed traveler—library tourist!—"tell us truly," the "aboriginal" self is in essence "black" and "savage"; it is suckled with the she-wolf's teat. Kerouac's idea in *On the Road* is more temperately expressed, certainly more sentimental, than Emerson's in "Self-Reliance." But for both men "whiteness" is a condition of decadence—an unsoundness of mind and body. Nothing in *On the Road* encourages me to regard Kerouac as particularly enlightened on these questions; he'd let the hundred and ten years that separated him from "Self-Reliance" go to waste. But of course, Kerouac never sought clarity or rigor in thought in *race* matters. He's less inward-looking than Huckleberry Finn.

As Sal and Dean move deeper into Mexico, Sal tells us that it was "not like driving across Carolina, or Texas, or Arizona, or Illinois; but like driving across the world and into the places where we would finally learn ourselves among the Fellahin Indians of the world, the essential strain of the basic primitive, wailing humanity that stretches in a belt around the equatorial belly of the world" (252). Primitivism, color, the earth, authenticity, and sexual vigor (as we move below the "belt"): the constellation is familiar in American writing, as the foregoing chapters have, I hope, established. Reading *On the Road* I think of such passages as the following from Jean Toomer's *Cane*, where Toomer conveys his character Dan Moore's impressions of a black woman seated near him in a theater: "A soil-soaked fragrance comes from her. Through the cement floor her strong roots sink down. They spread under the asphalt streets. . . . Her strong roots sink down and spread under the river and shoot in blood-lines that waver south. Her roots shoot down" (85). The idea in *Cane* is the same one we encounter in *On the Road*, as in much of Beat writing, which in this case Toomer anticipates. A certain problem of social and psychological alienation is set forth in these works, a problem associated with a specifically white middle-class culture; and the therapy proposed in each book is a psychosexual pastoral, a return to the earth, to the soil, to sexual vitality, and to color. *On the Road* and *Cane* look among the Fellahin for what can "stir the root life of a withered people" (76), to borrow Toomer's words.

In the long passage quoted above, Sal Paradise says he had always "dreamed" of becoming "a man of the earth." The remark is more revealing than he intends, because the episode describing his life with Terry in California surely follows the logic of his dreams about what the lives of hard laborers are really like. In this way, ideology gives us a dream of the world rather than a "direct" or unmediated experience of it. Dreams are fictions rooted in the world beyond the dream, with all its "horrible importunities," and they are somehow designed (so to speak) to accommodate us both to that world and to those importunities; in turn, a fiction is also a "con," which, I will argue, brings us full circle back to the question of literary belief and credulity that *On the Road* implicitly raises.

When, in the sequence with Terry, Sal reports that he "sighs like an old Negro cotton-picker" (88), one is entitled to wonder just how an old Negro cotton-picker sighs. What is the "method," as the actors say, for Sal's little piece of stage business? The question is to the point because this is precisely the sort of role-playing (or displacement) that *On the Road* exists to make possible—but also to hold up for scrutiny. Sal loses himself in blackness, shedding the "white" ambitions (161) that had saddled him through life until now. But notice that Sal's way of dreaming about Mexican-American and black laborers is an eminently white way of dreaming about them. To put the matter most uncharitably to him and to Kerouac: white Americans reduce Mexican-American and black farm workers to poverty only to flatter them with suggestions that their lives are idyllic and charmed, free of white worry, white responsibility, white inhibitions—in a word, with suggestions that they are "natural," *and therefore natural in their place*. How distant is this idea, really, from those expressed by Jefferson Davis in the passage from his *Rise and Fall of the Confederate Government* that I discuss in my introduction? I am also reminded (again) of the patronizing reflection Charles Chesnutt has his white narrator John deliver in *The Conjure Woman* (1899), in a passage I quoted already to other purposes. John is speaking of Uncle Julius, a former slave who serves as his coachman: "He was a marvelous hand in the management of horses and dogs, and manifested *a greater familiarity with them than mere use would seem to account for*, though it was doubtless due to the simplicity of a life that had kept him close to nature" (my emphasis; 30). Uncle Julius might well smile ironically at these remarks—or bitterly, depending on how tolerant he felt disposed to be—because they present Julius's life as a slave in extraordinarily romantic terms: as a "simple" life lived "close to nature" in an almost genetic sympathy with the animals. John offers us a dream about slavery, not an account of it. This way of thinking about hard labor informs Sal Paradise's idealizing response to a later generation of agricultural workers. A deep continuity connects Chesnutt's John to Kerouac's Sal—two white Northerners at liberty (and at play) among the Fellahin peoples of the world. Of course, Chesnutt qualifies John's way of thinking about Uncle Julius with irony. No equivalent irony is at work in *On the Road*: Sal pretty clearly speaks for his author in episodes like this one. These episodes mark a weird Beat revival of the plantation tale of the post-Reconstruction era. Sal's remarks about the California cotton field transport him to that other place and time, misty with elegiac grace: "There was an old Negro couple in the field with us.

They picked cotton with the same God-blessed patience their grandfathers had practiced in ante-bellum Alabama." If we hadn't already recognized Kerouac's implied reader as "white," we certainly must do so now. The civil rights movement was well underway: civil disobedience, not "God-blessed patience," was the order of the day, though a naive reader of this novel would never know it. One point of the civil rights movement was to make naiveté impossible. Would that it had succeeded more completely.

White Americans have often described themselves as repressed even as they oppress others. There is a mythic truth in this Hegelian idea that the master enslaves himself. But the politics of it are dubious. This is the dreamwork of a cruel social order, because it presents a way of thinking that erases oppressive conditions—a way of thinking that strategically forgets the "horrible importunities" of life on the other side of the line. Such a dream of the world makes it impossible to see what is really happening: entrapment becomes freedom, and poverty an idyll chiefly to be envied. As Kerouac's reader identifies with Sal, he or she inhabits a particular structure of feeling. To occupy it is to enter into a specific set of relations to the world presented in *On the Road*. It doesn't matter that this is an imaginary world: every world that we can be "aware of" is an "imagined" one in some sense. Kerouac encountered real men and women in the cottonfields of California, but he took them up into a dream of what he might be as Sal Paradise, and of what America he and they might dwell in together. Our relation to "real" men and women can be as imaginary as our relation to Sal Paradise and Dean Moriarty, characters who themselves stand in an "imaginary" relation to "real" men—Jack Kerouac and Neal Cassady. (In early drafts of the novel Kerouac had used his friends' names. His publisher required that he change their names and obtain releases for the use of their stories.)

The peculiar generic status of *On the Road* is pertinent here: as nonfiction fiction it subtly but clearly registers the slippage between the real and the imagined, between waking and dreaming life. *On the Road* equivocally offers itself as a document of America, but it is really a fiction of it. In the California interlude the relation into which we are invited to enter with "old Negro cotton pickers" and with Terry and her son is a relation of idealizing envy. Kerouac does not ask us to pity them, to champion them, or anything else. He asks instead that we wistfully love them best (and need them most) just as they are. Implicit in this relation is a specific practice: this imaginary relation to real laborers is as necessary to the maintenance of the agricultural system that employs them at three dollars a day as are any governmental or police agencies. Gary Snyder's remarks about his friend

Kerouac in *A Place in Space* are terribly misleading. "There is [in Kerouac] no self-pity or accusation or politics," Snyder writes, "simply human beings and facts." He goes on to suggest, incredibly, that Kerouac had "abandoned all classes" in his own mind and life (10).

A Marxist would say: there is nothing much in *On the Road* to disrupt the reproduction of existing relations of production and much that actually *helps* to reproduce those relations. But we can turn to Ralph Ellison for language more specific to American contexts. He writes, speaking of the "black mask" of minstrelsy: "Its function was to veil the humanity of Negroes thus reduced to a sign, and to repress the white audience's awareness of its moral identification with its own acts and with the human ambiguities pushed behind the mask" (*Shadow and Act* 48). This "repression of [its] white audience's awareness" makes *On the Road* a conservative novel. Sal Paradise never really sees the poverty in the California work camps, though he lives in and around them for several weeks. This blindness is what enables him to reflect with such amused charm on what he considers the quaint *mañana* culture of the Mexican-American workers: "It was always *mañana*. For the next week that was all I heard—*mañana*, a lovely word and one that probably means heaven" (85). As he sees them, these workers are carefree, happy, true-hearted, and ecstatic (to use terms Sal elsewhere favors). Everything can wait, in this world of God-blessed patience. *On the Road* gives us no way to comprehend or anticipate the struggles that would culminate in the 1967 strike organized in California by Cesar Chavez and the United Farmworkers. These struggles are unthinkable within the terms established in Kerouac's novel. In *On the Road*, as in earlier stories and novels of the "plantation tale" genre, we are met with a deceit, a diversion of attention *away* from the economic resources necessary to American capitalism (agricultural and industrial) and toward what *conceals* that necessity: we come to regard segregation not as a source of wealth, or as an indispensable factor in the reproduction of the relations of production, but as a thing somehow warranted by nature—whether this warrant is forthrightly conceived as "anti-black," as for example in the apologetics of the Negrophobic architects of the New South, or whether it is obliquely conceived, as in *On the Road*, as somehow anti-white and "pro-Fellahin." Kerouac depends upon this great diversion of attention, or both depends upon it and is himself a casualty of it. Nothing illustrates this better than the section of the novel devoted to Terry and her fellow Mexican-American farm workers in California, or to the remarks about the "happy," "true-hearted" African American inhabitants of Denver (and by extension of ghettoes elsewhere in the United States) (162). In short, what's consistent across the 130 years spanning 1830 to 1960 is this: attention has been directed not at people of color as laborers but at laborers as people of color, whether the operating assumptions attached to the badge of color are an unredeemable degradation, as in the novels of Thomas Dixon, or, as in *On the Road*, a most happy election (the idea that the "Fellahin" have it spiritually better than their white administrators, now reimagined as the *real* losers in the American transaction).[8]

Robert Holton finds in Kerouac's cotton-field fantasy a "depthless" "nostalgia" characteristic of postmodernity (276–77). The suggestion is intriguing. (It derives, in part, from Frederic Jameson's arguments in *Postmodernism; or, the Cultural Logic of Late Capitalism*.) But though I sympathize with Holton, I cannot agree that Kerouac's curious "nostalgia" is peculiarly postmodern, or distinctly associated (*pace* Jameson) with "*late* capitalism." It is a nice problem. But I would say that Kerouac's brand of Fellahin nostalgia has been doing its ideological work at least since the 1840s, as the passage quoted above from "Self-Reliance" is intended to suggest. I am persuaded—by George Fredrickson, David Brion Davis, Du Bois, and other historians—that Kerouac's thinking about the "Fellahin" is, in its essentials, quite in harmony with ideology supporting white supremacy in both the antebellum *and* the post-Reconstruction periods. True, Kerouac revised—even reversed—certain values which formerly attached to "whiteness" and "blackness." But whiteness and blackness are for him constituted pretty much as they were for Americans of Emerson's or Hawthorne's or Howells's day: color has to do with the life of the body, of the senses; whiteness, with the life of the mind. And bear in mind what James Baldwin will not let us forget about "color" in American history: the sheer *persistence* of its basic ideological contours. This persistence, among other things, disinclines me to think of Kerouac's experience of race as "postmodern," or even as very novel at all. Such changes as he does ring on the old white tunes chiefly illustrate the resourcefulness of white supremacy (as an economic system), which comfortably contains even the King of the Beats.

In the episode about Terry we are indirectly made aware of the struggles she undergoes, even if they aren't described as she might describe them: hard labor from dawn to dusk for three dollars a day and no security. *On the Road* achieves at least this much distance from its ideological basis. It almost wakes up from its peasant dreams, as Kerouac, at times, comes close to *exhibiting* the novel's ideological grounds (so to speak) rather than simply articulating them. These moments are like crises of faith. But even so, such details about the hard lives of migrant farm workers as we do become aware of in reading this part of *On the Road* never color the episode as a whole, or very much perturb its air of beatific complaisance: its sleep may be disturbed but it is never interrupted. Sal's sojourn on the plantation is underwritten by his aunt back in New Jersey. He has a sponsor. We smile at the irony, and wonder if Kerouac intends the irony at Sal's expense, when Sal says: "I was through with my chores in the cottonfield. I could feel the pull of my own life calling me back. I shot my aunt a penny postcard across the land and asked for another fifty" (89). Feeling the pull of her own life calling her back is a luxury that Terry—not to mention those patient, "Negro" cotton pickers—never has. But then again she really is Mexican, whereas the dreamer Sal is, as he himself puts it, only Mexican "in a way"—that is to say, only figuratively (88). That makes all the difference. There are Mexicans "in a way" (Sal) and then there are Mexicans (Terry); there is freedom (what Sal has), and then what might be termed freedom "in a way" (what Terry has). In this case, similitude is not identity, though *On the Road* seems at times to mistake the point. In fact, the novel may be said to exist in order to make precisely this sort of mistake.

Daltonism

The passage idealizing migrant farm labor, and others like it, involve a certain blindness on Kerouac's part. It isn't, I think, merely a matter of blindness on Sal's part, though I see how that argument might be made. There are facts about the struggles of the Fellahin that for ideological reasons *On the Road* cannot allow itself to see. This is what keeps Kerouac's book well within the assumptions of American liberalism, as Norman Mailer, a more radical thinker than Kerouac, describes them in "The White Negro," his controversial essay about the culture of the hipster. "What the liberal cannot bear to admit [about America]," Mailer writes, "is the hatred beneath the skin of a society so unjust that the amount of collective violence buried in the people is perhaps incapable of being contained, and therefore if one wants a better world one does well to hold one's breath, for a worse world is bound to come first" (*Advertisements* 321). This is what *On the Road* cannot bear to admit. This is the nightmare, the "horrible importunity," that Kerouac's Apollonian dreamwork supplants.

At times, Kerouac's turning away from this grim possibility is keenly felt by the reader, quite as if it were willful, or dishonest. It is hard to tell exactly how we are to take a reference to "the happy, true-hearted Negroes of America" (162). Is it an example of Sal's naiveté or of Kerouac's? The easy way in which Kerouac's narrator takes liberties with the truth in telling this story about America is an artistic fraud. There is a cheat in this "nonfiction fiction." Kerouac's vision is affected by the color blindness that Richard Wright ingeniously *characterized* in Native Son as "Daltonism" (also known as deuteranopia). (The word refers to an organic color blindness, and, as we have seen, Wright borrows it in naming the philanthropic family that hires Bigger Thomas in the novel's first section, and whose daughter, Mary Dalton, Bigger kills.) Whether we are meant to feel the hollowness of Sal's remark about happy, true-hearted Negroes is not entirely clear. But one can conclude that Kerouac and Sal never met Bigger Thomas or had somehow refused to recognize him even when they did meet him, whether in Wright's novel or in America itself. The refusal evolves out of diffidence, shame, fear, perhaps out of hypocrisy. It is a mode of what the existentialists call bad faith.[9] We want to turn on Sal, as Roy Johnson turns on Dean Moriarty, with charges that he is an amusing "con artist" at best, to employ the inadvertently resonant phrase that Sal had himself earlier applied to Dean. I am reminded, here, of Julius Lester's assessment of Twain's treatment of Jim in *Huckleberry Finn*. Lester points out that Jim is, to borrow Huck's own words, essentially "white inside," and then he explains: "[Twain's] is a picture of the only kind of black that whites have ever truly liked—faithful, tending sick whites, not speaking, not causing trouble, and totally passive. He is the archetypal 'good nigger,' who lacks self-respect, dignity, and a sense of self separate from the one whites want him to have" (44). Twain's vision in this novel, we can now say, is yet another species of "Daltonism." Surely, in a modified fashion, the same visual disorder affects Kerouac's sight in *On the Road*. Twain's Jim is (in certain respects) the "literary" father of the "true-hearted" negroes Kerouac so fondly (and so Americanly) fantasizes into existence, albeit with such different delineations.

The failure to recognize Bigger Thomas—his invisibility to white men and women—forms the main theme of *Native Son*, which is an incisive critique of the literary tradition to which Mark Twain's Jim and Kerouac's strategically *mis*-recognized "happy negroes" alike belong. Kerouac and Sal are like Wright's Jan Erlone, the young white Communist who awkwardly tries to befriend Bigger Thomas in the first part of the novel. Jan and Mary Dalton—surely acting in bad faith—ask Bigger to take them to a place where real people eat, by which they mean colored people; they speak liberally of how emotional black folk are; somewhat absurdly, they even invite Bigger to join them in singing "Swing Low, Sweet Chariot" as he drives them around Chicago's Loop (*Early Works* 517). Only after Bigger has killed Mary, only after he has tried to implicate Jan in the killing, only after he has killed a second time, is Jan able really to see the man he had so condescendingly idealized: "Bigger, I've never done anything against you and your people in my life," Jan says when he first visits Bigger in prison. "But I'm a white man and it would be asking too much to ask you not to hate me, when every white man you see hates you. I know my . . . my face looks like theirs to you, even though I don't feel like they do. But I didn't know we were so far apart until that night. . . . I can understand now why you pulled that gun on me" (713–14).

Sal Paradise never meets this understanding. He never comprehends the hatred of which both Norman Mailer and Wright speak, as is clear from his astonishing remarks at the beginning of part three of *On the Road*: "At lilac evening I walked with every muscle aching among the lights of 27th and Welton in the Denver colored section, wishing I were a Negro, feeling that the best the white world had offered was not enough ecstasy for me, not enough life, joy, kicks, darkness, music, not enough night" (161).[10] Well, neither has Jan Erlone ever had "enough night": enough night is exactly what Bigger Thomas gives him. *Native Son* is a nightmare about America in comparison to which *On the Road* is but a daydream—innocent, naive, charming. Afraid of the darkness by which it is also seduced, *On the Road* reads as if written under the palliating glow of an ideological night-light. In *On the Road* the promise of the "better world" to which Mailer refers in "The White Negro" is essentially willed into existence as a mirage, out along the western horizon, by the sheer force of Sal's and Dean's (and Kerouac's) beatific faith. And that "joyous" and "wild" America, where black and white live together "voluntarily" (as Sal memorably puts it early in the book), is, even within the terms of this fiction and faith, nothing other than a utopia or "supreme fiction." *On the Road* is nostalgic for a place that never was, which accounts for its distinctive and very American mood of *elegiac optimism*: a mixture of regret for what is missing and fond anticipation of what, according to our covenant with the gods, we suppose to lie ahead. Kerouac's utopia is as fragile, hermetic, and unreal as the hours Huck Finn spends alone on the river with Jim. That utopia, like those hours on the raft, is what we remember best about the book. But it is hardly what the book documents.

On the Road, then, is touched by shamed nostalgia: shame because we are reading a white writer condemn whiteness, nostalgia because the mood is so thoroughly unprogressive. *On the Road* invites us to suppose that in America blacks have actually been somehow "freer" than whites (and this in 1957). It accommodates us to their suffering—and therefore to the political economy that occasions the suffering—by imbuing it with the prestige of martyrdom, as if suffering were a gift. In *Existential Errands*,

Mailer wickedly suggests that blacks are "sufficiently fortunate to be alienated from the benefits of American civilization" (307). Without Mailer's irony, and without his intention to outrage, *On the Road* makes the same claim. Something sentimental in this false consciousness oddly lends *On the Road* its pathos. All this admiration and wonder, all this talk about freedom, all this regret about the repression the white man visits on himself: these things work, abashed, in the shadow of real oppression in America.

In *Nobody Knows My Name*, James Baldwin says what must be said of Sal's wish to exchange worlds with the "happy Negroes of America": "[It is] absolute nonsense, and offensive nonsense at that: I would hate to be in Kerouac's shoes if he should ever be mad enough to read this aloud from the stage of Harlem's Apollo Theater. And yet there is real pain in it, and real loss, however thin" (*Essays* 278). Had Kerouac read this passage of Sal's in Harlem he might have known what Jan Erlone felt the night Bigger Thomas pulled a gun on him. But Kerouac's pain is real enough, "however thin," as Baldwin concedes, with his characteristic generosity; and it is affecting. There is remarkable sincerity in this novel, though it doesn't reveal exactly what Kerouac thought it revealed. We pity him, as Baldwin does, for reasons he wouldn't accept. For here it all is at last: Sal, animated by unspeakable desire, in a dreary funk about his "white" inhibitions—whiteness is always felt as an inhibition—slumming around in Denver's "colored section." It is a perfect model for what Kerouac does in *On the Road*. That he may be aware of this—he places his alter ego Sal in exactly the same position—lends the book its air of shame. Kerouac's heroism is the odd heroism of a con artist trying to believe, against mounting evidence to the contrary, that his own patter might just be true. Still half asleep in his peasant dream, he ignores (if he ever heard it) the sound of the alarm clock with which Wright famously opens *Native Son*; the alarm never penetrates his oblivion. Call black Americans free in the mid-1950s, as Sal does, and you have, to borrow Ralph Ellison's indispensable trope, rendered them invisible. At times, it is hard not to think that *On the Road*, so well fitted to this end, is somehow "intended" to accomplish it ("intended" not by Kerouac but by the culture of which he is a part, and of which his novel is so characteristic an expression).

Or, to come at this another way: Kerouac idealizes the lives of the Fellahin peoples of the world (whether Mexican, Mexican-American, Indian, Arab, or African American) in a gesture that is at once a *criticism* of his own repressive culture of "whiteness," as he understands it, *and* an oblique *justification*, by means of the idealization I have described, of the abuses that that same culture commits against the Fellahin—both without and within its national borders. This is characteristic of the tangled problem of thinking through race in American culture. The dialectic of oppression leads us back to the masochism, or "self-abuse," of the oppressors themselves: sadism and masochism intersect and merge. More precisely, a specifically *white* cultural dialectic of oppression leads us from sadism to masochism by preferring examination of the "self-inflicted" psychic wounds of whites to examination of the wounds (of all kinds) that white America has inflicted on others. This may account for white liberals' poignant attachment to *Huckleberry Finn*. True, they acknowledge, with Julius Lester and others, that the novel is infected by the white supremacy it condemns. But they save it for the culture (and for K-12) by turning attention toward the masochistic way in which this racism has distorted the heart and mind of Huck (and of Mark Twain himself) more than toward the sadistic way in which it destroyed the lives of black Americans. Again: this has the effect, if not the intention, of keeping white experience at the center of the debate, and *On the Road* works in exactly this way. The episode describing Sal Paradise's time with Terry in California (for example) is informed by the *same* "white" subjectivity that Sal tries forthrightly to *escape* in the novel. And here we find another important point of contact with *Huckleberry Finn*, a novel that exhibits, as readers have come to acknowledge, the same "white" consciousness that Twain undoubtedly attacks in it. Twain can no more escape these determinations than Huck can. *Huckleberry Finn* and *On the Road* are therefore fine examples of how even insubordinate writers like Twain and Kerouac "'freely' [internalize] an appropriate 'picture' of their social world and their place in it," to borrow a phrase from James Kavanaugh (Lentricchia and McLaughlin 312).

Given the ideological drift of the novel, Kerouac's later turn toward the right in politics is less puzzling, and his hostility to the black radicals of the 1960s less surprising. (He could deal with Uncle Tom, not with Nat Turner.) Anyone who has read the biographical literature on Kerouac knows the racist diatribes he was sometimes given to indulging in toward the end of his life. (These were partly associated with the mental and physical deterioration that followed years of alcoholism. Even so, one hears in them a prescient vote for Donald Trump.) Barry Miles recounts the most infamous such episode in *Jack Kerouac: King of the Beats*: "In the summer of 1962, [Kerouac] got his fourteen-year-old nephew Paul to help him build a cross from two-inch-by-four-inch wooden posts which he then covered with cloth. They drove to a wall which roughly divided the Black neighbourhood from the White section of Orlando [where Kerouac was then staying]. There Jack soaked the cloth in kerosene, stood the cross on the wall, and set fire to it. As his homemade fiery cross burnt, Jack danced up and down, yelling racist obscenities" (278).[11] The dreamy plantation-tale ethos of *On the Road* should never be confused with more viciously forthright, not to mention delirious, manifestations of American racism. But among the novel's troubling lessons for contemporary readers is how continuous—and how coherent—the culture of "racism" actually is, across a spectrum running from embarrassing, to bad, to abominable. Take it all in, and Jack Kerouac's consciousness—his way of being aware of the social world he inhabited—was thoroughly American, *delirium tremens* and all. We simply have to own it: he registers our national failures like a mirror. That he should register our national promise, too, is a thoroughly American paradox.

Before moving ahead, I should acknowledge here an observation of Omar Swartz's in *The View From On the Road: The Rhetorical Vision of Jack Kerouac*. After quoting Kerouac on "the happy, true-hearted, ecstatic Negroes of America," Swartz remarks: "This passage is obviously problematic in its representation of the African American, whom Kerouac portrays paternalistically, as he does *all* minorities; yet, he never does so maliciously, and this is the most extreme example of it in *On the Road*. His condescending tone must be discounted in light of Kerouac's larger poetic framework. Kerouac typically poeticized the world, and this is particularly evident in his books of reminiscence" (87; emphasis in the original). The fact that Kerouac treats "*all* minorities" this way is, to my mind, probably beside the point: the minorities in question are, as white America sees them, uniformly people of color—whether African American, American Indian, Hispanic, or "Fellahin"; and *that* is the rub. Moreover, the point is not to choose between a "malicious" or "racist" Kerouac and a Kerouac in whom "paternalistic" attitudes must finally be "discounted." The point is to trace out the continuities linking "paternalistic" attitudes to those larger patterns of white supremacy which somehow contain Kerouac, as they contain so many of us; and which contain as well so much of our literature, *even when that literature is in certain respects counter-cultural*. I would add in passing that the strongest literary work done in America is often precisely the work that makes us feel the confining limits of its own ideological horizons; *Huckleberry Finn* is a case in point. So it seems of limited use to say, with Swartz, that "Kerouac is not a racist but a romantic" (87). My way out of the dilemma is to suggest that, at its best, *On the Road* makes a claim on behalf of literary writing generally: to wit, that great writing often exists in an abstract—in a withdrawn or estranged—relation to the ideological medium in which it is suspended. Literary works may not transcend that medium, but, like Mark Antony and the dolphins to which Shakespeare compares him, they can show their backs above it. For this reason, even Louis Althusser allows "authentic" artworks a certain autonomous energy (221–27). They do not merely inculcate in us a particular way of seeing the world; they also make apparent the limits of what they find it possible to think, to feel, and to say. Really strong writing can say the truth—as Emerson puts it—even though it "try," at times, "to say the reverse" (*Essays* 881). Surely that is something to care about as a literary critic. *On the Road* may bind us to the American past, with its sad contingencies. But it can also make us "citizens, by anticipation, in the world we crave," to borrow a phrase from George Santayana (vi). Mill City always exists somewhere in *On the Road*, as I have suggested: "It was, so they say, the only community in America where whites and Negroes lived together voluntarily; and that was so, and so wild and joyous a place I've never seen since" (51). But again to the matter of race.

Squiggling Like Saxophones

Driving through southwestern Louisiana, Sal Paradise relates the following exchange between himself and Dean Moriarty: "'Man do you imagine what it would be like if we found a jazzjoint in these swamps, with great big black fellas moanin' guitar blues and drinking snakejuice and makin' signs at us?' 'Yes!' There were mysteries around here" (141). This is the sort of parable Sal and Dean tell themselves once they get to Mexico. Their primitive ideal stands in antithesis to whiteness, which is, dialectically, as much the subject here as blackness. Elsewhere Sal speaks of the "essential strain of the basic primitive, wailing humanity" that stretches around the equator among the "Fellahin" peoples of the world (252). This strain, the strain of African American music in the novel, is what Sal and Dean listen to jazz in order to hear. They have lived, it seems, in exile from themselves. In an odd revision of antebellum "colonization" schemes, it is white men who require "repatriation" to Africa; and, selfishly, they require it for the health of their own bodies more than for the health of the body politic. Whiteness, here, is a condition of alienation: from the body, from sexuality, from the primitive alter ego. *On the Road* takes for granted that we are a nation under the domination of what, in his own oblique analysis of the constitution of whiteness, Wallace Stevens called "old Christian women." The association will not seem absurd if we take another look at his "A High-Toned Old Christian Woman" (1923):

> Poetry is the supreme fiction, madame.
> Take the moral law and make a nave of it
> And from the nave build haunted heaven. Thus,
> The conscience is converted into palms,
> Like windy citherns hankering for hymns.
> We agree in principle. That's clear. But take
> The opposing law and make a peristyle,
> And from the peristyle project a masque
> Beyond the planets. Thus, our bawdiness,
> Unpurged by epitaph, indulged at last,
> Is equally converted into palms,
> Squiggling like saxophones. And palm for palm,
> Madame, we are where we began. Allow,
> Therefore, that in the planetary scene
> Your disaffected flagellants, well-stuffed,
> Smacking their muzzy bellies in parade,
> Proud of such novelties of the sublime,
> Such tink and tank and tunk-a-tunk-tunk,
> May, merely may, madame, whip from themselves
> A jovial hullabaloo among the spheres.
> This will make widows wince. But fictive things
> Wink as they will. Wink most when widows wince. (47)

"A High-Toned Old Christian Woman" concerns a specifically WASPish mode of being white. While it is necessary to Stevens's purposes that this Christian be a woman, the poem comes fully alive only as we realize what those squiggling saxophones bring into it. Stevens's imaginative excursion into a 1920s jazz joint is an excursion across the color line, though this is only implied: it is a sophisticated act of literary minstrelsy. Whiteness, as it attaches to High-Toned Christian Women, is felt chiefly as a constriction of the sensual. That is the meaning of those "flagellations." Whiteness is ascetic, and the masculine voice that roundly teases the old woman promises a release from a civilizing regime that is completely recognizable. Stevens's speaker follows Huck Finn, though he marches to the beat of his own drummer. Having already been subject to the regime of the Widow Douglas and Miss Watson, Huck lights out for the territory when Sally Phelps, another Old Christian Woman, threatens to civilize him. But Huck's flight from femininity is also a flight from whiteness, and not simply from the horrifying "fish-belly" whiteness of his brutish father Pap. Huck's only real happiness in the novel—though he doesn't entirely assimilate this fact—is the time he spends with Jim on the margins of the river, and on the margins of civilization itself. The same may be said of Kerouac and Sal in *On the Road*, where "whiteness" names a suit of clothes too good to be comfortable.

In *On the Road*, release from white civility is specifically felt as an awakening of sexual vitality. At one point in the novel Galatea Dunkel and her high-toned "sewing circle" attempt to chasten Dean Moriarty. "You have absolutely no regard for anybody but yourself and your damned kicks," Galatea says. "All you think about is what's hanging between your legs and how much money or fun you can get out of people and then you just throw them aside" (174). The cultural distance between this white, feminine reproach and the scene of jazz-joint ecstasy that follows it in the novel is the same distance that separates Stevens's High-Toned Old Christian Woman from those "disaffected" flagellants, "smacking their muzzy bellies in parade." The answer to high-toned white women is jazz. Stevens speaks of "squiggling" saxophones. The figure refers at once to the shape, the sound, and the effect of the saxophones: their squiggling sounds make his speaker squiggle in Dionysian dance. The introduction of these saxophones into the poem accomplishes a double reorientation. With a single gesture Stevens's speaker moves toward blackness and toward masculinity: unleashing his sexual vitality, he repudiates white feminine prudery. This repudiation is felt even in the language of the poem (just as we feel the rhythms of the tenor-man's ecstasy enter Kerouac's "be-bop" prose as he describes the scene in a San Francisco jazz joint called Jamson's Nook). Stevens's intense consonance and onomatopoeia register his Dionysian indulgence of a verbal "bawdiness," "unpurged by epitaph," that makes a fine response to the old widow's ascetic flagellants: he coaxes a happy, scat-singing sort of poetry out of the bodies of the words themselves as the poem closes out.

To become hip to jazz, for these white writers, is to enter into a new relation to the body and to sexuality. This makes it possible for Norman Mailer to say, referring to the supposed etymology of the term, that jazz is orgasm; in a word, this is what Stevens also says. He brings into his poem all of these associations with the merest allusion to those "squiggling saxophones": such is the economy of the language of race in American writing. *On the Road* unfolds these same associations into a restless journey away from whiteness into the "Fellahin" darkness of the alter ego. And we might put it still another way, this time moving from Kerouac back to Stevens: "A High-Toned Old Christian Woman" is exactly the sort of reverie into which Sal Paradise falls in Denver, when, at "lilac evening," he wishes he were "a Negro, feeling that the best the white world had offered was not enough ecstasy for me, not enough life, joy, kicks, darkness, music, not enough night" (161). Still, the better to understand Sal's malaise (and Stevens's) it is good to turn again to James Baldwin and his friend Norman Mailer, and with them (and a few others) conclude this book.

CONCLUSION

In *The Fire Next Time*, Baldwin suggests that "the price of the liberation of the white people is the liberation of the blacks—the total liberation, in the cities, in the towns, before the law, and in the mind" (*Essays* 342). The idea is that "intercultural" oppression and "intrapsychic" repression are complementary disorders. In "The White Negro," Mailer, like his friend Baldwin, sets about to dismantle these twin structures of racist and psychic repressions—white over black, conscious over unconscious. He does so in a dual maneuver: he asserts the primacy of the historically or morally subordinate terms and then abolishes subordination altogether. And "The White Negro" helps us see how the racial politics of *On the Road* are perhaps more progressive than at first they seem. "The nihilism of Hip," Mailer says, "proposes as its final tendency that every social restraint and category be removed, and the affirmation implicit in the proposal is that man would then prove to be more creative than murderous and so would not destroy himself" (*Advertisements* 319). The revolution Mailer describes would take aim against all prohibitions having to do with sex and race. And his remarks suggest that the blackface tradition of the "white negro" is by no means without insubordinate implications. Mailer's essay brings to a fiercer, much more troubling pitch the argument with white Christianity that Stevens has in "A High-Toned Old Christian Woman" (which remains the utterance of an aesthete and insurance man, not a rebel). What follows The Revolution is total affirmation of Life, to use Mailer's Lawrentian term for it: "disaffected flagellants," smacking their muzzy bellies in parade.

Mailer believed (maybe only provocatively) that a sexual revolution would reverse the savage turn the West took in the first five decades of the twentieth century. For him, psychic repression, racist repression, and military-industrial rapacity were three aspects of the same pathology: they all added up to The Bomb. This argument remains radical today and explains why, in the fifth section of "The White Negro," Mailer says that the emergence of blacks into full participation in American life would revolutionize the country: this emergence, were it genuinely to occur, would mark the abolition of the range of repressions that has constituted the very psyches of Americans, determining what it means to be both "white" and "black." (It would also turn more than one Deep South state "blue," as we now say—with attendant effects for our politics: Texas, Georgia, Florida, North Carolina: who can say?) An integrated America will necessarily be a different America because what it means to be "American" has until now involved a complementary blend of social oppression and psychic repression. This is what Baldwin has in mind when he writes, in *No Name in the Street*: "In the generality, as social and moral and political and sexual entities, white Americans are probably the sickest and most dangerous people, of any color, to be found in the world today" (*Essays* 386).

Baldwin makes it impossible for us to read books like *On the Road* naively. But he also helps us read them with sympathy. He writes in *The Fire Next Time*: "The white man's unadmitted—and apparently, to him, unspeakable—private fears and longings are projected onto the Negro. The only way he can be released from the Negro's tyrannical power over him is to consent, in effect, to become black himself, to become a part of that suffering and dancing country that he now watches wistfully from the heights of his lonely power and, armed with spiritual traveler's checks, visits surreptitiously after dark" (*Essays* 341). "Spiritual traveler's checks" are what Sal Paradise cashes in the jazz joints he patronizes after dark. His need for them betrays his poverty, which is also the poverty of the nation. So, psychological integration follows upon, and can only follow upon, racial integration: this hope, which Kerouac shares with Baldwin, is what most marks *On the Road* as belonging to the era of the civil rights struggle. The real heart of the novel comes (as I've already suggested) in that early passage about Mill City, California: "the only community in America where whites and Negroes lived together voluntarily; and that was so, and so wild and joyous a place I've never seen since" (54). Sal's wild, joyous America is exactly that: a utopia—what we've never seen *outside* the pages of Kerouac's fiction, and what we've never seen *inside* the pages of Wright's and Chesnutt's. In *Nobody Knows My Name*, Baldwin rightly suggests that, in *On the Road*, Kerouac is "ruminating" on "the loss of the garden of Eden" (*Essays* 278). Eden is where we are headed, though we sometimes mistake it for where we have already been. Only a possibility and a promise, America has existed nowhere within our geographical or chronological horizons. But in their fictions, as opposed to their frauds, Americans have at times powerfully believed that possibility into existence. This is the abiding faith of *On the Road*—faith in the redemptive fiction of Dean Moriarty, a beat-beatific "white negro," a man psychically and socially integrated, whole and healed. To read *On the Road*, for the white reader it anticipates and requires, is therefore to dwell in possibility, "at sunset" in paradise America, as Kerouac's resonantly named narrator says. This Eden exists nowhere, and when we get there we'll find Dean Moriarty publishing his books "in heaven"—which brings us to the conclusion, or westernmost horizon, of the novel itself.

The last paragraph in *On the Road* is peculiarly evocative. The road (we know) opens up in spring and always calls us West. But here, Sal Paradise speaks from the winter of his discontent as he charts the Eastern streets of New York City, thinking again of Dean.

> So in America when the sun goes down and I sit on the old broken-down river pier watching the long, long skies over New Jersey and sense all that raw land that rolls in one unbelievable huge bulge over to the West Coast, and all that road going, all the people dreaming in the immensity of it, and in Iowa I know by now the children must be crying in the land where they let children cry, and tonight the stars'll be out, and don't you know that God is Pooh Bear? the evening star must be drooping and shedding her sparkler dims on the prairie, which is just before the coming of complete night that blesses the earth, darkens all rivers, cups the peaks and folds the final shore in, and nobody, nobody knows what's going to happen to anybody besides the forlorn rags of growing old, I think of Dean Moriarty, I even think of Old Dean Moriarty the father we never found, I think of Dean Moriarty. (278)

The verbs applied to the coming of night ("blesses," "cups," "folds," etc.) suggest a tender, maternal act. It is an act in keeping with the idea, gently impressed on us by the language, that the narrator—and Dean Moriarty, and even Old Dean Moriarty—has in some sense become a child again, and that, like the fabled children of Iowa (where America first goes to vote), he knows that God is Pooh Bear beneath the prairie's sparkler stars. The literary mode, here as elsewhere in the novel, is part lullaby, part national anthem, and part elegy—a patriotic lullaby-elegy. Sal is the father-child America, singing itself to sleep in its own life, as Wallace Stevens once put it. (Truly American parents like Kerouac and Stevens themselves believe the bedtime stories they tell the children.) The mythic, sad optimism of *On the Road* is inseparable from sentiments like these. We are made to feel at times that the book is willfully naive, as when Sal, at the road's end, adopts his Huck-like persona in a gesture that limits the point of view of the narrative as a whole: we sense at last in its closing strains that the novel is told to us as by a faithful child. (What is it about white American male writers and childhood? Why the appeal of naive heroes, whether Huck or Sal? From what knowledge do these authors wish to protect themselves?) And it is not only the absent father we feel the need of in this last paragraph—Old Dean Moriarty—but the lost mother and brother as well, as the final phrases of the novel plainly show that Sal's imaginative sympathy with Dean is now complete: he speaks the language of the orphan, with specifically American inflections of longing and dislocation. And the wholesome American dream that the father-child Sal has, with its prairies, stars, sparklers, and nighttime Iowa blessings, is just the impossible dream of *On the Road*: its wild utopia, the joyous America that exists nowhere beyond the border of this fiction, but where Dean and Huck and Jim; where Jan Erlone, Mary Dalton, and Bigger Thomas; where Frederick Douglass, Sandy Jenkins, William Lloyd Garrison, and even Edward Covey; where Uncle Julius and George Tryon; where Trayvon Martin and George Zimmerman; where Eric Garner and the police who killed him—where all these folk, where white and black alike, at last find their happy, true-hearted, ecstatic place together. *On the Road* sings its white readers to sleep dreaming of this world elsewhere: the place where America has the only reality it has in fact ever had: we have always dwelt merely in possibility, as migrant farm laborers in California, though not in *On the Road*, know full well. *On the Road* is therefore a novel steeped in forgetfulness, an Apollonian dream willfully set against a whole world of torment. It tells us a bedtime story about the power of our supreme national fiction to inspire belief, the better to bring into view its never-realized but always possible object, just over the western horizon. We simply have to keep telling ourselves that America can exist, as Baldwin knew when he wrote *The Fire Next Time*: "We, the black and the white, deeply need each other here if we are really to become a nation—if we are really, that is, to achieve our identity, our maturity, as men and women" (342).

NOTES

Introduction

1. See Michael W. Kraus, Julian M. Rucker, and Jennifer A. Richeson (Director of the Social Perception and Communication Lab), "Americans Misperceive Racial Economic Equality," *Proceedings of the National Academy of Sciences* (September 2017), 10324.

2. My ideas about American white supremacy derive chiefly from the works I study in the present book (by Douglass, Du Bois, Chesnutt, Wright, and Baldwin). I also owe much to Douglas Blackmon's superb *Slavery by Another Name* (2008), Edward Baptist's *The Half Has Never Been Told: Slavery and the Making of American Capitalism* (2014), and Heather Ann Thompson's *Blood in the Water: The Attica Prison Uprising of 1971 and Its Legacy* (2017). All three books are grounded in remarkable archival work. I am indebted also to David Roediger's *Wages of Whiteness* (revised edition, 1999). Most important to me has been the work of the late George Frederickson, particularly his *The Black Image in the White Mind* (1987). I would name here also Thomas Gossett's *Race: The History of an Idea in America* (1997 edition). I find political scientist Michael Tesler's *Post-Racial or Most Racial?: Race and Politics in the Obama Era* (2012) helpful in understanding how forthright white supremacy ("OFR," or "Old Fashioned Racism," as he puts it) has evolved, in the post-Civil Rights Era, into subtler forms of bigotry captured by such terms as "symbolic racism," "cultural racism," "laissez-faire racism," and—Tesler's preferred phrase—"racial resentment" (19–20). I agree with Tesler that, though more nuanced terms than "white supremacy" are now often necessary, the *effect* of "racial resentment" is the same as was the effect of OFR: it "is used to justify the pervasive racial inequities in American society" (Tesler 20). Among the most valuable books about American slavery (to me) is Peter H. Wood's *Black Majority: Negroes in Colonial South Carolina from 1670 through the Stono Rebellion* (1974). Its range is considerably larger than its title suggests, and Wood's use of primary sources is nonpareil. Reading *Black Majority* is a revelation of just *how* good good scholarship can be. While a student at the University of South Carolina in the early 1980s,

I first visited St. Helena Island (and Port Royal Sound), while reading Willie Lee Rose's classic *Rehearsal for Reconstruction: The Port Royal Experiment* (1964; reissued in 1999). I'll never forget the experience.

3. The Portuguese and Spanish had employed African slave labor in sugar production for many decades prior to 1620 on the Atlantic islands and in Brazil. Methods of production pioneered there were later adapted to and refined on plantations in the West Indies and in the North American British colonies and, later still, in the United States. See Sidney W. Mintz, *Sweetness and Power* (1985), 30–39; for a broader history of sugar production, see 19–73.

4. For a richly detailed history of redlining, see Richard Rothstein, *The Color of Law* (2017).

5. Amendment 4 on November 6, 2018, restored the right to vote to most (not all) ex-convicts, upon completion of parole and/or probation.

6. This act lowered the corporate tax rate from 35% to 21%, while ensuring that any modest benefits accruing to middle-class and working-class Americans would fall to zero in 2027. It also created a massive budget deficit that already—as of 2018—provides cover for Republican demands to cut Great Society programs that benefit the poor. See Paul Krugman's December 4, 2017, column in *The New York Times*: "Republicans Are Coming for Your Benefits."

7. See Christian Weller (professor of public policy at the University of Massachusetts), "Budget Estimates Show New Tax Cuts for Wealthiest Americans Threaten Middle-Class Retirement," *Forbes*, September 25, 2018.

8. Privatization of and within the prison system produced, in 2015, $629 million in profits, according to estimates compiled by IBISWorld, a market-research company whose data is widely used in the United States by such firms as Corrections Corporation of America (recently renamed CoreCivic), a for-profit company founded in 1983 by Thomas Beasley, one-time head of the Republican Party in Tennessee. Trump's election was (within twenty-four hours) a godsend to CCA/CoreCivic (and companies like it). "As terrific as Donald J. Trump has been for the stock market," wrote Jeff Sommer for *The New York Times* in "Trump's Win Gives Stocks in Private Companies a Reprieve," "he has been absolutely spectacular for a troubled niche: companies that run for-profit prisons and immigration detention centers for states and the federal government. In the market rally on the day after the election, the stock with the best performance was Corrections Corporation of America, the nation's biggest prison company. It soared 43 percent that day. Shares of the GEO Group, its main competitor, rose 21 percent. These two big private prison companies have had a rough time until recently. In August [2016], after the Justice Department put out a monitoring report that found safety and security problems at their facilities, the Obama administration said it would start to phase out the use of private prisons. So Mr. Trump's surprise victory represented a radical change in fortunes for them—a boon for investors and a potential nightmare for critics" (December 3, 2016). A lawsuit filed against GEO Group in 2014, and granted class action status in February 2017, alleges that

the company violated federal anti-slavery laws by compelling undocumented immigrants detained at its facilities to labor for as little as one dollar per day. (See Kristine Phillips, "Thousands of ICE Detainees Claim They Were Forced into Labor.") Still, the company's market value rises. "The worse the news for immigrants and their lawyers," writes Sommer in the *New York Times* (March 10, 2017), "the better it has been for the two companies. When a member of the Trump administration issues a memo or executive order, gives a speech or tweets about the crackdown on immigrants, shares of the two companies rise: Since the election, CoreCivic's stock price has climbed 120 percent, and GEO's has gained 80 percent. Already in 2017, CoreCivic is up about 30 percent; GEO has gained about 20 percent." And in these developments, too, we see relations of production associated with (capitalist) white supremacy, given (again) that our prison population is so disproportionately composed of persons of color.

9. See also note 23, chapter 4, below.

10. See Philip A. Klinker and Roger M. Smith, *The Unsteady March: The Rise and Fall of Racial Equality in America* (1999), 1–9 (and *passim*). They write: "Our story is . . . consistent with the old adage of civil rights workers, 'Two steps forward, one step back.' We stress, however, that thus far the two steps forward have come in concentrated bursts of ten to fifteen years [roughly 1776–89, 1861–77, and 1954–68]. The one step back, in contrast, has repeatedly been a lengthy stride covering a period of sixty to seventy-five years. Hence the normal experience of a typical black person in US history has been to live in a time of stagnation and decline in progress toward racial equality. That reality helps explain the deep pessimism about race visible in the outlook even of more affluent blacks today and in much of America's past" (5).

11. See Robert Caro, *The Years of Lyndon Johnson: Master of the Senate* (2003), 164–222, 232–303.

12. See Ta-Nehisi Coates, *We Were Eight Years in Power* (2017), 173–74. Coates relies on data gathered by the Pew Research Center. The magnitude of the white/black "wealth gap" varies according to how one measures it. For a detailed analysis, see Dedrick Asante-Muhammad et al., *The Road to Zero Wealth: How the Racial Divide is Hollowing Out the America's Middle Class*, a white paper issued by the Institute for Policy Studies in September 2017. See also "On Views of Race and Inequality: Blacks and Whites Are Worlds Apart," a report issued by the Pew Research Center on June 27, 2016. The report touches on the wealth gap but ranges considerably further in assessing the degree to which Americans are even aware that it (and other measures of inequality) exists.

13. See Richard Adams, "Rand Paul Versus the Civil Rights Act."

14. See Caro, *The Years of Lyndon Johnson: Master of the Senate*, 246, 250, 253, 276, 281–85, and 286–88. Caro describes a stag party LBJ organized in 1950 to introduce Texas oilmen to Georgia Senator and staunch racist Richard Russell: "It was a group that held views quite similar to Russell's on Communism and labor unions and Negroes and the importance of ending government interference with

free enterprise, a group that had long considered Russell the leader of the good fight on these issues and had been looking forward to meeting him" (305). Among the attendees was Herman Brown of Brown & Root—later Keller, Brown & Root (KBR), for decades a subsidiary of Halliburton.

15. See Jordan Weissmann, "Countrywide's Racist Lending Practices Were Fueled by Greed." See also the Department of Justice's December 21, 2011 online press release (number 11-1694): "Justice Department Reaches $335 Million Settlement to Resolve Allegations of Lending Discrimination by Countrywide Financial Corporation": "Countrywide discriminated by charging more than 200,000 African-American and Hispanic borrowers higher fees and interest rates than non-Hispanic white borrowers in both its retail and wholesale lending.... [These] borrowers were charged higher fees and interest rates because of their race or national origin, and not because of the borrowers' creditworthiness or other objective criteria related to borrower risk. The United States also alleges that Countrywide discriminated by steering thousands of African-American and Hispanic borrowers into subprime mortgages when non-Hispanic white borrowers with similar credit profiles received prime loans."

16. All the same, the reception accorded Baptist's *The Half Has Not Been Told* suggests how much controversy still meets arguments that slavery and white supremacy were and are foundational to the nation's political economy and to capitalism. See the afterword Baptist added to the 2016 paperback edition of his book (421–37).

17. In this I follow, and hope to complement, Eric Sundquist's work in *To Wake the Nations: Race in the Making of American Literature* (1993).

18. Davis's views are hardly quaint. We meet with them again in Patrick J. Buchanan's "A Brief for Whitey"—an article written in response to then-candidate Barack Obama's celebrated speech on race, delivered in Philadelphia on March 18, 2008. "America has been the best country on earth for black folks," Buchanan writes. "It was here that 600,000 black people, brought from Africa in slave ships, grew into a community of 40 million, were introduced to Christian salvation, and reached the greatest levels of freedom and prosperity blacks have ever known." "A Brief for Whitey" first appeared in the conservative journal *Human Events* on March 21, 2008. Buchanan competed in the Republican Party's presidential primaries in 1992 and 1996—winning about 3,000,000 votes in both contests—and secured the Reform Party's nomination for president in 2000. He is still an influential voice on the right, and, of course, a perennial television pundit; the views he espouses in his web-log show that his thinking (as to race) has hardly changed. See his essay there "Has the West the Will to Survive?" (June 22, 2018). *New York Times* columnist Charles Blow has rightly diagnosed Buchanan and his kind (Laura Ingraham et al.) as suffering from "white extinction anxiety" (see his June 24, 2018, column of the same name).

19. See Hugh Thomas, *The Slave Trade* (1997), 804. And as Edward Baptist notes, by 1807 "four out of every five people who came from the Old World to the New had come from Africa, not Europe" (41).

20. The hysteria was hardly limited to the South. I quote, here, from the *Columbia Democrat and Bloomsburg General Advertiser* (Bloomsburg, Pennsylvania), of August 18, 1860. For a concise overview of anti-Republican/anti-Lincoln propaganda, see Charles B. Dew, *Apostles of Disunion: Southern Secession Commissioners and the Causes of the Civil War* (2001). "No commissioner articulated the racial fears of the secessionists better, or more graphically, than Alabama's Stephen F. Hale," writes Dew. "When he wrote of a South facing 'amalgamation or extermination,' when he referred to 'all the horrors of a San Domingo servile insurrection,' when he described every white Southerner 'degraded to a position of equality with free negroes,' when he foresaw the 'sons and daughters' of the South 'associating with free negroes upon terms of political and social equality,' when he spoke of the Lincoln administration consigning the citizens of the South 'to assassinations and her wives and daughters to pollution and violation to gratify the lust of half-civilized Africans,' he was giving voice to the night terrors of the secessionist South" (80).

21. See Julie Hirschfeld Davis, et al., "Trump Alarms Lawmakers with Disparaging Words for Haiti and Africa."

22. The economy of which is detailed in William Dusinberre's *Them Dark Days: Slavery in the American Rice Swamps* (2000). Mortality rates among slaves in the Carolina rice fields were among the highest in the antebellum South. "Inhospitable" indeed.

23. Of course, Davis had opposed the entire Compromise of which this bill was a part, and not only because it admitted California as a free state. He writes, in *The Rise and Fall*: "The compensation which it was alleged that the South received [for admitting a free California] was a more effective law for the rendition of fugitives from service or labor. But it is to be remarked that this law provided for the execution by the General Government of obligations which had been imposed by the Federal compact [i.e., the Constitution] upon the several States of the Union. The benefit to be derived from a fulfillment of that law would be small in comparison with the evil to result from the plausible pretext that the States had thus been relieved from a duty which they had assumed in the adoption of the compact of union" (1: 16).

24. On December 26, 1860, six days after South Carolina seceded, Davis introduced the following into the record: "*Resolved*, That it shall be declared, by amendment of the Constitution, that property in slaves, recognized as such by the local law of any of the States of the Union, shall stand on the same footing, in all constitutional and Federal relations, as any other species of property so recognized; and, like other property, shall not be subject to be divested or impaired by the local law of any other State, either in escape thereto, or by the transit or sojourn of the owner therein. And in no case whatever shall such property be subject to be divested or impaired by any legislative act of the United States, or any of the territories thereof" (Committee of Thirteen, 36th Congress, Second Session, Report No. 288, page 3).

25. In *The Negro* (1915), Du Bois gave American chattel slavery its proper name (promulgators of agrarian paternalism be damned): "The greatest experiment in Negro slavery *as a modern industrial system* was made on the mainland of North America and in the confines of the present United States" (my emphasis; 183). Douglas Blackmon documents the continuing importance to industry of twentieth-century neo-slavery in the South (often to the benefit of Northern capital). For example, he details the system of convict labor used, in Alabama and elsewhere, to work iron mines and steel mills (in some of which US Steel had investments [335–36]).

26. Former Confederate General Matthew Butler undertakes a like inversion in testimony given in July 1871, before the Select Committee sent from Washington to investigate the Ku Klux Klan: "I think, in reality, the authors of the rebellion were the active instruments of emancipation, and, therefore, I think the negroes should be more thankful to us; and so I said on the stump last summer," while campaigning for the office of lieutenant governor of South Carolina (Poland and Scott 1201). Butler's overture to the ungrateful black voters of South Carolina failed. He lost to Alonzo Jacob Ransier (1834–82), the state's first black lieutenant governor (1870–72), and, later, a United States Congressman (1873–75). Ransier was born a free person of color in Charleston (parents unknown, though likely of Haitian background); he spent his last years in poverty there, working as a street cleaner, while Butler sat in the Senate. Fortune is indeed a strumpet.

27. Michelle Alexander writes: "White supremacy, over time, became a *religion* of sorts. Faith in the idea that people of the African race were bestial, that whites were inherently superior, and that slavery was, in fact, for blacks' own good, served to alleviate the white conscience and reconcile the tension between slavery and the democratic ideals espoused by whites in the so-called New World" (my emphasis; 26).

28. Du Bois writes, in *Black Reconstruction*: "The crisis came in 1860, not so much because Abraham Lincoln was elected President on a platform which refused further land for the expansion of slavery, but because the cotton crop of 1859 reached the phenomenal height of five million bales as compared with three million in 1850. To this was added the threat of radical abolition as represented by John Brown. The South feared these social upheavals but it was spurred to immediate action by the great cotton crop," which seemed to promise immediate economic independence. "Starting with South Carolina," Du Bois continues, "the Southern cotton-raising and slave-consuming states were forced out of the Union" (48). It might seem odd that DuBois should speak of secessionists as being "*forced* out of the Union"; here, historical materialism informs his rhetoric (hence the de-emphasis of more personal, more immediate agencies). Another statistic bears mention: "In 1860," as Walter Scheidel points out, "slaves accounted for a staggering 48.3 percent of all private wealth in the Southern states, significantly more than the total value of all farmland and associated buildings" (177).

29. Pro-slavery men demonized Lincoln in the same terms in the weeks following his election. Stephen Hale, the pro-secession commissioner (mentioned above), petitioned Governor Beriah Magoffin of Kentucky on December 27: "The election of Mr. Lincoln [is] an open declaration of war, for the triumph of this new theory of government destroys the property of the South, lays waste her fields, and inaugurates all the horrors of a San Domingo servile insurrection, consigning her citizens to assassinations and her wives and daughters to pollution and violation to gratify the lust of half-civilized Africans" (quoted in Dew 97–98).

30. The panic, and the fantasy of chaos, are indeed enduring. For example, from the earliest hours of the Attica uprising in 1971, the FBI—in addition to New York State and Governor Rockefeller—leapt into action; something deep was clearly felt to be at stake: "Rockefeller's men were not the only ones interested in monitoring the response of grassroots and civil rights organizations to the Attica uprising," notes Heather Ann Thompson in *Blood in the Water* (2017). "So was the Federal Bureau of Investigation (FBI). In fact, it was remarkable that federal agencies were so involved in what was happening in this one state prison in the middle of rural New York. Immediately, the FBI stepped up its already extensive surveillance of groups suspected to be sympathetic to prisoners and leaned on its informants in New York, Chicago, and San Francisco to gather information on the Attica rebels. Even more astoundingly, whatever intelligence the FBI gathered, credible or not, was then relayed to authorities at the highest levels of the United States government, including President Richard Nixon, Vice President Spiro Agnew, and US Attorney General John Mitchell, as well as the Defense Intelligence Agency, the Department of the Army, the Department of the Air Force, the Naval Investigative Service, the Secret Service, and the National Security Agency. The Albany office of the FBI alerted other bureau directors that Rockefeller's right-hand man, Robert Douglass, also wanted to be kept apprised of any 'information bearing on the Attica situation' that they gleaned from their 'extremist informants'" (81). White conservatives—and the government institutions that embodied their will—saw in Attica not a problem in criminal justice, or a problem limited to prison conditions at Attica, or even at Attica *and other places like it*; no, they felt at once that the men at Attica posed a threat to the State *as such*, a threat to national security: order at Attica meant order everywhere, and disorder at Attica must therefore mean disorder everywhere (and "order" in this context meant: white control of black men).

31. See Ta-Nehisi Coates, *We Were Eight Years in Power*, 26, 155, 201, 227–88, 270, 275, 296.

32. See Paul Dugan, "Sins of the Fathers: The Confederacy Was Built on Slavery. How Can So Many Southern Whites Still Believe Otherwise?" (2018). See also Booth Gunter and Jamie Kizzire, *Whose Heritage? Public Symbols of the Confederacy* (2016).

33. Republican pollster Frank Luntz first advised his clients to use the term "job creators" instead of "capitalists" or "the wealthy." Interestingly, a search for the term "job creators" at newspapers.com, date-limited to capture the 2011–12

presidential campaign season, returns 6,414 hits, with the highest concentrations occurring in papers published in two important "swing states" (Florida and Ohio). For 2013—not a campaign year—the figure is 1,249 hits.

34. Mondale received only 34% of the white vote in 1984 (Tesler 229).

35. See Tad Friend, "Donald Glover Can't Save You: The Creator of 'Atlanta' Wants TV to Tell Hard Truths," March 5, 2018, *The New Yorker*.

36. I have in mind the process David Brion Davis calls "animalization." See his *The Problem of Slavery in the Age of Emancipation* (2014), 3–44. The process of "animalization" persists, whether through such media as the "Willie Horton" ad the George H. W. Bush campaign ran in 1988 (at the instance of Lee Atwater), or in the "super-predator" scare of the 1990s, or in the hounding of the Central Park Five: African American teenagers who, before and during their trial for rape and assault (1989–90) of a white woman, were branded a "wolf-pack" out for "prey." Chief among the bloodhounds was Donald Trump, who, in a full-page $85,000 ad, published in the New York *Daily News* on May 1, 1989, before the trial had even begun, called for New York to reinstate the death penalty. Trump has yet to acknowledge what the world and New York City know: the Central Park Five were innocent, their "confessions" were coerced, they were exonerated by DNA evidence in 2002, and, in 2014, were paid $41 million to settle a lawsuit they'd brought against the city for malicious prosecution. See Amy Davidson, "Donald Trump and the Central Park Five," *The New Yorker*, June 23, 2014. See also Oliver Laughland, "Donald Trump and the Central Park Five: The Racially Charged Rise of a Demagogue," *The Guardian*, February 17, 2016.

37. *Collected Essays*, 341. All quotations of Baldwin in the present volume are from this edition of his five books of non-fiction.

38. I speak advisedly in calling the Trump administration "white nationalist" in disposition. In *Identity Crisis: The 2016 Presidential Campaign and the Battle for the Meaning of America* (2018), John Sides, Michael Tesler, and Lynn Vavreck—arguing from an immense body of polling data, much of it extending back decades—show conclusively that "racial resentment" (not "economic anxiety") animated the movement that brought Trump to power (69–97). The book is unequivocal: the Trump campaign "activated" and made "more "salient" (as political scientists say) a "white identity politics" long latent in the Republican Party. The data the authors present warrant Ta-Nehisi Coates's (not entirely ironic) designation of Trump as our "first white president." "Trump's appeal to white identity in 2016 was not unprecedented," the authors of *Identity Crisis* point out. "Both Pat Buchanan in 1996 and George Wallace in 1968 campaigned on threats to white Americans and thereby made white identity an important part of their electoral support. But neither Buchanan nor Wallace won a major-party nomination, much less the presidency. Trump's success may mean that appeals to white identity, including the suggestion that white dominance is increasingly threatened by nonwhites, is a rising force in American politics" (90). On "prison gerrymandering," see Heather Ann Thompson, "How Prisons Change the Balance of Power in

America," *The Atlantic*, October 7, 2013. See also Thompson's *Blood in the Water: The Attica Prison Uprising of 1971 and Its Legacy* (2016): 558–71. As for Trump's claims about "illegal aliens" voting for his opponent, see Amy Sherman, "Trump Voter Fraud Allegations," *Politifact Florida* (a site affiliated with the *Tampa Bay Times*), June 22, 2017.

Chapter One

1. Douglass, *Autobiographies*, ed. Henry Louis Gates, Jr. (New York: Library of America, 1994), 1078. Further references to this source will be given in parentheses in the text using the abbreviation *A* and a page number.

2. Compare Jefferson Davis's paean to cotton in a speech delivered in the Senate on May 7, 1860: "Since [the Revolutionary] era . . . a fiber then unknown in the United States, and the production of which is dependent upon the domestic institution of African slavery, has come to be cultivated in such amounts, to enter so into the wearing apparel of the world, so greatly to add to the comfort of the poor, that it may be said to-day that that little fiber, cotton, wraps the commercial world and binds it to the United States in bonds to keep the peace with us which no Government dare break" (*Rise and Fall* 1: 573).

3. Parallel passages occur in Mark and in Luke.

4. As David Roediger puts it in *The Wages of Whiteness* (revised edition 1999): "No answer to the 'white problem' can ignore the explanatory power of historical materialism" (6).

5. As Du Bois also points out, "there was another motive which more and more strongly as time went on compelled the planter to cling to slavery. His political power was based on slavery." Owing to the three-fifths provision in the Constitution, "with four million slaves [the planter] could balance the votes of 2,400,000 Northern voters" (*Black Reconstruction* 41).

6. In *The Problem of Slavery in the Age of Emancipation* (2014), David Brion Davis writes: "Garrison's free black supporters were even more focused on the issues of education and improvement and much more concerned with social equality and civil rights" than on abstruse questions about Constitutional law. "They were also far more pragmatic in their approach to reform and would become impatient and sometimes mystified by the white abolitionists' ideological debates and divisions" (192). From 1849 forward, Douglass exemplified the pragmatic and practical approach Davis speaks of, as when he began to urge abolitionists not to abstain from voting (as Garrison would have had them do), but, when confronted with any particular set of alternatives at the polls, to choose whichever was on the whole the more inimical to slavery, however impure its abolitionism might be.

7. Eric Sundquist was among the first to accord *My Bondage and My Freedom* its due. See his *To Wake the Nations* (particularly the section titled "Frederick Douglass's Revisions," 83–93). On the composition and nature of *My Bondage and*

My Freedom, see also David Blight, *Frederick Douglass: Prophet of Freedom* (251–64). I regret that I was unable to benefit more fully from Blight's new biography; it was published in October 2018, after the present book had already gone into production.

8. John Stauffer has been seeing to this, in his *The Works of James McCune Smith: Black Intellectual and Abolitionist* (2006), edited and annotated, and with an introduction, by Stauffer (and with a preface by Henry Louis Gates, Jr.). See also Stauffer's chapter on Smith in his *The Black Hearts of Men: Radical Abolitionists and the Transformation of Race* (2001).

9. By this date, the internal slave trade worked through vertically integrated corporations that offered such specialties as "fancy girls." Austin Woolfolk (1796–1847) owned one such corporation, which "included systematic channels of communication and exchange, widespread advertising, consistent pricing, cash payments, and fixed locations. He and his relatives concentrated people at fixed points in preparation for making large-scale shipments" (Baptist 183). Woolfolk "created a number of innovations that produced increasingly efficient market connections between the old states [of the upper South] and the slave frontier [along the Mississippi delta]. He set up branches of his firm in both selling and buying areas, allowing his trading activities to run more or less continuously. In districts ripe with buyable slaves, such as Maryland's Eastern Shore, Austin Woolfolk and his brother John used advertisements to generate a groundswell of brand recognition" (Baptist 179). For a well-documented history of such innovations as these in the slave trade, see Baptist, 171–92. Incidentally, Douglass discusses Woolfolk's operations, which he personally witnessed, in an appendix to *My Bondage*. Reprinted there is a lecture he gave on "The Internal Slave Trade" on July 5, 1852, in Rochester, New York: "To me the American slave trade is a terrible reality. . . . I lived on Philpot street, Fell's Point, Baltimore, and have watched from the wharves the slave ships in the basin, anchored from the shore, with their cargoes of human flesh, waiting for favorable winds to waft them down the Chesapeake [bound for Mobile and New Orleans]. There was, at that time, a grand slave mart kept at the head of Pratt street, by Austin Woldfolk [*sic*]. His agents were sent into every town and county in Maryland, announcing their arrival through the papers, and on flaming handbills, headed, 'cash for negroes'" (437). Advertisements in the Maryland newspapers of the day corroborate Douglass's account (as Baptist also does). On April 14, 1832, this notice ran in *The Frederick Town Herald* (Frederick, Maryland): "300 NEGROES WANTED. I wish to purchase them from the age of 13 to 25 years. Persons having such to sell, shall have *Cash* and the *Highest Prices*, by applying to the subscriber, Pratt-street Baltimore. . . . *Liberal Commissions* will be *paid* to those who will aid in purchasing for the subscriber. AUSTIN WOOLFOLK" (emphases in the original 3). Woolfolk owned a plantation in Rosedale, Louisiana, in addition to his Baltimore residence and slave markets.

10. Douglass intimated in his *Narrative* (1845) that Anthony was his father, but the question of his paternity remained unresolved, and Douglass spoke and

wrote of it in varying ways over the decades. See David Blight, *Frederick Douglass* (2018), 13–15.

11. Douglass wavers on the question of whether our social contracts "corrupt" or "redeem" us. It is likely the case that, for him, men need "social restraints" and checks against their "natural" inclination to commit "outrages," whereas women, "naturally" benevolent, must "learn" how to be cruel. Douglass is (let us say) a Romantic when it comes to women, a Freudian when it comes to men. Such anyway is the implication of Douglass's treatment of his Baltimore mistress, Sophia Auld (*A* 222).

12. David Blight agrees. Douglass, he writes, "was a man of the nineteenth century, a thoroughgoing inheritor of Enlightenment ideas" (*Frederick Douglass* 228).

13. See Janet Cornelius, *"When I Can Read My Title Clear": Literacy, Slavery, and Religion in the Antebellum South* (1991), 32–33.

14. See Matthew 4:1–4: "Then was Jesus led up of the Spirit into the wilderness to be tempted of the devil. And when he had fasted forty days and forty nights, he was afterward an hungered. And when the tempter came to him, he said, If thou be the Son of God, command that these stones be made bread. But he answered and said, It is written, Man shall not live by bread alone, but by every word that proceedeth out of the mouth of God."

15. Gustavus Dorgan (1819–98), born and raised in Baltimore, was (more or less) Douglass's exact contemporary; he married in 1848, had four children, and worked as a carpenter in the shipyards (Douglass worked there, too). Joseph Bailey was born in Baltimore in 1818; the census reports that he still lived there in 1850 (with his wife and son). Dorgan and Bailey were sons of the men who operated "Durgin & Bailey's shipyard" (as Douglass recalled it in 1855) in Philpot Street, Fells Point, Baltimore. I have been unable to find records for the other two boys Douglass mentions.

16. See Donne's "Batter My Heart, Three Person'd God."

17. Douglass's first owner, Aaron Anthony (1767–1826), worked as general overseer on the Lloyd plantation, called Wye House. When Douglass was born, its proprietor was Edward Lloyd V (1779–1834). His father (Edward Lloyd IV) had been a member of the Continental Congress, and Lloyd himself served as the 13th governor of Maryland (1809–11) and as US Senator from the state (1819–26). Census records and slave schedules indicate that in 1820 (when Douglass was about two years old), Lloyd owned 146 slaves; by 1830, not long after Douglass was separated from his mother, the number had increased to 558, placing Lloyd near the top of slaveholders (and capitalists) in the upper South (only the wealthiest of the rice planters and cotton magnates of the Deep South exceeded him in human property).

18. The account Douglass here gives is borne out by Du Bois in *Black Reconstruction* (1935): "From an economic point of view," writes Du Bois, the "planter class had interest in consumption rather than production. They exploited

labor in order that they themselves should live more grandly and not mainly for increasing production. Their taste went to elaborate households, well-furnished and hospitable; they had much to eat and drink; they consumed large quantities of liquor; they gambled and caroused and kept up the habit of dueling well down into the nineteenth century. Sexually they were lawless, protecting elaborately and flattering the virginity of a small class of women of their social clan, and keeping at command millions of poor women of the two laboring groups of the South" (35).

19. Edward Napoleon Covey (1806–75), son of Henry Covey (1775–1850) and Eleanor Ellen Edmondson (1772–1850), who seem to have admired the French dictator. Born in Kings Creek, Talbot County, Maryland, Covey married Susan Caulk (1809–69), the daughter of a successful farmer, in 1832; the couple settled on their own farm in St. Michaels District, as Douglass indicates, and had—Covey was quite the patriarch—fourteen children. The 1830 census indicates that Covey owned six slaves and, by 1850, his real estate was valued (for purposes of taxation) at $25,000. Covey himself was a man of some thrift (in addition to paternal fecundity). He later took second place at the Easton Cattle Show and Fair on November 18, 1848, for having produced, that year, and with slaves, 1,500 bushels of wheat and 300 of corn on his 268 acres. Douglass was touring England at the time, *Narrative* in hand. On Tuesday, March 6, 1866, Covey, now aspiring to political influence, sat on a committee in Talbot County that drew up resolutions endorsing the Reconstruction measures of President Andrew Johnson, opposing negro suffrage, and condemning Maryland Senator John Andrew Jackson Creswell's support of the Freedman's Bureau Bill, then before the Congress.

20. The date was 1834. Jenkins may well have been born in Africa; the international slave trade ceased (in America) in 1808, and Jenkins certainly seems much older than twenty-six. Douglass tells us that Jenkins, though owned by a "William Groomes" of Easton, Talbot County, was, in 1834, hired out to, or at any rate living with, a man named "Kemp." 1840 census records confirm that a William Groome (no "s") lived in Talbot County at the time, and owned three male slaves aged 36–54 (a standard age bracket on the slave schedules, and one into which Douglass's "old advisor" would fit). Six Kemps, some doubtless related, maintained households in Talbot County in the 1830s (three with slaves); I cannot say which Douglass has in mind. There remains one suggestive clue, to add to what Douglass tells us of Sandy. In 1870—in the hamlet of Trappe, Talbot County, Maryland, about ten miles from St. Michaels and Covey's farm—there resided an African American woman named Harriet Jenkins, born in 1799, and working, at the age of 71, as a domestic servant. Is it possible that she, married to a slave named Sandy, comforted Frederick Bailey, as he then would have been known, in the summer of 1834? All three of Groome's slaves are of her age, born at about the turn of the century, as was she.

21. See Richard Brodhead's introduction to the Duke University Press edition of *The Conjure Woman* for an illuminating discussion of Chesnutt's difficulties in this respect.

22. I borrow the term "romantic racialism" from George Frederickson. See his *The Black Image in the White Mind* (1987), 97–129.

23. I always cite Dickinson's poetry by page number (though on occasion I also refer to poems by the number assigned them in Thomas Johnson's edition).

24. I have in mind, *mutatis mutandis*, Nathaniel Hawthorne's great allegory of paranoia and suspicion, "Young Goodman Brown" (1835), in which our New World American enterprise—insofar as the Puritan settlement in Salem might be said to represent it—is alternatively (and undecidably) presented as depraved and wholesome; Herman Melville's *The Confidence Man* (1857), in which America figures, at least on my reading of it, as the con-game any "democracy" founded upon an economy of hereditary bond-slavery must be (the first incarnation of the confidence man appears in black-face); Douglass's great oration (already cited), "What to the Slave is the Fourth of July?" (1852) ("Go where you may . . . search out every abuse, and when you have found the last, lay your facts by the side of the everyday practices of this nation, and you will say with me, that, for revolting barbarity and shameless hypocrisy, America reigns without a rival"); *The Adventures of Huckleberry Finn* (1885), in which there is no socially accredited place in America for a fugitive soul such as Huck (and, of course, add to *Huck Finn* such other works by Twain as "The United States of Lyncherdom" and "To the Person Sitting in Darkness" [in which the national flag is re-imagined—pirate-fashion—with skulls and crossbones for stars]); any number of essays and books by Du Bois; Jack London's *The Iron Heel* (1908); John Jay Chapman's *William Lloyd Garrison* (1913); Sinclair Lewis's *It Can't Happen Here* (1935); Henry Miller's *The Air Conditioned Nightmare* (1945); Allen Ginsberg's *Howl* (1956) and *The Fall of America* (1973); Norman Mailer's "The White Negro" (1957) (collected in *Advertisements for Myself*) and *Armies of the Night* (1968) (in which America figures as a proto-fascist "corporation land"); Phillip Roth's alternative history *The Plot Against America* (2004); Thomas Pynchon's *V.* (1963), *The Crying of Lot 49* (1966), *Gravity's Rainbow* (1973), and *Vineland* (1990); Hunter S. Thompson's *Fear and Loathing in Las Vegas: A Savage Journey to the Heart of the American Dream* (1971), *Fear and Loathing on the Campaign Trail* (1973), and *Kingdom of Fear: Loathsome Secrets of a Star-Crossed Child in the Final Days of the American Century* (2003); and Gore Vidal in a number of essays and books condemning the American "national security state." On the softer side of this tradition (insofar as it has one) lie the many condemnations of America as stiflingly conformist (a nation whose mores and institutions are adapted to punish eccentricity, rebellion, or agnosticism with regard to the American civil religion). Sinclair Lewis's novels *Main Street* (1920) and *Babbit* (1922) provide the type for fictions of this kind. And then we have H. L. Mencken, for whom the follies and fallacies of democracy (and Comstockery) in America were an unending source of mirth (and indignation); see, for example, his "Puritanism as a Literary Force," collected in *A Book of Prefaces* (1917). I haven't even begun to number the dystopian fables of America that come to us out of Hollywood.

25. In *Roughing It* (1872) and "The Private History of a Campaign that Failed" (1885) he tells the tale.

26. As for Stevens's radicalism on labor and economic questions, see Du Bois, *Black Reconstruction* (1935), 197–98.

27. For a good history of Anacostia, see Louise Hutchinson, *The Anacostia Story* (1977). Freedmen and freedwomen moved into Anacostia following the Civil War. General Oliver O. Howard, head of the Freedmen's Bureau, quietly purchased 375 acres of land there for resale to them. That land opened for development in 1867, and, occasional violence against them notwithstanding, some 500 African American families had established residences in Anacostia by 1870 (Hutchinson, 81–83). The Freedmen's Bureau subsidized private schools for black children there (*publicly* funded schools were entirely restricted to white students). In 1871, President Grant appointed Douglass to represent Anacostia on the first Legislative Council established to govern the District of Columbia. Six years later Douglass made his home in Anacostia: he bought the nine-acre estate owned by one of the original developers of the area (John Van Hook); it never went out of the possession of the family. Douglass's sons Lewis, Charles, and Frederick, Jr., also soon established homes in Anacostia's Hillsdale neighborhood (Hutchinson, 89, 111). The construction of the Anacostia Freeway in the 1960s isolated the neighborhood. White flight soon segregated Southeast DC and Anacostia, which today is 92% African American (with a population in excess of 100,000).

Chapter Two

1. The significance of this experiment in democracy justifies an extraordinary claim Du Bois makes in *The Souls of Black Folk* (1903) with regard to the Freedmen's Bureau, one of the principal instruments through which the Radical Reconstruction was implemented: "Less than a month after the weary Emancipator [Lincoln] passed to his rest, his successor [Andrew Johnson] assigned Major-Gen. Oliver O. Howard to duty as Commissioner of the new Bureau. He was a Maine man, then only thirty-five years of age. He had marched with Sherman to the sea, had fought well at Gettysburg, and but the year before had been assigned to the command of the Department of Tennessee. An honest man, with too much faith in human nature, little aptitude for business and intricate detail, he had had large opportunity of becoming acquainted at first hand with much of the work before him. And of that work it has been truly said that '*no approximately correct history of civilization can ever be written which does not throw out in bold relief, as one of the great landmarks of political and social progress, the organization and administration of the Freedmen's Bureau*'" (my emphasis; 378). Du Bois quotes (here) a March 2, 1871, resolution exonerating Howard, and the Bureau, of corruption charges levied by his and its political opponents. The resolution was written by the House Committee on Education and Labor during the forty-first Congress,

Samuel Mayes Arnell (1833–1903) of Tennessee, chair. Arnell had been a staunch Unionist during the war (though Tennessee born).

2. Luke Poland and John Scott, *Testimony Taken by the Joint Select Committee to Inquire into the Condition of Affairs in the Late Insurrectionary States, South Carolina, Volume I* (1872), 97. The man under interrogation, Edwin W. Seibels (of Edgefield County, South Carolina), had served in the Confederate Army; before the war he'd been a planter of considerable wealth.

3. Thomas Wentworth Higginson gives the following account of Rivers in his *Army Life in a Black Regiment* (1869): "He is a man of distinguished appearance, and in old times was the crack coachman of Beaufort, in which capacity he once drove [Confederate General P. G. T.] Beauregard from this plantation to Charleston, I believe. They tell me that he was once allowed to present a petition to the Governor of South Carolina in behalf of slaves, for the redress of certain grievances; and that a placard, offering two thousand dollars for his recapture, is still to be seen by the wayside between here and Charleston. . . . There is not a white officer in this regiment who has more administrative ability, or more absolute authority over the men; they do not love him, but his mere presence has controlling power over them. He writes well enough to prepare for me a daily report of his duties in the camp; if his education reached a higher point, I see no reason why he should not command the Army of the Potomac. . . . No anti-slavery novel has described a man of such marked ability. He makes Toussaint perfectly intelligible; and if there should ever be a black monarchy in South Carolina, he will be its king" (57–58).

4. Hamburg would remain a majority African American town in the decades to come, though its population dwindled. Severe flooding—the town lay but several feet above the level of the Savannah River, on whose east bank it was built—destroyed what remained of it in 1929, and the citizens relocated up the bluffs, some two hundred yards, and rebuilt their settlement in what is now the Carrsville neighborhood of the (still largely segregated) city of North Augusta, which was incorporated in 1906. For decades the sole memorial erected in connection with the Hamburg Massacre was an obelisk, dedicated in 1916, honoring the only white man to die in the melee. The inscription reads: "In Memory of Thomas McKie Meriwether who on 8th July 1876, gave his life that the civilization builded by his fathers might be preserved for their children's children unimpaired. . . . What more can a man do than to lay down his life. In life he exemplified the highest ideal of Anglo-Saxon civilization. By his death he assured to the children of his beloved land the supremacy of that ideal." At the ceremony dedicating the monument, Matthew Calbraith Butler's son, Pierce Butler, a physician, delivered a speech celebrating Meriwether and the "Red Shirt" terrorist/redeemers. To this day the obelisk remains the most conspicuous public monument in the town, situated on the hill where Georgia and Carolina Avenues diverge, on a rise looking back down toward Augusta, Georgia. Not until 2011 were historical markers placed in the Carrsville section of North Augusta commemorating both Hamburg and the African American victims of the 1876 massacre.

5. Here and at the close of this chapter I draw details of the Hamburg Massacre and related events from contemporary newspaper reports and government documents; from Fox Butterfield, *All God's Children* (1995); from Francis Butler Simkins, *Pitchfork Ben Tillman* (1944); from Eric Foner, *Reconstruction* (1988); from Stephen Kantrowitz, *Ben Tillman & the Reconstruction of White Supremacy* (2000); and from Stephen Budiansky, *The Bloody Shirt* (2008) (the best account of the events, in my view).

6. In this connection, see George Frederickson, "The Vanishing Negro: Darwinism and the Conflict of the Races," and "The Negro as Beast: Southern Negrophobia at the Turn of the Century," both in *The Black Image in the White Mind* (1987).

7. For a splendid account of the book's reception, see David Levering Lewis, *W. E. B. Du Bois: Biography of a Race, 1868–1919* (2013), 277–96.

8. In *The White Image in the Black Mind* (2000), Mia Bay writes: "White supremacist literature of the nineteenth century asserted that blacks were inferior to whites in much the same way that women were inferior to men—less intelligent and rational, more childlike and emotional" (40). The same could be said of twentieth century writing. For an early example, see John W. Burgess, *Reconstruction and the Constitution* (1905): "There is no question, now, that Congress did a monstrous thing, and committed a great political error, if not a sin, in the creation of this new [black] electorate [in the late 1860s]. It was a great wrong to civilization to put the white race of the South under the domination of the Negro race. The claim that there is nothing in the color of the skin from the point of view of political ethics is a great sophism. *A black skin means membership in a race of men which has never of itself succeeded in subjecting passion to reason; has never, therefore, created any civilization of any kind*" (my emphasis; 133).

9. In the Compson "Appendix" he supplied for *The Portable Faulkner* (1946), Faulkner, in the entry where Dilsey's name appears, writes only two words—and pluralizes her such that she stands in for and typifies his African American characters: "They endured" (756). For a discussion of the matter, see *Faulkner and Ideology* (1995), Donald M. Kartiganer, Ann J. Abadie, eds. (249–50).

10. All quotations of Brooks' poetry are from her *Selected Poems*.

11. For reasons unclear to me, Du Bois, in quoting the poem, breaks its eight-foot lines into four-foot lines, thereby losing the end-rhymes as Lowell had them in the original. See *The Poems of James Russell Lowell* (1912), 96.

12. Martin Luther King, Jr. quoted the same lines from Lowell's poem in Los Angeles on February 26, 1965: "We shall overcome because James Russell Lowell is right: 'Truth forever on the scaffold, wrong forever on the throne. Yet, that scaffold sways the future and behind the dim unknown standeth God within the shadow, keeping watch above his own'" (Warren 180).

13. We find the idea everywhere in discourse about race (whether medical, literary, or pseudoanthropological). At times it takes a vicious form, as here, but at others the spuriously eulogistic form that Frederickson calls, in *The Black*

Image in the White Mind (1987), "romantic racialism." In a discussion of the abolitionist Theodore Parker's writings and orations, Frederickson says: "Although he believed that it was a good thing, in the main, that the national stock was predominantly Anglo-Saxon, Parker apparently thought that this 'strong, real, Anglo-Saxon blood' needed to be mixed with that of the other American races, including the Negroes and the Indians, 'just enough to temper [it],' and 'furnish a new composite tribe, far better I trust than the old.' Parker could not specify what the Negro in particular would contribute to this new blend, but he had, whether he realized it or not, opened the way for a romantic racialist concept of the mulatto character that would challenge the fundamental white supremacist belief in the evils of intermarriage." Frederickson continues: "Praise of the mulatto as a superior human type was occasionally forthcoming in antislavery writings of the 1850s" (120–21). He cites C. G. Parsons's *Inside View of Slavery* (1855), for which, as Frederickson points out, Harriet Beecher Stowe provided a flattering introduction: "The mulattoes especially—and they constitute a large proportion of the slave population—are the best specimens of manhood found in the South. The African mothers have given them a good physical system, and the Anglo-Saxon fathers a good mental constitution" (65–66). Note that *paternity* is here imagined as Anglo-Saxon; few white men would admit of the reverse in the 1850s, or for more than a century afterward (*black* paternity of mixed-race offspring was always deemed intolerable).

14. For more on the relation between imperialism in the Philippines and the reinstitution of white supremacy in the American South, see Frederickson, *The Black Image in the White Mind* (1987), 305–11, and C. Vann Woodward, *The Origins of the New South* (1951), 324–26.

15. This section of Byron's poem concerns the Ottoman subjection and occupation of Greece.

16. For details, see Lewis, *W. E. B. DuBois: Biography of a Race* (2013), 356–57.

17. By the time he published *Black Reconstruction*, thirty-two years later, Du Bois had answered the question. Hippomenes and golden apples it would be. So began Du Bois's move toward the Communist Party. In *The Souls of Black Folk* charity and hope, it seems, still held him. But of course, that book appeals to the better angels of our nature; where it exhorts, *Black Reconstruction* condemns.

18. Du Bois is an eco-critic *avant la lettre* of Southern culture and agriculture. His arguments are borne out by Eugene Genovese in "Cotton, Slavery and Soil Exhaustion," in *The Political Economy of Slavery* (1967), 85–105. As for ecology and race more generally—and as for abuse of the land and those who work and inhabit it—economists Michael Ash and James K. Boyce point out (in an October 2018 paper) that "it is well documented that racial and ethnic minorities in the United States experience disproportionate exposure to toxic air emissions from industry. . . . Longitudinal analysis has found that new hazardous facilities tend to be sited disproportionately in what were already predominantly minority communities." They show further that "the share of pollution risk accruing to minority

groups generally exceeds their share of employment and greatly exceeds their share of higher paying jobs" at the facilities that produce the toxins (10636).

19. The phrase dates to 1670, when the Reverend Samuel Danforth delivered his election sermon: "A Brief Recognition of New-Englands Errand into the Wilderness."

20. In fact, the Nazis looked to America for an example, when crafting the Nuremberg laws that underwrote Hitler's regime. See Whitman, *Hitler's American Model* (2017).

21. See the *Congressional Record—Senate* for 1900 (page 3223). In the same speech, Tillman rebukes Senator John Coit Spooner of Wisconsin. Spooner—a distinguished veteran of the Union Army—had said: "The negro during the war had won the eternal gratitude and appreciation of his old master. There never was a day during the war, Mr. President, nor a night, on which the negro slaves of the South could not have disbanded the Confederate army. They could have resorted to the torch; they could have resorted to all manner of violence. But they did not.... They knew, even to the humblest of them, that our Army was an army of liberation; they knew that when the flag of the United States came into their vicinity it meant freedom to them; and yet they were a kindly, faithful people, resisting all temptations to remember the past. They had nothing in their hearts of vengeance. All I mention that for is to say this in regard to it, that when the struggle was made to take by fraud and to take by violence, even to the extent of the shotgun, from the negroes, their participation in the government . . . it was violence against right. The colored man had the same right to vote, Mr. President, under the laws of the United States that the white man qualified to vote possessed. The colored man has the same right to come to the Senate of the United States and sit here as a Senator in the place occupied by the Senator from South Carolina as the Senator has under the Constitution and laws of the United States. I will not talk about a resort to fraud. That is peaceable, at least. I never yet, however, have been able to find justification for the use of the shotgun, for murder, against the man who had a right to vote, and who sought, under our Constitution and our flag, to exercise that right" (3219). So why the rape hysteria *now*, why all the murder, the lynching? Tillman had the answer: "[Senator Spooner] gave us a picture of the condition of the slave during the war, and of the debt of gratitude which the Southern people owe to those slaves, who had charge of our wives and children and homes, and, to their everlasting credit, during those four long and bloody years not one solitary crime was reported against them of the kind that is now reported every week.... [It] cannot be denied that the slaves of the South were a superior set of men and women to freedmen of to-day, and that the poison in their minds—the race hatred of the whites—is the result of the teachings of Northern fanatics. Ravishing a woman, white or black, was never known to occur in the South till after the reconstruction era. So much for that phase of the subject" (3233).

22. As I write in my introduction to *The Cambridge Companion to American Poets* (2015): "Out of all this, Paul Laurence Dunbar composed the most exemplary lyric poem to emerge in the late nineteenth century, 'We Wear the Mask,'

collected in *Lyrics of Lowly Life* (1896) with a preface (of course!) by a smiling Howells: 'We wear the mask that grins and lies, / It hides our cheeks and shades our eyes,— / This debt we pay to human guile . . .' In his preface, Howells assures the reader, first, that Dunbar is African in descent, without 'admixture of white blood' (xiv), and that his achievement in poetry without white blood is evidence of 'the essential unity of the human race' (xvii). But the concession comes with a codicil, altogether of its day (the *Plessy v. Ferguson* decision was handed down in 1896): the unity of the races notwithstanding, Howells argues, 'a precious difference of temperament' exists 'between [them] which it would be a great pity ever to lose, and . . . this is best preserved and most charmingly suggested by Mr. Dunbar in those pieces of his where he studies the moods and traits of his race in its own accent of our English'"—that is, in the dialect poetry, which compasses "the range of the race," as Howells phrases it, not in the poetry written in standard English (xvii–xviii). Could there be a finer literary-critical counterpart to the "separate but equal" doctrine established by *Plessy*? So much the better, as Howells later remarks, that Dunbar has a "finely ironical perception of the negro's limitations, with a tenderness for them which I think so very rare as to be almost quite new" (xviii). To which the book makes answer unheard: "'With torn and bleeding hearts we smile / And mouth with myriad subtleties' (167)," 6–7.

Chapter Three

1. McClurg, who owned a bookstore and publishing house in Chicago, had risen to the rank of Brigadier General for services in combat at Perryville, Chickamauga, Missionary Ridge, Chattanooga, and Bentonville. He was with Sherman's army during its March to the Sea. A man of literary tastes, he carried with him, throughout the war, a copy of Palgrave's *Golden Treasury*. He was born in 1845, mustered in and organized a company at age seventeen, in August 1862 (he was named its captain), and died in 1917. He was by sentiment an abolitionist, and an admirer of Sumner. He left a memoir of his military service, which was printed in *Reminiscences of Chicago During the Civil War* by Mabel McIlvaine (1914): "Those who enlisted were of course nearly all young men," McClurg writes, "just entering upon, or just about to enter upon, the activities of life. Hope and ambition were urging them forward in some chosen career which should bring competence and ease in later life. They longed to stay at home and to enter upon their life work; but something higher and nobler than their own self-interest beckoned them to the field where the life and integrity of their beloved country must be fought for in bloody battles. They could not be deaf to the calls which were sounding all around them. The periodical press was full of patriotic appeals. Every rostrum resounded with the fervid eloquence of anxious lovers of their country. Orators, like [abolitionists] Wendell Phillips and Henry Ward Beecher, and statesmen, like Lincoln and Seward, poured forth the most soul-stirring pleas to save the Union" (98).

2. I encountered Ruskin's remark in Daniel Aaron's *The Unwritten Civil War* (1972), 337.

3. A large body of fiction reflects the new North/South rapprochement. See Nina Silber, *The Romance of Reunion: Northerners and the South, 1865–1900* (1997). See Blight, *Race and Reunion* (2001), 211–54. In *The Origins of the New South* (1951), C. Vann Woodward writes: "The North had taken up the White Man's Burden, and by 1898 was looking to Southern racial policy for national guidance in the new problems of imperialism resulting from the Spanish American War. Commenting on the Supreme Court's opinion upholding disfranchisement in Mississippi [*Williams v. Mississippi* (1898)], the *Nation* pronounced it 'an interesting coincidence that this important decision is rendered at a time when we are considering the idea of taking in a varied assortment of inferior races in different parts of the world'—races 'which, of course, could not be allowed to vote.' . . . A speech in defense of American imperialism by [Republican Senator] George F. Hoar 'most amply vindicated the South,' said Senator John L. McLaurin of South Carolina. He thanks the Massachusetts statesman 'for his complete announcement of the divine right of the Caucasian to govern the inferior races'" (324).

4. See, for example, what is perhaps the best chapter in Du Bois's *Black Reconstruction* (1935): "The Black Proletariat in South Carolina" (381–430).

5. All quotations of Crane's writings are from *Great Short Works of Stephen Crane*.

6. One might suspect a sophisticated error in the text here: did Crane write "reflexively," and overlook the mistake in print? The semantic and discursive nearness of "philosophical" to "reflection" persuade me otherwise; the printed text is surely correct.

7. Diaries and letters written by soldiers on both sides of the war abound with tales of encounters between enemy pickets. Any contemporary reader of Crane at all familiar with the literature of the war might well have assessed the dimwitted exchange Crane offers against others in the same genre; and he would have understood the scene in *Red Badge* for what it is—farcical. For contrast, I reprint here an anecdote related in *The Personal Memoirs of U.S. Grant* (first published in 1885). It dates to the Chattanooga campaign (November 1863): "After we had secured the opening of a line over which to bring our supplies to the army, I made a personal inspection to see the situation of the pickets of the two armies. As I have stated, Chattanooga Creek comes down the centre of the valley to within a mile or such a matter of the town of Chattanooga, then bears off westerly, then north-westerly, and enters the Tennessee River at the foot of Lookout Mountain. This creek, from its mouth up to where it bears off west, lay between the two lines of pickets, and the guards of both armies drew their water from the same stream. As I would be under short-range fire and in an open country, I took nobody with me, except, I believe, a bugler, who stayed some distance to the rear. I rode from our right around to our left. When I came to the camp of the picket guard of our side, I heard the call, 'Turn out the guard for the commanding general.' I replied, 'Never mind the

guard,' and they were dismissed and went back to their tents. Just back of these, and about equally distant from the creek, were the guards of the Confederate pickets. The sentinel on their post called out in like manner, 'Turn out the guard for the commanding general,' and, I believe, added, 'General Grant.' Their line in a moment front-faced to the north, facing me, and gave a salute, which I returned. The most friendly relations seemed to exist between the pickets of the two armies. At one place there was a tree which had fallen across the stream, and which was used by the soldiers of both armies in drawing water for their camps" (420–21).

8. See Virginia Eubanks, *Automating Inequality: How High-Tech Tools Profile, Police, and Punish the Poor* (2017), 18. She describes the nineteenth-century practice of hiring children out to work on farms in chapter 1, "From Poorhouse to Database."

9. See Charles Larocca, "Stephen Crane's Inspiration," *American Heritage* (May/June 1991). Larocca explains: "Ironically, in 1983 the Common Council of Port Jervis voted to change the name of that park from Stephen Crane Memorial Park at Jervis Square to Orange Square Veterans Park, after some local citizens argued that *The Red Badge of Courage* was an antiwar novel that glorified cowardice and desertion and that 'Stephen Crane did a disservice to the many honorable veterans when he wrote *The Red Badge of Courage*.' Wilson Turner, commander of the local Veterans of Foreign Wars post, complained that 'Stephen Crane was not a veteran. He did not fight in the Civil War. He sat in the park and got information from the veterans that were there.'" One wonders whether the controversy in Port Jervis spun off the much larger controversy—very much agitated in 1983—over whether or not Maya Lin's Vietnam Veterans Memorial (dedicated in 1982) dishonored soldiers.

10. See Crane and Stallman, *Omnibus*: 192. Henceforth cited, within the body of the book, as "*Omnibus*."

11. Readers had to wait until 2014 for Paul Sorrentino's *Stephen Crane: A Life of Fire* for a study as ambitious and as extensive as Stallman's had been, though I should mention two fine, shorter biographies: Linda Davis's *Badge of Courage: The Life of Stephen Crane* (1998), and Christopher Benfey's *The Double Life of Stephen Crane* (1992).

12. See Crews's annotated edition of the novel, 128.

13. In this connection, see Woodward, *Origins of the New South* (1951), 154–68; 403.

14. Quoted in Wertheim, *A Stephen Crane Encyclopedia*, 86.

15. Here, as throughout this chapter, I'm trying to account for what Fredric Jameson would call (in his high academic) "the historicity" of the form and style of *Red Badge*, and to describe as precisely as I can the "historical moment" that allowed for "the emergence" of "the linguistic possibilities" of which Crane so ably avails himself, and of the "situation-specific function" of his new "aesthetic" (9).

16. I borrow the term from Sacvan Bercovitch's landmark 1978 book *The American Jeremiad*, now issued in a second, 2012 edition, with a new preface, by the University of Wisconsin Press.

Chapter Four

1. My account of James City relies on Roberta S. Alexander's *North Carolina Faces the Freedmen: Race Relations During Presidential Reconstruction, 1865–67* (1985) and Patricia C. Click's *Time Full of Trial: The Roanoke Island Freedmen's Colony, 1862–1867* (2001).

2. In South Carolina, the freedmen met a fate similar to the one that befell the inhabitants of James City. See Du Bois, *Black Reconstruction* (1935), 393–95.

3. All quotations of Chesnutt's short stories and novels—with the exception of *The Colonel's Dream*—are from Chesnutt, *Stories, Novels, and Essays* (2002). That volume includes *The Conjure Woman*, *The Wife of His Youth*, *The House Behind the Cedars*, and *The Marrow of Tradition*.

4. See also Mel Watkins, *On the Real Side: A History of African American Comedy from Slavery to Chris Rock* (1999): "The hip street persona [Eddie] Murphy affects at the beginning of both his popular *Beverly Hills Cop* films is a slick, apparently frenetic, fast-talking black con man engaged in outthinking and outtalking some dangerous, if somewhat inept, white criminals. This situation . . . harks back to one of the earliest black comic modes—the black slave outwitting a more powerful and presumably more knowledgeable master, or the even more venerable tradition of the black trickster" (19).

5. Galton (1822–1911)—a second-cousin to Charles Darwin—was among the most influential scientists of Victorian England. He coined the term "eugenics," established it as a field (in theory and in practice), and made significant contributions to statistics, psychology, anthropology, and criminology (he established the evidentiary value of fingerprints in British courts).

6. John makes the capital error of attempting to entertain his wife by reading *First Principles* aloud to her in "The Gray Wolf's Ha'nt" (79). She, for her part, prefers to listen to Uncle Julius. For a discussion of Chesnutt's satirical purposes as regards Spencer, see Dean McWilliams, *Charles W. Chesnutt and the Fictions of Race* (2002), 90–92.

7. Shannon Sullivan writes: "Understanding the biological inheritance of the effects of white racism [through the mechanism of epigenetics] means first and foremost appreciating how something social can become physiological" ("Inheriting Racist Disparities in Health: Epigenetics and the Transgenerational Effects of White Racism" [2013], 193). Chesnutt gives us—as if in anticipation of the alarming implications of epigenetics—an example of how, in Henry, "the social" becomes "the physiological." I call the new science of epigenetics alarming because it suggests that diseases associated with poverty and oppression can, in fact, become heritable: low birth-weight babies, premature delivery, diabetes, cardiovascular disease, decreasing life expectancy, etc. See Goosby; Kuzawa and Sweet; Sullivan (essay and book, as listed in the bibliography); and Ross. If the findings of these scientists are borne out, we shall have a fuller (and grimmer) understanding of the dogged persistence, and the appalling harm, of white supremacy.

8. Remarks in the concluding pages of *The Personal Memoirs of Ulysses S. Grant* (1885) sum up the developments nicely: "Prior to the rebellion the great mass of the people were satisfied to remain near the scenes of their birth. In fact an immense majority of the whole people did not feel secure against coming to want should they move among entire strangers. So much was the country divided into small communities that localized idioms had grown up, so that you could almost tell what section a person was from by hearing him speak. Before, new territories were settled by a 'class'; people who shunned contact with others; people who, when the country began to settle up around them, would push out farther from civilization. Their guns furnished meat, and the cultivation of a very limited amount of the soil, their bread and vegetables. All the streams abounded with fish. Trapping would furnish pelts to be brought into the States once a year, to pay for necessary articles which they could not raise—powder, lead, whiskey, tobacco and some store goods. Occasionally some little articles of luxury would enter into these purchases—a quarter of a pound of tea, two or three pounds of coffee, more of sugar, some playing cards, and if anything was left over of the proceeds of the sale, more whiskey. Little was known of the topography of the country beyond the settlements of these frontiersmen. This is all changed now. The war begot a spirit of independence and enterprise. The feeling now is, that a youth must cut loose from his old surroundings to enable him to get up in the world. There is now such a commingling of the people that particular idioms and pronunciation are no longer localized to any great extent; the country has filled up 'from the centre all around to the sea'; railroads connect the two oceans and all parts of the interior; maps, nearly perfect, of every part of the country are now furnished the student of geography" (778–79).

9. As for the ideological and political function of *Birth of a Nation*, Chesnutt had much to say. On April 3, 1917, shortly before America entered the Great War, he wrote to Munson A. Havens, an officer in the Cleveland Chamber of Commerce:

Dear Sir,

The Chamber of Commerce, as the foremost representative body of business and professional men of the community, stands very properly in the forefront of the movement for preparedness, for patriotism and the united action of the people in the crisis at present confronting the United States. In view of this position of the Chamber, I think it proper to call your attention, and through you the attention of the Board of Directors or the proper committees of the Chamber to the following facts.

The moving picture film called *The Birth of a Nation*, because of its vicious and anti-social character was refused approval by the board of moving picture censors, or whatever its title is, of the State of Ohio, during the last administration, but has been pounding at the gates of Ohio for several years, and finally under this administration has been passed by the present board of censors, and is announced for early exhibition in Cleveland. It seems to me a most unwise and unpatriotic thing to permit its production, at this time especially, without protest, for the following reasons.

The picture was made of course to make money, and to make it by stirring up race prejudice and race hatred, which it seems to me is a most unwise and most unpatriotic thing at this juncture in our national affairs. The principal action of the picture is devoted to exploiting the alleged misconduct of colored Union soldiers during the reconstruction period (to say nothing of its glorification of that organization of traitors known as the Ku-Klux-Klan). The principal villain of the story, the would-be rapist, is portrayed as a colored captain in the Union army. There are already four colored regiments in the regular army with a military history in past wars of which they and the nation may well be proud. There are several complete regiments of colored militia, and battalions in several other states, and similar units proposed in other places. With war declared there will undoubtedly be a large accession to these. The colored people are loyal citizens, without perhaps a great deal of encouragement, in some quarters, to loyalty, indeed in spite of serious discouragement; but it seems to me and those on behalf of whom I speak, that such an insult to the national uniform when worn by men of color, as the public exhibition of such a picture as *The Birth of a Nation, which, as a work of pictorial art is a superb and impressive thing, and all the more vicious for that reason, should not be permitted at this time, when all citizens should stand together to support the honor of the nation.*

When it is also taken into consideration that there are numbers of colored men in the community who have recently come to the North because of our disorganized labor market, it would seem a matter of doubtful wisdom to do or to permit anything that is likely to breed discontent and ill feeling among these people.

It has seemed to me and to prominent citizens with whom I have talked, some of them members of the Chamber, that it would be a wise and patriotic thing for the Chamber of Commerce to use its influence with the city administration, or the police department, or whatever authority has power in the matter, to discourage this sort of thing at this juncture, and to prevent, if possible, the exhibition of this film. (my emphases; *An Exemplary Citizen*, 134–35)

10. For details of these negotiations, see Brodhead's introduction to *The Conjure Woman.*

11. Frances E. W. Harper's novel *Iola Leroy* abounds with stories of men and women seeking family members from whom slavery and war had separated them; indeed, the plot of the novel hinges on a quest for just such a reunion as Chesnutt here considers.

12. Of 226,167 black inhabitants of Kentucky in 1860, only 10,684 were free (4.7%). On the other hand, as Du Bois observes in *Black Reconstruction* (1935), "the loss of capital through runaway slaves was a constant menace to the system" of slavery in Kentucky (567). Grandison will deprive Col. Owen of many thousands of dollars, once he effects his plans.

13. Twain wrote the book on the "Walter Scott disease." In *Life on the Mississippi*, published first in 1883, he says: "Sir Walter had so large a hand in making Southern character, as it existed before the war, that he is in great measure responsible for the war. . . . The Southerner of the American Revolution owned slaves; so did the Southerner of the Civil War; but the former resembles the latter as an Englishman resembles a Frenchman. The change of character can be traced rather more easily to Sir Walter's influence than to that of any other thing or person" (*Mississippi Writings* 501). It is all but impossible to conceive that, in writing his Col. Owen up, Chesnutt did not have Twain's celebrated remarks about Walter Scott in mind.

14. Of special pertinence to "The Passing of Grandison" is the testimony of a fugitive slave named Lewis Clarke, who, like Grandison, fled Kentucky: "Of course, the slaves don't tell folks what's passing in their minds about freedom; for they know what'll come of it, if they do. I said a slave was like a brute; and so he is, in many things; but he ain't altogether that much like a brute, neither. The fact is, slavery's the father of lies. The slave knows he ought to have his freedom; and his master knows it, jest as well as he does; but they both say they don't; and they tell me some folks this way believe 'em. The master says the slave don't want his freedom, and the slave says he don't want it; but they both of 'em lie, and know it. There never was anything beat slavery for lying; and of all folks in the world, there's nobody deceived quite so bad, as the masters down South; for the slaves deceive them, and they deceive themselves. Some have thought their slaves were so much attached to them, that nobody could coax them away; and them very slaves now reside in Canada" (quoted in Blassingame 153). Clarke gave these remarks in a speech printed in two parts in *The National Anti-Slavery Standard* (October 20 and 27, 1842).

15. Notwithstanding the pretension among so many planters to its refinements—the family of Charles Manigault, a Charleston rice planter, spoke French while dining—the example of France had filled the antebellum South with fear, owing to Toussaint's success in Haiti; he had taken *liberté, égalité, fraternité* a little too seriously. After the Civil War, at least in 1871, the French communards served the turn (see Philip M. Katz, *From Appomattox to Montmarte* [1998]). In "Of the Coming of John," the one work of fiction collected in Du Bois's *The Souls of Black Folk* (and discussed in some detail in the second chapter), the (black) John of the title—he has a white counterpart of the same name—assumes charge of a school for African America children in the (fictional) Georgia hamlet of Altamaha. He works at the pleasure of the local white judge, who instructs him as follows: "I like the colored people, and sympathize with all their reasonable aspirations; but you

and I both know, John, that in this country the Negro must remain subordinate, and can never expect to be the equal of white men. . . . Now, John, the question is, are you, with your education and Northern notions, going to accept the situation and teach the darkies to be faithful servants and laborers as your fathers were?" (531). Word soon reaches the judge that something is amiss, and it smacks of the Gallic menace:

"Heah that John is livenin' things up at the darky school," volunteered the postmaster, after a pause.

"What now?" asked the Judge, sharply.

"Oh, nothin' in particulah,—just his almighty air and uppish ways. B'lieve I did heah somethin' about his givin' talks on the French Revolution, equality, and such like. He's what I call a dangerous Nigger" (532).

16. See Frederickson, *The Black Image in the White Mind* (1987), 277.

17. *Independent* 51, May 18, 1899, 1354–55.

18. See also John L. Hodge and Donald K. Struckmann, "Flight from the Body: Racism and Sexism," in Hodge et al, eds., *Cultural Bases of Racism and Group Oppression* (1975): "The dualism of mind and body in Western philosophy is explicitly expressed as a dualism within the self, a dualism of the self's internal constitution. But . . . this same dualism has been incorporated into the 'external' world. Different social classes and different peoples have been seen and treated in terms of this dualism of mind and body. Whites have generally likened black people to the body, and have viewed them in the same way they have viewed their own bodies, namely, as something inferior and evil to be hated, controlled, and kept separate" (196–97). See also Richard Dyer, *White* (1997), 14–40 *passim*, as for example here: "*Christianity* (and the particular inflection it gives to Western dualist thought) is founded on the idea—paradoxical, unfathomable, profoundly mysterious—of incarnation, of being that is in the body yet not of it. This provides a compelling cosmology, as well as a vivid imagery and set of narrative tropes, that survive as characteristics of Western culture. All concepts of *race*, emerging out of eighteenth-century materialism, are concepts of bodies, but all along they have had to be reconciled with notions of embodiment and incarnation. The latter became what distinguish white people, giving them a special relation to race. Black people can be reduced (in white culture) to their bodies and thus to race, but white people are something else that is realised in and yet is not reducible to the corporeal, or racial. . . . At some point, the embodied something else of whiteness took on a dynamic relation to the physical world, something caught by the ambiguous word 'spirit.' The white spirit organises white flesh and in turn non-white flesh and other material matters: it has *enterprise*" (emphases in the original; 14–15).

19. William Byrd wrote the Earl of Egmont in 1736: "They import so many Negroes [into the colony of South Carolina], that I fear this Colony will some time or other be confirmed by the Name of New Guinea. I am sensible of many bad consequences of multiplying these Ethiopians amongst us. *They blow up the pride,*

and ruin the Industry of our White People, who seeing a Rank of poor Creatures below them, detest work for fear it should make them look like Slaves" (my emphasis). Peter H. Wood quotes the letter in his *Black Majority* (1974), 244. As Wood indicates, Byrd's purpose was, in part, to commend the decision, on the part of the trustees, *not* to permit slavery in the new colony of Georgia.

20. On May 17, 1902, the *Atlanta Constitution*—the paper of record in the New South—published this unsigned editorial, praising a decision made by the Virginia state board of education to defund liberal arts education for African Americans: "The experiment that has been made to give the colored students classical training has not been satisfactory. Even though many were able to pursue the course, most of them did so in a parrot-like way, learning what was taught, but not seeming to appropriate the truth and import of their instruction, and graduating without sensible aim or valuable occupation for their future. The whole scheme has proved a waste of time, efforts, and the money of the state. . . . [African American students] will not be able to calculate the procession of the equinoxes, scan Virgil or give the exact differentiations between psychology and pneumatology—but they will be able to shingle a barn, lay an even course of bricks, make a horseshoe nail and launder a shirt. . . . Their field is not, and in the south will never be, that of poesy, rhetoric and statesmanship. The fitting they need, therefore, is for the places which they can and must occupy—in the furrow, at the forge and *wherever the hand serves the brain and eye*" (my emphasis; 6). Incidentally, Du Bois quotes part of this editorial in "Of the Training of Black Men," chapter 6 of *Souls*, and then marshals considerable sociological data about college-educated African Americans to refute it (431–38).

21. Earlier in *The Fire Next Time* Baldwin writes, to similar effect: "White Americans seem to feel that happy songs are happy and sad songs are sad, and that, God help us, is exactly the way most white Americans sing them—sounding, in both cases, so helplessly, defenselessly fatuous that one dare not speculate on the temperature of the deep freeze from which issue their brave and sexless little voices. Only people who have been 'down the line,' as the song puts it, know what [blues] music is about. I think it was Big Bill Broonzy who used to sing 'I Feel So Good,' a really joyful song about a man who is on his way to the railroad station to meet his girl. She's coming home. It is the singer's incredibly moving exuberance that makes one realize how leaden the time must have been while she was gone. There is no guarantee that she will stay this time, either, as the singer clearly knows, and, in fact, she has not yet actually arrived. Tonight, or tomorrow, or within the next five minutes, he may very well be singing 'Lonesome in My Bedroom,' or insisting, 'Ain't we, ain't we, going to make it all right? Well, if we don't today, we will tomorrow night.' Americans do not understand the depths out of which such an ironic tenacity comes, but they suspect that the force is sensual, and they are terrified of sensuality and do not any longer understand it. The word 'sensual' is not intended to bring to mind quivering dusky maidens or priapic black studs. I am referring to something much simpler and much less fanciful. To be sensual, I

think, is to respect and rejoice in the force of life, of life itself, and to be present in all that one does, from the effort of loving to the breaking of bread" (*Essays* 311).

22. Quoted in Josiah U. Young III's *James Baldwin's Understanding of God* (2016), 105.

23. North Carolina no longer resorts to violence to secure elections for the party of white supremacy, or at any rate for the party (GOP) with which white voters chiefly identify in the state. But that didn't stop the state from trying to load the dice during Obama's presidency. Section 5 of the Voting Rights Act of 1965 required that North Carolina (like most states in the former Confederacy) secure "preclearance" from the US Department of Justice for any alterations made to voting regulations. The purpose of Section 5 of the VRA was, of course, to ensure that voter suppression by other means than violence ("literacy" tests, poll taxes, etc.) could not be codified in the South (or in any other states with a history of race-based voter suppression). On June 25, 2013, in its *Shelby County, Alabama v. Eric Holder, Jr., Attorney General* decision, the US Supreme Court, under John Roberts, neutered Section 5 of the VRA (without eliminating it). Within *days*, North Carolina—and many other southern states, in addition to states elsewhere under Republican Party control—moved to pass laws whose effect was to curtail voting by African Americans (and the poor more generally). That effect has now, in the case of North Carolina, been found "intentional." On July 29, 2016, the US Fourth Circuit of Appeals struck down a battery of new voting regulations imposed in North Carolina immediately after the *Shelby County* decision was handed down. Judge Diana Motz, writing for the court, explained its decision, in the matter of *NAACP et al. v. Patrick McCrory, Governor of North Carolina*: "In North Carolina, restriction of voting mechanisms and procedures that most heavily affect African Americans will predictably redound to the benefit of one political party [the Republican Party] and to the disadvantage of the other [the Democratic Party]. As the evidence in the record makes clear, that is what happened here. After years of preclearance and expansion of voting access, by 2013 African American registration and turnout rates had finally reached near-parity with white registration and turnout rates. African Americans were poised to act as a major electoral force. But, on the day after the Supreme Court issued *Shelby County v. Holder*, 133 S. Ct. 2612 (2013), eliminating preclearance obligations, a leader of the [Republican] party that newly dominated the legislature (and the party that rarely enjoyed African American support) announced an intention to enact what he characterized as an 'omnibus' election law. Before enacting that law, the legislature requested data on the use, by race, of a number of voting practices. Upon receipt of the race data, the General Assembly enacted legislation that restricted voting and registration in five different ways, all of which disproportionately affected African Americans. In response to claims that intentional racial discrimination animated its action, the State offered only meager justifications. Although the new provisions target African Americans with almost surgical precision, they constitute inapt remedies for the problems assertedly justifying them and, in fact, impose cures for problems

that did not exist. Thus the asserted justifications cannot and do not conceal the State's true motivation. . . . Faced with this record, we can only conclude that the North Carolina General Assembly enacted the challenged provisions of the law with discriminatory intent" (10–11). Absent this injunction, African American voters would again have had nowhere to turn for redress, in North Carolina (a "swing state"), during the presidential elections of 2016. I bring the matter up only to suggest that—all differences in tactics allowed for in the intervening century—*The Marrow of Tradition* remains startlingly contemporary. For details about recent developments in North Carolina, see William J. Barber II with Jonathan Wilson-Hartgrove, *The Third Reconstruction: Moral Mondays, Fusion Politics, and the Rise of a New Justice Movement* (2016).

24. On June 13, 1866, Thaddeus Stevens all but wept in frustration: "I had fondly dreamed that when any fortunate chance should have broken up for a while the foundation of our institutions, and released us from obligations the most tyrannical that ever man imposed in the name of freedom, that the intelligent, pure and just men of this Republic, true to their professions and their consciences, would have so remodeled all our institutions as to have freed them from every vestige of human oppression, of inequality of rights, of the recognized degradation of the poor, and the superior caste of the rich. In short, that no distinction would be tolerated in this purified Republic but what arose from merit and conduct. This bright dream has vanished 'like the baseless fabric of a vision.' I find that we shall be obliged to be content with patching up the worst portions of the ancient edifice, and leaving it, in many of its parts, to be swept through by the tempests, frosts and the storms of despotism. Do you inquire why, holding these views and possessing some will of my own, I accept so imperfect a proposition [as the 14th Amendment]? I answer, because I live among men and not among angels" (quoted in *Black Reconstruction* 300–301). So the Fourteenth Amendment passed in all its imperfection. Northern capitalists got what they wanted: the old Southern planter class (hostile to tariffs and in favor of debt repudiation) would come back into the Union severely weakened, at least for a decade or so (by disabilities imposed on former Confederates in article 3, and by the black vote, however tenuously protected by article 2). New England got what it wanted: the franchise would (as per article 1 of the amendment) include *naturalized* men (giving to the old industrial interests duly proportionate representation, shored up by recent immigration from Europe).

25. See "Felony Disenfranchisement Laws in The United States," a fact sheet published by The Sentencing Project (April 28, 2014): "2.2 million African Americans, or 7.7% of black adults, are disenfranchised, compared to 1.8% of the non-African American population. In three states—Florida (23%), Kentucky (22%), and Virginia (20%)—more than one in five African Americans is disenfranchised." See also Michelle Alexander, *The New Jim Crow* (158–61, 192–93). As she points out, "the United Nations Human Rights Committee has charged [in 2006] that U.S. disenfranchisement policies are discriminatory and violate

international law" (158). Fortunately, even as the present book was in production, voters in Florida passed an initiative—Florida Amendment 4 (November 6, 2018)—re-enfranchising (most) ex-convicts. But there is much work still to do. See *A Critical Assessment of the U.S. Commitment to Civil and Political Rights*, a detailed report prepared by the Lawyers' Committee for Civil Rights Under Law and published in 2006 (see especially pages 57–73 of that report). The Committee was founded at the request of President John. F. Kennedy in 1963 (the year of the March on Washington).

26. *The Colonel's Dream* (New York: Doubleday & Page, 1905), 117. The Library of America edition of Chesnutt—from which all other quotations of his fiction are drawn in this chapter—does not reprint *The Colonel's Dream*. I cite here its first edition.

27. They appeared for the first time in 1999, in an edition prepared for Princeton University Press by Dean McWilliam.

28. Chesnutt deploys the metaphor of the procrustean bed also in *The Marrow of Tradition*. Dr. Adam Miller, traveling by train from North to South, entertains the following thought: "Surely, if a classification of passengers on trains was at all desirable, it might be made upon some more logical and considerate basis than a mere arbitrary, tactless, and, by the very nature of things, brutal drawing of a color line. It was a veritable bed of Procrustes, this standard which the whites had set for the negroes. Those who grew above it must have their heads cut off, figuratively speaking,—must be forced back to the level assigned to their race; those who fell beneath the standard set had their necks stretched, literally enough, as the ghastly record in the daily papers gave conclusive evidence" (512).

Chapter Five

1. All quotations from *Black Boy (American Hunger)*, *Lawd, Today!*, *Uncle Tom's Children*, *Native Son*, *The Outsider*, "How Bigger Was Born" and "The Ethics of Living Jim Crow" are from the Library of America's two-volume edition of Wright's works (cited in the bibliography). I should also point out here (as I do later) that "American Hunger" was the working title for *Black Boy*. Indeed, when the book was in production it bore that name. Wright retitled it *Black Boy* when, in 1945, the Book of the Month Club chose to publish the book (along with Harper & Brothers) and requested that he omit the long section detailing his experiences in the North. Over the years, Wright published portions of the omitted section in magazines, but the first complete edition of it came only in 1977 when Harper & Row issued it as *American Hunger*. When the Library of America published its edition of Wright in 1991, the two sections were for the first time reunited (as they had been before the Book of the Month Club intervened) and titled *Black Boy (American Hunger)*. In what follows (in this chapter) I discuss Wright's negotiations with the Book of the Month Club in greater detail.

2. For details about Wright's life, I rely on his own writings and on Rowley's biography.

3. Compare Mary, in her sexual advances toward (and sexual interest in) Bigger Thomas, to the woman who tries to seduce the unnamed narrator of Ralph Ellison's *Invisible Man*. The narrator's response to her is, at times, as vexed, angry, titillated, and confused as Bigger's is to Mary: "I nodded, seeing her turn without a word and go toward a vanity with a large oval mirror, taking up an ivory telephone. *And in the mirrored instant I saw myself standing between her eager form and a huge white bed, myself caught in a guilty stance, my face taut, tie dangling; and behind the bed another mirror which now like a surge of the sea tossed our images back and forth, back and forth, furiously multiplying the time and the place and the circumstance.* My vision seemed to pulse alternately clear and vague, driven by a furious bellows, as her lips said soundlessly, I'm sorry, and then impatiently into the telephone, 'Yes, this is she,' and then to me again, smiling as she covered the mouthpiece with her hand, 'It's only my sister; it'll only take a second.' And my mind whirled with forgotten stories of male servants summoned to wash the mistress's back," the narrator says; "chauffeurs sharing the masters' wives; Pullman porters invited into the drawing room of rich wives headed for Reno—thinking, But this is the movement, the Brotherhood. And now I saw her smile, saying [into the phone], 'Yes, Gwen, dear. Yes,' as one free hand went up as though to smooth her hair and in one swift motion the red robe swept aside like a veil, and I went breathless at the petite and generously curved nude, framed delicate and firm in the glass. It was like a dream interval and in an instant it swung back and I saw only her mysteriously smiling eyes above the rich red robe. *I was heading for the door, torn between anger and a fierce excitement, hearing the phone click down as I started past and feeling her swirl against me and I was lost, for the conflict between the ideological and the biological, duty and desire, had become too subtly confused*" (my emphasis; 416–17). The episode recalls so many of the details of *Native Son* as to seem a calculated response to it, carried off with Ellison's characteristic irony and wit: "Why did they [white men] have to mix their women into everything? Between us and everything we wanted to change in the world they placed a woman: socially, politically, economically. Why, goddamit, why did they insist upon confusing the class struggle with the ass struggle, debasing both us and them—all human motives?" (418).

4. The curious interplay of accident and act recalls the great, pivotal scene in Theodore Dreiser's *Sister Carrie* (1900), in which Hurstwood accidentally-on-purpose steals the cash from the office safe. See chapter 27 ("When Water Engulfs Us We Reach For a Star"). Dreiser, of course, was a major influence on Wright.

5. I adapt terms from Kenneth Burke's *Language as Symbolic Action* (1966), 64.

6. Quoted in *Richard Wright's Black Boy (American Hunger): A Casebook*, ed. by William Andrews and Douglas Taylor (2003), 71.

7. Most of the details of these transactions derive from my own research in the archives at Princeton's Firestone Library and at Yale's Beinecke Library (done

in 1990–91). Hazel Rowley, Andrew Warnes, William E. Dow, Alice Mikal Craven, Yoko Nakamura, Janice Radway, and other scholars have since covered the same ground, and I have benefitted from their work.

8. Printed in Madigan's edition of Canfield Fisher's letters, 233.

9. Quoted in Andrew Warnes, *Richard Wright's Native Son: A Routledge Study Guide* (2007), 95.

10. Wright supplied the following substitution for the first edition of *Black Boy* (where it appears on pages 164–65):

"Nigger, you think you'll ever amount to anything?" he asked in a slow, sadistic voice.

"I don't know, sir," I answered, turning my head away.

"What do niggers think about?" he asked.

"I don't know, sir," I said, my head still averted.

"If I was a nigger, I'd kill myself," he said.

I said nothing.

"You know why?" he asked.

I still said nothing.

"But I reckon niggers don't mind being niggers," he said suddenly and laughed.

In a June 25, 1944 letter to his editor, Edward Aswell, Wright explains: "The insert did not happen on the job where it is now placed; the dialogue is lifted from another situation altogether, but I think its tone and manner make it fit here" (letter held in the Richard Wright Papers, Yale Collection of American Literature, Beinecke Rare Book and Manuscript Library [henceforth cited as "Richard Wright Papers"]). This alteration, made at the behest of the Book of the Month Club, should not be ranked with *another* set of revisions Wright made (earlier, and in typescript) to protect his memoir from all possible legal troubles. Aswell retained the law firm of Greenbaum, Wolff, and Ernst to determine what passages of the manuscript might be susceptible to libel charges, or to charges of obscenity. Wright altered names, circumstances, and places in accordance with the suggestions of the firm, and of Aswell himself. The correspondence held in the Harper and Brothers archives at Princeton and at Yale provides a fairly complete and clear record of these negotiations. Wright made nearly all of the revisions himself, and those minor adjustments made by Aswell were always submitted to Wright for approval. The larger changes requested by the book club are another matter.

11. I examined this correspondence myself in 1990–91, but some of it, including this letter, has since been published. I quote Aswell's letter from *Richard Wright in a Post-Racial Imaginary*, ed. Alice Mikal Craven et al., 86.

12. Much earlier (in the winter and spring of 1939) first Wright's agent, Paul Reynolds, and then Aswell had suggested to Wright that he shorten the lawyers' speeches. Reynolds wrote to Wright when he first read the manuscript: "I personally think that Max's address and the address of the D.A. should be cut very severely." And in a conference with Wright in April, Aswell very likely made a

similar suggestion; anyway, he wrote to the author on June 21, after he'd read the revised manuscript: "I am glad you were able to cut some of the newspaper items. As for the lawyers' speeches—well, you're the doctor and what you say goes" (quoted in Rowley, 165). It's pretty clear that in preparing the final draft of the novel Wright decided against cutting the speeches as severely as Aswell hoped he might. At this point the typescript went to the manufacturing department. It was in page proofs by the time the Book of the Month Club requested a new round of revisions. In making them, in September, Wright did in fact cut some 4–5 pages from Max's and the D.A.'s speeches. It may be that he reconsidered the advice given him by Reynolds and by Aswell; it may even be that the book club requested that he cut them. At any rate, Wright's attention would naturally have been drawn to the courtroom speeches when he cut the D.A.'s allusions to the Regal Theatre episode.

13. Publication of the restored text of *Native Son* (in the Library of America edition [1991]) occasioned a number of re-assessments of the book (uniformly positive). For some of them, see Warnes (mentioned above), *Richard Wright's Native Son: A Routledge Study Guide* (a collection of essays).

14. These practices, and their successors in the 1940s, 1950s, and 1960s (colloquially known as "redlining"), are well described by Ta-Nehisi Coates in "The Case for Reparations" (*The Atlantic*, June 2014; now reprinted in his *We Were Eight Years in Power*). As mentioned earlier, Richard Rothstein has published the most comprehensive book to date about redlining and its persistent legacies: *The Color of Law* (2017). As for the artificial inflation of rent in *contemporary* American cities, see Matthew Desmond's brilliant (and beautifully written) *Evicted: Poverty and Profit in an American City* (2017).

15. In *A Feeling for Books: The Book-of-the-Month Club, Literary Taste, and Middle-Class Desire* (1997), Janice Radway reviews the matter: "Surviving documents tell us little about the motives of individual judges [on the Book of the Month Club's selection committee], but they apparently informed Aswell and Wright that they hoped" the excisions of sexually charged passages "would enable the book to reach a larger audience without offending the more conservative members within it. There were limits, apparently, to the kinds of identification middlebrow personalism could promote" (286).

16. To study the efforts of American legislators—in the early twentieth century—to codify "whiteness" and "blackness" is to see how absurd the business was and is. A person recognized as legally white in Florida would, on crossing the state line into Georgia in 1927, become black, for example. See John Hope Franklin and Isidore Starr, *The Negro in Twentieth Century America: A Reader on the Struggle for Civil Rights* (1967), part 1: "What is a Negro?," 4–13. See also James Q. Whitman, *Hitler's American Model* (2017), 77–80, 106–9, 118–20 (though indeed Whitman touches on American racial legal codes and jurisprudence throughout the book).

17. The figure Max uses; it approximates the total African American population in the late 1930s.

18. After reading a typescript of the novel, Jack Fischer sent a detailed note to Wright. "Some fairly drastic cutting would help the book a lot," he said. "It now runs to about 220,000 words, according to my rough estimate; if you can bring it down to something in the neighborhood of 150,000 words, I am confident that the impact of the story would be infinitely greater." As for diction: "The description of the subway wreck would be more effective," Fischer argued, "if it were presented more concisely. Piling one grizzly adjective on top of another doesn't make the scene seem any more horrible; it just makes it seem overdone and unreal." Another matter worried him: "Could the long exposition of Damon's philosophy, beginning at page 616 [in the typescript], be shortened considerably? All these points are made, explicitly or implicitly, throughout the book. It might be well to summarize them here, but couldn't they be put more concisely, and perhaps broken up with more dialogue? Such a long speech sounds unrealistic, and is likely to be skipped by many readers" (Richard Wright Papers). Wright did add a bit more dialogue, but the "exposition" remained otherwise unchanged. The consultant Fischer paid to edit the typescript (identity unknown) summarized the work he did as follows: "Wright goes for melodramatic adjectives in a big way; have cut some of red rages, black despairs, hot angers, and so on. . . . Wright is mad for physical activity; he has the habit of minutely describing each move a person makes and this frequently slows down the action unnecessarily. When it added nothing to our understanding or esthetic appreciation to know that 'Cross opened his mouth, took out his cigarettes, put one in his open mouth, took out his matches, struck one, and started to smoke' I shortened it to 'Cross started to smoke.' Also, [Wright] has a battery of pet words for describing these actions which aren't particularly good; have cut excessive use of 'his body jerked,' 'she sobbed, wailed or whimpered,' 'her chest heaved' and others of a like ilk. . . . In his expository passages, Wright frequently uses an almost texty vocabulary; this sounds like self-conscious use of big words, so I frequently cut the most unnatural of them. Have used contractions, for 'wasn't it' sounded better than 'was it not.' Have changed the more formal 'ought he' to 'should he'" (Richard Wright Papers). In its 1991 edition of *The Outsider* (the one I use), the Library of America restored many of the passages that Wright cut at the insistence of his editor (Fischer) or that were cut (in-house at Harper) without his knowledge. (See the "Note on the Texts" to *Richard Wright: Later Works*, 869–74.) For an assessment of the value of this restoration, see Maryemma Graham's introduction to the 1993 HarperPerennial edition of the novel, xi–xxix.

Chapter Six

1. The idea is native to American pragmatism. William James writes, in *The Will to Believe* (1896): "So far as man stands for anything, and is productive or originative at all, his entire vital function may be said to have to deal with maybes. Not a victory is gained, not a deed of faithfulness or courage is done, except

upon a maybe; not a service, not a sally of generosity, not a scientific exploration or experiment or text-book, that may not be a mistake. It is only by risking our persons from one hour to another that we live at all. And often enough our faith beforehand in an uncertified result *is the only thing that makes the result come true*" (emphasis in the original; 59).

2. *Jack Kerouac: Road Novels: 1957–1960*, ed. Douglas Brinkley, 107. All quotations of Kerouac are from this edition.

3. The crowd attending the inauguration exceeded one million. It was the first to be televised; the broadcast reached ten million additional viewers. The 1949 inaugural parade was also the first to include an air-force flyover (some 600 warplanes). Thousands of troops swelled the progress down Pennsylvania Avenue.

4. I acknowledge, here, a debt to Gary Lindberg's *The Confidence Man in American Literature* (1982), which taught me much. Lindberg's discussion of Neal Cassady and *On the Road* may be found on pages 259–70 of the book. My arguments diverge from Lindberg's in that they highlight in any reading of Kerouac the great American con-game of "race."

5. As others have pointed out, Kerouac borrowed the term "fellahin" from Spengler's *The Decline of the West* (1928). See Robert Holton for a discussion of Kerouac's investment in Spengler (270–72, 277).

6. Holton has also pointed out the affiliation to blackface minstrelsy (269).

7. The African Americans Kerouac encountered may well have been recruited by the big California planters from the cotton-growing states of the Deep South (a boll weevil infestation had devastated cotton production there in the 1920s and 1930s).

8. In 2017, Ryan F. Lei and Galen V. Bodenhausen published a study bearing on this in *The Frontiers of Psychology*. They found that "participants high in economic prejudice produced strongly class-differentiated mental images. They imagined the poor to be Blacker than middle income and wealthy people. They also imagined them to have less positive psychological characteristics" (1). They conclude: "This study indicates that social class connotes race, such that the category 'poor people' is mentally represented as relatively Black, even though there are many more poor White than poor Black people in the US. . . . Our results comport with the notion that resentments regarding policies designed to help the poor are tied up with racial prejudice" (6).

9. To an extent, I am again following a line of argument sketched out by Robert Holton: "[Kerouac's] suggestion [in speaking of "happy Negroes"] seems to be that African Americans are insulated from disappointment because they are lacking in aspiration, a notion that can be sustained only at a considerable distance from the actually existing African American community. Nor could these fantasies of the placid fellahin survive exposure to the African American literary culture of the time which included Richard Wright, Ann Petry, Chester Himes, and Ralph Ellison, writers whose articulations of disappointment and frustration are, to put

it mildly, unmistakable" (269–70). Among my aims is to bring *On the Road* decisively into contact with that literary culture.

10. In *The Problem of Slavery in the Age of Emancipation*, David Brion Davis speaks of "a bias against professionalism, technocracy, improvement, and moral respectability" that "has often prevented historians from appreciating the aspirations and genuine accomplishments of Westernized black nationalists who understood the world they faced, as well as the kind of skills and knowledge needed to empower the powerless, to break through the constricting coils of dependency, including those cultivated by well-meaning whites in search of authentic emotion or an antimodernist soul" (126–27). Whether we may speak of Kerouac (on the whole) as a "well-meaning" white remains an open question. But what Kerouac has Sal Paradise say about 27th and Welton certainly reflects a "bias against professionalism" and "moral respectability," and reflects all the more certainly a "search," in African American culture, for something like "authentic emotion" and "an antimodernist soul." In fact, the quest for an "antimodernist soul"—which for Sal cannot be "white"—is one form a vestigial white supremacy takes in *On the Road*, one way in which the novel may be said not merely to exemplify, but to shore up, what Davis calls "the constricting coils of dependency." Which of course James Baldwin perfectly understood.

11. The source for the story about the cross-burning is Paul Blake, the nephew involved. Gerald Nicosia interviewed him while working on *Memory Babe* in 1978 (739). In writing up the episode, Nicosia offers it as evidence that the "endless cognac and Irish whiskey [had driven Kerouac] out of his mind at last" (634). That suggestion is as over-generous as it is humane. It would be hard to demonstrate that the insanity of which Nicosia speaks is not *somehow* of a piece with what Baldwin calls the "utter" and "offensive" "nonsense" of *On the Road* (*Essays* 278).

BIBLIOGRAPHY

Aaron, Daniel. *The Unwritten War: American Writers and the Civil War*. New York: Knopf, 1972.

Adams, Richard. "Rand Paul Versus the Civil Rights Act." *The Guardian*, May 20, 2010. Web.

Alexander, Michelle. *The New Jim Crow: Mass Incarceration in the Age of Colorblindness*. New York: The New Press, 2012.

Alexander, Roberta S. *North Carolina Faces the Freedmen: Race Relations During Presidential Reconstruction, 1865–67*. Durham, NC: Duke University Press, 1985.

Allen, James, Hilton Als, Leon F. Litwack, and John Lewis. *Without Sanctuary: Lynching Photography in America*. Santa Fe, NM: Twin Palms, 2000.

Althusser, Louis. *Lenin and Philosophy and Other Essays*. New York: Monthly Review Press, 1971.

Andrews, William L., and Douglas Taylor. *Richard Wright's Black Boy (American Hunger): A Casebook*. New York: Oxford University Press, 2003.

Asante-Muhammad, Dedrick, et al. *The Road to Zero Wealth: How the Racial Divide is Hollowing Out the America's Middle Class*. Institute for Policy Studies. September 2017. Web.

Ash, Michael, and James K. Boyce. "Racial Disparities in Pollution Exposure and Employment at US Industrial Facilities." *Proceedings of the National Academy of Sciences* 115, no. 42 (October 2018): 10636–41. Also available online. Digital object identifier:10.1073/pnas.1721640115.

Baldwin, James. *Collected Essays*. New York: Library of America, 1998. Reprinted here are *Notes of a Native Son, Nobody Knows My Name, The Fire Next Time, No Name in the Street,* and *The Devil Finds Work*. All quotations of Baldwin are from this edition.

Baptist, Edward. *The Half Has Never Been Told: Slavery and the Making of American Capitalism*. New York: Basic Books, 2016.

Barber, William J., and Jonathan Wilson-Hartgrove. *The Third Reconstruction: Moral Mondays, Fusion Politics, and the Rise of a New Justice Movement*. 2016.

Barlow, Joel. *The Columbiad: A Poem*. London: R. Phillips, 1809.
Barringer, Paul B. *The Sacrifice of a Race*. Raleigh, NC: Edwards & Broughton, 1900.
Bay, Mia. *The White Image in the Black Mind: African-American Ideas About White People, 1830–1925*. New York: Oxford University Press, 2000.
Beatty, Paul. *The Sellout*. New York: Farrar, Straus, and Giroux, 2015.
Beauvoir, Simone de. *The Second Sex*. New York: Random House, 1952.
Beer, Thomas. *Hanna, Crane and the Mauve Decade*. New York: Knopf, 1941. This volume brings together Beer's best-known books, among them the biography of Stephen Crane quoted above in chapter 3 (which Beer published first in 1903).
Benfey, Christopher. *The Double Life of Stephen Crane*. New York: Knopf, 1992.
Bercovitch, Sacvan. *The American Jeremiad*. Madison: University of Wisconsin Press, 1978.
Bierce, Ambrose. *Civil War Stories*. New York: Dover, 1994.
Blackmon, Douglas A. *Slavery by Another Name: The Re-Enslavement of Black Americans from the Civil War to World War II*. New York: Anchor Books, 2008.
Blassingame, John W. *Slave Testimony: Two Centuries of Letters, Speeches, Interviews, and Autobiographies*. Baton Rouge: Louisiana State University Press, 1976.
Blight, David. *Frederick Douglass: Prophet of Freedom*. New York: Simon and Schuster, 2018.
Blight, David W. *Race and Reunion: The Civil War in American Memory*. Cambridge: Belknap Press of Harvard University Press, 2001.
Blow, Charles. "White Extinction Anxiety." *New York Times*. June 24, 2018. Web.
Brodhead, Richard. Introduction to Charles Chesnutt, *The Conjure Woman and Conjure Tales*. Durham, NC: Duke University Press, 1994.
Brooks, Gwendolyn. *The Bean Eaters*. New York: Harper, 1960.
———. *Report from Part One*. Detroit: Broadside, 1970.
———. *Selected Poems*. New York: Harper Perennial Modern Classics, 2010.
———. *A Street in Bronzeville*. New York: Harper, 1945.
Buchanan, Patrick J. "A Brief for Whitey." *Human Events*. March 21, 2008. Web.
———. *Official Website*. "Has the West the Will to Survive?" June 22, 2018. Web.
Budiansky, Stephen. *The Bloody Shirt: Terror After Appomattox*. New York: Viking, 2008.
Burke, Kenneth. *A Grammar of Motives*. New York: Prentice-Hall, 1945.
———. *Language as Symbolic Action*. Berkeley: University of California Press, 1966.
Burgess, John W. *Reconstruction and the Constitution, 1866–1876*. New York: Scribner's, 1905.
Butterfield, Fox. *All God's Children: The Bosket Family and the American Tradition of Violence*. New York: Knopf, 1995.

Calhoun, John C., and Richard K. Crallé. *Speeches of John C. Calhoun: Delivered in the House of Representatives and in the Senate of the United States.* Volume 4. New York: D. Appleton, 1854.

Carnegie, Andrew. *Autobiography of Andrew Carnegie.* Boston: Houghton Mifflin Company, 1920.

———. *The Gospel of Wealth and Other Timely Essays.* New York: The Century Company, 1901.

Caro, Robert A. *The Years of Lyndon Johnson: Master of the Senate.* New York: Vintage Books, 2003.

Carroll, Charles. *The Negro a Beast.* St. Louis, MO: American Book and Bible House, 1900.

Chapman, John Jay. *William Lloyd Garrison.* New York: Moffat, Yard, and Company, 1913.

Chesnutt, Charles W. *The Colonel's Dream.* New York: Doubleday & Page, 1905.

———. *The Conjure Woman and Other Conjure Tales.* Edited and with an introduction by Richard H. Brodhead. Durham, NC: Duke University Press, 2006.

———. *An Exemplary Citizen: Letters of Charles W. Chesnutt, 1906–1932.* Edited by Jesse S. Crisler, Robert C. Leitz, and Joseph R. McElrath. Stanford, CA: Stanford University Press, 2002.

———. *The Journals of Charles W. Chesnutt.* Edited by Richard H. Brodhead. Durham, NC: Duke University Press, 2001.

———. *Stories, Novels, and Essays.* New York: Library of America: 2002. Reprinted here are *The Conjure Woman, The Wife of His Youth and Other Stories of the Color Line, The House Behind the Cedars,* and *The Marrow of Tradition.* Unless otherwise noted, all quotations of Chesnutt are from this edition.

———. *"To Be an Author": Letters of Charles W. Chesnutt, 1889–1905.* Edited by Joseph R. MacElrath. Princeton, NJ: Princeton University Press, 1997.

Cleveland, Henry. *Alexander H. Stephens in Public and Private, With Letters and Speeches.* Chicago: National Publishing Company, 1866.

Click, Patricia C. *Time Full of Trial: The Roanoke Island Freedmen's Colony, 1862–1867.* Chapel Hill: University of North Carolina Press, 2001.

Coates, Ta-Nehisi. "The Case for Reparations." *The Atlantic,* June 2014; reprinted in *We Were Eight Years in Power,* 163–208. New York: Random House Inc., 2017.

———. *We Were Eight Years in Power: A Journey Through the Obama Era.* New York: Random House Inc, 2017.

Conkle, Daniel O. "Three Theories of Substantive Due Process." *North Carolina Law Review* 85, no. 1 (2006): 63–148.

Conrad, Joseph. *The Selected Letters of Joseph Conrad.* Edited by Laurence Davies. Cambridge, UK: Cambridge University Press, 2015.

Cooper, Anna J. *A Voice from the South.* Xenia, Ohio: Aldine Printing House, 1892.

Cornelius, Janet D. *"When I Can Read My Title Clear": Literacy, Slavery, and Religion in the Antebellum South.* Columbia: University of South Carolina Press, 1991.

Crane, Stephen. *Great Short Works of Stephen Crane*. New York: Harper and Row, 1965.

———. *Letters*. Edited by R W. Stallman, and Lilian Gilkes. New York: New York University Press, 1970.

———. *The Red Badge of Courage: An Episode of the American Civil War*. Edited with an introduction and annotations by Frederick C. Crews. Indianapolis: The Bobbs-Merrill Company, 1964.

———. *War Is Kind*. Drawings by Will Bradley. New York: F. A. Stokes, 1899.

Crane, Stephen, and R. W. Stallman. *Stephen Crane: An Omnibus*. New York: Knopf, 1952.

Craven, Alice M., William E. Dow, Yoko Nakamura, and Amritjit Singh. *Richard Wright in a Post-Racial Imaginary*. New York: Bloomsbury Academic, 2014.

Darwin, Charles. *The Descent of Man: Selection in Relation to Sex*. London: John Murray, 1896.

Davidson, Amy. "Donald Trump and the Central Park Five." *The New Yorker*, June 23, 2014. Web.

Davis, David Brion. *The Problem of Slavery in the Age of Emancipation*. New York: Alfred Knopf, 2014.

Davis, Jefferson, *The Rise and Fall of the Confederate Government: Volume 1*. New York: D. Appleton, 1881.

———. *The Rise and Fall of the Confederate Government: Volume 2*. New York: Appleton and Company, 1881.

Davis, Julie Hirschfeld, et al. "Trump Alarms Lawmakers with Disparaging Words for Haiti and Africa." *New York Times*, January 11, 2018. Web.

Davis, Linda. *Badge of Courage: The Life of Stephen Crane*. Boston: Houghton Mifflin, 1998.

Delbanco, Andrew. "The American Stephen Crane: The Context of *The Red Badge of Courage*." In *New Essays on The Red Badge of Courage*, edited by Lee C. Mitchell, 49–76. Cambridge: Cambridge University Press, 1986.

———. *Required Reading: Why Our American Classics Matter Now*. New York: Farrar, Straus & Giroux, 1997.

Desmond, Matthew. *Evicted: Poverty and Profit in the American City*. New York: Broadway Books, 2017.

Dew, Charles B. *Apostles of Disunion: Southern Secession Commissioners and the Causes of the Civil War*. Charlottesville: University Press of Virginia, 2001.

Dewey, John. *The Quest for Certainty: A Study of the Relation of Knowledge and Action*. London: George Allen, 1929.

Dickinson, Emily. *The Poems of Emily Dickinson: Including Variant Readings Critically Compared with All Known Manuscripts*. Edited by Thomas H. Johnson. Cambridge, MA: The Belknap Press of Harvard Univ. Press, 1955.

Douglass, Frederick. *Autobiographies*. Edited by Henry Louis Gates. New York: Library of America, 1994. Reprinted here are *Narrative of the Life of Frederick Douglass, An American Slave*, *My Bondage and My Freedom*, and *The Life and

Times of Frederick Douglass. Unless otherwise indicated, all quotations of Douglass's writings are from this edition.

———. *The Life and Writings of Frederick Douglass: Volume 3*. Edited by Philip S. Foner. New York: International Publishers, 1975.

Dray, Philip. *At the Hands of Persons Unknown: The Lynching of Black America*. New York: Modern Library, 2003.

Dreiser, Theodore. *Sister Carrie; Jennie Gerhardt; Twelve Men*. New York: Library of America, 1987.

Du Bois, W. E. B. *Black Reconstruction in America: 1860–1880*. New York: Atheneum, 1992.

———. *Dark Princess: A Romance*. Jackson: University Press of Mississippi, 1995. Originally published in 1928 by Harcourt Brace.

———. *Dusk of Dawn*. In *Writings*. Edited by Nathan Huggins. New York: Library of America, 2007.

———. *John Brown*. New York: Modern Library, 2001.

———. *The Negro*. Philadelphia: University of Pennsylvania Press, 2001.

———. *The Souls of Black Folk*. In *Writings*. Edited by Nathan Huggins. New York: Library of America, 2007.

Dugan, Paul. "Sins of the Fathers: The Confederacy Was Built on Slavery. How Can So Many Southern Whites Still Believe Otherwise?" November 28, 2018. *Washington Post Magazine*. Web.

Dunbar, Paul L. *Lyrics of Lowly Life*. With an introduction by William D. Howells. New York: Dodd, Mead and Co, 1897.

Dusinberre, William. *Them Dark Days: Slavery in the American Rice Swamps*. Athens: University of Georgia Press, 2000.

Dyer, Richard. *White*. London: Routledge, 1997.

Eagleton, Terry. *Ideology: An Introduction*. London: Verso, 2007.

———. *Literary Theory: An Introduction*. Malden, MA: Blackwell Publishing, 2015.

Ellison, Ralph. *Invisible Man*. New York: Random House, 1952.

———. *Shadow and Act*. New York: Random House, 1953.

Emerson, Ralph W. *Emerson in His Journals*. Selected and edited by Joel Porte. Cambridge, MA: Belknap Press of Harvard University Press, 1982.

———. *Essays and Lectures*. New York: Library of America, 1983.

Eubanks, Virginia. *Automating Inequality: How High-Tech Tools Profile, Police, and Punish the Poor*. New York: St. Martin's Press, 2017.

Faulkner, William. *The Portable Faulkner*. Selected and edited by Malcolm Cowley. New York: Viking Press, 1946.

Fitzhugh, George. *Cannibals All: Or, Slaves Without Masters*. Richmond, VA: A. Morris, 1857.

Foner, Eric. *Reconstruction: America's Unfinished Revolution, 1863–1877*. New York: Harper & Row, 1988.

Frankfurter, Felix. *Mr. Justice Holmes and the Supreme Court*. Cambridge, MA: Harvard University Press, 1931.

Franklin, John H, and Isidore Starr. *The Negro in Twentieth Century America: A Reader on the Struggle for Civil Rights*. New York: Vintage Books, 1967.

Frederickson, George M. *The Black Image in the White Mind: the Debate on Afro-American Character and Destiny, 1817–1914*. Hanover, NH: Wesleyan University Press, 1987.

———. *Racism: A Short History*. Princeton, NJ: Princeton University Press, 2015.

Friend, Tad. "Donald Glover Can't Save You: The Creator of 'Atlanta' Wants TV to Tell Hard Truths." *The New Yorker*, March 5, 2018. Web.

Frohock, W. M. "*The Red Badge* and the Limits of Parody." *Southern Review* (Winter 1970): 137–48.

Frost, Robert. *Collected Poetry, Plays, and Prose*. Edited by Richard Poirier and Mark Richardson. New York: Library of America, 1995.

Galton, Francis. *Hereditary Genius: An Inquiry into Its Laws and Consequences*. London: Macmillan, 1869.

Garrison, Francis J., and Wendell P. Garrison. *William Lloyd Garrison: 1805–1879; the Story of His Life*. Vol. 1. New York: The Century, 1885.

———. *William Lloyd Garrison: 1805–1879; the Story of His Life*. Vol. 3. New York: The Century, 1889.

Genovese, Eugene D. *The Political Economy of Slavery: Studies in the Economy and Society of the Slave South*. New York: Vintage Books, 1967.

Ginsberg, Allen. *Collected Poems, 1947–1997*. New York: HarperCollins Publishers, 2007.

Goosby, Bridget J., and Chelsea Heidbrink. "Transgenerational Consequences of Racial Discrimination for African American Health." *Sociology Compass* 7, no. 8 (2013): 630–43. PMC. Web. Sept. 25, 2018. Available at the NIH Public Access website.

Gossett, Thomas F. *Race: The History of an Idea in America*. New Edition. New York: Oxford University Press, 1997.

Graham, Maryemma. "Introduction." In Richard Wright, *The Outsider: The Restored Text, Established by the Library of America*. New York: HarperPerennial, 1993.

Grant, Ulysses S. *Personal Memoirs of U. S. Grant and Selected Letters, 1839–1865*. New York: The Library of America, 1990.

Gunter, Booth, and Jamie Kizzire. *Whose Heritage? Public Symbols of the Confederacy*. Montgomery, Alabama: Southern Poverty Law Center, 2016.

Harper, Frances E. W. *Iola Leroy, Or, Shadows Uplifted*. Philadelphia, PA: Garrigues, 1892.

Harris, Corra Mae, "A Southern Woman's View." *The Independent*. Edited by William Hayes Ward. May 18, 1899: 1354–55.

Higginson, Thomas W. *Army Life in a Black Regiment*. Boston: Fields, Osgood & Co, 1870.

Hodge, John L., and Donald K. Struckmann. "Flight from the Body: Racism and Sexism." In Hodge, Struckmann, and Trost, *Cultural Bases of Racism and Group Oppression*.

Hodge, John L, Donald K. Struckmann, and Lynn D. Trost. *Cultural Bases of Racism and Group Oppression: An Examination of Traditional "Western" Concepts, Values, and Institutional Structures which Support Racism, Sexism, and Elitism*. Berkeley, Calif: Two Riders Press, 1975.

Hofstadter, Richard. *The Age of Reform: From Bryan to F.D.R.* New York: Vintage Books, 1955.

Holton, Robert. "Kerouac among the Fellahin: 'On the Road' to Post-Modern." *Modern Fiction Studies* 41 no. 2 (1995): 265–83.

Howells, William D. *Criticism and Fiction*. New York: Harper and Brothers, 1892.

Hutchinson, Louise. *The Anacostia Story, 1608–1930*. Washington, DC: Smithsonian Institution Press, 1977.

James, William. *Pragmatism*. In *Writings: 1902–1910*. New York: Library of America, 1996.

———. *The Will to Believe: And Other Essays in Popular Philosophy*. New York: Longmans, Green, and Co, 1896.

Jameson, Frederic. *The Political Unconscious: Narrative as a Socially Symbolic Act*. London: Cornell University Press, 1981.

Jefferson, Thomas. *Notes on the State of Virginia*. Richmond, VA: J. W. Randolph, 1853.

Jones, Jacqueline. *A Dreadful Deceit: The Myth of Race from the Colonial Era to Obama's America*. 2013; New York: Basic Books, 2015.

Jordan, Winthrop D. *White over Black: American Attitudes toward the Negro, 1550–1812*. Chapel Hill: University of North Carolina Press, 1968.

Kantrowitz, Stephen D. *Ben Tillman and the Reconstruction of White Supremacy*. Chapel Hill: University of North Carolina Press, 2000.

Kartiganer, Donald M., and Ann J. Abadie. *Faulkner and Ideology*. Jackson: University Press of Mississippi, 1995.

Katz, Philip M. *From Appomattox to Montmartre: Americans and the Paris Commune*. Cambridge, MA: Harvard University Press, 1998.

Kazin, Alfred. *An American Procession*. New York: Knopf, 1984.

———. *On Native Grounds: An Interpretation of Modern American Prose Literature*. San Diego: Harcourt Brace & Company, 1995.

Kendig, Catherine. "Race as a Physiosocial Phenomenon." *History and Philosophy of the Life Sciences* 33, no. 2 (2011): 191–21.

Kerouac, Jack. *On the Road*. In *Road Novels, 1957–1960*. Edited by Douglas Brinkley. New York: Library of America, 2007.

Kettle, Martin. "Echoes of Slavery as Bush Nominees Back Confederacy." *The Guardian*, January 12, 2001. Web.

Kipling, Rudyard. *Mandalay*. Garden City, NY: Doubleday, Page & Co, 1921.

Klinker, Philip A., with Rogers M. Smith. *The Unsteady March: The Rise and Decline of Racial Equality in America*. Chicago: University of Chicago Press, 1999.

Kraus, Michael W., Julian M. Rucker, and Jennifer A. Richeson. "Americans Misperceive Racial Economic Equality." *Proceedings of the National Academy of Sciences* 114, no. 39 (September 2017): 10324–31. Also available on the web.

Krugman, Paul. "Republicans Are Coming for Your Benefits." *The New York Times*, December 4, 2017. Web.
Kuzawa, Christopher W., and Elizabeth Sweet. "Epigenetics and the Embodiment of Race: Developmental Origins of U.S. Racial Disparities in Cardiovascular Health." *American Journal of Human Biology* 21 no. 1 (2009): 2–15.
Lai, K. K. Rebecca, and Jasmine C. Lee. "Why 10% of Florida Adults Can't Vote: How Felony Convictions Affect Access to the Ballot." *New York Times*. October 6, 2016. Web.
Larocca, Charles. "Stephen Crane's Inspiration." *American Heritage*. May/June 1991.
Laughland, Oliver. "Donald Trump and the Central Park Five: The Racially Charged Rise of a Demagogue." *The Guardian*. February 17, 2016. Web.
Lawyers' Committee for Civil Rights Under Law. *A Critical Assessment of the U.S. Commitment to Civil and Political Rights*. New York, 2006.
Lei, R. F., and Bodenhausen, G. V. "Racial Assumptions Color the Mental Representation of Social Class." *Frontiers in Psychology* 8, no. 519 (April 2017). Also available online. Digital object identifier: 10.3389/fpsyg.2017.00519.
Lentricchia, Frank, and Thomas McLaughlin. *Critical Terms for Literary Study, Second Edition*. University of Chicago Press, 1995.
Lester, Julius. "Morality and Adventures of 'Huckleberry Finn.'" *Mark Twain Journal* 22, no. 2 (1984): 43–46.
Lewis, David Levering. *W. E. B. Du Bois: Biography of a Race, 1868–1919*. New York: Henry Holt and Company, 2013. Volume one of a two-volume biography.
Lichtman, Alan. *The Embattled Vote in America: From the Founding to the Present*. Cambridge, MA: 2018.
Lincoln, Abraham. *Abraham Lincoln's Speeches*. New York: Dodd, Mead, 1923.
Lindberg, Gary. *The Confidence Man in American Literature*. New York: Oxford University Press, 1982.
Logan, Rayford W. *The Negro in American Life and Thought: The Nadir, 1877–1901*. New York: Dial Press, 1954.
Lowell, James Russell. *The Poems of James Russell Lowell*. London: Henry Frowde, 1912.
Luntz, Frank. "Why Republicans Should Watch Their Language." *Washington Post*, January 13, 2013. Web.
Madigan, Mark J., ed. *Keeping Fires Night and Day: Selected Letters of Dorothy Canfield Fisher*. Columbia: University of Missouri Press, 1993.
Mailer, Norman. *Advertisements for Myself*. 1959; New York: Penguin Books, 2018.
———. *Cannibals and Christians*. New York: Dell, 1966.
———. *Existential Errands*. Boston: Little Brown, 1972.
Marans, Daniel. "Donald Trump's Closing Ad Has Anti-Semitic Overtones." *Huffington Post*. November 5, 2016. Web.
Marvell, Andrew. *The Complete Poems*. Edited by Elizabeth S. Donno. London: Penguin, 2005.

Marx, Karl. *The Portable Karl Marx*. Edited by Eugene Kamenka. New York: Penguin, 1983.
McClurg, Alexander C. "The Red Badge of Hysteria." In *Stephen Crane: The Contemporary Reviews*. Edited by George Monteiro. Cambridge, UK: Cambridge University Press, 2009.
McFeely, William S. *Frederick Douglass*. New York: Norton, 1990.
McIlvaine, Mabel. *Reminiscences of Chicago During the Civil War*. Chicago: R. R. Donnelley, 1914.
McPherson, James M. *Battle Cry of Freedom: The Civil War Era*. New York: Oxford University Press, 1988.
McWilliams, Dean. *Charles W. Chesnutt and the Fictions of Race*. Athens: University of Georgia Press, 2002.
Melville, Herman. *Battle-pieces and Aspects of the War*. New York: Harper & Brothers, 1866.
Mills, C. Wright. *The Racial Contract*. Ithaca, NY: Cornell University Press, 1999.
Milton, John, Elijah Fenton, and Samuel Johnson. *Paradise Lost*. London: John Bumpus, 1821.
Mintz, Sidney W. *Sweetness and Power: The Place of Sugar in Modern History*. New York: Penguin, 1985.
Mitchell, Lee C., ed. *New Essays on the Red Badge of Courage*. Cambridge, UK: Cambridge University Press, 1986.
Montaigne, Michel *The Complete Works of Michael De Montaigne*. Edited by William Hazlitt, translated by Charles Cotton with amendments by Hazlitt. New York: Worthington Co., 1889.
Monteiro, George, ed. *Stephen Crane: The Contemporary Reviews*. Cambridge: Cambridge University Press, 2009.
Morrison, Toni. *Playing in the Dark: Whiteness and the Literary Imagination*. New York: Vintage, 2015.
Motz, Diana Gribbon. See *NAACP et al. v. Patrick McCrory*.
Murray, Albert. *Collected Essays & Memoirs*. Edited by Paul Devlin and Henry Louis Gates, Jr. New York: Library of America, 2016.
NAACP et al. v. Patrick McCrory, Governor of North Carolina [2016] No. 16-1468 (UNITED STATES COURT OF APPEALS FOR THE FOURTH CIRCUIT). The Honorable Diana Gribbon Motz, Circuit Judge, authored the opinion.
Ngũgĩ, wa Thiong'o. *Decolonising the Mind: The Politics of Language in African Literature*. London: J. Currey, 2011.
Nicosia, Gerald. *Memory Babe: A Critical Biography of Jack Kerouac*. Berkeley: University of California Press, 1994.
Nietzsche, Friedrich. *The Birth of Tragedy and the Genealogy of Morals*. Translated by Francis Golffing. Garden City, NY: Doubleday, 1956.
Nott, Josiah C. "The Future of the South." *DeBow's Review of the Southern and Western States*. Vol. X. New Series. 1851.

Parker, Hershel. "Getting Used to the 'Original Form' of *The Red Badge of Courage*." In *New Essays on The Red Badge of Courage*, edited by Lee Clark Mitchell, 25–47. New York: Cambridge University Press, 1986.

Parsons, C. G. *Inside View of Slavery, Or, a Tour Among the Planters*. Introductory note by Harriet B. Stowe. Boston: John P. Jewett and Company, 1855.

Pew Research Center. "On Views of Race and Inequality: Blacks and Whites Are Worlds Apart." Washington, DC: June 27, 2016. Web.

Phillips, Kristine. "Thousands of ICE Detainees Claim They Were Forced into Labor." *The Washington Post*. March 5, 2017. Web.

Poland, Luke P., and John Scott. *Testimony Taken by the Joint Select Committee to Inquire into the Condition of Affairs in the Late Insurrectionary States, South Carolina, Volume I*. Washington: U.S. Government Printing Office, 1872.

———. *Testimony Taken by the Joint Select Committee to Inquire into the Condition of Affairs in the Late Insurrectionary States, South Carolina, Volume II*. Washington: U.S. Government Printing Office, 1872.

Pollack, Norman. *The Populist Mind*. Indianapolis: Bobbs-Merrill, 1967.

Radway, Janice A. *A Feeling for Books: The Book-of-the-Month Club, Literary Taste, and Middle-Class Desire*. Chapel Hill: University of North Carolina Press, 1997.

Raff, Jennifer. "Nicholas Wade and Race: Building a Scientific Façade." *Human Biology* 86, no. 3 (2014): 227–32.

Richardson, Mark. "Introduction." In *The Cambridge Companion to American Poets*, edited by Mark Richardson, 1–9. New York: Cambridge University Press, 2015.

Robinson, Nathan J. *Superpredator: Bill Clinton's Use and Abuse of Black America*. Sommerville, MA: Current Affairs Press, 2016.

Roediger, David R. *Class, Race, and Marxism*. New York: Verso 2017.

———. *The Wages of Whiteness: Race and the Making of the American Working Class*. Revised edition. New York: Verso, 1999.

Rose, Willie Lee. *Rehearsal for Reconstruction: The Port Royal Experiment*. Athens: University of Georgia Press, 1999.

Ross, Janell. "Epigenetics: The Controversial Science Behind Racial and Ethnic Health Disparities." *The Atlantic*. March 20, 2014. Web.

Rothstein, Richard. *The Color of Law: A Forgotten History of How Our Government Segregated America*. New York: Liveright, 2017.

Rowley, Hazel. *Richard Wright: The Life and Times*. Chicago: University of Chicago Press, 2008. The book was first published by Henry Holt in 2001.

Santayana, George. *Interpretations of Poetry and Religion*. New York: Scribner's, 1922.

Scheidel, Walter. *The Great Leveler: Violence and the History of Inequality from the Stone Age to the Twenty-First Century*. Princeton, NJ: Princeton University Press, 2017.

The Sentencing Project. Washington, DC. "Felony Disenfranchisement Laws in The United States." April 28, 2014. Web.

Sherman, Amy. "Trump Voter Fraud Allegations." *Politifact Florida* (a site affiliated with the *Tampa Bay Times*). June 22, 2017. Web.

Silber, Nina. *The Romance of Reunion: Northerners and the South 1865–1900*. Chapel Hill: University of North Carolina Press, 1993.

Simkins, Francis B. *Pitchfork Ben Tillman, South Carolinian*. Baton Rouge: Louisiana State University Press, 1944.

Smith, James McCune. *The Works of James McCune Smith*. Edited by John Stauffer. New York: Oxford University Press, 2006.

Snyder, Gary. *A Place in Space: Ethics, Aesthetics, and Watersheds: New and Selected Prose*. Washington, DC: Counterpoint, 1995.

Sommer, Jeff. "Trump Immigration Crackdown Is Great for Private Prison Stocks." *New York Times*. March 10, 2017. Web.

———. "Trump's Win Gives Stocks in Private Prison Companies a Reprieve." *New York Times*. December 3, 2016. Web.

Sorrentino, Paul. *Stephen Crane: A Life of Fire*. Cambridge: Harvard, 2014.

Spengler, Oswald. *Decline of the West*. New York: Alfred A. Knopf, 1928.

Stallman, Robert W. *Stephen Crane: A Critical Bibliography*. Ames: The Iowa State University Press, 1972.

Stauffer, John. *The Black Hearts of Men: Radical Abolitionists and the Transformation of Race*. Cambridge: Harvard University Press, 2004.

Stevens, Wallace. *Collected Poetry and Prose*. New York: Library of America, 1997.

Stewart, George R. *American Place-Names: A Concise and Selective Dictionary for the Continental United States of America*. New York: Oxford University Press, 1985.

Strong, Josiah. *Our Country: Its Possible Future and Its Present Crisis*. New York: Published by Baker & Taylor for the American Home Missionary Society, 1885.

Sullivan, Shannon. "Inheriting Racist Disparities in Health: Epigenetics and the Transgenerational Effects of White Racism." *Critical Philosophy of Race* 1, no. 2 (2013): 190–218.

———. *The Physiology of Sexist and Racist Oppression*. New York: Oxford University Press, 2015. See particularly chapter 3, "The Epigenome: On the Transgenerational Effects of Racism."

Sumner, William G. "The Absurd Effort to Make the World Over." In *Sumner Today: Selected Essays of William Graham Sumner, with Comments by American Leaders*. Edited by Maurice R. Davie. Westport, CT: Greenwood Press, 1971.

Sundquist, Eric J. *To Wake the Nations: Race in the Making of American Literature*. Cambridge, MA: Harvard University Press, 1993.

Swartz, Omar. *The View from on the Road: The Rhetorical Vision of Jack Kerouac*. Carbondale: Southern Illinois University Press, 2001.

Taibbi, Matt. *I Can't breathe: A Killing on Bay Street*. New York: Spiegel and Grau, 2017.

———. *Insane Clown President: Dispatches from the 2016 Circus*. New York: Spiegel & Grau, 2017.

Tesler, Michael. *Post-Racial or Most-Racial?: Race and Politics in the Obama Era*. Chicago: University of Chicago Press, 2016.

Thomas, Hugh. *The Slave Trade*. New York: Simon and Schuster, 1997.

Thompson, Heather Ann. *Blood in the Water: The Attica Prison Uprising of 1971 and Its Legacy*. New York: Vintage, 2017.

———. "How Prisons Change the Balance of Power in America." *The Atlantic*. October 7, 2013. Web.

Thompson, Hunter S. *Kingdom of Fear: Loathsome Secrets of a Star-Crossed Child in the Final Days of the American Century*. New York: Penguin, 2003.

Timrod, Henry, and Paul H. Hayne. *The Poems of Henry Timrod. Edited, with a Sketch of the Poet's Life, by P. H. Hayne. New Revised Edition*. New York, 1873.

Tomasky, Michael. "Fighting to Vote." *New York Review of Books* 65, no. 17 (November 8, 2018): 8–12. Also available on the Web.

Toomer, Jean. *Cane: An Authoritative Text: Backgrounds, Criticism*. New York: W. W. Norton & Co, 1987.

Twain, Mark. *Mississippi Writings*. New York: The Library of America, 1982.

United States Department of Justice. *Justice Department Reaches $335 Million Settlement to Resolve Allegations of Lending Discrimination by Countrywide Financial Corporation*. December 21, 2011 (press release number 11-1694). Web.

Vosburgh, R. G. "The Darkest Hour in the Life of Stephen Crane." In *The Book Lover: A Magazine of Book Lore*. San Francisco, The Book-Lover Press, 1901.

Warner, Gerald. "Hoist It High and Proud: The Confederate Flag Proclaims A Glorious Heritage." *Breitbart*. July 1, 2015. Web.

Warnes, Andrew. *Richard Wright's Native Son: A Routledge Study Guide*. New York: Routledge, 2007.

Warren, Mervyn A. *King Came Preaching: The Pulpit Power of Dr. Martin Luther King, Jr*. Downers Grove, IL: Intervarsity Press, 2001.

Washington, Booker T. *Up from Slavery: An Autobiography*. Cambridge, MA: The Riverside Press, 1901.

Watkins, Mel. *On the Real Side: A History of African American Comedy from Slavery to Chris Rock*. Chicago: Lawrence Hill Books, 1999. Second edition, and with a new afterword by Watkins.

Weissmann, Jordan. "Countrywide's Racist Lending Practices Were Fueled by Greed." *The Atlantic*. December 23, 2011. Web.

Weller, Christian. "Budget Estimates Show New Tax Cuts for Wealthiest Americans Threaten Middle-Class Retirement." *Forbes*. September 25, 2018. Web.

Wertheim, Stanley. *A Stephen Crane Encyclopedia*. Westport, CT: Greenwood Press, 1997.

Whittier, John G., and Nathan H. Dole. *Poems of John Greenleaf Whittier*. New York: T. Y. Crowell, 1902.

Whitman, James Q. *Hitler's American Model: The United States and the Making of Nazi Race Law*. Princeton, NJ: Princeton University Press, 2017.

Whitman, Walt. *Leaves of Grass*. Brooklyn, New York, 1855.

———. *November Boughs*. Philadelphia: D. Mckay, 1888.

Williams, Ryan C. "The One and Only Substantive Due Process Clause." *Yale Law Journal* 120, no. 408 (2010): 408–512.

Wood, Peter H. *Black Majority: Negroes in Colonial South Carolina from 1670 Through the Stono Rebellion*. New York: W. W. Norton, 1974.

Woodward, C. Vann. *Origins of the New South, 1877–1913*. First issued in 1951. Baton Rouge: Louisiana State University Press, 2013.

Woolfolk, Austin. "300 Negroes Wanted." *The Frederick Town Herald* (Frederick, Maryland). April 14, 1832: 3.

Wright, Richard. *Black Power: A Record of Reactions in a Land of Pathos*. New York: Harper, 1954.

———. *The Color Curtain: A Report on the Bandung Conference*. Cleveland: World Publishing Company, 1956.

———. *Early Works: Lawd Today!, Uncle Tom's Children, Native Son*. Edited by Arnold Rampersad. New York: Library of America, 1991. Included in this volume also are two important essays: "The Ethics of Living Jim Crow" (which Wright collected in the second edition of *Uncle Tom's Children*) and "How Bigger Was Born."

———. *Haiku: This Other World*. New York: W. W. Norton, 2011.

———. *Later Works: Black Boy, The Outsider*. Edited by Arnold Rampersad. New York: Library of America, 1991.

———. *The Long Dream: A Novel*. Garden City, New York: Doubleday, 1958.

———. *Savage Holiday*. Chatham, New Jersey: Chatham Bookseller, 1954.

———. *White Man, Listen!* Garden City, New York: Doubleday & Company, 1957.

Young, Josiah U., III. *James Baldwin's Understanding of God*. New York: Palgrave Macmillan, 2014.

INDEX

1776 (musical by Sherman Edwards), 67

Aaron, Daniel, 118, 145, 282n2
abolitionism, schools of: colonizationist, 28, 256; Garrisonian, 28–31, 33, 34, 35, 36, 47, 48, 61, 62, 63, 64, 85, 211, 271n6; gradualist, 24, 28; New England, 46; political, 29–31, 36, 47, 66, 271n6
Adams, Dock, 74–75, 106
Agnew, Spiro T. (US vice president), 269n30
agrarian myth (Richard Hofstadter on), 124–25
Alexander, Michelle, 2–3, 268n27
Alexander, Roberta S., 166, 284n1
Allen, James, 187
Allen, James, works by: *Without Sanctuary: Lynching Photography in America*, 187
Althusser, Louis, 256; and ideological state apparatuses, 27
alt-right (US political movement), 13
Amendment 4, State of Florida (2016), 2, 291–92n25
America, dystopian visions of, 275n24
Americans for Prosperity (Koch Brothers-funded Super Pac), 14, 150. *See also* Super Pacs

Anacostia (neighborhood in Washington, DC), 71–72, 276n27
Anderson, Sherwood, 153, 208
Anglo-Saxon triumphalism, 105, 113, 146–47, 168, 186, 277n4. *See also* white supremacy, psychology and ideology of
Anthony, Aaron (one-time owner and possible father of Frederick Douglass), 44, 272–73n10
Anthony, Susan B., 71
anti-foundationalism, 161
Ash, Michael, 279n18
Aswell, Edward (as editor of Richard Wright), 218, 220, 224, 226, 228, 231, 294n10, 294n11, 294–95n12, 295n15
Atlanta University (as described by Du Bois), 15, 75, 76, 91, 100–102
Attica Correctional Facility, 1971 uprising at, 269n30
Auld, Hugh (as "master" of Frederick Douglass), 49–50, 51
Auld, Sophia (as wife of "master" of Frederick Douglass), 49–50, 273n11
Auld, Thomas (as "owner" of Frederick Douglass), 49, 54–55
authorship, vocation of, 115, 117, 147, 162, 174–75, 213–15

Bailey, Joseph (white childhood friend of Frederick Douglass), 51, 273n15
Baldwin, James, 17, 19, 105, 193, 196, 205, 249, 253, 258, 259, 260, 262, 263n2, 270n37, 289n21, 298n10, 298n11
Baldwin, James, works by: *Fire Next Time, The*, 17, 19, 105, 193, 259, 260, 262, 289n21; *No Name in the Street*, 260; *Nobody Knows My Name*, 253, 260
Baldwin, William (Tuskegee Institute Trustee, industrialist), 77
Baptist, Edward, 4, 39, 263, 266, 272
Barlow, Joel, 42, 48, 52
Barlow, Joel, works by: *The Columbiad*, 42, 59
Barringer, Paul B. (of the University of Virginia and Virginia Tech), 152
Barringer, Paul B., works by: *Sacrifice of a Race, The*, 152
Battles and Leaders of the Civil War (popular book series, nature of, and as source for *The Red Badge of Courage*), 118
Bay, Mia, 278n8
Beat Generation/Beats (US, literary movement), 19, 246, 249, 261
Beatty, Paul, 16, 82, 166
Beatty, Paul, works by: *The Sellout*, 16, 82, 166
Beauvoir, Simone de, 87, 88, 231
Beauvoir, Simone de, works by: *The Second Sex*, 87–88
Beer, Thomas, 140–42, 160
Beer, Thomas, works by: *Stephen Crane*, 140–42
Bentonville, Battle of (US Civil War), 165
Bierce, Ambrose (Union Army, lieutenant), 144–47
Bierce, Ambrose, works by: "Chickamauga," 146–47; "What I Saw of Shiloh," 145–46
Bigger Thomas (literary character, creation of Richard Wright), 195, 207, 211–17, 227–31, 251, 252, 253, 262, 293n3
Bingham, Caleb, 48
Birth of a Nation, The (1915 film by D. W. Griffith), 173; Charles Chesnutt on, 285–86n9
birtherism (lie, as propagated by Donald J. Trump), 20
Black Arts Movement (US), 85
black codes (repressive state laws, circa 1865–66), 165–66
Black Lives Matter (political movement, US, 2013–present), 15
Blackmon, Douglas A., 2, 187, 263n1, 268n25
Blackmon, Douglas A., works by: *Slavery by Another Name: The Re-Enslavement of Black Americans*, 187
Blight, David, 113–15, 118, 272n7, 273n12, 282n3
Blue State/Red State divide. *See* Red State/Blue State divide
Boer War (second; 1899–1902), 93
Book of the Month Club (as publisher of Richard Wright), 217, 218–20, 222–23, 227, 228, 230, 292n1, 294n10, 295n12, 295n15
Booth, John Wilkes, 109
Bork, Robert, 4
Boyce, James K., 279n18
Brahms, Johannes, 129
Brodhead, Richard, 171, 172, 274n21, 286n10
Brooks, Gwendolyn, 84–86, 196, 212, 278

INDEX

Brooks, Gwendolyn, works by: *Bean Eaters, The*, 84; "Lovers of the Poor, The," 84–85, 86, 212; *Report from Part One*, 85; *Selected Poems*, 85, 278n10; "Sundays of Satin Legs Smith, The," 84–85

Brooks, Preston (assailant of Charles Sumner), 71

Brown, John, 10, 94–95, 145, 268n28. See also Harpers Ferry, 1859 Insurrection at

Brown v. Board of Education (US Supreme Court case, 1954), 184, 240

Bryan, William Jennings, 125

Buchanan, Patrick J., 266n18, 270n38

Burke, Kenneth, 62, 214, 293n5

Burroughs, William S., 241

Bush, George H. W. (US president), 270n36

Butler, Benjamin (Union Army general), 145

Butler, Matthew Calbraith (Confederate Army general, Red Shirt terrorist, US Senator from South Carolina), 75, 78, 268n26, 277n4

Butler, Nathaniel (Confederate veteran, Red Shirt terrorist), 106–7

Butler, Pierce, 277n4

Butler, Thomas, 74

Byron, George Gordon (Lord), 58, 93, 279n15

Cable, George Washington, 175

Calhoun, John C. (US Senator, South Carolina), 4, 9, 14, 23

capitalism/capitalists/capital, 1–5, 6, 7, 10, 11, 12, 13–14, 15, 77, 78, 90–91, 92, 94, 98, 99, 113, 114–15, 141, 142, 167, 176, 183, 189, 195, 197, 198, 218, 220, 227–28, 230, 232, 247–48, 249, 265n8, 266n16, 268n25, 269n33, 273n17, 287n12, 291n24

Carey, Harry (film actor), 226

Carnegie, Andrew (industrialist, founder US Steel), 13–14, 76, 95; as supporter of Booker T. Washington, 15, 76–77, 95

Carnegie, Andrew, works by: *Gospel of Wealth and Other Timely Essays*, 13–14, 76

Carr, Elias (Governor of North Carolina, 1893–97), 164

Carroll, Charles, 187, 190, 193, 229

Carroll, Charles, works by: *The Negro a Beast*, 187–88

Cartwright, Samuel, 187

Casler, John O. (Confederate Army, private, 33rd Regiment, Stonewall Brigade), 118

Cassady, Neal, 239, 247, 297n4

Cedar Hill (final home of Frederick Douglass), 16, 71–72

Central Intelligence Agency (CIA), 237

Central Park Five (exonerated defendants in "New York jogger" case), 270n36

Chamberlain, Daniel H. (Reconstruction governor, South Carolina), 74

Chamberlain, Joshua Lawrence (Union Army, General), 110

Chancellorsville, Battle of (US Civil War), 116, 118

Chapman, John Jay, 23, 114, 275n24

Chappelle, Dave, 166

Chavez, Caesar (union organizer), 248

Chesnutt, Charles, 6, 13, 17, 19, 35, 61, 157, 164–203 *passim*, 209, 213, 218, 222, 246, 260, 263n1, 274n21, 284n3, 284n6, 284n7, 285–86n9, 287n13, 292n28

Chesnutt, Charles, works by: "Baxter's Procrustes," 18, 202–3; *Colonel's Dream, The*, 175, 200–202, 284n3, 292n26; *Conjure Woman, The*, 18, 61, 165, 166, 171, 174–75 (making of), 177, 246, 274n21, 284n3, 286n10; "Goophered Grapevine, The," 165, 167–70; "Gray Wolf's Ha'nt, The," 170; "Hot-Foot Hannibal," 170; *House Behind the Cedars, The*, 18, 184–93, 284n3; *Marrow of Tradition, The*, 18, 175, 193–200, 202, 284n3, 291n23, 292n28; "Passing of Grandison, The," 173, 174, 179–84, 284n12, 287n13, 284n14; *Paul Marchand, F.M.C.*, 202; "Po' Sandy," 170; "Postbellum Pre-Harlem," 196; *Quarry, The*, 202; "Wife of His Youth, The," 175–79; *Wife of His Youth and Other Stories, The*, 179, 284n3

Christianity, 7, 8, 9, 26, 51, 53, 64, 65, 146, 186, 187, 190, 256–57, 259, 266n18, 288n18; and *Red Badge of Courage*, 128–30

civil rights, African-Americans and/or civil rights movement, 4, 15, 18, 24, 91, 152, 178, 218, 240, 247, 260, 263n2, 265n10, 269n30, 271n6, 291–92n25

Civil Rights Act (1866), 2
Civil Rights Act (1957), 4
Civil Rights Act (1964), 4
Civil War (US), 6, 13, 17, 23, 28, 70, 73, 75, 83, 92, 110, 113–16, 118, 119, 139, 140, 141, 144–47, 162, 165, 185, 187, 194, 200, 209, 267n20, 269n29, 276n1, 281n1, 283n9, 285n8, 287n13

Clawson, Thomas (in the Wilmington Race Riots of 1898), 194
Coates, Ta-Nehisi, 265n12, 269n31, 270n38, 295n14

Coker, Simon (Reconstruction-era Republican politician, South Carolina), 106–7
Colbert, Stephen, 150
Cold War, 241
Collins, John, 33, 34
Columbian Orator, The (schoolbook), 16, 48, 52, 59, 65, 66
Committee of Fifteen (congressional framers of the 14th Amendment), 198
Communist Control Act (US Congress, 1954), 240
Communist Party USA, 210, 211, 213, 218, 232, 236, 279n17
Compromise of 1850 (US Congress; passed), 8, 267n23
Confederate Monuments, controversies about, 13, 269n32
Confederate States of America (1861–65), 11, 14, 25, 73, 115
Conrad, Joseph, 129, 163
Constitution (Confederate States of America), 11, 24–25
Constitution (US), 10, 12, 20, 25, 28, 29–31, 74, 83, 114, 116, 195, 267n23, 271n5, 280n21; 13th Amendment to, 30, 207; 14th Amendment to, 4–5, 30, 141, 197–98, 291n24; 15th Amendment to, 30, 74, 141; debates about relation of slavery to, 28–31, 83; fugitive slaves, provisions regarding, 10, 28; "three-fifths" provision of, 20, 27, 271n5
convict labor, use of, 2, 186, 201, 264–65n8, 268n25
Cooke, John Esten, 140, 141, 142
Cornelius, Janet Duitsman, 49, 273n13
Cosdry, William (white childhood friend of Frederick Douglass), 51
cotton (as slave-produced commodity), 11, 12, 22–23,

INDEX

24, 27, 38, 39, 48, 96, 103, 244, 246–47, 268n28, 271n2, 279n18; and commodity fetishism, 24; as cultivated in California, 297n7
Countrywide Financial (racial discrimination and), 5, 266n15
Covey, Edward Napoleon ("the Negro breaker"), 35, 36, 54–60, 63–66, 262, 274n19, 274n20
Crane, Hart, 234
Crane, Stephen, 5, 6, 17, 19, 110–63 *passim*, 238, 282, 283
Crane, Stephen, works by: "Blue Hotel, The," 117, 131, 148, 151; "Bride Comes to Yellow Sky, The," 116, 130, 132, 147–51; "Experiment in Misery, An," 125; *Maggie: A Girl of the Streets*, 125, 133, 158, 205; *The Monster*, 6, 17, 133, 151–61, 163; "Open Boat, The," 117, 121, 148, 149, 151, 155, 163; *Red Badge of Courage*, 5, 17, 110–16, 117–45 *passim*, 162–63, 282n6, 283n9; *War Is Kind*, 155
Creek War (1813–14), 23
Crittenden Compromise (US Congress, 1861; failed), 10
Custer, Elizabeth Clift (née Bacon), 140
Custer, George Armstrong (Union Army general), 140
Cuvier, Georges, 9

Daltonism (deuteranopia, form of color-blindness), 251
Darwin, Charles, 9, 176, 284n5. *See also* social Darwinism
David, David Brion (historian), 249, 270n36, 271n6, 298n10
Davis, Jefferson, 6–12, 13, 14, 15, 95, 113, 173, 246, 266n18, 267n23; on cotton, 271n2
Davis, Jefferson, works by: *Rise and Fall of the Confederate Government*, 6–12, 113, 173, 246, 267n23, 271n2
Declaration of Independence (American), 43, 48, 64, 96, 97, 99
Delbanco, Andrew, 117, 119, 127, 139, 142, 162
Democratic Leadership Council (founded 1985), 15
Democratic Party (US), 6, 100, 193, 196; and 1898 Wilmington Race Riots,194; and disenfranchisement, 208; in Reconstruction-era South Carolina, 74–75; as target of voter suppression in North Carolina, 2013–16, 290n23; white supremacy and, 4, 92, 113
deuteranopia. *See* Daltonism
Dewey, John, 189, 190, 192, 193
Dewey, John, works by: *The Quest for Certainty*, 189–90
Dickinson, Emily, 67, 68, 69, 70, 116, 234, 275n23
Dixon, Thomas, 249
Donne, John, 51, 273n16
Dorgan, Gustavus (white childhood friend of Frederick Douglass), 51, 273n15
Dos Passos, John, 209, 210
Dostoevsky, Fyodor, 231
double-consciousness, Du Bois's concept of, 81, 84, 86, 107
Douglass, Charles (son of Frederick), 276n27
Douglass, Frederick, 5–6, 16, 22, 24, 26, 28, 29, 30, 31–72 *passim*, 85, 94–95, 114, 115, 117, 142, 157, 160, 192, 207, 209, 211, 217, 218, 220, 222, 223, 235, 262, 263n2, 271n6, 271–72n7, 273n11, 273n18, 274n19, 275n24, 276n27; paternity of, 272–73n10

Douglass, Frederick, works by: and anti-Catholicism, 51, 53, 54, 59; *Life and Times of Frederick Douglass, The*, 31, 51, 53–54; *My Bondage and My Freedom*, 5–6, 16, 22, 28, 30, 31–64 passim, 65–67, 117, 271–72n7, 272n9; *Narrative of the Life of Frederick Douglass, An American Slave*, 29, 31–32, 35, 36–37, 57, 272n10, 274n19; newspapers edited by, *The North Star*, 30

Douglass, Frederick, Jr. (son of Frederick), 276n27

Douglass, Lewis (son of Frederick), 276n27

Dowling, Mike (in the Wilmington Race Riots of 1898), 194

Dray, Philip, 187

Dray, Philip, works by: *At the Hands of Persons Unknown: The Lynching of Black America*, 187

Dred Scott v. Sanford (Supreme Court case, 1857), 4, 48

Du Bois, W. E. B., 1, 6, 15, 16–17, 19–20, 27, 35, 45, 48, 66, 73–109 passim, 110–12, 114, 142, 144, 155, 157, 159, 162, 165, 172, 184, 188, 192, 195, 207, 208, 215, 218, 221, 222, 223, 237, 249, 263n2, 268n25, 271n5, 273n18, 275n24, 276n1, 278n11, 279n17, 282n4, 284n2, 287n12, 289n20. *See also* double-consciousness, Du Bois's concept of; psychological wage, Du Bois's concept of

Du Bois, W. E. B., works by: *Black Reconstruction*, 1, 20, 27, 73, 74, 75, 79, 82, 83, 84, 92, 111, 159, 172, 173, 198, 208, 268n28, 271n5, 273n18, 276n26, 276n1, 279n17, 282n4, 284n2, 287n12; *Dark Princess*, 88–89; *Dusk of Dawn*, 76, 77, 78, 91, 94, 188; *John Brown*, 94–96; *Negro, The*, 268n25; *Philadelphia Negro, The*, 79; *Souls of Black Folk*, 5, 6, 15, 17, 19, 20, 35, 48, 75–76, 78–82, 85, 86–88, 89, 90, 91–92, 93–94, 95–106, 108, 110–11, 112, 142, 155, 157, 162, 165, 207, 215, 276n1, 279n17, 287n15, 289n20; *Suppression of the African Slave Trade*, 79

Dumas, Alexandre, 203

Dunbar, Paul Laurence, 18, 81, 157, 166, 280–81n22

Dunbar, Paul Laurence, works by: 18, 166; *Lyrics of Lowly Life*, 280–81n22; "We Wear the Mask," 18, 166, 280–81n22

Dunning, William (pro-Southern historian of Reconstruction), 172

Eagleton, Terry, 15, 161–62

Eagleton, Terry, works by: *Literary Theory: An Introduction* (2nd edition), 161–62

Ebola Zaire (virus), 156

ecology and race, 279–80n18

Eliot, T. S., 129, 160, 209, 210

Eliot, T. S., works by: *The Wasteland*, 209

Ellison, Ralph, 196, 236, 248, 253, 293n3, 297n9

Ellison, Ralph, works by: *Invisible Man*, 236, 293n3; *Shadow and Act*, 248

Emancipation Proclamation (US, January 1, 1863), 141

Emerson, Ralph Waldo, 21–22, 34, 46, 47, 67, 68, 112, 115, 117, 150, 234, 239, 241, 244–45, 249, 256

Emerson, Ralph Waldo, works by: "Fate," 68; "Self-Reliance," 244, 249

Engels, Friedrich, 122, 233

INDEX 319

epigenetics (as vector for physiological effects of racism), 284n7
eugenics, 77, 168, 187, 284n5
existentialism, 81, 216, 220, 231–32, 251

fake news, so-called, and "alternative facts," 244
Farity, Charles (white childhood friend of Frederick Douglass), 51
Faulkner, William, 9, 84, 209, 210, 278n9
Faulkner, William, works by: *The Sound and the Fury*, 209
Federal Bureau of Investigation (FBI), 237, 269n30
Fischer, Jack (as editor of Richard Wright), 231, 233, 296n18
Fish, Stanley, 161
Fisher, Dorothy Canfield, 219–20, 223, 294n8
Fisk University, 76, 102, 218
Fitzgerald, Edward, 106
Fitzgerald, Edward, works by: (as translator) *Rubaiyat of Omar Khayyam*, 106
Force Bill (US Congress, 1890; failed). See Lodge Force Bill
Forrest Gump (novel by Winston Groom, and title character of), 240
Foster, George, 33
Fourteenth Amendment. See Constitution, US
France, radicalism of in the white American imagination, 287–88n15
Franco, Francisco, 236
Frederickson, George, 188, 249, 263n1, 275n22, 278n6, 278–79n13, 288n16
Frederickson, George, works by: *The Black Image in the White Mind*, 188, 263n1, 275n22, 278n6, 278–79n13, 288n16; concept of "romantic racialism," 278–79n13
Freedmen's Bureau (US, 1865–72), 86, 276n27, 276n1
Frémont, John C. (Union Army general), 145
Freneau, Philip, 48
Frohock, W. M., 121, 123
Frost, Robert, 122, 239
Frost, Robert, works by: *North of Boston*, 122
Fugitive Slave Bill of 1850, 10, 39, 179, 183

Galileo, 25
Galton, Francis, 168, 187, 284n5
Galton, Francis, works by: *Hereditary Genius: An Inquiry into Its Laws and Consequences*, 168
Garner, Eric (killed by Staten Island police, 2014), 184, 262
Garrison, William Lloyd, 23, 28, 29–30, 32, 33, 34, 36, 71, 262, 271n6; newspaper edited by, *Liberator, The*, 28, 29, 32, 33
gender, 69, 87–88, 89, 93, 97, 98, 196, 258. See also patriarchy; white supremacy, and sexuality/the body
General Education Board, 90–91, 102
Genovese, Eugene, 38, 279n18
Gettysburg, Battle of, 114, 115–16
Getzen, Henry (and the Hamburg Massacre), 74
Ghana, 76, 235, 237
Ginsberg, Allen, 70, 239, 275n24
Ginsberg, Allen, works by: *Fall of America, The*, 275n24; *Howl and Other Poems*, 239, 242, 275n24; "Supermarket in California, A," 70
Glover, Donald (aka Childish Gambino), 16

INDEX

Glover, Donald (aka Childish Gambino), works by: *Atlanta*, 16; "This Is America," 16
Goethe, Johann Wolfgang (von), 89, 101, 102
Goldwater, Barry, 4, 15
Gompers, Samuel, 125
Gone With the Wind (novel by Margaret Mitchell), 83
Grady, Henry, 77
Grant, Ulysses S. (US president), 73, 74, 76, 111, 162, 276n27
Grant, Ulysses S., works by: *Personal Memoirs of U.S. Grant*, on Blue/Grey camaraderie on the battlefield, 282–83n7; on the vanishing of strong regional differences in America, as a consequence of the Civil War, 285n8
Great Migration (of African-Americans to northern cities, early 20th century), 208
Great Recession (2008), 5, 20. *See also* Countrywide Financial
Great Society (policies of President Lyndon B. Johnson), 4, 15, 203, 264n6
Griffiths, Julia (associate of Frederick Douglass), 36

Haiti, 9, 28, 185, 267n21, 268n26, 287n15
Hamburg, town of (South Carolina), 74–75, 106–7, 277n4, 278n5
Hamburg Massacre (1876), 74–75, 106–7, 277n4, 278n5
Hardy, Thomas, 185
Harper, Frances E. W., 157, 286n11
Harper, Frances E. W., works by: *Iola Leroy*, 286n11
Harpers Ferry, 1859 Insurrection at, 10, 94. *See also* Brown, John
Harrington, Ollie (friend of Richard Wright), 237
Harris, Catherine, 125
Harris, Cora Mae, 192; as defender of lynching, 188–89
Harris, Joel Chandler, 18, 77, 113, 172
Harvey, William, 25
Hawthorne, Nathaniel, 46, 249, 275n24
Hawthorne, Nathaniel, works by: "Young Goodman Brown," 239, 275n24
Hayes, Rutherford B. (US president), 6
Hegel, Georg Wilhelm Friedrich, 87, 247
Henry, Patrick, 64, 66, 67
Herbert, George, 130
Higginson, Thomas Wentworth (Union Army colonel; commander of an African-American regiment), 277n3
Hitchcock, Ripley (as editor of Stephen Crane), 128, 132
Hofstadter, Richard, 124, 125
Holmes, Oliver Wendell, Jr. (Supreme Court Justice), 4–5
Holton, Robert, 249, 297n5, 297n6, 297n9
Hoover, J. Edgar, 237
Hose, Sam (lynching victim, 1899), 188, 189
Howard, Oliver O. (Union Army Major General; head of the Freedmen's Bureau), 276n1
Howells, William Dean, 108, 249, 280–81n22
Howells, William Dean, works by: preface to Paul Laurence Dunbar's *Lyrics of Lowly Life*, 280–81n22
Huckleberry Finn (literary character, creation of Mark Twain), 70, 78, 245, 251, 252, 254, 257, 262, 275n24
Hughes, Howard, 64

Hughes, Langston, 61, 209
Hume, David, 102
humor, African-American, 166, 284n4
Hurricane Katrina, 20
hydrogen bomb, 259; 1952 detonation at Eniwetok Atoll, 240

ideology, operations of (in the Marxist sense), 10–11, 15, 27, 69, 139, 141, 142, 176, 239, 245, 246, 250, 252, 254, 255–56, 285–86n9, 283n15. *See also* Marx, Karl (and/or Marxism)
IKEA, 133
Internal Security Act (US Congress, 1950), 240
Iowa Caucus (and US presidential campaigns), 125

Jackson, Andrew (US president), 23, 83
Jackson, Thomas Jonathan "Stonewall" (Confederate Army Lieutenant General), 118
James, Horace, 164
James, William, 79, 112, 114, 143, 155–56, 157 161, 296n1
James, William, works by: *Pragmatism*, 155–56, 161; *Will to Believe, The*, 112, 296–97n1
James City (North Carolina; named for Horace James), 164–65, 194, 284n1, 284n2
Jameson, Frederic, 249, 283n15
jazz (white people's ideas about), 256–58, 260
Jefferson, Thomas (as author and slaveholder, pre-presidential years), 10, 23–24, 27
Jefferson, Thomas, works by: *Notes on the State of Virginia*, 23–24, 25
Jenkins, Harriet (possible wife of Sandy Jenkins), 274n20

Jenkins, Sandy (slave and friend of Frederick Douglass), 58–66, 209, 262, 274n20
Job, Book of (in relation to Richard Wright's works), 235
John Reed Clubs, 210
Johnson, Lyndon Baines (US president), 15, 265–66n14
Jones, Jacqueline, 5

Katz, Philip M., 287n15
Kavanaugh, James, 254
Kazin, Alfred, 68, 127, 144, 160
Kennedy, John F. (US president), 76, 291–92n25
Kerouac, Jack, 18, 19, 238–58 *passim*, 260, 261, 297n2, 297n4, 297n5, 297n7, 297n9, 298n10, 298n11
Kerouac, Jack, works by: *On the Road*, 18–19, 239–58 *passim*, 259, 260–62, 298n9, 298n10, 298n11; Cold War and, 241–42; genre and, 247; patriotism and, 242; and plantation tales, 243–47
King, Martin Luther, Jr., 15, 19, 76, 210, 278n12
Kipling, Rudyard, 47, 89, 156, 157, 161
Korean War (1950–53), 240
Kraus, Michael W., 1, 263n1
Krugman, Paul, 264n6
Ku Klux Klan (first incarnation of, 1860s), 74, 75, 111, 195, 268n26, 286n9

Langdon, Olivia (wife of Mark Twain), 70
Lardner, Ring, 162
Lee, Robert E. (Confederate Army General in Chief), 20
Leitz, Robert, 174
Lester Julius, 251
Letterman, David, 150, 162
Lewis, David Levering, 90

Lewis, Sinclair, 17, 153, 208, 275n24
Liberator, The. See Garrison, William Lloyd, newspaper edited by
Liberty Party (US 1840–48), 29–30
Lichtman, Alan, 3
Lincoln, Abraham (US president), 6, 7, 8, 9, 10, 11, 12, 30, 71, 109, 110, 111, 114–16, 118, 144, 145, 160, 177, 209, 267n20, 268n28, 269n29, 276n1, 281n1
Lincoln, Abraham, works by: Gettysburg Address, 115–16, 144; Second Inaugural Address, 177
Lloyd, Edward IV, 273n17
Lloyd, Edward V, 52, 273n17
Lloyd family of Maryland (employers of Douglass's first master), 52–53, 273n17
Lochner Doctrine, 4
Lochner v. New York (Supreme Court case, 1905), 4
Lodge Force Bill (US Senate, 1890; failed), 141, 198
London, Jack, 275n24
Lost Cause, cult of (Confederacy), 126, 141, 142
Louverture, Toussaint, 9, 277n3, 287n15
Loving v. Virginia (Supreme Court case, 1967), 69
Lowell, James Russell, 86, 87, 278n11, 278n12
Lowell, James Russell, works by: "Present Crisis, The," 86
loyalty oaths, as passed by several US states (early Cold War era), 240
Luntz, Frank (as Republican pollster), 269n33
lynching, 4, 5, 17, 70, 78, 100, 106, 109, 116, 151, 159, 186, 188, 189, 200, 280n21

Mailer, Norman, 64, 69, 250, 252–53, 258, 259–60

Mailer, Norman, works by: *Armies of the Night*, 275n24; *Existential Errands*, 252–53; "White Negro, The," 250, 252, 259–60, 275n24
Martin, Trayvon (killed by George Zimmerman, 2012), 262
Marvell, Andrew, 137
Marvell, Andrew, works by: "Upon Appleton House," 137
Marx, Karl (and/or Marxism), 1, 10–11, 25, 87, 107, 122, 161, 229, 233, 248. *See also* Althusser, Louis; cotton, and commodity fetishism; ideology, operations of (in the Marxist sense)
Marx, Karl, works by: *Communist Manifesto* (with Engels), 122, 233; *German Ideology, The*, 10–11
mass incarceration, advent and effects of, 2. *See also* prison industry (for profit)
Mather, Cotton, 66
McClurg, Alexander (Union Army Brigadier General, publisher, reviewer of *Red Badge of Courage*), 111–12, 113–14, 115, 123, 126, 127, 141, 142, 143, 144, 281n1
McElrath, Joseph, 174
McKinley, William (US president), 117
McVeigh, Timothy (American terrorist), 109
Meadman, Dhima Rose (first wife of Richard Wright), 218
Melville, Herman, 46, 94, 115, 234, 275n24
Mencken, H. L., 122, 124–25, 127, 139, 207–8, 275n24
Mencken, H. L., works by: *Book of Prefaces, A*, 207
Meriwether, Thomas McKie (and Hamburg Massacre), 277n4
Mexican-American War (1846–48), 86
Miles, Barry, 254

INDEX 323

Miller, Henry, 275n24
Mills, C. Wright, 12
Milton, John, 191
Milton, John, works by: *Paradise Lost*, 190–91
minstrelsy (black face), 34, 146, 152, 157, 159, 161, 169, 173, 199, 243, 248, 257, 297n6
Mintiz, Sidney, 264n3
Mississippi Plan, The (as model for reinstitution of white supremacy after Reconstruction), 208
Mitchell, John (US Attorney General), 269n30
Mitchell, Lee Clark, 116
Mondale, Walter (as 1984 Democratic Party presidential nominee), 15, 270n34
Montaigne, Michel de, 192–93
Montaigne, Michel de, works by: *Apology for Raimond Sebond*, 192–93
Moody, William Vaughan, 114, 142, 144, 160, 162
Moore, Marianne, 1
Motz, Hon. Diana (judge, US Fourth Circuit of Appeals), 290n23; legal opinion quoted, 290n23
mulattoes, discussions of, 39, 98, 184, 188, 195, 279n13
Murphy, Eddie, 284n4
Murray, Albert, 10, 16

NAACP et al. v. Patrick McCrory, Governor of North Carolina (case decided by the US Fourth Circuit of Appeals, 2016), 290n23
National Association for the Advancement of Colored People (NAACP), 94, 107, 202, 207, 290n23
National Security Agency (NSA), 269n30

National Security State, the US as, 240–41, 269n30
naturalism (literary movement), 116, 147, 220
neo-Confederates, 13, 269n32
neo-pragmatism, 161–62
New Criticism, The, 129
New Deal (policies of FDR), 4, 13, 15, 144, 217
Ngugi, wa Thiong'o, 82
Ngugi, wa Thiong'o, works by: *Decolonising the Mind*, 82
Niagara Movement (founders of the NAACP), 93
Nietzsche, Friedrich, 232, 238, 238, 242
Nietzsche, Friedrich, works by: *Birth of Tragedy, The*, 238
Nixon, Richard Milhous (US president), 15, 269n30
Nott, Josiah C., 27

Obama, Barack (US president), 14, 264n8, 266n18, 290n23
Obergefell v. Hodges (Supreme Court case, 2015), 69
Oberholtzer, Ellis Paxson, 94
Oklahoma City Bombing, and white supremacy (1995), 20, 109
Orr, Nathaniel (American artist and illustrator), 38, 40, 41

Page, Thomas Nelson, 18, 113, 142, 172
Paine, Thomas, 47–48
Parker, Hershel, 128, 132
Parks, Rosa, 240
passing (as a "white" person), 185
patriarchy, 16, 68, 87–88, 90, 98, 186, 258, 278n8. *See also* gender; white supremacy, and sexuality/the body
Paul, Rand (US Senator, Kentucky), 4, 265

Paul, Ron (as presidential aspirant), 4
Paul, Saint, 18, 53, 189, 190, 192
Paul, Saint, works by: *Romans*, 190
Pease, Elizabeth, 31
Philippine-American War (1899–1902), 70, 99, 102, 117, 143, 144, 196, 279n14
Phillips, Wendell, 31, 281
plantation myth/plantation tales, 5, 13, 18, 113, 142, 171–75, 180–85, 196, 199, 244, 246–47, 248, 255
Plato/Platonism, 46, 100, 168, 190, 192
Plessy v. Ferguson (US Supreme Court case, 1896), 149, 281n22
Pollard, Percival, 145
polygenetic theory of creation (and white supremacy), 27, , 193, 229; and pre-Adamites, 187
Poor People's Campaign (US, 1968), 15
Pope, Alexander, 37
Poplar, Ellen (second wife of Richard Wright), 218
Populism (1890s), 78, 116, 123, 125, 130, 151, 194
prison industry (for-profit), 19, 264–65n8
prison-gerrymandering, 20, 270–71n38
Protocols of the Elders of Zion, 109
Pryor, Richard, 166
psychological wage, Du Bois's concept of, 84, 159, 172–73, 189, 223
Pullman, George, 149, 163
Pullman Palace Car Company, The, 149, 150, 163
Pynchon, Thomas, 275n24

Qafzeh, cave of, 189

racial wealth gap (US), 4, 265n12
Randolph, A. Philip (US civil rights leader), 218

Ransier, Alonzo Jacob (Reconstruction-era Republican politician, South Carolina), 268n26
rape, white hysteria/fantasies about, 105, 186, 200, 213, 226, 280n21
Reagan, Ronald (US president), 15, 176, 203
Reconstruction (US, 1865–76), 1–2, 4, 5, 13, 20, 27, 73–75, 82–83, 93, 95, 99, 106, 108, 111, 113–14, 141, 146, 157, 159, 166, 167, 172, 177, 195, 198, 208, 276n1, 274n19, 276n1
Red Shirts (white supremacist terrorist movement, South Carolina, 1876), 194, 195, 277n4
Red State/Blue State divide, 124, 260
redlining (means of creating and protecting all-white neighborhoods), 295n14
refugee slaves, status of (US Civil War), 145–46
Republican Party, 3, 4, 5, 71, 73–74, 113, 117, 159, 177, 194, 196; in election of 1860, 8; and elections of 1992 and 1996, 266n18; and hostility to social welfare programs, 203, 264n6; and political euphemism, 14; Radical wing of in 1860s, 114, 210; in South Carolina during Reconstruction, 106; and voter suppression efforts, 290n23; white identity politics and, 270n38
Republican Tax Cuts and Jobs Act of 2017, 3, 264n6, 246n7
Reynolds, Paul (as agent of Richard Wright), 233, 294–95n12
Richeson, Jennifer A., 1, 263n1
Rivers, Prince (Union Army veteran, Reconstruction-era Republican politician, South Carolina), 75, 277n3

INDEX

Rochester, Earl of (John Wilmot), 143
Rockefeller, John D. (founder, Standard Oil), 79, 125
Rockefeller, Nelson Aldrich (Governor of New York), 269n30
Roediger, David, 1
Roediger, David, works by: *Class, Race and Marxism*, 1; *Wages of Whiteness*, 263n1, 271n4
romantic racialism. *See* Frederickson, George; concept of romantic racialism
Roosevelt, Franklin Delano (US president), 13, 218; and Executive Order 8802 (June 1941), 218
Roosevelt, Theodore (US president), 117, 202
Rorty, Richard, 161, 162
Rosenberg, Ethel, 240
Rosenberg, Julius, 240
Roth, Phillip, 275n24
Rothstein, Richard, 264n4, 295n14
Rowley, Hazel (as biographer of Richard Wright), 205, 237, 293n2, 294n7, 295n12
Rucker, Julian M., 1, 264
Ruskin, John, 111, 282n2
Russian (Bolshevik) Revolution, 107
Ryan, Paul (US politician, Republican Party, Speaker of the House 2015–19), 167

Santayana, George, 18–19, 256
Sartre, Jean-Paul, 231
Scheidel, Walter, 268n
Scott, Walter, 182; Scott's novels as "cause" of the Civil War, 287n13
Shakespeare, William, works by: *Antony and Cleopatra*, 256; *Coriolanus*, 67; *Hamlet*, 192; *Julius Caesar*, 55; *Macbeth*, 108, 161, 209; *Tempest*, 6

Shaw, Robert Gould (Union Army, commander of Massachusetts 54th Infantry Regiment), 110
Shelby County (Alabama) v. Eric Holder (Supreme Court case, 2013), 3, 290n23
Sherman, William Tecumseh (Union Army, Major General), 162, 165, 257n1, 276n1, 281n1; March to the Sea of (1864–65), 281n1
Shiloh, Battle of (US Civil War), 140, 141, 145–46
Simms, William Gilmore, 182
slave trade, internal/domestic (US), 39, 272n9; international, 8, 266n19
slavery (American), 1, 2, 7–13, 16–17, 20, 21–72 *passim*, 74, 75, 77, 83, 87, 96–98, 102, 107, 113, 118, 142, 160, 162, 165, 170, 179–84 *passim*, 187, 188, 195, 196, 207–8, 222, 235, 246, 263n2, 266n18, 268n25, 269n29, 271n2, 271n6, 277n3, 278–79n13, 279n18, 286n11, 287n12, 287n14, 288–89n19; effects on free labor of, 288–89n19
slavery (in antiquity), 190
slavery (as practiced by the Portuguese and Spanish), 264n3
Smith, Adam, 25
Smith, Gerritt (US politician, Liberty Party; associate of Frederick Douglass), 29–30, 71
Smith, James McCune, 35, 63–64, 67, 272n8
Smith, James McCune, works by: Introduction to *My Bondage and My Freedom* (Frederick Douglass), 35–36, 63
Snyder, Gary, 247–48
social Darwinism, 76, 77, 78, 89, 116, 176–77, 229. *See also* Darwin, Charles
Southern Education Board, 90–91, 102

326 INDEX

Spanish-American War (1898), 79, 144
Spencer, Herbert, 5, 170, 284n6
Spooner, John Coit (US Senator, Wisconsin), debate with Senator Ben Tillman, 280n21
Stallman, R. W., 127, 128, 129, 132, 134, 144, 283n10, 283n11
Standard Oil Trust, 76, 90, 151. *See also* Rockefeller, John D.
Stanton, Elizabeth Cady, 71
Stauffer, John, 272n8
Stein, Gertrude, 234
Stephens, Alexander H. (Confederate States of America, vice president), 11, 15, 24–25, 30, 113
Stevens, Thaddeus (Radical Republican congressman, 1860s), 71, 114, 160, 198, 276; on defects of the Fourteenth Amendment, 291n24
Stevens, Wallace, 234, 256–58, 259, 261
Stevens, Wallace, works by: "A High-Toned Old Christian Woman," 256–58, 259
Stevenson, Robert Louis, 199
Stewart, George, 38
Stowe, Harriet Beecher, 83, 279n13
Strong, Josiah, Rev., 146–47
Strong, Josiah, Rev., works by: *Our Country: Its Possible Future and Its Present Crisis*, 146–47
style (prose, literary, analysis of), 5, 7–11, 36–38, 54–58, 84–86, 101, 115, 117, 134, 135–39, 144, 147–49, 151–61, 181–83, 168–69, 207, 209, 231, 233–34, 243–44, 256–58, 261–62 283n15
Sullivan, Shannon, on epigenetics and the heritability of the effects of racism, 284n7
Sumner, Charles, 71, 83, 114, 160, 198, 281n1
Sumner, William Graham, 149–51, 160

Sumner, William Graham, works by: "Absurd Effort to Make the World Over, The," 149–51, 160
Sundquist, Eric, 34, 62, 179, 193, 266n17, 271n7
Super Pacs, 3, 14, 150
super-predators, hysteria about (US, 1990s), 270n36
Swartz, Omar, 255

Taibbi, Matt, 188
Taibbi, Matt, works by: *I Can't Breathe: A Killing on Bay Street*, 188
Tax Cuts and Jobs Act of 2017 (Republican), 3; effects of, 264n6; and entitlement reform, 264n6
terrorism (US, as perpetrated by white supremacists), 6, 74, 78, 109, 116, 151, 159, 194, 219, 277n4
Tesler, Michael, 14, 263n1, 270n34, 270n38
Thompson, Heather Ann, 188, 263n1, 269n30, 270–71n38
Thompson, Heather Ann, works by: *Blood in the Water: The Attica Uprising of 1971*, 187–88, 263n1, 269n30, 270–71n38
Thompson, Hunter S., 275n24
Thoreau, Henry David, 115
Till, Emmett, 5, 76, 240
Tillman, Benjamin (Red Shirt terrorist, US Senator, South Carolina), 75, 78, 107–8, 161; debate with Senator John Coit Spooner, 280n21
Timrod, Henry, 24, 25
Timrod, Henry, works by: "The Cotton Boll," 24
Tomasky, Michael, 3
Toomer, Jean, 82, 245
Toomer, Jean, works by: *Cane*, 82, 245
Tourgée, Albion, 114, 176
Toussaint. *See* Louverture, Toussaint

Trader Horn (1931 film, directed by W. S. Van Dyke), 226
tragic mulatto, as stock character (American fiction), 184–85, 195. *See also* mulattoes, discussions of
Truman, Harry S. (US president), inauguration of, 240, 297n3
Trump, Donald J. (US president), 3, 9, 244, 254, 264–65n8; and Central Park Five, 270n36; and racist "birther" lie, 20; rhetoric of ("border-wall," "travel-ban," immigrant "caravan"), 12–13; white identity politics and, 270n38
Turner, Frederick Jackson, 83
Turner, Nat, 28, 94, 254
Turner Diaries, The (by William Luther Pierce), 109
Tuskegee Institute, 15, 76, 77, 78, 89, 90, 91, 95, 101
Twain, Mark, 64, 70, 71, 114, 122, 143, 144, 159, 161, 239, 251, 254
Twain, Mark, works by: *Adventures of Huckleberry Finn*, 55, 70–71, 78, 83, 122, 159, 161, 239, 251, 254 (and white readers' attachment to), 275n24; *Life on the Mississippi*, 287n13; "Man that Corrupted Hadleyburg, The," 159; "Private History of a Campaign that Failed, The," 276n25; *Roughing It*, 276n25; "To the Person Sitting in Darkness," 275n24; "United States of Lyncherdom, The," 275n24

Uncle Julius (literary character, creation of Charles Chesnutt), 17, 18, 165–73, 177, 180, 213, 246, 262, 284n6
United Farmworkers (union, organized by Caesar Chavez), 248
US Steel (corporation; as beneficiary of neo-slavery), 268n25

USSR (Soviet Union), 240, 241

V.F.W. (Veterans of Foreign Wars), Port Jervis, New York chapter, attitude toward Stephen Crane, 127, 283n9
Vatican, The, 53
Vesey, Denmark, 64
Vidal, Gore, 275n24
Vosburgh, R. G., 135
voter suppression, 3; 20, 77, 208, 271; felony disenfranchisement, 2, 264n4, 291–92n25; in North Carolina, 290–91n23; and supposed "voter fraud," 14
Voting Rights Act (US, 1965), 3, 4, 290

Waddell, Alfred Moore (in the Wilmington Race Riots of 1898), 194
Wagner, Richard, 106
War of 1812 (1812–15), 23
War on Drugs (US, 1980s–2000s), 2
Ward, William Hayes, 188, 189
Washington, Booker T., 14–15, 76–77, 78, 88, 89, 90–91, 92, 93, 94, 95, 100, 101, 103, 106
Washington, Booker T., works by: Atlanta "Compromise" Speech, 14–15, 78, 91, 106; *Frederick Douglass*, 94; *Up From Slavery*, 76, 91
Washington, Madison, 63
Watkins, Mel, 284n4
Watson, Thomas E. (Populist politician, Georgia), 78
wealth gap. *See* racial wealth gap
Welles, Orson, 218
Wells, Ida (Barnett), 71, 157, 160
white extinction anxiety (Charles Blow's concept of), 266n18
white flight (in the wake of the civil rights movement), 276n27

white nationalism, 15, 20, 270n38
white supremacy, psychology and ideology of, 6, 7–12, 16–17, 18, 24–25, 81, 88–89, 105, 146–47, 160, 172–73, 179, 186, 189–93, 196, 199, 206, 214, 222–23, 229–30, 249, 253–55, 263n2, 265n8, 266n18, 267n20, 268n27, 278n8, 279n13, 297n8, 298n10; and epigenetics, 284n7; and imperialism/colonialism, 17, 70, 76, 79, 92, 96, 99, 101, 102, 113, 117, 142–43, 146, 196, 199, 222, 279n14, 282n3; intra-racial, 176–77, 178; and sexuality/the body, 5–6, 8, 34–35, 39, 43, 46, 47, 64, 68, 87–89, 97–98, 99, 101–6, 170, 178, 185–86, 188–89, 190–93, 211, 221, 222–24, 227–28, 229, 235, 245, 249, 256–58, 267n20, 269n27, 270n36, 280n21, 288n18, 289–90n21, 293n3, 295n15. *See also* Anglo-Saxon triumphalism; convict labor, use of; ecology and race; gender; Mississippi Plan; polygenetic theory of creation; redlining; whiteness (as structure of feelings)
whiteness (as structure of feelings), 6, 36, 178, 229–30, 244–45, 249, 252–53, 256–58, 260, 288n18. *See also* white supremacy, psychology and ideology of
Whitman, Walt, 20, 35, 47, 64, 66, 67, 68, 70, 115, 117, 234, 239
Whitman, Walt, works by: *Leaves of Grass*, 35, 117
Whittier, John Greenleaf, 25–26
Whittier, John Greenleaf, works by: "The Haschish," 25–26
Williams, Bert, 166
Wilmington (North Carolina) Race Riots of 1898, 193–94, 200

Wilson, Edmund, 117
Winterich, John T., 132
Wood, Peter H., 166, 180, 181, 263n1
Wood, Peter H., works by: *Black Majority: Negroes in Colonial South Carolina*, 166, 180–81, 263n1
Woodward, C. Van, 279n14, 283n13; on US imperialism and race, 282n3
Woolfolk, Austin (US slave-trader, businessman), 272n9
World War I, 93, 107, 219; deleterious effects on recruitment of African-American soldiers by D. W. Griffith's *Birth of a Nation*, 285–86n9
World War II, 93, 220, 223, 244
Wright, Julia (daughter of Richard Wright and Ellen Poplar), 218, 236
Wright, Nathan (father of Richard Wright), 221–22, 223, 235
Wright, Rachel (daughter of Richard Wright and Ellen Poplar), 218
Wright, Richard, 6, 18, 19, 35, 80, 195, 196, 204–37 *passim*, 251–52, 253, 260, 263n1, 292n1, 293n2, 293n4, 294n10, 294–95n12, 295n15, 296n18, 297n9
Wright, Richard, works by: *Black Boy (American Hunger)*, 204–5, 207, 218–23, 235, 236, 292n1, 294n10; *Black Power: A Record of Reflections in a Land of Pathos*, 235, 237; *Color Curtain, The*, 237; "Ethics of Living Jim Crow, The," 206, 210, 292n1; *Haiku: This Other World*, 236; "How Bigger Was Born," 211, 213–15, 292n1; *Lawd, Today!*, 209–292n1; and Library of America editions of, 211, 220, 224, 292n1, 295n13, 296n18; *Long Dream, The*, 237; *Native*

Son, 195, 211–18, 218 (stage adaptation of), 223–31, 251–52, 253, 292n1, 294–95n12, 295n13, 295n15; *Outsider, The*, 231–35, 236, 292n1, 296n18; *Pagan Spain*, 236, 237; *Savage Holiday*, 235; *Uncle Tom's Children*, 206, 210–11; *White Man, Listen!*, 80, 237

Yeats, William Butler, 129

Zimmerman, George (killer of Trayvon Martin), 262